T0375850

'Life-long dedication to the struggle for democracy, human rights and justice and for challenging the religious dogma including the theological justification for apartheid. In the 1970s, Nolan became the central figure for young black and white Christians seeking liberation.'
Citation when awarded the 'Order of Luthuli in Silver' by then President **Thabo Mbeki** in 2003

'His deep care for humanity radiated from the Dominican Order, as his spiritual home, to communities and institutions across the country and around the globe with whom he built friendships, partnerships and alliances.
He was not afraid to act. Indeed, his was a life of action. Nor was he afraid to think, to reflect, to learn, to disagree and to be proved wrong.
We are blessed to have his ideas live on in his writings. While his books were seminal to our liberation, they are equally valuable as guides for the individual and institutional renewal of our democratic society.'
President Cyril Ramaphosa

'The news of the passing of Fr Albert Nolan OP reached us this morning with a mixture of joyful and sad feelings. Joyful because Fr Nolan, in his lifetime, with his clarity of thought driven by compassion, was a beacon of hope for the poor and the oppressed in a world and country that is still characterised by gross inequality and injustice. His example of life made the poor feel at home with him.'
Bishop Sithembele Sipuka
President, South African Catholic Bishops' Conference

'Through the years I got to know Albert better. Not only was he a great intellectual and academic, but he had the special gift of being able to speak and write profound thoughts and ideas in a way that was easily understandable to people. There was no complicated language disguising or softening what he taught—he was straight forward and to the point. He lived what he taught, especially through his simple lifestyle. Always kind and gentle, he had a wonderful sense of humour.'
Archbishop Stephen Brislin
Cape Town

'Father Albert Nolan, the beacon of hope that was the light of this country in the darkest of days, will continue to shine that light of hope onto South Africa through his works, and a society that must be galvanised to reflect the impact of his lifelong call for a caring society, where the social structures that feed the ego, greed and the self-centredness of 'me-ness' are replaced with just structures that cater for the common good.'
SACC General Secretary Bishop Malusi Mpumlwana
Johannesburg

'I remember Albert Nolan with deep admiration and appreciation, indeed, awe. His theological insight in the struggle against Apartheid was clear, uncompromising and deeply embedded in his reading of the gospel and years of spiritual discipline. He was one of the most unassuming and humble theologians I have ever met, without pretence he simply tried to follow Jesus. We can truly celebrate his life and witness as a faithful disciple of Christ. Having struggled so courageously for justice, may you rest in a well-deserved peace, brother Albert.'
John de Gruchy
Emeritus Professor University of Cape Town

Jesus before Christianity started me on a lifelong quest to learn as much as I could about the historical Jesus. And that quest continues today. Such quests are sometimes denigrated as contrary to faith. Why? Mainly because study of the historical Jesus is placed into false contrast with devotion to the "Christ of faith", the one who has risen from the dead and is alive to us through the Holy Spirit. But of course the "Jesus of history" and the "Christ of faith" are one and the same.'
James Martin SJ
Writer, and editor-at-large of the Jesuit magazine *America*

'In the late 1980s I was a student in Geneva and was a member of YCS. In 1986 and 1987 we dedicated most of our time and reflections to analysing and struggling against the oppressive apartheid system and supporting our YCS friends in South Africa. A delegation of them came to visit us. Still today I vividly remember some conversations. Albert Nolan came to Switzerland and took time to be with us . . . his love and his radical clarity shook many of us out of our comfort zone.'
Véronique Schoeffel
Switzerland

Reluctant Prophet

Mike Deeb OP
Philippe Denis OP and Mark James OP

Dominican Series

The Dominican Series is a joint project by Australian Dominican women and men and offers contributions on topics of Dominican interest and various aspects of church, theology and religion in the world.

Series Editors: Mark O'Brien OP and Gabrielle Kelly OP

1. *English for Theology: A Resource for Teachers and Students*, Gabrielle Kelly OP, 2004.
2. *Towards the Intelligent Use of Liberty: Dominican Approaches in Education*, edited by Gabrielle Kelly OP and Kevin Saunders OP, 2007.
3. *Preaching Justice: Dominican Contributions to Social Ethics in the Twentieth Century*, edited by Francesco Campagnoni OP and Helen Alford OP, 2008.
4. *Don't Put Out The Burning Bush: Worship and preaching in a Complex World*, edited by Vivian Boland, 2008.
5. *Bible Dictionary: Selected Biblical and Theological Words*, Gabrielle Kelly OP in collaboration with Joy Sandefur, 2008
6. *Sunday Matters A: Reflections on the Lectionary Readings for Year A*, Mark O'Brien OP, 2010.
7. *Sunday Matters B: Reflections on the Lectionary Readings for Year B*, Mark O'Brien OP, 2011.
8. *Sunday Matters C: Reflections on the Lectionary Readings for Year C*, Mark O'Brien OP, 2012.
9. Scanning the Signs of the Times: *French Dominicans in the Twentieth Century*, Thomas F O'Meara OP and Paul Philibert OP, 2013.
10. *From North to South: Southern Scholars Engage with Edward Schillebeeckx*, edited by Helen F Bergin OP, 2013.
11. *The ABC of Sunday Matters*, Mark O'Brien OP, 2013.
12. *Restoring the Right Relationship: The Bible on Divine Righteousness*, Mark O'Brien OP, 2014.
13. *Dominicans and Human Rights: Past, Present, Future*, edited by Mike Deeb OP and Celestina Veloso Freitas OP, 2017
14. *Promise of Renewal: Dominicans and Vatican II*, edited by Michael Attridge, Darren Dias OP, Matthew Eaton and Nicolas Olkovich, 2017
15. *A Stumbling Block: Bartolomé de las Casas as Defender of the Indians*, Mariano Delgado, 2019.

Disclaimer:

Views expressed in publications within the Dominican Series do not necessarily reflect those of the respective Congregations of the Sisters or the Province of the Friars.

Reluctant Prophet

Tributes to Albert Nolan OP

Edited by Mike Deeb OP, Philippe Denis OP and Mark James OP

UJ Press

Adelaide | Johannesburg
2023

© Copyright remains with the individual authors for their own contributions and to ATF Press for the collection.

ISBN:
- 978-1-922737-88-5   Softcover
- 978-1-922737-89-2   Hardcover
- 978-1-922737-90-8   Epub
- 978-1-922737-91-5   PDF

Published and edited by

Making a lasting impact
An imprint of the ATF Press Publishing Group
owned by ATF (Australia) Ltd.
PO Box 234
Brompton, SA 5007
Australia
ABN 90 116 359 963
www.atfpress.com

UJ Press
Johannesburg
South Africa

Table of Contents

List of Abbreviations and Definitions   xiii

List of Photographs   xvii

1. Foreword   xix
   Timothy Radcliffe OP
2. Introduction   xxv
   Mike Deeb OP
3. Homily Preached at the Requiem Mass   xxxi
   Mark James OP

Section 1 The Early Years

4. Beginnings   3
   Virginia Zweigenthal
5. *Aggiornamento*   9
   Andrew Prior
6. Stellenbosch   15
   Joseph Falkiner OP
7. A Saint and a Doctor of the Church   21
   Brian Robertson

Section 2 Student Chaplain

8. An Inspiration to a Generation of Students   25
   Mike Deeb OP
9. A Spirituality of Action for International Catholic Student
   Movements   33
   Kevin Ahern
10. A Chaplain who Inspired IMCS Pax-Romana   43
    Ravi Tissera Warnakulasooriya

viii   *Reluctant Prophet*

11. Law as Servant	49
Brian Currin	
12. *Jesus before Christianity*	53
Robert Ellsberg	
13. An Echo from Australia	59
Paul Burke	
14. Supporting the Spread of YCS	63
Cecil Sols	
15. Integrating Life and Faith	65
Francis Vusumuzi Zitha	
16. In Tune with the *Sensus fidelium*	67
Lois Law	
17. A Mentor and a Friend	73
Peter Sadie	
18. A Humble Servant of God	77
Mike Mailula	
19. Taming a Wild Cannon	81
Norman Malatjie	
20. In the Footsteps of Jesus	87
Shepi Mati	

Section 3   Mayfair

21. 124 Central Avenue	97
Joseph Falkiner OP	
22. Outward Going, Yet a Haven	103
Ian Linden	
23. Declining Election as Master of the Order	107
Nicholas Punch OP	
24. A Man with Whom I Could Engage	111
Neil Mitchell OP	
25. 'What I do is Me'	119
Ann Wigley OP	
26. More than a Colleague	123
Celia Smit OP	
27. A Theology Rooted in Dominican Life	127
John O'Leary	
28. A Sound Sounding Board	131
Michael Lewis SJ	
29. The Struggle *Ad Intra* and *Ad Extra*	133
Kevin Dowling CSsR	

30. An Evangelical Discovering Contextual Theology	141
Moss Ntlha	
31. A Significant Impact on Evangelical Movements	145
Aaron Mokabane	

Section 4 Theologising in the Midst of the Struggle

32. On Context in Context	153
James R Cochrane	
33. Hope Against Hope!	161
Frank Chikane	
34. The Story of the *Kairos Document*	171
Molefe Tsele	
35. Common Ground for the Common Good	179
Smangaliso Mkhatshwa	
36. In Hiding	185
Brigid Rose Tiernan SNDdeN	
37. A Different Way of Doing Theology	189
Larry Kaufmann CSsR	
38. Prophetic Ecumenism	197
Edwin Arrison	
39. A Grounded Intellectual	203
Leslie Dikeni	
40. The Christian Action Movement	211
Benita Pavlicevic and Peter Stewart	
41. Co-conspirator for God's Reign of Justice	215
Roxane Jordaan	
42. *God in South Africa*: Then–and Now	219
Anthony Egan SJ	
43. Operative 42	229
Horst Kleinschmidt	
44. Converging Journeys Towards the 'Sacred'	237
Raymond Suttner	

Section 5 Opening Space for Debate

45. The 'Option for the Poor' Debate	249
McGlory Speckman	
46. Eschatology for Urgent Times	259
Paul B Decock OMI	
47. Biblical Interpretation as Prophetic Process	269
Gerald O West	

48. The Known and Unknown God	279
Charles Villa-Vicencio	
49. God the Stranger	287
Michael Worsnip	
50. The God who Dignifies and Humanises Us	295
Trevor Peter Amafu Ntlhola	
51. *Rakhmah*: A Palestine-Inspired Spirituality	301
Stiaan Van der Merwe	

Section 6 *Challenge*

52. Telling the *Challenge* Story	313
Renate Cochrane	
53. Mentoring a Young Journalist	319
Khotso Kekana	
54. A Trusted Partner	323
Jacques Briard	
55. Skilling Religious Journalists	327
Theo and Ruth Coggin	

Section 7 Spiritual Renewal

56. A Prophet for our Planet's *Kairos* Moment	337
Marilyn Aitken	
57. Converted to the Universe Story	345
Miriam MacGillis OP	
58. Processes of Conversion and Hope	351
Malusi Mpumlwana	
59. A Prophet Micah for Today	361
Peter-John Pearson	
60. An Incarnational Spirituality	365
Sidwell Mokgothu	
61. A Man who Respected Women as Thinkers	375
Susan Rakoczy IHM	
62. A Teacher, a Colleague and a Friend	379
Sylvester David OMI	
63. The Pietermaritzburg Spirituality Book Club	381
Graham Lindegger and Sharon Grussendorf	
64. A Spirituality of Simplicity and Service	385
Isaac Mutelo OP	
65. Like Meister Eckhart, an Exemplary Dominican	389
Therese Sacco	

Table of Contents xi

66. Compassion, Humility and Justice *Lionel Green-Thompson*	393
67. Over a Glass of Wine *Michael Murphy SPS*	399
68. A Tremendous Companion *Hyacinth Ennis OFM*	405
69. At Peace *Stephany Thiel OP*	407

Section 8

70. Conclusion *Philippe Denis OP*	415
71. Time Lines *Albert Nolan OP*	421

Biographical Details of Contributors	425

Section 9

Indices	
Names	449
Subject	455

List of Abbreviations and Definitions

ACTS: Association of Catholic Tertiary Students
AIDS: Acquired Immunodeficiency Syndrome
AFM: Apostolic Faith Mission of South Africa
ANC: African National Congress
ACTS: Association of Catholic Tertiary Students
Acts: Acts of the Apostles
ART: Antiretroviral Treatment
AZASO: Azanian Students Organisation
BCM: Black Consciousness Movement
CAM: Christian Action Movement
CARE: Catholic Action for Racial Education
CASA: Catholic Students Association
Cathsoc: Catholic Student Society
CBS: Contextual Bible Study
CCFD: Catholic Committee against Hunger and for
            Development
CDF: Congregation for the Doctrine of the Faith
CE: Concerned Evangelicals
CI: Christian Institute of Southern Africa
CIDSE: International Cooperation for Development and
            Solidarity
CIIR: Catholic Institute of International Relations
CLG: Christian Life Group
COSAS: Congress of South African Students
CSsR: Congregation of the Most Holy Redeemer,
            Redemptorist.
DSI: Dominican Sisters International

DRC:	Dutch Reformed Church
EATWOT:	Ecumenical Association of Third World Theologians
EED:	Evangelischer Entwicklungsdienst
EWISA:	Evangelical Witness in South Africa
Ex:	Book of Exodus
Ezra:	Book of Ezra
FEDOSA:	Federation of Dominicans in South Africa
Fedsem:	The Federal Theological Seminary
FFP:	Freedom Front Plus
Heb:	Letter to the Hebrews
ICT:	Institute for Contextual Theology
ICY:	Inter-Church Youth
IFA:	Interfederal Assembly
IHM:	Congregation of the Sisters, Servants of Immaculate Heart of Mary
IMCS:	International Movement of Catholic Students
IPBES:	Intergovernmental Platform on Biodiversity and Ecosystem
IPCC:	Intergovernmental Panel on Climate Change
ISB:	Institute for the Study of the Bible
IYCS:	International Young Catholic Students
Jer:	Book of Jeremiah
Jn:	Gospel of John
JOC:	Jeunesse Ouvrière Chrétienne
Joceto:	Johannesburg Central Township (Name of a Community)
JODAC:	Johannesburg Democratic Action Committee
JTSA:	Journal of Theology for Southern Africa
KP:	Kairos Palestine document
Kweekskool:	Seminary (in Afrikaans) for Dutch Reformed Ministers
LGBTQIA:	lesbian, gay, bisexual, transgender, queer, (questioning), intersex, asexual, and agender
Lk:	Gospel of Luke
MIEC-JECI:	Movement International des Etudiants Catholiques-Jeunesse Etudiante Catholique Internationale
Mk:	Gospel of Mark
Mt:	Gospel of Matthew
MG:	Master General
MO:	Master of the Order

MUCCOR:	Ministers United for Christian Co-responsibility
MK:	Umkhonto we Sizwe
NDCs:	Nationally Determined Contributions
NCFS:	National Catholic Federation of Students
NEUSA:	National Educational Union of South Africa
NGO:	Non-Governmental Organisation
NUSAS:	National Union of South African Students
OCU:	Orthodox Church of Ukraine
OMI:	Oblates of Mary Immaculate
OP:	Order of Preachers
PAC:	Pan Africanist Congress
PCI:	Pax Christi International
PACSA:	Pietermaritzburg Agency for Christian Social Awareness
PhD:	Doctor of Philosophy
RCC:	Roman Catholic Church
ROL:	Review of Life.
Rom:	*Paul's Letter to the Romans*
SACBC:	Southern African Catholic Bishops' Conference
SACC:	South African Council of Churches
SACLA:	South African Christian Leadership Assembly
SADF:	South African Defence Force
SAFCEI:	Southern African Faith Communities Environment Institute
SAHA:	South African Historical Archives
SAKD:	South African Kairos Document
SACP:	South African Communist Party
SASL:	South African Sign Language
SASSA:	South African Social Security Agency
SCM:	Student Christian Movement
S-J-A:	See-Judge-Act
SJA groups:	See-Judge-Act groups
SLUCSM:	Sri Lanka University Catholic Students Movement
SNDdeN:	Sisters of Notre Dame de Namur
SPOBA:	St Peter's Old Boys Association
SUCA:	Students Union for Christian Action
TCFA:	Tertiary Catholic Federation of Australia
TEP:	Theology Exchange Program
TEASA:	The Evangelical Alliance of South Africa

TRC:	Truth and Reconciliation Commission
UCM:	University Christian Movement
UCT:	University of Cape Town
UCCSA:	United Congregational Church of South Africa
UDF:	United Democratic Front
Udusa:	Union of Democratic University Staff Associations.
UKZN:	University of KwaZulu-Natal
UMC:	United Methodist Church (Mozambique)
UNISA:	University of South Africa
UNEC:	Unión Nacional de Estudiantes Católicos
VCA:	Vaal Civic Association
Veiligsheid:	Reference to Security Police (in Afrikaans)
Veritas:	Truth (in Latin)
WAACSA:	We Are All Church South Africa
Wits:	University of the Witwatersrand
WAACSA:	We Are All Church South Africa
WARC:	World Alliance of Reformed Churches
WLTP:	Women's Leadership and Training Programme

List of Photographs

Page xii. Portrait, Albert. Source: Archives of the Vice-Province of the Dominican Order in Southern Africa (Archives).

Page xxx. Mike Deeb with Albert Nolan in 2021. Source: Archives/Mike Deeb.

Page 2. Family photographs. Source: Iris Prinsloo (Albert's sister).

Page 14. Photos 1 and 2 Albert as a student and at his ordination. Source: Archives. Photos 3 and 4, Albert. Source: Iris Prinsloo (Albert's sister).

Page 22. Photo 1: Albert. Source: Archives. Photos 2 and 3, family photographs. Source: Iris Prinsloo (Albert's sister).

Page 24. St Nicholas Priory, Stellenbosch. Source: Archives.

Page 42. Stellenbosch. Source: Archives.

Page 48. Stellenbosch. Source: Archives.

Page 52. *Jesus before Christianity*, book cover.

Page 58. Albert in Australia, 1998. Source: Lorna Payne.

Page 72. Albert with Mark James and Thomas Chuma. Source: Archives/Mike Deeb.

Page 80. Portrait, Albert. Source: Archives.

Page 96. Mayfair. Source: Archives.

Page 110. Albert, Damian Byrne and Emil Blaser. Source: Archives.

Page 126. Stellenbosch. Source: Archives.

Page 130. Albert with Gregory Brooke OP. Source: Archives.

Page 150. Albert concelebrating Mass at the NCFS National Conference. Source: Archives/Mike Deeb.

Page 152. Frank Chikane. Source: University of Cape Town Libraries Digital Collections.

Page 170. Albert at UDF Million Signature Campaign. Source: Wits University.

Page 188. Portrait, Albert.
Source: *National Catholic Reporter*/Archives.
Page 196. Albert Johannesburg Justice and Peace conference.
Source: Archives/Mike Deeb.
Page 202. Portrait, Albert. Source: Archives.
Page 210. Wedding photo. Source: Archives.
Page 218. *God in South Africa*, book cover.
Page 228. Group photo. Source: Archives.
Page 236. Albert with Raymond Suttner. Source: Nomboniso Gasa.
Page 246. Albert at an ordination. Source: Archives.
Page 248. Portrait, Albert. Source: Archives.
Page 258. Albert talking in Rome. Source: Archives/Mike Deeb.
Page 268. Albert at a meeting with Master of the Order.
Source: Archives/Mike Deeb.
Page 278. Mayfair community Mass. Source: Archives.
Page 310. Albert with YCS members. Source: Archives.
Page 312. Albert with Emil Blaser and Stephen Paradza.
Source: Archives.
Page 318. Portrait, Albert. Source: Archives.
Page 332. Mayfair. Source: Archives.
Page 326. Journalism course. Source: Quo Vadis Communications.
Page 334. Portrait, Albert with *Challenge* magazine cover.
Source: Archives.
Page 336. *Challenge* magazine. Source: Archives.
Page 360. *Jesus Today*, book cover.
Page 374. Albert's 83rd birthday with Chris Langefeld.
Source: Therese Sacco.
Page 378. Albert with a group of novices. Source: Archives.
Page 384. Albert, Roger Houngbedji and Quirico Pedregosa.
Source: Archives/Mike Deeb.
Page 404. Portrait, Albert at Stellenbosch. Source: Archives.
Page 412. Albert with Theo Coggin. Quo Vadis Communications.
Page 414. Albert with a young Dominican brother. Source: Archives.
Page 424. Albert with Mike Deeb. Source: Archives.
Page 446. Albert at Kairos Document anniversary.
Source: Malusi Mpumlwana.
Page 448. Albert with Neil Mitchell 2014.
Source: Archives/Neil Mitchell.
Page 454. Portrait, Albert. Source: Archives/Neil Mitchell.
Page 463. Portrait, Albert, 2014. Source: Archives/Neil Mitchell.

Foreword

Timothy Radcliffe OP

The Church is engaged in the biggest listening exercise in the history of humanity. Hundreds of millions of Catholics in every country on the planet are being asked by Pope Francis to help us hear what the Spirit is saying to the Church today. This is the Synodal path on which the Pope is asking us to embark, so that the Body of Christ may discern the will of God for humanity and creation. It is also a sign of hope for humanity in a difficult and dangerous moment when the future is obscure.

Most people are excited by this extraordinary journey the Church is undertaking, but some are nervous. Where will it take us? What does it look like? Many Church leaders doubtless think that they know best and wonder why it is necessary to consult the faithful.

Albert understood profoundly why it is so vital and right that this listening to the People of God is happening. This collection of pieces written by Albert's friends and colleagues gives us a glimpse of why Albert, like Pope Francis, was a thoroughly Vatican II Catholic. He was studying in Rome when the Council was taking place and, like Pope Francis, he believed that we are only at the beginning of implementing its vision. Fundamental to this is the conviction that if the Holy Spirit is poured on every baptised Christian, every one of us should have a voice in discerning the will of God for the Church and the world. Albert advised Larry Kaufmann to ask what ordinary people think about Jesus. What are their questions and their insights? He is reported as saying that 'the Spirit of truth moved through the faith questions which ordinary people were asking'. Theological truth is attained not just by academics working in libraries but in conversations about our faith and hope on the streets and in our homes.

Albert told Mark James OP: 'If people want to know who I was, what I believed and what I stood for, they can read my books.' I would add 'and meet my friends'. So, this is an unusual book since it contains pieces by Albert's former students and colleagues, his Dominican brothers and sisters, academics and activists, Catholics and Christians of other denominations. It is rare to have a collection of such different sorts of contributions, ranging from the highly personal to the academic. But this is what the People of God is like, a deeply and beautifully diverse community of pilgrims on the way to the Kingdom, conversing as we travel.

People are often anxious and even angry that it takes so long for the Church to change. All these meetings and endless documents and yet still so many people, especially women, continue to feel marginalised and not fully recognised. Albert felt this too, but he understood the slowness of all organic change. He wrote at the end of *Jesus Today: A Spirituality of Radical Freedom*, 'God's Work sometimes appears to be very slow. Perhaps that is because we do not always appreciate the immensity of what we are involved in. Yet, precisely because it is God's work, the future is secure'.

Having read the contributions to this collection, I feel humbled to be asked to write a Foreword. Everyone writing here has, as far as I can see, shared with Albert in the struggle for justice, especially in the cruel world of Apartheid. Albert called for an active engagement in the struggle. The authors in this book are mainly those who responded with a resounding 'yes'. Robert Ellsberg quotes Albert: 'I am concerned about people, the daily suffering of so many millions of people, and the prospect of much greater suffering in the near future. My purpose is to find out what can be done about it.' *Veritas*, Truth, is the motto of the Order, and Albert wished to be true to what people lived and suffered, true to how they expressed themselves, true to their dreams and to their faith.

But I am deeply aware that I have spent much of my Dominican life in the safety of the ivory towers of Oxford University. What right have I to speak? Only that I am one of so many brethren who loved and admired Albert, even from afar.

Forty years ago, Albert came to stay in Blackfriars, our Priory in Oxford. I was the Prior and so his host. We were all excited by a visit from this famous brother but I was a little nervous. Might he not think that we were rather mediocre and compromised, living in relative comfort and safety in this privileged environment? The night of his arrival I took him to the pub. This was a typically Dominican act of welcome. St Dominic is said to have first thought of founding the Order in a pub, when he argued all night with the publican who was a Cathar. The pub to which Albert and I went was called The Royal Oak, named in honour of the tree in which the fugitive King Charles II hid to escape his enemies who wished to kill him. Even though Albert was not a Royalist, he too had had to hide from those who wished to kill him.

My memory of that first encounter was of Albert's simple, whole-hearted joy. It so overflowed that when the time came for the pub to be closed for the night, the publican invited us to stay on and share some more drinks with him. I had never had that honour before or since. Albert did not accuse us for not being in the frontline of the struggle. The challenge that he made was all the more powerful for being embodied in who he was, his joy and freedom, rather than in words which might have cast us down. He accepted his Oxford brethren as we were and so invited us to be more. As a group of his friends write in this book, he was 'the least prejudiced person we knew'.

In 1983 Albert was elected Master of the Order. Nick Punch OP reports on how he asked to be excused from taking on this role because of the inescapable duty of opposing Apartheid in his homeland. His brethren showed their respect for his engagement in this combat by electing him as Master and even more so in accepting his reasons for not accepting. Nick tells us that the brother whom they then elected, Damian Byrne, said that we should be obedient to Albert! So, I write on behalf of all of his Dominican brothers and sisters who were so proud of him, and challenged by him, even if we were not with him in South Africa at his side.

When I was provincial of the English Province, I was invited to come to South Africa to spend some time with the brethren and help them reflect on how to plan for the next Provincial Chapter. At this stage in my life, I had never planned a Chapter myself and so I felt rather a fraud, but I could not resist the invitation. Albert collected me from Johannesburg airport and we drove south for several hours to the meeting. On the way a young boy suddenly ran out into the road and was hit by our car. I held his bleeding body in my arms as Albert drove him to the nearest hospital and ensured that he would receive the best possible care. On the way back after the meeting, we went to visit the boy, to be sure that he was recovering well. I was moved by his profound and unhesitating compassion for the boy and his personal response to the lad's suffering.

Then I stayed with the community in Mayfair, the poor neighbourhood in which the provincial was based. Several pieces in this book recount what a simple way of life the brethren lived there. Albert shared a bedroom with two or three of the brethren, which was my idea of a nightmare. In our prayers, the psalms were recited slowly and reverently. The Magnificat, the song of the young Mary, was the prayer that daily enunciated their faith in the one who 'raises the lowly'. I was overwhelmed by the joy of the brethren. I often told provincials who lived in more luxurious quarters that nowhere had I seen a more joyful provincial community than in Mayfair. How can the gospel be 'Good News', the original meaning of the word, if the preacher is not joyful? I was amused to discover that our brother Finbar (who had passed on a few years before) had to be kept from answering the phone since he would be inclined to answer all questions truthfully, as a good Dominican, even if this meant revealing the presence of someone sought by the security police!

Albert was highly intelligent, a gifted scholar, but he was, as Edwin Arrison remarks, 'uncomplicated'. He was simply himself. There were no hidden sides to him, as far as I could see. Ann Wigley OP quotes the wonderful lines by the Jesuit poet Gerard Manley Hopkins, 'What I do is me, for that I came' (*As Kingfishers catch fire*). He was a witness to the gospel in how and who he was. His words rang true, with an authority like those of our master, Jesus. No wonder he was seen as a threat by the regime and so had to hide for a while with the Notre Dame community in Melville, Johannesburg. Albert told me once that he was now too well known to be assassinated openly, but he lived with the knowledge that an 'accident' might be arranged.

In 1992, I moved to Rome as the newly elected Master of the Order. I had no valid reason to ask to be excused! One of my first visits to the Vatican was to meet Cardinal Ratzinger, later Pope Benedict XVI. I had expected the meeting to be difficult. I had swallowed the idea current in the press at the time that he was God's Rottweiler. In fact, during my nine years of encounters with him, I discovered that he was the easiest person with whom to deal in the Vatican, always humble, simple and open to dialogue if one was open to dialogue with him.

He did however express his concerns with Albert's famous book *Jesus before Christianity* (1976). My duty was always to stand up for the brethren, and so I argued that any action that was undertaken against the book would increase its sales, which I was sure the Cardinal did not wish to do. He agreed, smiling. But I have always been a little uneasy about the search for 'the historical Jesus', which the book does undertake. I felt that there is always the danger that in trying to find Jesus prior to the interpretations of the Gospels and tradition, one will usually end up with the person whom one wishes to find. I was therefore rather relieved to read in this collection of essays, Paul Burke's expression of his own hesitations. Albert would never mind one posing questions and having a good argument about them.

After reading the frequent references to this book in the essays collected here, I have finally, rather late in the day, understood why for so many people, reading the book was such a transformative experience. Here they met *That man Jesus*, in the words of Mark James OP. Albert enabled an encounter with the One who changed the world and who changes us if we dare to meet him. Ellsberg writes, 'I felt I was meeting him [Jesus] for the first time'. It is this encounter with the person of Jesus that was for Albert so central, as indeed it was for Pope Benedict!

Albert could bring about such an authentic encounter with the Lord because his own experience of Christ radiated from his very being. This is why he was such an attractive preacher and a beloved friend of so many. Bishop Sylvester David describes Albert as 'a man I could not help but love and want to follow'.

Albert had qualified for his doctorate at the Dominican University in Rome, but since he did not wish to waste money on publishing it, the honour was never officially bestowed. It was typical of Albert not to bother about any such titles. So, it was a tremendous joy to invite him back to the Angelicum to lecture, together with another remarkable Dominican theologian Herbert McCabe. We celebrated on the balcony with Damian Byrne, who had been elected when Albert had declined the position.

It was my joy to keep regularly in touch with Albert in later years. In Chicago he shared with me his vast delight that Gustavo Gutiérrez, the Father of Liberation Theology, had entered the Order. As the years passed, Albert increasingly stressed the inseparability of political liberation from spiritual freedom. In one of his last messages to me, he explained that because of his state of health,

I am no longer chaplain here in this retirement home which belongs to the Newcastle Dominican Sisters. I am now a resident. I don't preside at Mass any longer. But I am very happy here. Well looked after. I have nurses and caregivers and morning and evening prayer and sometimes Mass. I have plenty of time to read and to deepen my spiritual life.

Here is the witness of his final days, when this most active of people could no longer do much, and yet his life is filled with joy and gratitude to the end. We give thanks to God for you, dear Albert.

Introduction

Mike Deeb OP

Albert Nolan died on 17 October, 2022. His death resulted in an outpouring of emotion, in many, many tributes, that was fascinating to witness—in memorials, social media groups, in the press and even in the minutes of a government cabinet meeting. These reflected just how much he meant to so many people. Immediately after the funeral, I was approached by Hilary Regan of ATF Press in Australia about the possibility of producing a book of essays in honour of Albert. I came to know Hilary while working with him in editing a book, published in three languages, on *Dominicans and Human Rights* between 2016 and 2020. After resisting his request and trying to fob him off on to other Dominicans, I was eventually persuaded to help him, especially since I felt I owed it to Albert and to the many people whose tributes yearned for his legacy to be sustained. This resulted in a four-month, almost full-time project. Thankfully, my Dominican brothers, Mark James and Philippe Denis, agreed to assist me in an editorial team and with invaluable support from our journalist friend, Terence Creamer, and daily encouragements from our indefatigable publisher, Hilary—to all of whom I am greatly indebted—this book has seen the light of day!

We decided to seek articles that would honour Albert in the different aspects of his life—chronologically, along with his different areas of activity—and to throw the net wide, expecting that the majority would decline. However, very few declined and we have ended up with a book of seventy contributions from seventy-one people (two with two articles each and three articles each written jointly by two people).

The book therefore consists of a variety of genres: historical accounts, personal biographical stories, reflections on Albert's preoccupations, and several academic articles grappling with Albert's thought and contribution. This diversity provides a rich kaleidoscope of Albert the brother, the Dominican preacher, the priest, the chaplain, the pastor, the mentor, the theologian, the intellectual, the political activist and the friend.

The collection

This privileged collection of first-hand accounts from each stage of his life has yielded many gems. The interview Virginia Zweigenthal conducted with Albert's sister, Iris, on his early years is one of them, along with the accounts of his contemporaries in his early years as a priest in Stellenbosch (Joseph Falkiner, Andrew Prior and Brian Robertson).

Albert really made his mark as a chaplain to university and, later, secondary school students in the National Catholic Federation of Students (NCFS) and the Young Christian Students (YCS), and at least fourteen of these students offer insights into the role he played in their lives at that time and ever since. His impact further afield—in the International Movement of Catholic Students (IMCS–Pax Romana) and even among students in Australia is also recounted.

There are also many stories of Albert in his Dominican life, especially as the provincial, when he established the Mayfair community which impressed many as a witness to solidarity with the poor. Furthermore, interesting light is shed on his friendship and collaboration with Dominican sisters and his accompanying role to novices from his time as novice master. And his broader engagement within the Catholic Church is also highlighted, particularly with the Southern African Catholic Bishops' Conference (SACBC), with leaders of other religious congregations who were contemporaries of Albert, such as the Redemptorists and the Jesuits, and with the Oblates of Mary Immaculate (OMI) at St Joseph's Theological Institute in Cedara.

Nearly thirty per cent of the articles are written by Albert's ecumenical partners, those of other denominations and faiths or with no professed faith, especially from his time working for the Institute for Contextual Theology (ICT) and as editor of *Challenge* magazine. The testimonies of the evangelicals who were touched by Albert are particularly interesting. This was the period when he was also an underground operative, and the accounts of Frank Chikane and Horst Kleinschmidt particularly reveal this.

Then we have stories of those who personally accompanied Albert during the writing and publication of his celebrated books as well as those whose engagements with Albert provoked lots of interesting disagreements and debate. Despite the differences, the admiration for Albert still shines through.

Finally, there are several stories that follow Albert's spiritual evolution with regard to the environment, gender issues, contemplation and eventually his aging process. These bring out the wholesomeness of his spirituality.

Many of the articles border on being hagiographic with several explicitly describing Albert as a modern-day saint, a prophet and doctor of the Church. Yet, even if less effusive or even critical of him, all the contributors reveal their deep respect and love for Albert.

Reluctant prophet

Since so many contributions refer to Albert as a 'prophet', it is unsurprising that this word is part of the title of this volume. One may ask, 'Is this designation not overused?' Not if our experience matches that of Ann Wigley who says that he was not afraid to speak Truth as he understood it, regardless of the consequences—even exposing himself to severe criticism by many in the Church. Nevertheless, most—even bishops—could not ignore him, even if they did not always like what he was saying.

In condemning the political and economic structures prevailing in South Africa and in the world, Albert primarily saw himself following in the footsteps of the biblical prophets. He loved them—especially Jeremiah, and he always insisted that Jesus, in affirming John the Baptist, directly aligned himself with the prophetic tradition in the Bible.

Designating Albert as a 'prophet' is furthermore unsurprising since, like the biblical prophets, his starting point was always 'reading the signs of the times'. All his books are a profound witness to this: from *Jesus before Christianity*, which he begins by highlighting 'Catastrophe' in the world and Jesus' response to it; to *God in South Africa*, where he highlights the particular signs of the times in South Africa under Apartheid; to *Jesus Today*, where he identified the new signs of the times: globalisation, search for spirituality, rampant individualism and the absence of a consciousness of the interconnectedness of the universe. Having identified these 'signs', Albert did not stop there. He then attempted to offer alternatives.

Many of the stories in this book point to his prophetic initiatives: reminding the world of the humanity of Jesus; having the courage to establish the Mayfair Dominican community in a poor neighbourhood; declining his election as Master of the Dominican Order; spearheading a way of doing theology different from traditional theological education; collaborating in the underground with the liberation movement to topple Apartheid; active support for the struggle of women for full equality; promoting the Universe Story in the face of derision. These and many other initiatives fill these pages without exhausting them since some of his prophetic actions could not find their way here. One such initiative was the establishment, in 1981, of a formation house in Maseru, Lesotho. This was a non-racial community that could function without police harassment and also welcome vocations from other Southern African countries.

Some might question his stance as prophetic in the light of his close relationship with the ANC and his apparent sympathy for Marxism (which several of the authors in this book assume)—especially in an age when communist practice has largely been discredited globally and is associated only with authoritarian regimes. In the 1970s and 1980s, Albert certainly did believe that Marxism offered a profound analysis of the systemic causes of the poverty and suffering of millions. And he agreed with analysts who saw an integral link between the development of Apartheid and capitalist development in South Africa. However, while he continued to see the socialist value of sharing—and not the individualism promoted by capitalist ideology—being more in tune with the Kingdom of God that Jesus proclaimed, Albert would not identify himself as a Marxist. In fact, he would say that Marxism, while articulating truths about society, was not radical enough. Jesus offered a path that went much, much deeper, transforming the hearts of all people.

That Albert was a prophet, therefore, few may dispute. But, in some respects, the profile does not fully fit. One often associates a prophet with a person who, being appalled by evil abounding, is serious and even grumpy. Many stories in this book paint a picture of Albert that contradicts this, pointing to his joyfulness and his signature outbursts of laughter. Also, one often associates a prophet with an abrasive and aggressive person who is always at the forefront upbraiding people, yet Albert never sought the limelight. Author after author in this book point to his humility. Even though he was a world-renowned theologian, he had no airs and people immediately felt comfortable with him—even if he was challenging them.

This humility was also reflected in Albert's political activity. While he was passionate about the struggle for change in South Africa, seldom would he be seen in political rallies or marches. He always played a background role, as attested to by Molefe Tsele, Smangaliso Mkhatshwa and Frank Chikane. His activism was primarily with his pen—writing his books, editing the *Kairos Document* and *Challenge* magazine, initiating a journalism course—and in promoting a different way of doing theology. His unobtrusiveness was particularly evident in his underground activism, as Horst Kleinschmidt and Ian Linden reveal, which was done without any of his own brethren knowing about it.

Albert was a very private person. Just three months before he died, when I sent him a draft chapter of my own memoirs, in response he remarked, 'You are clearly a people's person which I am not. I am, in comparison, a very private person'. He didn't like talking about himself and he would never promote himself.

In a documentary by the Irish Catholic media organisation, *Radharc* (described in Joseph Dunn's book, *No Lions in the Hierarchy*), an interview with Albert is entitled, 'Like Jeremiah, I am a very reluctant prophet'. This comes from a comment he made:

> If I look into my heart of hearts, I would prefer a peaceful relationship with authority, it makes life so much easier. If sometimes I speak up, I assure you it's not because I like being a rebel, but because I feel that is what I must do, that is what God is calling me to do. And if there's any sense in which that is prophetic, then like Jeremiah I'm a very reluctant prophet, and I wish to God that I didn't have to do it.[1]

This resonated with all the experiences mentioned of Albert's humility and hence we decided to entitle this book, *Reluctant Prophet*.

It is our hope that all these stories and reflections will preserve the legacy of Albert and re-ignite the memories we have of him. And we hope that they will inspire the reader—even if Albert was not known personally—to catch and emulate his humble and prophetic spirit as we struggle to make the Reign of God—proclaimed by Jesus and championed by Albert—more present in our world.

---

1. Dunn, Joseph. *No Lions in the Hierarchy* (Dublin: Columba Press, 1994), 270.

Albert with Mike Deeb after his solemn vows, 20 January 1990.

Homily Preached at the Requiem Mass

Our Lady of Mercy Catholic Church, Springs,
Wednesday 19 October 2022

Mark James OP

Today we come to bid farewell to our brother, Albert Nolan. Many of us would not know this, but Albert was actually born Dennis James Harry Nolan on 2 September 1934. He was born to South African parents of Irish descent and grew up in Gardens in Cape Town. He went to high school at St Joseph's Marist Brothers in Rondebosch and after school he worked in a bank for a few years. He was actively involved in St Mary's parish and he read the writings of a prominent spiritual writer at that time—Thomas Merton. Merton was originally a non-believer whose father was an artist born in New Zealand and his mother was from the United States. After having lived a wayward life—a bit like St Augustine—Merton underwent a profound spiritual transformation. After his baptism as a Catholic, Merton desired to be a priest. At first, he considered being a Franciscan but later chose to become a Cistercian or Trappist monk and joined the monastery of Gethsemane in Kentucky in the USA. He developed a writing ministry and in his first number of books he romanticised religious life as leaving behind the world and moving into the perfection of God's Kingdom—namely, the Church or the monastery. But over the years, he developed a deeper appreciation of the presence of Christ as not just leaving the world behind, but really immersing oneself more fully in the world as Jesus did—coming among us as Word made flesh—pitching his tent among us.

By reading Thomas Merton, Albert realised that he had a call to be a religious. He wanted to follow Christ and give his whole life in his service. But Albert did not see himself being a monk. He did not want to spend his life in a monastery—singing, reading the Bible and praying. He wanted to bring the Word of God to others and he searched for a religious order that would assist him to do this. Eventually, he discovered the Dominican Order. The Dominicans were dedicated to study, to prayer and to proclaiming Christ, the Word of God. They also had as their motto *Veritas*, or Truth, which appealed to Albert.

Albert entered the novitiate in 1954, where he received his religious name of Albert. He was professed in 1955 and ordained in 1961. Shortly after his ordination he was sent to study at the Angelicum, the Dominican University in Rome, to do his licentiate and his PhD in biblical theology. I remember him telling us at the dinner table one day that being in Rome in those years was one of the most formative events of his life. While he was there, the Second Vatican Council got underway and he was influenced by the debates and the new ideas that were emerging at the time. Albert realised that this was a seminal moment in the history of the Church as it was undergoing a radical transformation.

When he finished his studies in about 1963 or 1964, he came back to South Africa and was sent back to Stellenbosch, where he had done his novitiate and his priestly formation as a Dominican. He worked a bit with the parish, but he was also doing teaching in our *studium* (house of studies) in Stellenbosch at the time, were we had a number of students, including thirteen novices. Albert would have taught these students and novices.

On one occasion while in Stellenbosch, Albert decided to attend the New Testament Society's conference that was taking place at the University of Stellenbosch that year. And, as he tells the story, he went to this conference as a New Testament scholar himself and he listened to the talks. And, he said, he started to feel more and more uncomfortable as one speaker after the next spoke. He said he felt 'something was amiss'—something did not sit well for him. He felt uneasy about what was being said in the talks. The emphasis of the scripture scholars who spoke focused on the philological approach to scripture. This meant researching each word in the scriptural text, analysing it so that one can understand the meaning in Greek and see its relationship and its associations with accounts in the Old or New Testament. While it was interesting what some of the scholars were coming up with, Albert said, he felt that they were missing the point of the text. The passage they were reflecting on was the one from Matthew's Gospel (11:25): 'you hide these things from the learned and the clever and you reveal them to mere children'.

Albert decided that there must be another way of doing scripture, rather than just the scholarly way. And this typified Albert's approach to Scripture and theology for the rest of his life. He realised that the Scriptures were powerful because they were the Word of God. The Word of God was alive and active, and the Word of God was there to touch people's hearts, to change them and to bring them to conversion. The Word of God transformed people's hearts so that they can change the world and to transform the reality in which they live. For Albert, Scripture was not just for academics. He wanted ordinary people to be able to read the Bible and to understand its significance for their lives. And that was what made his preaching, what made his theology, so vibrant—it freed people to be truly themselves. Perhaps he learnt this from Thomas Merton, who himself believed that the Scriptures exist to help us follow Christ, which means to become authentically oneself, to become a person who is alive and active in Christ.

Albert passed on this great enthusiasm for Scripture, for theology, to the university students when he became chaplain to the Catholic students at Stellenbosch University in the 1970s. Albert really touched the lives of these students, enabling them to understand that the reality of faith was not something that you practised in church on Sunday, but that which you had to live in your daily life. That Scripture was not only to be read but to be lived. This meant not saying of scripture: 'Oh, what lovely words; how inspiring and awesome they are!' No, the Word of God was more challenging that—it was a challenge to recognise your true dignity and authenticity as a human being, but then to go out and recognise the dignity and authenticity of every other human being in the world today. Live the Word of God!

We must remember that Albert was preaching this message during the time of Apartheid. Apartheid as the official ideology of the country at the time held that whites were the special loved ones of God and black people were second class at best. Albert always believed the scriptures: that every person created in God's image and likeness is a child of God. For Albert, all God's children need to have their dignity respected and their rights upheld. It was beholden to every Christian to ensure that they do this. This truth he believed was central to the teaching of Jesus. In his writings, Albert was always keen to point out that 'this is not *me* who is saying this to you' but *That man Jesus*. This was the phrase that he used as the title of his talks that he gave to the university students at the NCFS conference in 1972. All his preaching, all his theology, pointed to *That man Jesus*.

Albert's theological approach was really to motivate all people—white, black, rich, poor—to anticipate or to look forward to the coming of God's Kingdom or Reign of love, justice and peace among us. In the first book that he wrote called *Jesus before Christianity*, a revision of his lecture notes on *That man Jesus* that he gave to the NCFS conference, Albert starts with a warning of impending catastrophe awaiting us if we persist in the direction we are presently travelling in South Africa. For him, if we are to avert a future catastrophe, we need to take the present moment seriously by undergoing a radical change of heart and mind. 'Now is the time.' Later this would be referred to as the *kairos*.

Albert was influential in writing parts of the *Kairos Document*, or at least being its final editor. He often preached that:

> Now is the time, now is the *kairos*. Now is the opportunity for us to change our hearts, to live in a new way. We must take this opportunity now and not delay because we might not have enough time. It might be too late when we eventually wake up.

And so, throughout his life, Albert sought to bring theology down from its lofty academic heights and bring it to the people; bring it to us who were students; bring it to workers; bring it to all people in the country, to understand that theology was not just to be read, to be prayed about, but more importantly, to be lived.

When I came to Wits University in 1981, I joined the Catholic Student Society on campus. Albert's book was influential in shaping our faith as idealistic students. We used to say jokingly, 'The Protestant churches walk around with the Bible under their arms, we have *Jesus before Christianity*!' Albert's interpretation of the Scriptures for us, reminded us, as white South Africans, that we should not buy into the ideology of Apartheid, that we had to stand against it, and resist it even to the point of giving up our lives. Albert could be uncompromising in his preaching. It is interesting that in today's Gospel (Lk 6:20–23), we have 'blessed are the poor, blessed are the hungry, blessed are those who weep now, blessed are you when people hate you'. But the 'woes' have been left out. 'Woe to you who are rich, woe to you who are satisfied, woe to you who are comfortable.' Albert would not have left those words out, for sure. He will have reminded us that the gospel is not just about consolation and comfort, it was also about challenge.

Another opportunity arose when Albert attended a conference in 1975 in Peru, where he had contact with the thinking of the theologians in South America, particularly Gustavo Gutiérrez. Gutiérrez was a diocesan priest at the time, who wrote a book called *A Theology of Liberation*. In this book, Gutiérrez highlighted the challenges facing the Church in the Latin American context. Gustavo was himself involved in an organisation linked to the Young Christian Students (YCS), which employed the Cardijn methodology called See–Judge–Act. Gutiérrez also emphasised the need to bring the Word of God down from its lofty heights, to become a word that nourishes the lives of people, especially the poor and marginalised, to look at the reality in which they live, to evaluate it, and to understand it in the context of the Bible, and in terms of the context of Scripture. And then the third step, most important of all, not just to leave it at an academic level, but to *act*, to bring it into the lives of people, to make a difference in our world.

And in that sense, See–Judge–Act became a means within the Church to point the way to Christ in a more prophetic way. Not just to write statements of protest against injustices, but to realise that we have to do something about it. It is not enough for us just to condemn or to moralistically point fingers. Rather, Christians have to be actively involved and change the reality in which the poor and oppressed live. It meant becoming like *That man Jesus*, who was concerned about the suffering of others, who wanted the humanity of the poor and sinners of his time recognised. But it also meant seeing through the ideologies of oppression, so that in a system like Apartheid not only are the poor dehumanised but so is the oppressor.

To follow *That man Jesus* meant to free and liberate all people from oppression so that they can live as Christ did—by being more compassionate, more loving, more forgiving and to strive for social justice. Albert believed Jesus did not die on the cross because he just went against the doctrines of Judaism, but because he stood up for those who were in greatest need. And so, we see in Albert's theology, a concern for the suffering of humanity, for people's suffering, and that we as Christians cannot stand above it aloof, but to do something about ending this suffering.

In using the See–Judge–Act method in theology, Albert wrote his second book called *God in South Africa* in 1989. It was an attempt to write a South African contextual theology. Together with others he was part of the Institute for Contextual Theology (ICT) in Johannesburg, to try and develop this type of theology that follows the See–Judge–Act method, that brings the Bible to the people and speaks to the context of humanity's suffering. Contextual theology seeks to be a prophetic witness, a radical living out of the life-giving and transforming Word of God. As the struggle against Apartheid was intensifying, Albert also wanted people to be aware that God was active and at work bringing about transformation in the South African context through the struggle. He also wanted to give people hope in the midst of the pain and suffering they were enduring.

Years later in 2008, Albert received an official recognition from the Dominican Order for his work as a theologian. He was granted an honorary title as a Master of Sacred Theology by the Master of the Order. At the reception of his award, he gave a talk at St Vincent School for the Deaf in Johannesburg, entitled 'Hope in an age of despair'. It was a talk that typified Albert himself. Hope characterised the person that Albert was! He was a person who never despaired, because he had a deep trust and faith in *That man Jesus* and in the work of God. He believed that God was *in* all the situations in which we find ourselves so there was no need to fear. Yes, we are faced with catastrophe; yes, we are in danger; yes, we need to do something urgently; but if we respond to God's invitation to *do* something, God will provide the increase. It is really about God doing his work for us. We are only his assistants. It is all God's work, not ours.

In this respect, Albert had this unshakeable hope in life reminiscent of today's first reading (Isa 25:6–9). Isaiah envisages the final redemption God's people will receive even though they presently are being assaulted by the forces of chaos. The people of Judah are facing an invasion by the Assyrians. This is one of the most traumatic times of their history, where ten tribes of the northern kingdom have already been conquered and destroyed. Only Judah and Benjamin have survived so far, but they are under threat.

In the midst of this chaos and the Assyrian genocide being afflicted upon the people of Israel, Isaiah speaks these prophetic and hope-filled words. In the midst of their trauma—Isaiah speaks of God's salvation as a glorious banquet that will take place on Mount Zion. In this passage, Isaiah contrasts the present suffering, the trauma that Israel is undergoing, with a banquet of God's victory—a very hopeful message, in the face of an impending catastrophe. Rather than disaster, there will be a banquet of exuberant joy, where tables will overflow with rich food and glorious wine. Isaiah gives people hope by reminding them of God's glorious desire for his people.

But Isaiah also points out that God's liberation extends not just to the people of Israel, but to all people. God's saving actions will not just be for the salvation of Israel only but for all peoples on the earth, even Israel's enemies—the oppressive Assyrians, and the Moabites, and the Hittites. God's vision for the glory of Israel is for the glory of humanity. On this mountain, even death itself will be ultimately eaten or swallowed up. Death will be overcome by God's saving power. Even though darkness prevails, there is always hope in God's salvation. There is hope because God's message is a message of God's life-giving presence to his people.

Like Isaiah, Albert himself always pointed to the hope in any situation. I remember times when I used to complain when I was provincial, about this problem or that problem. Albert was always able to turn it around, and help me see the hope in the situation, or what needed to be done. He was always encouraging one never to give up hope, that you must give people another chance, or see the problem one is confronted with from a new angle or a different perspective.

In our world today, Albert's way of living for Christ, pointing to *That man Jesus*, is as necessary as it was when he wrote during the time of Apartheid. After 1994, and when the enthusiasm to build up the rainbow nation dissipated and the corruption of the ANC became so prevalent, Albert wrote another book, *Jesus Today*. It was obvious that the freedom many had fought so hard for was being eroded by the greed of a new elite that was jumping on the bandwagon to get rich quick. They did not care that they were hollowing out the institutions of our society and the organs of our civil society for personal gain and to the detriment of the common good. In this book, Albert acknowledged the need for structural change in society, but it was useless if it was not accompanied by a personal conversion of heart too. The corrupt and selfish values of this world need to be replaced by the values of the Reign of God. This means moving from a preoccupation with the demands of our little or false self and opting to live from what Merton called the true self. It means putting individualism and selfishness aside and living for the common good. For Albert, it is only when human beings can learn to act from their true selves rather than their egotistical selves that change can happen that will help our world avert poverty, corruption, war and ecological devastation.

In conclusion, let us end with the words of Albert. When once I asked him to write down his memoirs, he smiled wryly and said he did not want his life dissected and analysed. 'I am not important', he said, 'if people want to know who I was, what I believed and what I stood for, then they can read my books'.

So hopefully, I have given you a taste that will encourage you to go from here and do what Albert suggested: 'read my books and follow *That man Jesus*'.

Section One

The Early Years

Photos left to right: 1. Dennis aged 4 years.   2. Dennis with sister Iris, brother Ronnie and cousins Sheila and Jean.   3. Dennis as altar server wth Ronnie.

Beginnings

Virginia Zweigenthal

Fr Albert Nolan was the first born of three children of James (Jimmy) and Dorothy Margaret Nolan (neé Kiddle) and was named Dennis James Harry. He was born in a maternity home in Newlands Cape Town, on 2 September 1934. His brother, Ronnie, followed two years later. The family then moved to 26 Wandel Street in Gardens where his sister, Iris, was born two years later.

Albert, as most of us knew him, was a private person and his family background was largely unknown. Two rich resources for the writing of this article reflecting on his early life were a presentation he gave to the Jesuits in 1986, entitled 'My Experience of Being a Religious in South Africa', and an interview I conducted in March 2023 with Iris Prinsloo, Albert's eighty-five-year-old sister, at her home in a retirement village in Tableview, Cape Town.

This exploration of Albert's family and early life could provide a more contextual and rounded sense of Albert, the priest, theologian and intellectual; the person who impacted on theology as well as on the local and global Church, and who has touched so many people's lives. This chapter refers to him as both Albert and Dennis, and these names are used interchangeably. When he refers to himself, he is Albert; when Iris talks about him, he is Dennis; before he becomes a Dominican religious, he is Dennis and afterwards he is Albert.

I first met Iris when she came to our Cape Town memorial service to commemorate Albert's life in late November 2022. She brought black and white photographs of the family from their childhood to the service for everyone to look at before and after the service. They included portraits of him as a toddler and young child, pictures of him with siblings and cousins and after his ordination with his parents. There were newspaper photographs of Albert shaking John Paul II's hand at the Vatican and receiving the Order of Luthuli, shaking Thabo Mbeki's hand.

Iris, a slight woman with a broad smile, exuded a calm serenity. She spoke confidently and proudly at the memorial service about her brother, whose life she celebrated and embraced. It was clear that Albert was Iris' brother. She had a similar defined chin, and threw her head back when she laughed, much like my memory of Albert who too laughed often. She was delighted when I called her in February 2023 to ask if she would be up for talking about Albert, and we made a time for me to visit her in her home a few days later.

Iris told me that theirs was not a wealthy family. Their home, which still stands, is a semi-detached terraced Victorian house, in one of the oldest quarters of Cape Town, Gardens. An inner-city suburb, Gardens was named after and developed around the original Dutch East India Company gardens. That land, now a heritage park in contemporary Cape Town, was appropriated by the Dutch to grow vegetables for company vessels that docked in Cape Town on their way to the East. Bordering on the city centre, Gardens was not an upmarket area as it is now. The Nolans did not own their home, and Iris remembers the landlord coming to collect rent each month. The three children looked forward to his visit as he was fond of them, giving each child a few pennies every month. Dennis, the eldest received six pence, Ronnie, four, and Iris two pence!

Albert, in his talk to the Jesuits, also recalls their street in Gardens, which sounds much like a contemporary inner city setting. He remarks that early in life he confronted 'the hard realities of drunkenness, violence, sexual exploitation, poverty, prostitution and even murder'. While many neighbourhood children grew up to become professionals, there were some girls who became prostitutes and boys who became policemen.

Although Dorothy—their mother—was not a Catholic herself, the family was deeply involved in the Catholic Church. Their father, Jimmy, was the Catholic, and their local parish was St Mary's Cathedral, where all three children were baptised and confirmed. Both Dennis and Ronnie were altar boys and photographs of them serving at Mass are centre points of Iris' family photograph collection. Dorothy promoted the children's attendance at Mass, and Iris recalls her mother reminding the children to express thankfulness at church.

All three children were educated at Catholic schools. Dennis was first educated at St Mary's Convent, a Dominican girls' convent school, which admitted boys in the early grades. It is located next to the cathedral and was a short walking distance from their home and still operates today. After completing Grade Four, Dennis transferred to the Marist Brothers' junior school, in Hatfield Street, Gardens very near St Mary's. This school closed in 1983. The original Marist brothers' high school in Gardens moved in 1933 to St Joseph's College in Rondebosch where Dennis completed Standard Eight (modern-day Grade Ten).

Both boys, Dennis and Ronnie, left school at the end of Standard Eight, taking jobs at the Standard Bank to contribute to the family income. Dennis went to a correspondence college in the evening, putting himself through the last years of schooling and matriculated in 1952 at the age of eighteen. He worked for four years at the bank and for three of these years bought and sold stocks and shares for the bank's clients. Albert comments that he found that world 'vicious', with people delighting in crushing competitors financially. He perceived that 'survival of the fittest' was the order of the day.

Iris remembers that Dennis told their mother that it was while he was working in the bank that he 'had a calling'. This he put to his mother as, 'rather than helping people with money, [I'd like to] help them with themselves'. Dorothy confirmed with him that this was his own decision, checked with him that there was no coercion involved and gave Dennis her blessing.

Albert's mother, Dorothy was the centre of the family, and her values permeated their day-to-day life. Albert credits his mother with instilling him with the value of compassion, a deep emotional concern for people who suffer. Albert remembers his mother daily reminding the children of the starving millions in India. Iris framed this as her mother's kindness. She recalls Dorothy speaking about there being rich and poor people in the world and that one always needed to think about that. Examples of her concern for others are two stories that Iris relayed to me.

Across the road from their home in Gardens, there were flower sellers, who sold bouquets daily to customers even in the 1940s. Now, selling flowers is a long-standing occupation of people of colour in Cape Town, and even though this was a pre-Apartheid era, racial segregation was firmly entrenched in society. Dorothy went against those norms and regularly made the flower sellers a flask of coffee to see them through their long working days. To show their appreciation, they reciprocated, giving her a bunch of flowers which she loved and which gave her joy. Iris also reminisced about a scene of her mom scolding the police for roughing up a man of colour who 'had a few toots', admonishing them as he had done no harm. Dorothy maintained that it was important to 'be kind when you can and do what you can'.

Dorothy did not work when the Nolan children were young. Their father, Jimmy, was a carpenter, but his employment was not constant. Consequently, as Albert relays, the family was always in debt but did not think of themselves as poor. Iris remembers that Jimmy smoked and consequently suffered poor lung health. She remembers his difficult, laboured breathing as he slowly climbed the stairs to the bedrooms on the upstairs floor in the house. In time, his compromised health resulted in him giving up his carpentry work. Towards the end of his working life, he too worked at the Standard Bank, directing customers where to go. Jimmy died in Groote Schuur Hospital in Observatory, Cape Town, soon after Dennis—by then Albert—was ordained as a priest in 1961.

Life at home was not always easy. Besides financial woes, Albert indicates that his parents argued and their displays of anger frightened him as a young boy. As an adult, Albert says that he was known as someone who did not get angry. He avoided interpersonal conflict at all cost even among his fellow religious. He rather looked for a middle ground and a compromise to keep the peace. Later in life, he realised that many of his concerns and approaches grew out of his early life experiences and his social conditioning. He then learnt to speak out and focus his energy—his anger—against social and political systems that underlie human suffering and pain.

Despite the family circumstances, Iris recalls that there was always food on the table at home. Dorothy reminded the children that it was important to have one decent meal a day. Before setting out for school, Dorothy prepared the children's Jungle Oats for breakfast. It was dished out into three bowls, and Iris, who enjoyed her porridge hot, was there first. She remembers that Ronnie complained if it was cold, but Dennis did not mind!

Iris remembers Dennis, the schoolboy as a great reader, not particularly outgoing, although he had friends. She recalled two Polish girls who frequently passed their house looking for Dennis, who escaped when he saw them coming! He had a good friend in his eldest cousin, Jean, the daughter of his maternal aunt, and they spent many afternoons talking at family events, particularly at the Nolan Christmas.

The family stayed on at the Wandel Street house after Dennis entered his novitiate in 1954 at St Nicholas' Priory in Stellenbosch along with his lifelong friend Gregory Brooke. Dennis took on his religious name Albert and was finally professed in 1958. Iris remembers that news had spread in the neighbourhood that Dennis had decided to become a priest, and one young boy often came past their house asking Dorothy about him as he too wished to become a priest. The family visited Dennis in Stellenbosch when they could, taking him his favourite treats. Iris laughingly remembers their mom taking Albert a packet of Sunrise toffees for himself, and Albert retorting 'No ma, Dominicans share. We put it on the table!' Iris highlighted Albert's concern and love for the family. He offered to baptise his mom, which he later did. Although he no longer contributed to the family finances, he helped out where he could. Iris had moved to Stellenbosch and worked as a saleslady for Woolworths. Her husband Colin, who had worked for the Navy, needed work and Albert helped find him office work. After Dorothy became ill and Jimmy had died, Albert helped find a place for her at Villa Maria, a Catholic residential home in central Cape Town for women. She soon moved to live with Iris in Stellenbosch, but the family moved back to Cape Town into a small house once Iris' husband had re-joined the Navy and was based in Simonstown. Again, Albert helped his mom find a place in an old-aged home in Observatory. Soon afterwards, it was discovered that Dorothy had diabetes and cancer and she passed away, also at Groote Schuur hospital in 1989.

Albert maintained his relationships with his family and siblings. He officiated at the marriages of Ronnie to Edith and Iris to Colin as well as the weddings of Iris' two sons, Lance and Wayne. Iris and 'Dennis', as she continued to call him, often spoke on the phone, particularly when pension pay-outs were due. Both Iris and Albert physically went to collect their South African state pension—a South African Social Security Agency (SASSA) grant—an amount of less than R2000, or USD110 monthly, which is grossly inadequate to support families or individuals. She highlighted Dennis' concern with the family's health and welfare and on occasion he helped family members experiencing financial difficulties with his grant. He visited his family regularly when he was on leave, and Iris fondly remembers his visits and outings with him to visit other Dominican priests' families.

Iris has a set of birthday cards from Albert, some gently teasing about her love of animals. All signed, 'Dennis', they were always sent in time for her birthday until 2019. These are treasured mementos, symbols of his care and love for his 'little sister'. While he remembered her birthday, she had to remind him of other family members' birthdays which he had forgotten, and he was grateful for the reminder. She remembers Dennis as an 'even-keeled person', who guided her, encouraging her to call on her own strength and patience to manage life's difficulties. When she told Dennis that he was the clever sibling, followed by Ronnie, he retorted that he 'could never be a saleslady like you. Because if you put me behind the counter, I wouldn't know what to do. So that's your profession'. She remembers that he emphasised that she and every person was valuable and worthy, that people should always treasure and not limit themselves.

Albert's formative experiences as a child are evident in the man he became. He had insight into the world he was born into, which with reflection, enabled him to 'read the signs of the times' in South Africa. While his disposition was to avoid conflict, he learnt to speak out, harnessing his experience of injustice and using his sharp mind to confront Church and State. He was deeply appreciative and cognisant of the values and person that he saw in his mother, Dorothy. Like her, he responded to both individuals and communities with compassion, living and walking with them. Albert enabled people, wherever they found themselves to reflect, to 'do theology' and act to transform their circumstance and the world. His kind demeanour and his sense of humour were always present. These qualities also shone in Iris, his sister. She too loves her family and Church. She was so keen to help us know Dennis as she knew him.

Aggiornamento

Andrew Prior

Albert Nolan knew the word *aggiornamento*. He had learnt it after arriving in Rome in 1962 to study at the Angelicum, the Dominican University in Rome. But he did not learn it immediately. A few months elapsed between his arrival and Pope John XXIII announcing the beginning of the Second Vatican Council and his learning of the word.

When Albert went to study in Rome he met the medieval Church. On his first days at the University he visited the barber to have a tonsure, the top part of his head shaved bare like the medieval friars, and always wearing the Dominican habit in the priory and the Roman streets. And thus began his studies, attending lectures on dogmatic and moral theology given by habited, learned, elderly friars in fluent medieval Latin as spoken in the thirteenth century by Thomas Aquinas. Leaving Cape Town he now found himself in another world, the world of Latin, monkish habits and private prayers, in the formula of past ages. Then Pope John XXIII, aware of the outdated character of the Church, announced that the time had come to 'update, renovate and modernise' the Church. The word that he used was *aggiornamento* (update). And Albert learnt it.

Albert was in Rome for the opening of the Second Vatican Council on 11 October 1962. And he, like many Catholics, religious or secular, had to confront the new reality. 'Open the Church's windows; let in fresh air; shake off the imperial dust accumulated on the throne of St Peter!' And so Albert and his contemporaries in Rome, who had arrived at the centre of Roman Catholicism to find it dogmatic and hidebound in its traditions, were forced to confront the disturbing world of institutional change, theological criticism, and implement it. Critical institutional analysis, examining codes of belief and moral behaviour became the order of the day.

But the invitation to the new world brought words of warning. An example came from Denis Hurley, Archbishop of Durban: 'Go into the Church with your broom', he advised his flock, 'and sweep out the accumulated dust of the ages!' This was quickly followed by a qualification: 'But don't throw away the furniture, the sacred traditions of the past!'

Armed with this new vision and fully identifying with it, the young Albert Nolan returned to St Nicholas Priory in Stellenbosch, near Cape Town, in 1964. His aim was to implement the vision of the Vatican Council: respect tradition, remove what is defective in it, be open minded and engage in dialogue with the world.

Not long after returning Albert was contacted by aspirant *dominees* (pastors) from the Dutch Reformed *Kweekskool*, the training school for *predikants* (ministers) in their Church. Aware of the open mindedness of the Vatican Council, Albert agreed to a meeting. Two enthusiastic Afrikaans-speaking young men arrived, wearing dark suits, white ties and each grasping a Bible. Opposite them sat the habit-clad Dominicans eager to implement what Pope John had advised and what these young men wanted. The *predikant* students were the first to speak. They spoke in the manner of a sermon drawing to the attention of their seated audience the failures of the Roman Catholic Church, quoting extracts from their Bibles, and what they should do to become true, Bible-believing Christians. Then it was the Dominican students turn to speak with a vigour equal to that of the *predikant* students, pointing out the failures of the Reformation and their proponents. It was as if each group was in an opposite pulpit preaching to the other and expecting the other to listen and accept what they were saying with the humility of church-goers listening to the Sunday sermon. But they weren't in a church and neither group was prepared to accept what the other had said.

Leaving the meeting Albert knew that an impasse was reached; mutual preaching does not result in the one accepting, or even respecting, the views of the other. Preaching might work in a church, but not in a seminar room. How do you break it? He knew that only through open-minded discussion, mutual respect, listening and evaluating by both groups, could there be any hope for finding common ground. How do you find the means to do this? To his surprise, he discovered that there was a way. And, ironically, it came from a Professor at the University of Stellenbosch.

That man was a thirty-year-old South African, Johan Degenaar, educated at Stellenbosch and in the Netherlands, and now a professor in his own department. His early appointment as a professor was unusual. Returning from the Netherlands he lectured in the Philosophy Department but his method of teaching met with opposition from the *Kweekskool*. Their problem was that aspirant Dutch Reformed ministers were expected to do a course in philosophy, and their lecturer was Johan Degenaar. Finding that his teaching methods resulted in a critical approach to life and philosophy and, in their opinion, undermined the teachings of the Reformed Church, they campaigned to force him from the University. They were partially successful. The agreement was that Degenaar would leave the Philosophy Department and so release the aspirant *predikante* from his classrooms, and he would establish his own department, *Staatsfilosofie*, Political Philosophy.

His method of teaching was straightforward. Instead of seeing philosophy teaching as the dogmatic transmission of philosophical systems, he placed himself in the tradition of the ancient Greek philosophers, Anaximander and Socrates. 'The secret to understanding nature's secrets is through asking questions', Anaximander had said, 'Don't accept beliefs as truth simply because they are beliefs. Don't accept dogmatic assertions because of faith; question what you believe'.

Initially the size of Degenaar's classes were small because of the *Kweekskool* opposition to him but this benefitted his teaching method. Classes were turned into discussion groups; the most critical phrase used by Degenaar was 'What do you mean?' Questioning, examining through discussion became his critical tool. Ironically, even though many academics at the University opposed Degenaar and his teaching methods, there were many who supported him.

Two events forced the attention of the university academics on the country's racial policies. They were the police killings of sixty-nine pass law protestors at Sharpeville on 21 March 1960 and the arrest, trial and imprisonment of prominent anti-Apartheid activists, including Nelson Mandela, in 1964. Some Afrikaners, including academics at Stellenbosch, began to question the government's Apartheid policies, others demanded that the policy of racial segregation be implemented more strongly. Stellenbosch's academics found themselves in this turmoil of self-examination. Among them was Johan Degenaar.

Aware of the changing mood amongst some of his fellow academics, Degenaar set up a *Kring*, a small discussion group composed of lecturers and professors from different disciplines who were later to be called the *verligtes* (the enlightened), as opposed to the *verkramptes* (the hidebound traditionalists). Meeting monthly, they listened to a paper given by one of them before engaging in discussion. Participants included professors of the social and natural sciences, theology, mathematics, and literature. Invited too were Dominicans from St Nicholas Priory and some of the meetings occurred at the Priory. And so, questioning and examining intellectual disciplines became the order of the day.

When he returned from Rome, Albert Nolan was invited to the group. He and a few fellow Dominicans became enthusiastic participants. They too became involved in the process of self-examination, 'updating', and modernising. Each time Albert, or another Dominican, presented a paper they were confronted with Degenaar's standard question, 'What do you mean by . . .?' And so Albert found himself involved in the two historical paths, '*aggiornamento*' and 'critical thinking'. He knew what the Italian word meant; now he saw how this could apply to South African institutions: Instead of preaching to the proponents of Apartheid, communism or other political systems, engage with them by subjecting everything to testing and rational analysis. Individual conscience should be free from political or religious coercion. Reason, individualism, and scepticism should replace authoritarianism, autocratic government, or other forms of political and religious control.

This process had its attendant problems. Established institutions felt threatened. Critical analysis sometimes resulted in rejection of established churches like the Dutch Reformed Church and the Catholic Church. Some supporters of the political programme of Apartheid and nationalism defected from their institutions to the point where they themselves opposed their traditional racial philosophies and began the process of negotiation with those previously excluded from the political and economic systems. Some supporters and believers in religious systems rejected them for alternative philosophical systems. The Dutch Reformed Church was faced with the danger of losing members if it did not 'update or modernise'. The seeds of change were sown. It took time for them to put out shoots and germinate. But germinate they did during the 1970s and 1980s.

The Dominicans in Stellenbosch came under similar pressures from within the Catholic Church. Some began the process of critical reflection of *aggiornamento,* which took them down the path of individualism and making their own decisions about their lives, which resulted in them leaving the Order. Others however were more successful in harmonising *aggiornamento* and critical analysis. Among them was Albert Nolan.

His success enabled him to examine his personal beliefs, think for himself, and re-commit himself to his life as a Dominican. He was one who balanced *aggiornamento*, critical thinking and his religious commitments. For this he will be remembered as a believer, an intellectual and one of the great successful reformers.

What were the outcomes? An example is in the changing mood in the Dutch Reformed Church. In the 1990s and in the aftermath of the release from prison of Nelson Mandela, students from the *Kweekskool*, along with several Dominicans, were ready to accept the principles of critical thinking and to meet in spaces where ecumenism, changes in religious perceptions of race and how to build up a new South Africa were discussed.

Was this change because of the work of Albert Nolan or Johan Degenaar, or the changing mood of the times? Take your choice. Probably something from all of them.

Photos left to right   1. Albert as a Dominican student.   2. Albert's ordination.
　　　　　　　　　　3. Albert with his family after his ordination.   4. Albert at the marriage of his sister, Iris.

Stellenbosch

Joseph Falkiner OP

Albert Nolan joined the Dominican Order in 1954 at the age of nineteen. He had already worked for Standard Bank for four years, where he was known by his birth name of Dennis, but on being clothed in the habit of the Dominican Order at the start of his novitiate year he was given the name Albert after St Albert the Great. This was a symbolic way of indicating that he was to begin a totally changed way of life and indeed he did so. This clothing took place in the Dominican Priory at Stellenbosch in the Western Cape.

On completing his novitiate year on 1 March 1955 he made his first vows, after which he began his life of study. His first few years as a student of philosophy and theology were spent at the same Stellenbosch Dominican Priory under the guidance of a number of Dominican lecturers who had been sent from England to teach South African recruits to the Order. He was then sent to Rome for higher studies so that he himself could qualify as a lecturer and return to Stellenbosch to teach others.

The Stellenbosch property had been bought by the English Dominican Province in 1930 with the idea of it becoming the site of a future house of formation for South African Dominicans. On the property were a large nineteenth-century farmhouse and an eighteenth-century barn capable of being transformed into a church, as well as some outbuildings said to have been slave-quarters in previous times. The first recruits underwent all their formation in England but the plan was to erect a fairly large priory building capable of housing up to thirty brothers. This was only implemented in the late 1940s when the number of recruits increased. When Albert began his novitiate, a number of brothers were already undergoing their formation there.

The priory was not merely a residence but a house of studies with a classroom, a library and a community of lecturers and students, as well as two or three lay-brothers.

While he was in Rome the Second Vatican Council began. It brought enormous change into the Catholic Church, not only spiritually and intellectually, but also structurally. I think it made Albert realise that similar enormous changes must be implemented in Dominican formation and studies back home in South Africa. The novitiate and house of studies would certainly have to be moved away from Stellenbosch as Apartheid had become government policy in 1948 and the local municipality had prohibited any Africans whatsoever from residing in the town.

I joined the Order in 1963 while Albert was still in Rome and so was able to observe Albert's return to Stellenbosch in 1964. We lived together in that community until the end of 1969 when I was ordained and sent to assist the novice master at Payneville, outside Springs, where we had just established a non-racial novitiate. It was not in a Dominican priory but in temporary quarters in a parish. Albert however remained in Stellenbosch with a dwindling number of Dominican students until he was elected provincial in 1976. The relocation of the novitiate and the dwindling numbers created great uncertainty about the future of the priory.

There was no sudden change. During the late 1960s while I was still there I was not aware of any plan regarding where future students might do their studies. Albert was no politician and did nothing to promote himself or his ideas, but in retrospect I believe that he was working quietly in the background to influence our ideas. He knew that the days of the Stellenbosch priory were numbered and that he had to prepare us for a different future. At that time, he had no formal role in the running of the priory. He was not the prior. He was not the student master. He was not part of the revolt against religious life that resulted in the gradual departure of the prior, the student master, some of our lecturers and the majority of the students. He was just there, and for those of us that remained he became the one that we could look up to.

Albert believed that our spirituality should be based on studying firstly the 'signs of our times' and then studying how Jesus reacted to the 'signs of his time'. This double emphasis would result in us developing a much more mature spirituality and theology. The phrase 'signs of the times' was introduced to the Church by Pope John XXIII in the 1961 document *Humanae Salutis* that announced the coming Vatican Council II. Albert had been in Rome when that document was issued. After years of debate it was taken up by the Council's Pastoral Constitution on the Church in the Modern World in 1965. Albert introduced us to this concept from 1964 onwards.

The signs of our times that I remember us noticing included that we lived not only in a country dominated by racial Apartheid but that the town of Stellenbosch actually prohibited any black residents. There were not even any African domestic servants allowed in the town. All unskilled work was done by so-called 'coloured' people, that is people of supposedly mixed racial ancestry, and many of those in the Western Cape were not of mixed origin at all but were direct descendants of slaves brought from Indonesia in the seventeenth and eighteenth centuries. We noted that in some of their workplaces they were still treated as if they were slaves. Most importantly, as our house of formation was situated in Stellenbosch we would not be allowed to accommodate any African candidates wanting to become Dominicans.

Another sign of our times was the world-wide debate that had arisen among Catholic academics in the 1960s as to whether the church should focus on being a church 'for the poor', or alternatively a church with 'a preferential option for the poor' or more radically 'a church of the poor'. Albert was aware that in South Africa the socially and economically poor were the African people and the so-called 'coloured' people. Legislation had been passed by the apartheid government to keep Africans poor by allowing them only elementary education so that they would forever remain as unskilled labourers for the benefit of white-owned industries and white people in general. The 'coloured' people in Stellenbosch were marginally better off in that they were allowed to become skilled in certain specified trades in the building industry, but they still had to live apart from whites in a poor township known as Ida's Valley. The very poor among them were assigned to a shanty-town known as Cloetesville. Albert was adamant that this debate was not merely academic but should change the way that Catholic parishes and their parishioners treated the poor. We Dominicans ran the parish of Stellenbosch. Our prior was *de facto* the parish priest for the two local Catholic parishes. What were we to do?

A third sign of the times in which we were living was the remarkable 'Christian Institute' (CI) founded by Beyers Naudé in 1963 in Johannesburg. This originally had the aim of fostering reconciliation through interracial dialogue, research, and publications. It soon became seen as an enemy of the Apartheid State. For an ordained minister of the Dutch Reformed Church to have initiated such an institute was anathema. He had to choose between his pastoral ministry and his promotion of the CI. He chose the latter. Twice he visited the priory, in 1966 and again in 1968.

Having attended the first meeting of the Stellenbosch CI group in 1964 with two other friars, Albert led us Dominican students at Stellenbosch to read the flow of publications from the CI. One of our students even refused to make his solemn vows in the Dominican Order unless the Order could guarantee that he would be assigned specifically to work with the CI. That could not be allowed and that student left us. But Albert and Beyers became friends and some years later, after Albert became provincial and was living in Johannesburg, they combined to give support to the leaders-in-exile of the banned African National Congress (ANC).

These signs of our times at Stellenbosch really had an impact on Albert, as one can see by looking at his later life and the books he wrote. His 2006 book *Jesus Today* reveals how his thoughts about the signs of the times developed into a spirituality enabling readers to face up to the post-modern world with all its uncertainties. But that came later. The impact on us Dominican students in the 1960s was that he influenced a change in our ideas, not only by means of lectures, but also through casual remarks made during private conversations.

In the 1970s his main pastoral assignment was that of chaplain to the small number of Catholic university students at the Afrikaans-speaking University of Stellenbosch (US), giving them talks mainly about Jesus. His approach to them was based on the gospels as reflected in his 1976 book *Jesus before Christianity*. It is largely about how Jesus related to people who were poor, oppressed or marginalised; how Jesus responded to the signs of his time. Albert told me once that his talks to these university students gave him the inspiration to get it all into book form.

What I was not aware of at the time but discovered later was that to Albert the US was the intellectual and spiritual home of the racial concept of Apartheid including its philosophical and theological justification. This was where young men aspiring to become clerics in the Dutch Reformed Church did all their studies, and the choice made by the English Dominican Province many years previously for Stellenbosch to be the site of the Dominican House of Studies had been made to counter its influence.[1]

Albert made it his business to go into this matter. We Dominican students at the priory knew that Albert had frequent contacts with a certain Professor Johan Degenaar at the university. We knew that he attended meetings of a small discussion group, but hardly any of us knew what was being discussed. Only after Degenaar died in 2015 and I read his obituary did I begin to perceive what Albert must really have been occupied with during those Stellenbosch years. It was with what he could learn from Degenaar. It formed the basis of what he could later contribute to the writing of the *Kairos Document* with its attack on both 'State theology' and 'Church theology' as both types of theology that justified the racial divisions of society. Degenaar had been head of Philosophy at Stellenbosch University for many years before he was demoted to a lesser position for having consistently challenged Apartheid's racial dogma. Naturally Degenaar's subversive lectures and publications had been noted by Apartheid politicians and information was given to the security police. He was being watched. So when Albert began to be a regular visitor to Degenaar a security file was opened on him as well. This resulted in files being set up on all us Dominican students because of our friendship with Albert in the priory. Albert told us that a policeman had given him this information as a warning. I discovered it to be true because when I was moved by the provincial from Stellenbosch to be assistant priest in our new temporary novitiate at Payneville (a black and coloured township outside of Springs about fifty km from Johannesburg) some security police knocked on the door just to check on where I was living.

Albert also became involved in the parish apostolate. Stellenbosch had two Catholic parishes, an English-speaking parish based at the priory in the white town, and an Afrikaans-speaking parish in the coloured township of Ida's Valley. Both were served by Dominican priests from the priory. When Albert arrived back from Rome the priory had two other priests who could converse and preach in Afri-

---

1. Philippe Denis, *The Dominican Friars in Southern Africa* (Leiden: Brill, 1998), 120–123.

kaans but as the number of priests in the priory dropped, Albert remained the only fluent Afrikaans-speaker and had to do most of the pastoral work in Ida's Valley. He got to know the people there and soon discovered some housewives struggling to feed their children. Invariably the problem was that their husbands were alcoholics bringing in very little income and the last thing the wives wanted was another baby. Was this not just another sign of the times in which we lived? Albert told us that the only solution he could think of was to provide them with anti-booze tablets. He explained to us that when the husbands arrived home under the influence and likely to demand sex later that evening once the children were asleep, the wives would crush one of the tablets into powder and sprinkle it on to the husband's food. That powder would react with the alcohol making the man feel ill and he would lose his desire for sex.

But then in 1968 came Pope Paul VI's encyclical *Humanae Vitae*. It forbade Catholics from practising artificial forms of birth control. Only 'natural' methods of contraception like the rhythm method were permitted. Albert initiated a discussion of the whole priory community (priests and students together) to determine what our pastoral approach could be. The upshot was that we all signed a press statement which said in effect that *Humanae Vitae* should not be taken as the last word on the matter. This made headline news in the *Cape Times* newspaper and later in the Catholic press. The first that the Archbishop of Cape Town, Cardinal Owen McCann, knew of it was when a reporter asked him for his comments. He was naturally disturbed and told the prior that he should have been informed in advance.

Another result of this press statement was that our benefactors ceased to support us. They were shocked that we were negating a document signed by the pope. Some even assumed we had left the Catholic Church. The Cardinal got wind of that too, and said that we would have to reassure people that we were still loyal Catholics by always wearing Roman collars when we made trips into Cape Town. We had not been in the habit of doing that. But the priory lost some benefactors permanently.

Albert was elected Prior of Stellenbosch in October 1970 and in 1976 he was elected provincial. In this capacity he presided over the winding down of the priory and sale of the property in 1980.

A Saint and a Doctor of the Church

Brian Robertson

I first met Albert at the Dominican priory in Stellenbosch when I went there in the sixties to become a Dominican priest. Albert accompanied me spiritually for the three years of philosophy studies until I left the priory for the married life.

My most warm and enduring images are of Albert patiently guiding me during spiritual direction. I was and have always been struck by his happy, loving and self-effacing personality, a man at peace with himself who always made himself available whatever else he might be doing. I had not met anyone before who so clearly embodied the Christian way of life.

When Francoise and I married in 1967, Albert was the priest I wanted to officiate, and he obliged as always. Reading his groundbreaking and prophetic book *Jesus before Christianity* in 1976 was probably for me the first step of many towards a real understanding of Jesus' message which ultimately culminated in my decision in 2010 to propose the establishment of We Are All Church South Africa (WAACSA).

I don't need his canonisation to know that Albert is a saint and a doctor of the Church. St Albert, please continue to love and teach us.

Photos left to right   1. Albert in 1975.   2. Albert's mother, Dorothy.   3. Albert with his sister, Iris.

Section Two

Student Chaplain

St Nicholas Priory, Stellenbosch.

An Inspiration to a Generation of Students

Mike Deeb OP

I arrived at Stutterheim (in the modern-day Eastern Cape) on a cold July afternoon in 1975, filled with apprehension about the week ahead. The annual conference of the National Catholic Federation of Students (NCFS) had become the highlight of each year for me—this year for the third time. But now, as a twenty-two-year-old student in the final year of my BA degree, I arrived with a big quandary: Should I accept a job offer for the following year (including a promise to be sent to do an MBA) that was difficult to refuse, or should I accept a strong proposal that I make myself available as a candidate to be the next NCFS president—which would be impossible to combine with doing an MBA? This anxiety was increased when I became a pawn in a 'simulation game' orchestrated by Kallie Hanekom, the NCFS president at the time, which separated each of us on arrival, unknowingly, into a group of 'haves' or 'have-nots'—the former with many privileges and the latter with absolutely nothing! After a near-revolution, the experiential learning gained about the nature of our society left its mark. This set the tone for another conference of transformational experiences and insights around the theme, 'Liberation'. The highlight of the conference was an explosive talk on 'The Kingdom of God' by the national chaplain, Albert Nolan, which filled most of the hundred or more students present with a fervour for a faith that would last for months, years and even decades.

Despite the hectic schedule of the conference, Albert made time to sit down with me to sift through my dilemma, enabling me to come to a life-changing decision to abandon a future in 'business' and to commit to working in the Church as a vehicle for contributing to ending the unjust system of Apartheid in South Africa. I was not the only student thus assisted by Albert to discover God in Jesus, to let go of my preconceived images of God (such as a grey old man with a wagging finger waiting for me to break a rule) and to make commitments that would radically reshape my dreams and behaviour with a fervour for God's Kingdom. A whole generation of students in NCFS, in the broader Catholic university student movement and later, the secondary and university students in the Young Christian Students (YCS) would similarly be touched by Albert, especially when he was national chaplain of NCFS and of all Catholic Students (1973–1980) and of YCS (1977–1984).

Albert's journey with students started some years earlier when he was appointed in 1970 as the Catholic chaplain to Stellenbosch University, the intellectual powerhouse of Apartheid ideology which vigorously promoted Afrikaner nationalism. According to Kallie Hanekom (a Stellenbosch student who was NCFS President in 1974/75, and was close to Albert throughout his period as chaplain there), being regarded as a campus for the *volk* (the Afrikaner people), groups like the Catholic Society (Cathsoc) and the Jewish Society could not be officially registered on campus. In this context, Albert had already drawn close to Johan Degenaar, a controversial liberal-minded philosopher, who formed a regular discussion group of critical reflection, the *Kring*. He was also in continual dialogue with the Catholic students with whom he refined his political perspectives in tandem with his understanding of faith in Jesus. Kallie recalls Albert being preoccupied with understanding and confronting the group solidarity of the *volk* in order to develop a 'human solidarity'—that featured so strongly in his articulation of the Kingdom values of Jesus in his 1976 book, *Jesus before Christianity*.[1]

Albert's work with students began during a watershed year for NCFS. The Black Consciousness movement initiated by Steve Biko and his companions, along with Black Theology which was particularly promoted through the ecumenical University Christian Movement (UCM), had gained traction on all the black university campuses and this sentiment erupted at the 1970 NCFS national conference. Acrimonious divergent views of the black and white students led to the Cathsocs in the four black universities disaffiliating from NCFS in the following year. The remaining affiliates from the eight

---

1. Interview with Kallie Hanekom, Fish Hoek, Cape Town, 2 March 2023.

white universities then began a process of soul-searching. A more liberal leadership was elected in 1971, which asked Albert to lead the 1972 conference around the theme, 'That Man Jesus'. His talks fired up the students (and many chaplains) and laid the foundation for a new generation, especially after he eventually refined the material in 1976 into his best-selling book, *Jesus before Christianity*. It was translated into at least fifteen other languages and touched the lives of countless numbers of people in all corners of the globe. I personally caught the fire indirectly by attending a regional conference of the Cathsocs from the universities of Pretoria (Tukkies) and the Witwatersrand (Wits) in April 1973. Hearing the same material of 'That Man Jesus' communicated by the Pretoria chaplain, Jan Haen CSsR, inspired a dramatic conversion in me that set me on a path which I am still exploring today. The impression made by Albert also led the students to ask for him to be the national chaplain and the bishops appointed him in late 1973.

At the 1974 conference focused on 'Reconciliation' (my second national conference and I was the conference organiser), it was decided to send delegations to visit each of the four black campuses to start a process of reconciliation. I visited the University of the North (Turfloop) with two other Wits University students. These visits culminated in a gathering of representatives from all the black campuses and most of the white campuses in Mariannhill near Durban in March 1975, in the context of an NCFS Natal (now KwaZulu-Natal) regional conference focused on 'Christian Liberation' led by Albert and Kallie. The encounter with the stories of suffering of the black students, alongside Albert's exposition of Jesus who took the side of the poor and oppressed, was the biggest life-changing experience of my life. I left the weekend with a firm conviction that Jesus offered the fullness of life and, to follow him, I had to be part of destroying Apartheid. Most of the life choices I have since made can be linked to the spirit that caught me on that weekend. The meeting affirmed the need for black students to separate to 'determine' themselves, while giving white students time to 'redetermine' themselves. It also affirmed Themba Simelane from Fort Hare University to represent all South Africa's Catholic students at the upcoming Interfederal Assembly (IFA) of the International Movement of Catholic Students (IMCS-Pax Romana) in August 1975 in Lima, Peru.

The culmination of these decisions was the establishment in 1976 of the black Catholic Students Association (CASA) with the intention to find a black national chaplain. Meanwhile, Albert and his full-time assistants—Kallie from 1976–1977 and me from 1978–1980—offered assistance to consolidate the new organisation through support for the national leaders and visits to local branches. With its growth, CASA was soon admitted as a separate member of IMCS, alongside NCFS, at the IFA in 1982. The two movements continued to collaborate—such as organising their separate national conferences at the same time and venue—and eventually in 1993, seventeen years after CASA was established, they both decided to dissolve and to merge to form a new organisation, the Association of Catholic Tertiary Students (ACTS).

The Stutterheim national conference (mentioned above), which elected me as NCFS national president, followed just a few months after the Mariannhill meeting—in July 1975. The urgency felt was palpable for us white students to do much more than just talk, and to become more integrally involved in working for change away from Apartheid in South Africa. However, it was recognised that such a direction was already sparking some negative reactions amongst the membership in some local Cathsocs, and a lot of time was spent justifying the stands that NCFS was beginning to take. The conference therefore decided that a new structure had to be sought to take account of this development. So, a commission was set up which concluded that, while NCFS in its current form was playing a vital role in trying to draw all Catholic students together, there was a need to develop an additional small group dynamic with a new methodology within each Cathsoc for those wishing to express a deeper social justice commitment. The YCW[2] (Young Christian Workers) movement was identified as having a small group structure and a method

---

2. Founded by Fr Joseph Cardijn (later Cardinal) in Belgium in 1924, the Young Christian Workers is an international Catholic movement of young workers, which they run and direct themselves. Using the Review of Life (See–Judge–Act method) in small communities, the young workers share all aspects of their lives and plan and review action to change their situations. The initial success of the movement spawned the growth of several other movements of 'Specialised Catholic Action' in various other milieus or sectors (such as peasants, students, children, middle class youth, working class adults and middle-class adults) similarly structured in small groups applying the See–Judge–Act method.

(See–Judge–Act[3]) that could be learnt from, and so Kallie, now a full-time organiser for NCFS after handing the presidency over to me, went to work with the YCW leaders for some time to learn more about this structure and method. It was precisely at this same time, in August, that Albert accompanied Themba to the IMCS Interfederal Assembly in Lima, Peru along with two other NCFS students, Trish Struthers and Jean-Paul Franzidis, who attended as observers. There he encountered celebrated liberation theologians like Gustavo Gutiérrez, the chaplain of the local IMCS movement, and was struck by the 'Review of Life' or 'See–Judge–Act' method used by many movements of IMCS (most of whom were affiliated also to IYCS[4]) and the effect it had on their analysis, commitment and involvement. Therefore, on his return, Albert wrote a booklet on this method, and we set about starting a few pilot 'Christian Action Groups' in the Cathsocs of the universities of Stellenbosch, Durban and Wits (located in Johannesburg). With this experience, the 'method' was presented at the July 1976 NCFS Conference, resulting in See–Judge–Act (SJA) groups being started within the Cathsocs at all eight affiliated campuses. It was hoped that this dynamic would build leadership in each Cathsoc on an ongoing basis.

---

3. Developed by Joseph Cardijn, the See–Judge–Act method is a three-step tool of analysis as well as of spiritual and theological formation which is central to the identity of movements of Specialised Catholic Action and was explicitly affirmed as a significant evangelising tool by several documents of the Second Vatican Council (*Apostolicam Actuositatem* – AA29, *Ad Gentes* – AG21, and in the structure of *Gaudium et Spes*: See Stefan Gigacz, *The Leaven in the Council*, Chapter 9, 'The Three Truths in Gaudium et Spes', [Australian Cardijn Institute, 2021], 195). The method begins with 'Seeing' the concrete reality experienced by the members and analysing the root causes of the problems identified, then 'Judging' that reality in the light of the values of the Gospel or the Church's social teachings, and finally 'Acting' to change that reality in a way that is aligned with those Gospel values or church teachings. Also known as the 'Review of Life', an ingrained grasp of the method transforms it into a spirituality leading individuals and groups using it to internalise it as an ongoing instrument of reflection, action and reflection again.

4. The IYCS (International Young Catholic Students) was established in the context of a meeting of IMCS in 1946 in the wake of the Second World War. It is a global movement aiming to engage students (both at secondary and tertiary levels) to look at the world from the perspective of the poor, with a commitment to global solidarity, freedom, justice and peace. IYCS is also a movement of Specialised Catholic Action for whom the use of the See–Judge–Act method is fundamental.

The urgency for developing such leadership was highlighted just a few weeks earlier—in the last month of my presidency of NCFS—by the outbreak of the revolt of black secondary school students in Soweto on 16 June 1976 that rapidly spread to schools and universities throughout the country. This day is embedded in the South African consciousness as the symbol of the beginning of the escalation of the struggle that eventually brought down Apartheid. And, coincidentally, it was the very day that Albert was on the road while moving definitively from Stellenbosch to Johannesburg from where, initially as provincial of the Dominicans and as the national chaplain of Catholic students, he would exert even greater national influence on the Church and on society.

The decision to start See-Judge-Act groups in the Cathsocs on all NCFS campuses was immediately warmly welcomed by the leaders of YCW. They were in the process of re-emphasising the working-class identity of YCW and no longer felt comfortable having middle-class YCS school groups under their wing. Therefore, in a meeting in November 1976, they persuaded Albert and Kallie to agree to take over the YCS school groups and integrate them with university groups in the middle-class milieu, leaving YCW to organise both students and workers in the working-class milieu.

This new perspective given to the role of the university SJA groups—as a middle-class movement integrated with the YCS schools groups—set them more in the direction of becoming an autonomous movement and hence structurally distinct from NCFS and the Cathsocs. Consequently, on 31 January 1977, representatives from the SJA groups at the universities of Wits, Pretoria, Cape Town, Stellenbosch and Pietermaritzburg met in Johannesburg, along with the YCS schools organiser (Alan Ralphs), where they definitively decided to become YCS (Young Christian Students), and to seek affiliation to IYCS. It was accepted that Kallie be national secretary (and the organiser for Cape Town and Stellenbosch), that Albert be national chaplain, that Alan be a full-time organiser in schools and that I be a full-time organiser at Wits University (and assisting Pretoria and Natal).

In 1978, a new development took place that would have a significant broader impact. Kallie and I went to Valladolid in Spain where he (as the YCS National Secretary) participated in the World Council of IYCS and I (now as the NCFS full-timer and Albert's assistant for the Catholic student national chaplaincy) participated in the IMCS Interfederal Assembly. When Kallie learned that IYCS globally was a predominantly secondary school movement, and conscious of the mass politicisation of black secondary school students in South Africa since 1976, he realised that the priority of YCS in South Africa should be to spread in black schools. To achieve this, he conceived the idea to run a year-long course to train YCS organisers. Hence, in 1979, twelve organisers were trained and in the subsequent years YCS began to spread in schools of all races, but especially in black or 'coloured' schools. Albert played a central role in providing the theological formation for these students, for many of whom YCS was their first positive experience of 'Church', realising that they could be involved in the struggle and be Christian at the same time. This non-racial and ecumenical experience opened Albert up to a whole new world which led him and the whole of YCS to become integral to the struggle being waged in black townships in many parts of the country. Many of these YCS students, in turn, went to study at the black universities where they continued to spread the movement.

In 1980, Albert's term as national chaplain of NCFS finally came to an end, but he remained the national chaplain of YCS until 1984. He had meanwhile also become very involved with the Institute for Contextual Theology (ICT) where, with his experience in theological method in YCS, he was, in turn, able to make a significant contribution within the whole spectrum of Churches in the country and which led him too, to play an increasingly important—even if quiet—role in the struggle at large. It was this involvement that was appreciated by the Dominican General Chapter in 1983 where he was elected as Master of the Dominican Order, but was allowed to decline it. Without any interest in the status involved, he felt that there were enough brothers globally who could fulfil the role of governance and administration required, while the urgency of the struggle in South Africa could not afford the depletion of its ranks.

Conclusion

Without doubt, Albert Nolan has been the person who has most influenced my own life choices. Having met him in July 1973, I was privileged to collaborate continuously with him—weekly, if not daily for six years in student ministry (1975–1980)—when his role as national chaplain of NCFS and YCS coincided with my role as a student leader. From 1977 to 1980, I participated in a five-person weekly 'Review of Life' group that included Albert, where many of my convictions and commitments were clarified. It was Albert who drew me in to initiate, from 1981–1983, the Theology Exchange Programme (TEP[5]), which enabled a life-changing trip for me to Latin America to set up the programme; to get involved with the ICT (1981–1993), eventually as a member of its executive committee; and to sign the *Kairos Document* and collaborate in its release and promotion (1985). With the significant role that he was playing in my life, I was relieved that Albert was allowed to decline his election as the Master of the Dominican Order in 1983.

But it was not only Albert's down-to-earth theology and intellectual prowess that touched me. When I was an inexperienced twenty-three-year-old student in 1976, he took my simple theological insights seriously by asking me to read the final manuscript of *Jesus before Christianity*, and he even accepted and made changes from my critiques. His simplicity, his affirming, empowering and positive nature and his 'un-shockability' and 'freedom' allowed me to grapple with him as a friend on any issue or question without fear, and to grow in freedom—even to disagree with him. I cannot minimise his influence in my decision to become a Dominican, and it was therefore fitting that, at my eventual ordination to the priesthood in 1991, Albert was the Master of Ceremonies. After ten years of working closely with Albert as a student leader, and thirty-six years spent with him as a Dominican brother, I will sorely miss him—as will the generation of students that he inspired!

---

5. An ecumenical programme – the brainchild of Jim Cochrane (a Congregational Church minister and theologian) - that I was employed to set up in 1981 to enable South African theologians and church activists to visit and learn from the experience of doing contextual or liberation theology in Latin America. Initially it also focused on the Middle East and, later, on the Philippines.

A Spirituality of Action
for International Catholic Student Movements

Kevin Ahern

In August 1975, more than eighty student leaders from thirty countries gathered in Lima, Peru for the 28th Interfederal Assembly of the International Movement of Catholic Students (IMCS–Pax Romana) with the theme 'Christian Commitment in a World in Crisis'. Among those accompanying the students were several pioneering theologians, including Gustavo Gutiérrez, the chaplain of the hosting movement in Peru, the *Unión Nacional de Estudiantes Católicos*, Tissa Balasuriya OMI, IMCS Asia Regional Chaplain and Albert Nolan OP, Chaplain of the National Catholic Federation of Students (NCFS) in South Africa. This was a significant meeting in the life of IMCS, which was renewing its mission in a post-conciliar and post–1968 context. This process, particularly in Latin America, placed IMCS and the other movements of specialised Catholic action at the vanguard of the newly emerging framework that would become known as Liberation Theology.

For Nolan and the student movement in South Africa, this meeting revealed the importance of the See–Judge–Act method and what specialised Catholic Action describes as the spirituality of action. Nearly thirty years later in 2003, Nolan again participated in an international meeting of IMCS, this time in a joint training session with the International Young Catholic Students (IYCS) in Barcelona. In a series of talks, Nolan outlined the importance of this approach. 'We have a spirituality of action', he told the student leaders, 'because Jesus was a man of action, that is, a person of action'. Later, he concluded,

> if we can develop a spirituality of action that is closer to this model, following in the footsteps of Jesus, I have no doubt that our movements will be re-energised. And if our move-

ments are to be known by this type of spirituality of Jesus, we will become, I believe, a sign of hope in today's student environment.[1]

What is this spirituality and how does it connect with Nolan's wider theological project on the nature of Jesus?

The spirituality of action and specialised Catholic Action

One of the unique features of the spirituality of action is the way it was developed in the youth and student movements of specialised Catholic Action. Not to be confused with the more top-down model of general Catholic Action, the 'specialised' approach envisions models where young adults organise themselves in movements of, for, and by a specific milieu.

A pioneering experience of this approach is the Young Christian Worker (YCW or JOC) movement, which was founded in Belgium in 1925 as a prophetic and pastoral response to the dehumanising experiences confronting working class youth. Accompanying the young workers, Joseph Cardijn, the YCW chaplain, articulated a cell-based structure and methodology to actualise the agency of people marginalised by age (youth), social status (working class) and gender (in the case of women-led sections of YCW). This inductive method would come to be called the Review of Life or See–Judge–Act.[2]

Around the same time, university students were also developing their own autonomous movements. Following the catastrophe that was World War I, student leaders from twenty-one countries convened a peace conference in Fribourg, Switzerland. The delegates, many of whom had recently been fighting on opposite sides, believed that they could promote a more just and peaceful world by forming what would be later known as the International Movement of Catholic Students (IMCS–Pax Romana). At the heart of this initiative was the development of leadership within the student milieu, rather than

---

1. Albert Nolan, 'A Spirituality of Action', 21 August 2003, 1 and 6, 2003 International Committee, IMCS Archives, Paris.
2. For more on the YCW and the method, see Joseph Cardijn, *Laypeople into Action*, originally published 1963 (Adelaide: ATF Press, 2017); Stefan Robert Gigacz, *The Leaven in the Council: Joseph Cardijn and the Jocist Network at Vatican II* (Australian Cardijn Institute, 2021); Maria Cimperman, *Social Analysis for the 21st Century: How Faith Becomes Action* (Maryknoll, NY: Orbis Books, 2015).

on priests or adults. The student movement at the campus, national and international levels should be led and directed by students themselves. If no such groups existed, IMCS endeavoured to create them. In South Africa, IMCS worked with student leaders, to create the Students' Catholic Federation of South Africa in the late 1930s. This federation would formally join IMCS after World War II as the National Catholic Federation of Students (NCFS) and gave the international movement leaders like Anne Hope, who served as IMCS international vice president 1950–1952, and Michael Deeb OP, a former NCFS student leader who served as international chaplain from 1999–2007. IMCS also incorporated the Catholic Students Association (CASA), which was formed in 1976 to cater for the needs of black students and eventually merged with NCFS in 1993 to establish the Association of Catholic Tertiary Students (ACTS).

Following World War II, student groups more directly inspired by the YCW cell-based model formed IYCS at an IMCS Assembly in Fribourg in 1946. From there, the two international student movements began a dynamic (though sometimes contentious) collaboration. In Latin America, where many IMCS movements had previously adopted YCS structures, the two opened a joint regional office with the acronym MIEC–JECI.

Like the YCW, IMCS and IYCS aim to mobilise young adults for action in the society and in the Church. In its document on the laity, the Second Vatican Council affirmed this model wherein young people become the 'first apostles' to other young people.[3] While it may seem like an obvious method, the innovative approach of the 'apostolate of like to like' (student to student) has a radical edge as it confronts both clericalism and patriarchy by affirming the leadership and responsibility of young adults *'in life, Church's mission and in the world'*.[4] This 'participatory ecclesiology' is achieved in a profound way by methodological tools that promote praxis-oriented critical theological analysis, including the review of life, See–Judge–Act, and Action-Reflection-Action.[5]

---

3.   Second Vatican Council, *Apostolicam Actuositatem, The Decree on the Apostolate of Lay People* (Rome: Libreria Editrice Vaticana, 1965), www.vatican.va, No 12.
4.   IMCS Pax Romana, *International Statutes of IMCS Pax Romana* (International Movement of Catholic Students, 2007), https://www.imcs-miec.org/statutes/.
5.   Kevin Ahern, 'II. Toward a Participatory Ecclesiology: Catholic Students and the Quest for Ecclesial Adulthood', in *Horizons* 49/1 (June 2022): 188–202, https://doi.org/10.1017/hor.2022.6.

Following Vatican II, where IMCS, IYCS and YCW actively promoted lay participation, the spirituality of action took on new dimensions, especially in Latin America with the publication of Gutiérrez's *A Theology of Liberation*. 'It was from both the practice and theory of these groups', as Enrique Dussel points out, 'that the most important theological break in Latin American history was to emerge'.[6] To celebrate the 50th Anniversary of the movement, IMCS organised its 1971 Interfederal Assembly on the theme 'Liberation–How?' Using an inductive method, IMCS committed itself 'to work in the student environment and in society as a whole for the liberation of man [*sic*] from all domination, oppression and discrimination, whether material or moral'.[7]

At the following Assembly in Lima in 1975, more than eighty delegates from thirty-two national federations developed these new pastoral options.[8] Regional gatherings of students before the assembly and an 'exposure program' during the study session, helped to facilitate the inductive nature of the assembly. In Lima, the delegates articulated the liberative mission of IMCS more clearly, 'to be a sign of the Church committed to the transformation of the world starting from the university'.[9]

For Nolan, who accompanied Themba Simelane, Jean-Paul Franzidis and Trish Struthers to Peru, this assembly offered insights to apply in the South African context. He was particularly impressed by the work of the movements in Latin America, where these pedagogies were refined and upon his return, he worked to develop the YCS in South Africa as a more intensive experience within the wider IMCS affiliated student movement. The Lima meeting supported and gave greater meaning to the growing concern for NCFS's efforts of linking liberation of the poor and oppressed with the Kingdom of God.[10]

---

6. Enrique D Dussel, 'Recent Latin American Theology', in *The Church in Latin America, 1492–1992*, edited by Enrique D Dussel, translated by Paul Burns, Volume 1, A History of the Church in the Third World (Maryknoll, NY: Orbis Books, 1992), 392.
7. 'Resolutions Carried by the Directing Committee of IMCS', in *Convergence* (July 1971), 28.
8. Buenaventura Pelegri, *IMCS–IYCS: Their Option Their Pedagogy* (Hong Kong: IMCS Asia Secretariat, 1979), 9.
9. 28th Interfederal Assembly of IMCS (Lima), 'Toward a Re-Definition of the Movement' (International Movement of Catholic Students, 1975), 6, AIF 75/312/ FES, Pax Romana Archives, University of Fribourg.
10. Anthony Egan, 'The National Catholic Federation of Students: A Study of Political Ideas and Activities within a Christian Student Movement, 1960–1987' (Master Thesis, University of Cape Town, 1990), 108–109, https://open.uct.ac.za/ handle/11427/21836.

From a spirituality to a theology of action

While the student movements offered a spirituality of action, they did not necessarily have a robustly developed theology. By turning to Jesus as a person of action, Albert Nolan, like Gutiérrez, Balasuriya and others, offers a theological support structure to the spirituality implicit in the youth and student movements he worked with for over a decade. But to understand this, it is helpful to look at what is meant by action.

In his series of talks given at the 2003 IMCS and IYCS International Committees, Nolan draws from the work of the movements to offer a helpful distinction:

> Traditionally, in our movements, we distinguish between *actions* and *activities*. A good deed is based on careful reflection on an experience that demands a response, while an activity is the rest of the things one does without this formal process of reflection. Our method or pedagogy is described as Action–Reflection–Action or See–Judge–Act. We do not act without having first reflected on the situation, without Seeing or Judging.[11]

The process of reflecting (and acting), however, does not stop once an action is completed. Instead, as the student movements point out, we are called to reflect on what we have done and to discern how and where God is present in our agency; a process many describe as a circle or spiral. Nolan explains it this way:

> Another characteristic of our methodology is that we learn from our actions. The experience of doing often becomes an experience of the grace of God working with us, of hoping that things can change. Generally, we learn from our actions by reviewing them and carefully analysing what happened and why it happened in a certain way. Accordingly, the basis of a new action is our reflection on what we have done before.[12]

---

11. Nolan, 'A Spirituality of Action', 2. See also Michael Deeb, 'The Review of Life: A Spirituality and Method of Student Christian Communities', in *God's Quad: Small Faith Communities on Campus and Beyond*, edited by Kevin Ahern and Christopher Derige Malano (Maryknoll, NY: Orbis, 2018), 197–208.
12. Nolan, 'A Spirituality of Action', 2.

Thus, student movements like the YCS or IMCS have the potential to become schools of formation and action to empower young people to go deeper in exploring the liberating and transformative dimensions of Christian spirituality and lived discipleship. But this is not always easy. Engendering this spirituality among young people confronts a number of obstacles.

On the one hand, young adults are subjected to many cultural forces that do not support collective experiences of contemplation, reflection and analysis. In a fast-paced culture, finding the time needed to really 'see' and 'judge' is not easy. In *Jesus Today*, Nolan identifies this 'busyness' as a major obstacle in engaging the spirituality of Jesus: 'It distracts us from self-awareness and from awareness of the real world. It distracts us from awareness of God'.[13] More recently, in *Gaudete et Exsultate,* Pope Francis makes a similar observation:

> contemporary life offers immense possibilities for action and distraction, and the world presents all of them as valid and good. All of us, but especially the young, are immersed in a culture of zapping ... Without the wisdom of discernment, we can easily become prey to every passing trend.[14]

Here, it can be tempting, especially in the urgent struggles to overcome major social injustices, from racism and economic inequality to nuclear proliferation and climate change, to skip contemplation. The end result is a type of activism detached from both the depths of reality and the revelatory dimensions of Christian faith.

In his 2003 address to IMCS and IYCS, Nolan explores this by considering opposing dimensions. 'The opposite of a spirituality of action', he insists, 'is not a spirituality of contemplation'.[15] Prayer, contemplation and discernment are essential to enact the social transformation necessary to overcome the structures of sin threatening people and the planet. 'Perhaps what our spirituality of action needs most now', he told the student leaders,

---

13. Albert Nolan, *Jesus Today: A Spirituality of Radical Freedom* (Maryknoll, NY: Orbis Books, 2006), 91.

14. Pope Francis, *Gaudete et Exsultate* (Rome: Libreria Editrice Vaticana, 2018), No 167, https://www.vatican.va/content/francesco/en/apost_exhortations/documents/papa-francesco_esortazione-ap_20180319_gaudete-et-exsultate.html.

15. Nolan, 'A Spirituality of Action', 2.

is a deeper awareness of God. Perhaps we need to explore private prayer as well as public and liturgical prayer. Perhaps, like Jesus, we must go somewhere in order to be alone in silence, to be in touch with the great mystery behind all mysteries, the mystery that loves us like a father.[16]

On the other hand, there is an opposing risk. Instead of an activism detached from contemplation and reflection, there is a danger of a contemplation or spirituality bereft from lived discipleship: spirituality without action. For Nolan then,

> the opposite of a spirituality of action is an escapist spirituality, that is to say, the type of individualism and egocentric spirituality which wants to leave the transformation of the world entirely to God.

This takes many forms, including a fundamentalism that he describes as a 'thoughtless obedience to their idea of the Will of God and a blind obedience to all authorities, whether Church or State'.[17] At times this can lead to what *Jesus before Christianity* describes as a fatalism, which he sets up as opposing faith.[18] This attitude prevents people from seeing any value in social action, an attitude which can only reinforce the status quo and systems of oppression. Among Catholic student ministry, this fatalism and 'hopeless resignation'[19] is sustained by what a recent IMCS statement described as 'a spiritual consumerism where young adults become consumers and the ministers, a service provider'.[20] As with clericalism, students in consumer models of ministry are not supported as active agents, but rather passive participants in systems that they are not encouraged to change.

How can students navigate between these two extremes? Between an activism devoid of contemplation and the escapist spirituality absent of any actualised agency? Here, the work of Albert Nolan

---

16. Nolan, 'A Spirituality of Action', 4.
17. Nolan, 'A Spirituality of Action', 3.
18. Albert Nolan, *Jesus Before Christianity* (Maryknoll, NY: Orbis Books, 1992), 39–40.
19. Nolan, *Jesus Before Christianity*, 9.
20. 'Young Catholics and the Synod: Listening to Voices from Around the World', 1 October 2018, https://www.icmica-miic.org/2018/10/listening-to-voices-from-around-the-world-young-catholics-and-the-synod/.

offers an important contribution to the mission and pedagogies of the student movement. For him, Jesus, that 'upside down messiah', is key to developing an authentic spirituality of action.[21] Like his later book, *Jesus Today*, Nolan's 2003 address to IMCS and IYCS uplifts Jesus as an example of this integrated balance of contemplation and action.

As he does elsewhere, Nolan urged the students to reflect on 'Jesus' own spirituality, his 'spirituality of action', which he saw as rooted in two elements: Jesus' intimacy with the God he called Abba and his 'extraordinary compassion for people', especially the poor and oppressed. With many years of experience in accompanying university students, Nolan understood that they were well prepared to hear this message of Jesus as a person of action but also believed they needed to (re)discover Jesus with both of these dimensions if they were to actualise this potential. Later, in *Jesus Today*, Nolan describes this integration with the language of mysticism and prophecy and the way they 'form an inseparable whole in the life and spirituality of Jesus'.[22]

But of course, such a spirituality of action informed by both mysticism and prophetic compassion does not usually arise spontaneously. Such a spirituality is most often encouraged and sustained in the experience of small communities. This in many ways may be one of the best arguments for the continued relevancy of experiences of IMCS and IYCS.

Conclusion

In his 2019 post-synodal apostolic exhortation, *Christus Vivit*, Pope Francis challenged young people to be 'protagonists of change', 'to fight apathy' and 'to work for a better world'.[23] This in many ways summarises the message at the core of the student movement's spirituality of action and the wider theological and christological project offered by Albert Nolan.

Sadly, in far too many places the Church's youth and young adult engagement, if it exists, does not provide resources for this spirituality to develop. Instead it can give in to an activism detached from

---

21. Nolan, *Jesus Today*, 59.
22. Nolan, *Jesus Today*, 72. 2
23. Pope Francis, '*Christus Vivit*': *Post-Synodal Exhortation to Young People* (Rome: Libreria Editrice Vaticana, 2019), No 174.

faith and reality, forms of what Nolan identified as a spiritual escapism, models which pacify young adults into spiritual consumers, and hyper-emotive large scale gatherings with no space for real reflection and action. While the traditional movements of students and young workers struggle in many parts of the world, their distinctive legacy offers a model for mobilising young adults and should not be overlooked. As Nolan explained to the student leaders in 2003, this model can be a source of hope for the Church, particularly in this present moment as it seeks to deepen the participatory and synodal path.

1960s photo of Stellenbosch priory church with Nicholas Humphreys OP in the background.

A Chaplain who Inspired IMCS Pax-Romana

Ravi Tissera Warnakulasooriya

There are heroes that you have never met but have been influenced by all your life, even without you hearing their names, almost like they live through your actions and witness. As a leader of the International Movement of Catholic Students (IMCS Pax-Romana), my relationship with Albert Nolan is such an influence. Through his humble accompaniment and intellectual contributions to the thinking of the global Catholic student movement for almost five decades, Albert has left his mark in shaping the identity of the global movement together with his contemporary visionaries.

My encounter with Nolan's thought happened as I was researching the identity of the global Catholic student movement which is strongly bound with the idea of a 'Spirituality of Action'. In preparation for the celebration of the 100th anniversary of the Pax-Romana movement which was founded by Catholic tertiary students in 1921, we were re-reading how students globally have evolved through the century and reached the current identity. Unlike many other faith-based organisations, this identity has continuously been inspiring generations of Catholic student leaders around the world, whose spirituality has strongly compelled them to walk with the marginalised and take profound social, political, cultural and economic actions to respond to the injustices. These profound responses have been nourished by the lived experiences of committed men and women who have walked with the global Catholic student movement.

Catholic students founded the Pax-Romana movement to contribute to peace and justice around the world as a practice of faith. After a prior attempt in 1887[1] under the name 'International Union of

---

1. The founding president was Baron George de Montenach (Swiss Catholic Students Association).

Catholic Students', which didn't last long, a second successful attempt was made in 1921 by the same groups of Catholic students, which resulted in creating the 'Pax-Romana' movement. As education of any sort, especially higher education, was a luxury enjoyed by privileged classes in those days, the founding members of the Pax-Romana movement were predominantly well-meaning students from affluent groups in Europe and North America. After World War II, countries in Africa, Asia and Latin America were gaining their independence from the colonial or neo-colonial powers and the IMCS[2] Pax-Romana movement was expanding to those regions. This contributed to the development of solidarity among students from the global north and south. IMCS Pax-Romana was learning through the experiences of the members of the peripheries and was refining the identity of the global Catholic student movement to be much more relevant, as the movement was built on the idea of 'Catholic students in society'.

Albert Nolan was connected to IMCS Pax-Romana as a chaplain of the National Catholic Federation of Students (NCFS) in South Africa from 1973–1980. NCFS South Africa had become a member of IMCS Pax-Romana in 1948.[3] Initially, NCFS was the only Catholic student body in South Africa.[4] In 1977, Nolan was instrumental in establishing the Young Christian Students (YCS)[5] in South Africa after he attended an IMCS Pax-Romana Interfederal Assembly in Lima, Peru, in 1975. There he was introduced to the See–Judge–Act pastoral theological method of social transformation and he was inspired by Gustavo Gutiérrez, the chaplain of UNEC[6] Peru (the IMCS Pax-Romana

---

2. During the 25th Anniversary of Pax-Romana in 1947, the movement was divided into two branches: the International Movement of Catholic Students (IMCS Pax-Romana) for Catholic tertiary students and the International Catholic Movement for Intellectual and Cultural Affairs (ICMICA) Pax-Romana for Catholic graduates and professionals.
3. BC 927 Pax-Romana: IMCS Circular No 1, 26 April 1948.
4. This changed after black students began organising themselves into separate formations as Black Consciousness flourished. Students attending black campuses broke away from NCFS to form the Catholic Students Association (CASA) in 1976. Consequently, CASA then existed at historically black campuses whereas NCFS existed at historically white campuses. Even though Albert Nolan was not a chaplain of CASA, he was accompanying them as well.
5. From 1977–1984, Nolan served as the National Chaplain of YCS.
6. Unión Nacional de Estudiantes Católicos (UNEC) Peru.

national affiliate of Peru), who is regarded as one of the pioneers of Liberation Theology[7] and who later became a Dominican.

Nolan began his engagement with NCFS by giving a series of lectures on the historical Jesus to an NCFS national conference,[8] which he later turned into a book, *Jesus before Christianity*, published in 1976. Having lived through the breakaway from NCFS by the black Catholic students after 1970 when the Black Consciousness movement arose, Nolan sought during his tenure to help white Catholic students find a way of working with their black colleagues for the common goal of ending Apartheid. Eventually, the racial lines between the student groups were removed in 1993, bringing them to form one common Catholic student organisation which is known as the Association of Catholic Tertiary Students (ACTS) of South Africa and which is the current national affiliate of IMCS Pax-Romana.

While South Africa was combating Apartheid, other countries and regions were dealing with issues derived from colonial remnants. As Nolan was walking with South African students under Apartheid and supporting the growth of Liberation Theology in South Africa, his counterparts in other countries were bringing their contributions to the table. As a global platform, the Catholic student movement (both IMCS and IYCS) was a great incubator of ideas and a place of exchange for these visionaries. As the young and brave Catholic student leaders from various countries—inspired by their spiritual values—were challenging the systemic injustices, the chaplains of the student movements played important roles in accompanying them, conserving the memory of their experiences and facilitating a much-needed synthesis with the global character of the movement through their interactions over these global platforms.

Buenaventura Pelegri, the former international chaplain of IMCS and IYCS,[9] shares about this necessary synthesis which nourishes today's identity of the student movement in the following exhortation:

---

7. Anthony Egan, 'The National Catholic Federation of Students: A study of Political ideas and activities within a Christian student movement, 1960–1987', January 1990.
8. NCFS 24th Annual Conference—July 1972—Four Talks given by Albert Nolan under the general title 'That man Jesus'.
9. Buenaventura Pelegri served as the International Chaplain from 1971–1978.

Our Movements can and must be a 'workshop' of theology. Certainly not being cut off or isolated from the efforts being made by the Church nor with any pretension to be better. But I believe that the challenges faced by our militants in their lives and in their action within the milieu give them the fundamental elements for doing contemporary theology, understood as a critical (and scientific) reflection on faith.

It is an effort which should be made fundamentally by the militants, that is to say, by the laity. It requires a good grasp of the history of theological thought of the Christian community rooted in Sacred Scripture. We cannot expect that they would do theology alone. Chaplains must play an important role, especially those who have a good theological training. Even this will not be enough and it will be very important to collaborate with professional theologians. But it is from the "intuition" of our militants that a re-reading of the Bible, theology and the history of the Church should be made. That is to say, a rereading making sense to their age and from the perspective of the poor and oppressed. Efforts in this line have already been made in or by our Movements. One of the best-known examples is the 'Theology of Liberation' of Fr. Gustavo Gutiérrez, national chaplain of our Peruvian movement. But in the same line, we find theologians more or less closely linked to our Movements, such as Samuel Ryan (India), Tissa Balasuriya (Sri Lanka), Aguirre (Philippines), Albert Nolan (South Africa) and many others.[10]

Albert Nolan, together with his contemporaries like Gustavo Gutiérrez and Tissa Balasuriya, played a prophetic role in walking behind and parallel to the student leaders, facilitating the growth of the idea of a spirituality of action, which has guided generations of students until today. Their contributions were contextual and made a huge difference to the times they were serving. Their strong convictions helped us to find direction for the global Catholic student movement. The memory and profound legacy of these 'inspirational fathers' invites us to play the necessary prophetic role to nourish the next stages of our 'spirituality of action' as it is always built upon the lived

---

10. Buenaventura Pelegri, *IMCS-IYCS: Their Option their Pedagogy* (Hong Kong: IMCS Asia Secretariat, 1979), 141–142.

experiences of people at the peripheries. The global Catholic student movement celebrates the legacy of these giants which reminds us of the need to continue the prophetic role they have played in the global student movement's history. Hence, on the occasion of the 100th anniversary of the Pax-Romana movement, IMCS Pax-Romana decided to establish a 'Gutiérrez, Balasuriya, Nolan Initiative for Spirituality of Action', which will continue to promote the development of a progressive, communal and marginalised-centred spirituality for the global movement. Only weeks before his death, Albert agreed to allow his name to be part of this initiative. We are grateful that he had the opportunity to personally accept this token of our appreciation.

Community St Nicholas Priory in Stellenbosch.

Law as Servant

Brian Currin

I underwent twelve years of Catholic education—the first two at a convent and the subsequent ten years at a Christian Brothers College where the mantra 'spare the rod and spoil the child' was consciously embraced by virtually all the Brothers. They presented a God whose default position was to punish us if we committed the mortal sins that young adolescent men might be prone to commit. As a result, my adherence to Catholicism was born out of fear rather than belief and faith.

After a year in the army, in 1969 I arrived at Stellenbosch University to study law. The last thing I expected—in fact it never entered my mind—was that I would undergo a complete transformation of what I understood to be Catholicism. This was triggered when, as a first year law student, I met Fr Albert Nolan.

He exuded the antithesis of what I had previously experienced Catholicism to be. He was warm, he was humble, he was caring, he was intellectual in the most unassuming way, he was fun, he was a listener and he was empathetic. I could go on and on. On reflection, his ability to relate to students was remarkable. We all loved Albert, and that was not only the Stellenbosch students where he was the chaplain. He was also chaplain to the National Catholic Federation of Students (NCFS) and in that capacity he led three NCFS conferences which I attended, all of which had a profound impact on how I eventually chose to practice law, although I never appreciated his influence at the time.

The NCFS conference that set my professional life on a course, subconsciously at the time, was the 1972 conference whilst I was a law student. We had the privilege of workshopping, under his tutorship, the essential elements of Albert's first book, *Jesus before Christianity*, published in 1976.

Albert presented Christ to a group of idealistic young students as Jesus the man, rather than Jesus the Son of God. The impact on me was profound. What emerged in my mind was a vulnerable activist fighting for social justice. In retrospect, and remarkably, I saw no link between social justice and the law, to the extent that I contemplated changing courses.

Although this version of Christ as a political activist had an intellectual impact on my approach to religion, it was not until five years later, shortly after being admitted to the side bar as an attorney, that the seed planted by Albert somewhere deep inside of me began to germinate when I was confronted by the rampant oppression, state violence and gross human rights violations being perpetrated by the Apartheid regime.

Albert likened the leaders of Christ's time with the leaders of our time in the early 1970s. Their power and the security of their position as leaders was not a consequence of their legitimacy but rather the fear instilled on their subjects through oppressive laws enforced by brutal force. He did not use those words but that was the message. Twenty years later, arguments presented by the proponents of a constitutional democracy, of which I was one, for a liberated South Africa to replace Apartheid's parliamentary supremacy, took me back to that NCFS conference.

In *Jesus before Christianity* this quote particularly touched me:

> After enslaving themselves to the letter of the law, such people (leaders and scholars in Jesus's time) always go on to deny freedom to others. They will not rest until they have imposed the same oppressive burdens upon everyone (Mt 23:4, 15). It is always the poor and the oppressed who suffer most when the law is used in this manner.

> Jesus wanted to liberate everyone from the law—from all laws. But this could not be achieved by abolishing or changing the law. He had to dethrone the law. He had to ensure that the law would be our servant and not our master (Mk 2:27–28). We must therefore take responsibility for our servant, the law, and use it to serve the needs of humankind.[1]

---

1. Albert Nolan, *Jesus before Christianity* (Cape Town: David Philip, 1976). 71–72.

That was Albert's message in the early 1970s; make the law our servant and not our master, and that is precisely what we have in South Africa today. Our constitution, incorporating our bill of rights is supreme, no longer the powerful political elite, and for that reason we the people, through an independent constitutional court have the power to hold law makers to account. Unsurprisingly there are some among the political elite, especially in the wake of state capture, who want to wrestle back supreme power and make the law our master, precisely as it was under Apartheid—a crime against humanity.

The nourishment that germinated the seed planted by Albert also came in the form of another Catholic priest, Fr Smangaliso Mkhatshwa, early in 1977. Through him I received my first 'political' instruction. It landed on my desk by default while I was a young recently qualified attorney with eyes firmly fixed on commercial practice. Smangaliso, a fellow liberation theologian of Albert and a fearless activist priest, symbolised for me Jesus the man that Albert had introduced to me five years earlier. Almost overnight he changed the trajectory of my legal practice for which I will be eternally grateful.

One of the turning points for me was a failed court application to the then Transvaal Supreme Court for an interdict against the torture of Smangaliso, who had been stripped naked and tortured throughout the night on one of the hills overlooking Pretoria. Like the Christ described by Albert in *Jesus before Christianity*, Smangaliso could not call upon the Heavenly Father to intervene, and neither did he have the law as a servant.

The inability to achieve social justice and protect fundamental human rights in a legal system where the law was master rather than servant of the people, took me back to Albert's *Jesus before Christianity* and the text that touched me, which I repeat:

> After enslaving themselves to the letter of the law, such people (leaders and scholars in Jesus's time) always go on to deny freedom to others. They will not rest until they have imposed the same oppressive burdens upon everyone (Mt 23:4, 15). It is always the poor and the oppressed who suffer most when the law is used in this manner.

The extent to which most of our Apartheid era judges and magistrates 'enslaved themselves to the letter of the law' eventually drove me to transition from being a human rights lawyer attempting to apply the law, to being a human rights activist committed to transforming the law from master to servant of the people.

JESUS
BEFORE
CHRISTIANITY

*"The most accurate and balanced
short reconstruction of the life
of the historical Jesus."*
— Harvey Cox

ALBERT NOLAN

Jesus before Christianity

Robert Ellsberg

In the world beyond South Africa, Albert Nolan is undoubtedly best known for his classic work, *Jesus before Christianity*. Though the book emerged from his work in South Africa as a chaplain to the National Catholic Federation of Students (NCFS), it included no explicit reference to the South African context. No doubt that contributed to its wide, global appeal. And yet there is also no doubt that his motivation for writing was rooted in his passionate engagement with the cause of justice and liberation in his native land. That commitment was made explicit in his later book, *God in South Africa* (1988) and other activities that for some time forced him to operate underground, hiding from the security police.

Nolan's book aimed to present a 'thoroughly and profoundly human' Jesus, 'before he was enshrined in doctrines, dogmas, and ritual'. He presented Jesus, his preaching and ministry in the context of first-century Palestine, a world marked not just by differences about the role and meaning of religion, but by profound inequality and injustice. He intended to present this Jesus in a way that might speak to all people engaged with the challenges of history—not just Christians. Specifically, as he wrote in the original introduction, he had an,

> urgent and practical purpose . . . I am concerned about people, the daily sufferings of so many millions of people, and the prospect of much greater suffering in the near future. My purpose is to find out what can be done about it.

Jesus before Christianity was originally published in South Africa in 1976 by David Philip, Publisher. It was then licensed in the UK to Darton, Longman, and Todd, which in turn licensed the North American edition to Orbis Books in 1977 (Orbis eventually assumed full rights to the work). For Nolan's work, which was dedicated 'to the People of the Third World', Orbis was a natural home. The publishing arm of the Maryknoll Fathers and Brothers, Orbis was founded in 1970 specifically to amplify theological voices from 'the Third World'. Our programme was fundamentally shaped in its early years by our publication in 1973 of the English translation of Gustavo Gutiérrez's *Theology of Liberation*. This book laid the foundation for the ensuing wave of Liberation Theology from Latin America and elsewhere in the world. We were early publishers of works by James Cone, the father of 'Black Liberation Theology', and his books were quickly joined by the work of many South African theologians engaged in the Church struggle against Apartheid. Nolan's work, imbued with the spirit of Liberation Theology, but not evidently fixed in a specific context, served as an effective bridge for an English-speaking audience receptive to considering the social and political implications of Jesus' life and message.

Jesus before Christianity quickly found a broad, ecumenical audience, both in the Churches and in the classroom. Harvey Cox, the renowned Protestant theologian, played a significant role in spreading the word. He taught an undergraduate course at Harvard, 'Jesus and the Moral Life', which drew an annual enrollment of over 1,000 students each year. Nolan's book was one of his core texts.

The history of successive editions of *Jesus before Christianity* provides an interesting reflection of developments over the years, both in the world as well as in Nolan's own understanding.

In 1988, to mark its tenth anniversary, Orbis brought out a second edition. Nolan noted in the preface that the book's popularity amazed no one more than himself. While acknowledging that much in the world had changed, he 'still stood by the main lines of argument in the book', which was in some ways 'even more relevant now than it was ten years ago'.

Referring to the world, he noted the looming threat of nuclear war and the intensifying struggle in South Africa and the Third World for liberation. 'In South Africa', he wrote, 'the catastrophe is for many already upon us; for others it is on our very doorstep'. Nevertheless, he wrote, 'This does not substantially alter the perspective. In fact, I would argue that the slightly different perspective of today makes the message of Jesus even more pertinent than it might have appeared to be ten years ago.' By this time, however, sensitivities had certainly changed around sexist language, and for this he offered an apology.

In 1992, a third edition offered Nolan the opportunity to revise 'the sexist language and assumptions of the original'. As he noted:

> One of the really great signs of hope in the world today is the way in which women are claiming their rights and opening the eyes of men to the injustice of patriarchy in all its forms. How grateful we ought to be to God for this grace of our times.

And yet, with the passage of time, Nolan continued to look again at his book in the light of unfolding history. In 2001 Orbis brought out a 'Twenty-Fifth Anniversary Edition'. The world as a whole had changed in many ways—nowhere more dramatically than in South Africa. And yet he continued to feel that his book continued to speak to the present moment:

> While the threat of nuclear holocaust has receded somewhat, the threat to all forms of life on this planet is now overwhelming clear. And with the accelerated pace of economic globalization, we are faced more starkly than ever with the reality of the rich becoming richer and the poor poorer. That too spells disaster for the human race.

In his new preface, he wrote:

> John the Baptist's call for conversion in the face of an impending disaster and Jesus' joyful hopefulness about the future could hardly be more relevant in these fearful and confusing times. The same is true of the values Jesus preached.

Were he to rewrite the book, he said, he would especially give more attention to Jesus' relationship with women and elaborate 'on the experience of solidarity with humanity and nature as an experience of solidarity with the whole created universe, with the awe-inspiring unfolding of all things that we call the story of the universe'. Finally, he said, he would write about 'Jesus' experience of prayer'.

To a large extent, Nolan found the opportunity to explore these very themes in his subsequent work, *Jesus Today: A Spirituality of Radical Freedom* (2006). For those accustomed to associating Nolan only with the social context of Jesus' life and ministry, this book was written in a very different voice. While the need for social liberation was no less urgent, he now described his growing awareness of the need for 'personal liberation, and therefore spirituality'. His new book took a different approach to the Jesus of first-century Palestine, focusing this time on Jesus' own spirituality, 'his contemplative prayer, and his concern for the individual'. This work, he claimed, was no less contextual, though the context this time was 'today's world and not just South Africa'.

These two works, together, presented two halves of Nolan's prophetic voice—the voice of challenge and resistance, and the voice of hope and consolation. In a way, these two voices were integrated in his last published work. In 2009 Orbis brought out *Hope in an Age of Despair,* a collection of talks and writings edited by his Dominican brother, Stan Muyebe, and drawn from the past twenty-five years. The title essay from 2008 was the most recent piece—an apt reflection of a life-long ministry, confronting the injustices and oppression in the world and in South Africa, but always sustained by a deep spiritual conviction that hope is possible, that death and oppression do not have the last word,

> What matters in the long run . . . is not only that we are hopeful but that we act hopefully. The most valuable contribution that a Christian can make in our age of despair is to continue, because of our faith, to act hopefully, and in that way to be an encouragement to those who have lost all hope.

That was a good summary of the spirit that motivated Albert Nolan in his ministry and his writing. But it was not the last word on the impact of his work. With 150,000 copies in print, *Jesus before Christianity* in its various editions continues to hold the Orbis record as the best-selling title in our publishing history. And besides the Orbis editions and several other English-language editions, the book was translated into at least fifteen other languages: Arabic, Chinese (Taiwan), French, German, Hungarian, Indonesian, Italian, Japanese, Korean, Malayalam (India), Portuguese, Romanian, Spanish, Swedish and Urdu (Pakistan). What is the explanation for this success? He showed that Jesus lived in a time of oppression, social conflict, and perhaps even despair. He challenged a pious vision of Jesus, all too common in the churches, that imagines him floating above or outside of these conflicts. Insofar as we continue to live in such a world of conflict and injustice, Jesus's life and message continues to challenge this reality and to inspire us in the confidence that a different world is possible—if we 'act hopefully'.

In 2022, within weeks of Albert's death as it turned out, Orbis brought out a new edition of *Jesus before Christianity*. The text this time was unchanged, though the cover now recognised the book as 'An Orbis Classic'! The only new addition was a foreword by Sister Helen Prejean, a nun whose famous memoir *Dead Man Walking* has had enormous influence in changing attitudes about the death penalty—not only in the United States, but with palpable effect on Catholic Social Teaching itself.

It was this book, she said, that had opened her eyes to the social implications of the gospel. 'Even though I had been a nun for a long time, certain that I had given up everything to follow Jesus, in reading *Jesus before Christianity* I felt I was meeting him for the first time as a human being'. In her own personal journey of conversion, she wrote, Nolan's book was the 'entryway into the compassionate justice-loving heart of Jesus' that inspired her subsequent vocation as an activist and champion of the poor. No doubt, her testimony speaks for countless readers.

I first met Albert Nolan when he visited Maryknoll in 1988 for a summer of celebration for the work of Gustavo Gutiérrez (who would himself later join Nolan as a member of the Order of Preachers). World class theologians from around the world were gathered that summer. But no one impressed me more than Fr Nolan. He embodied a prophetic zeal for God's justice, as well as a 'spirituality of radical freedom'. It was a privilege and honour to work with him over many years—to support him in his work for justice and liberation through his publishing ministry. There is no way of measuring the impact of his work on successive generations of readers.

Upon learning of his death, I thought of his concluding words in *Jesus Today:*

> God's Work sometimes appears to be very slow. Perhaps that is because we do not always appreciate the immensity of what we are involved in. Yet, precisely because it is God's Work, the future is secure. There is hope for the universe and for each of us as individuals. When I die, my ego, my false self, will be destroyed once and for all, but my true self will continue forever in God, the Self of the universe.

Albert in Australia in 1998: Partly obscured Fr Bob Wilkinson, Br Mark O'Connor, Kevin McDonald, Francis Regan and Albert.

An Echo from Australia

Paul Burke

I am pleased to be able to contribute to this volume celebrating the life and work of Dominican theologian Albert Nolan. His book *Jesus before Christianity* was the focus of a national programme undertaken by the national organisation of Catholic university students, the Tertiary Catholic Federation of Australia (TCFA), in the heady era of the late 1970s. I was one of two full-time workers for TCFA at the time and can attest to the influence of Nolan's book in confirming the direction of the national movement to promote the 'Option for the Poor', a central tenet of the international organisation to which TCFA was affiliated—the International Movement of Catholic Students (IMCS). Because of fading memory and scattered records, this account must necessarily be a personal one.

TCFA was always a shoestring operation. Its main activity was a national conference which was typically attended by between 100 and 200 university students from Catholic groups on fifteen or so university campuses. The strongest groups were at universities where the local diocese provided a full-time university chaplain, a long history in the Australian Catholic Church. In the 1970s, although there were large numbers of university students from Catholic backgrounds, only a very small percentage of them attended the Catholic chaplaincy at their university, and then with varying degrees of involvement from attending Mass occasionally to it being one's primary social group on campus. Much seems to have depended upon the character of the particular chaplain. We were lucky to have a diverse group of thoughtful, encouraging and even inspiring men and one woman, a Blessed Sacrament sister (a few more women chaplains followed in the 1980s). Many of the chaplains were quite supportive of

TCFA's activities and direction. On the organisational side, TCFA had its own unpaid executive and full or part-time workers, who would suspend their university studies and would be funded by a low-tech version of today's Patreon, that is many members pledging small weekly amounts to support them.

From the contemporary perspective of quiet university campuses and busy students who typically have part-time jobs to support themselves, the spirit of the 1970s on university campuses was exciting and exploratory. Although it was well after the heyday of the moratorium demonstrations against the Vietnam War, university campuses were still places of political mobilisation and social experimentation. In Australia in that era, there were no tuition fees or the incurring of student debts. Students were generally freer to engage in extracurricular activities.

It was in these circumstances that TCFA took upon itself the task of transforming itself from an organisation to a social movement. But how? The Cardijn movements (Young Christian Workers, Young Christian Students) had their signature See–Judge–Act methodology and we were aware of other methodologies being used by radical Catholic organisations around the world, such as the Exposure Tour, in which middle-class students would be taken to sites of poverty to share the life of the poor for a limited period and reflect upon it. This is where *Jesus before Christianity* came in.

I am now not sure who actually suggested the book, but the idea was that we would encourage the constituent university groups to set up reading groups to work their way through the book and reflect upon it. This became our national programme to supplement our national conference and newsletter. In my recollection, most of the local university groups took up the idea and we were able to integrate it in some way in the next national conference. We were also able to present it as a coherent national strategy at a regional international meeting and have it acknowledged as such, even if we were otherwise seen as small fry on the international stage.

As to reactions and the impact of the book, it is difficult to recall. Certainly, a number of the 'militants', as we used to call those who are actively engaged (following trade union terminology and IMCS jargon), remember it fondly and still have in their possession the underlined copies of the book or photocopies of the book (sorry publishers). A number of the militants pursued careers in Aboriginal

Legal Aid organisations, medical services or other indigenous rights organisations. Quite a few went into L'Arche.[1] Others I think took the 'Option for the Poor' with them in their work in government departments, academia, UN organisations and in various practices of depth psychology. My assessment is that these people were already heading in that direction and that *Jesus before Christianity* encouraged them on the way. For TCFA, it sent out a signal to the university groups of our preferred orientation.

Sometimes this was not well received. One of the militants asked me why we were so willing to support broadly leftist protests but never protested against abortion. I had no convincing answer for him. While most of the university chaplains seemed happy enough to go along with *Jesus before Christianity*, one theologically literate student, Neil Ormerod, raised other objections. He was by no means a political conservative and I think had no particular objection to Liberation Theology as such. Rather, he thought that the task Albert Nolan had set himself, to subtract the accretions of the later organised Church to recover the original significance of the message of Jesus, was an impossible and hence misguided project. Neil had, in the same period as our reading groups on *Jesus before Christianity*, organised a reading group on Bernard Lonergan's *Insight* and he later gained an international reputation as a Lonergan scholar.

I had a sneaking suspicion then, and more so now, that he was right about the impossibility of Nolan's project but I still thought the national programme to be worthwhile. *Jesus before Christianity* provided an accessible and mercifully concise introduction to Liberation Theology which made it appropriate for a wider group of Catholic students who did not necessarily see themselves as developing a specialisation in theology. In contrast, I imagined the bewilderment of many of the participants in the *Insight* reading group and Ormerod later referred to the difficulty of Lonergan's work, describing him as the theologian's theologian.[2]

Having reread *Jesus before Christianity* recently, after a gap of forty years, I am conflicted with feelings of nostalgia, appreciation and

---

1. A global federation of communities including people with intellectual disabilities, founded by Jean Vanier, that exist in over thirty-eight countries on five continents.
2. Neil Ormerod, *Introducing Contemporary Theologies: The What and the Who of Theology Today*, revised and enlarged edition (Sydney: EJ Dwyer, 1977), 115.

apprehensiveness about the book. I am struck by the centrality of the political sphere as the privileged object of our praxis throughout the book and, what seems to be implicit, that political alignments and policies are somehow straightforward to formulate. I wonder if this was only ever true in extreme situations like Apartheid South Africa, which was the political background to Nolan's involvement with the Catholic student movement of South Africa. Now, and perhaps even then, questions of political strategy and the implementation of political equality and a sustainable economy are difficult to discern. The book passes quickly over the question of belief in a transcendent God (Chapter 12) but it seems to me that this is the major reason for the modern difficulty with religion and why all those Catholic university students never turned up to the chaplaincy.[3]

Moreover, the quest to recover the actual sayings of Jesus and the historical context tends to undervalue the literary qualities of the Gospels and therefore their reliance upon the idiom of the Old Testament and the potential fruitfulness of literary interpretation. I also wondered about bracketing the difficult history between Judaism and Christianity and concentrating on what was in the time of Jesus an internal critique of certain fundamentalist and literalist tendencies within Judaism. The Catholic Church has had to grapple with those same tendencies over the years and has struggled to develop a more respectful attitude towards Judaism. This is a difficult area and I feel sure that Nolan was not intending any disrespect. The same could perhaps be said about the Catholic Church grappling with patriarchal practices and the feminist critique. By going back to the historical Jesus this grappling is bypassed, notwithstanding that Nolan clearly identifies Jesus with the liberation of women. Some of the militants who read *Jesus before Christianity* were also inspired by the flowering of feminist theology which was happening around the same time. What Nolan did offer in the book was a concise focus on some of the central and enduring aspects of Christianity, which continue to provide an intimate challenge to us half a century after its publication.

---

3. *Cf* Charles Taylor, *A Secular Age* (Cambridge, Massachusetts: The Belknap Press of Harvard University Press, 2007).

Supporting the Spread of YCS

Cecil Sols

Fr Albert Nolan served as the national chaplain to the Young Christian Students (YCS) from 1977–1984. In the period during his chaplaincy, the country was going through a process of mass resistance against Apartheid. The youth were questioning the role of religion and the Church in the struggle.

In his response to the questions raised by the militant youth who at that time could not connect with the Church, Albert displayed great patience and tolerance. The Church at that time was seen broadly as removed from the plight of the oppressed but rather obsessed in its preaching about the concept of going to heaven. Albert provided hope in explaining the role of Christianity in our current situation. His teachings and presentations influenced the young students to be able to understand the Theology of Liberation, which was seldom preached in Churches back then. He was very convincing in his explanation of the role that Christians and the Church needs to play in our times.

He had a great impact on the thinking of young students from schools and universities, who began to apply the See–Judge–Act method to analyse and resolve problematic situations. This methodology encouraged critical thinking among the young students and they felt at home with his teaching.

As a member of YCS during this time I was empowered to begin understanding the contradictions in our society. We were always reminded to ask 'Why?' until we could get to the root causes of a problem. Albert greatly influenced me, as an organiser for YCS, to read further in order to broaden my understanding of the root causes of our societal problems. He introduced me to the broader world that influenced our situation in South Africa.

He generously shared his knowledge on issues as well as his possessions. I remember when I had to improve my driving skills, he volunteered his Volkswagen Bettle to use for practice.

Upon my release from five months in solitary detention without trial in Soweto and Sandton under section six of the Terrorism Act in 1981–1982, he continued to be a strong pillar of support as part of the YCS leadership team. I was deployed to Natal (now KwaZulu-Natal) to cool off and work with Francis Zitha. This deployment further enhanced my experience in dealing with young students from all social classes. I found a very welcoming situation to organise YCS. Most of the Church leaders knew a lot about his work and writings—from PACSA (Pietermaritzburg Agency for Christian Social Awareness) run by Peter Kerchhoff to the nuns at the Oakford Dominican School near Verulam. The mention of Albert's name opened doors and made it easier to organise for YCS as his opinion on the role of religion and the church was shared by most of those that supported the cause for a just world.

He was a strong pillar in YCS as he provided undivided support and strategic thinking to the organisation. He was a brilliant, sharp intellectual with an exceptionally humble character. He always provided a smile even in difficult situations. We would greatly appreciate that attentive character with a charming laugh and smile.

He was a chaplain who walked the talk in his preaching, which was reflected in his lifestyle. One of the influences he had on me was his ability to explain the role of different social classes in bringing about a just society. The option for the poor that he promoted, in one's lifestyle and consciousness, remained with me consistently.

His teachings influenced youth and student leaders of that time to want to be part of YCS as it operated in small groups which encouraged individual development. He inspired much hope for the youth who wanted to see a free non-racial democratic South Africa.

I was privileged to have attended the youth ministry course that he and the YCS leadership conducted in Cape Town, Johannesburg and Magaliesberg in 1979. We were a team of twelve participants that came from different provinces, trained to spread YCS in schools throughout the country.

In his lifetime he achieved what he was sent to do. His teaching and spirit will continue to live among us.

Integrating Life and Faith

Francis Vusumuzi Zitha

As a chaplain to the Young Christian Students (YCS), Fr Albert Nolan had a big impact on me as he displayed passion, compassion and trustworthiness in all he did. During our YCS leadership course as organisers in training in Magaliesberg in 1979, I remember how Fr Nolan would encourage and motivate us in our meetings and celebrations of the Eucharist. His theological teaching and readings from the Gospel would be fabulously exciting and bring tremendous hope. He would also provide brilliant ideas and information on how to go about giving and sharing hope together with belief in the Kingdom of God to the students we were working with.

In his celebration of the Eucharist during the YCS conferences and in the review of our work of organising students in the field, Fr Nolan would demonstrate how our life is integrated with our faith. I would witness his implementation and putting into practice of the See–Judge–Act method, which assisted in enlightening and deepening our Christian faith.

He also made an impact on me when he demonstrated the gospel values by moving out of Houghton and convincing other fellow Dominican priests to live in Mayfair to share the life of the poor and the needy. That action gave me courage and a spirit of selflessness to also serve and work towards the Kingdom of God here on earth.

Fr Nolan made me realise the effectiveness of prayer in a way that connects us to God the Father who created us, as human beings in his image, to love, respect and serve one another as he has done through his Son, Jesus Christ. As Christians we have certain expectations that when we pray and ask for something, God will then react immediately and answer our prayers. Fr Albert Nolan revealed to me that

God works and reveals himself through people we live with here on earth and through the environment surrounding us as humans. God also desires first to enter into a relationship with us as Christians who believe in the teaching of the gospel so that we can understand his work.

I would like to conclude the text by mentioning that his book *Jesus before Christianity* played a significant role in my life as a Christian and made me share with other people the values he portrayed in his book.

In Tune with the *Sensus Fidelium*

Lois Law

Attending a Catholic School and growing up in Johannesburg during the 1970s, I belonged to a Christian Life Group (CLG) through which I was fortunate to meet a number of other students across what would have been called the 'colour bar'. I heard first-hand accounts of the experiences of some of those students during the 1976 student uprising. This made a very profound impression on me. I felt a deep sense of social dislocation which led me to study social work at the University of the Witwatersrand (Wits), with a number of questions about faith, politics, injustice and the possibility of change and social transformation.

I first encountered Albert at a student Catholic Society weekend where he spoke about the idea of the Kingdom of God. Albert's primary thesis was that the Kingdom of God which Jesus spoke of was not heaven, but rather something to which we should strive to achieve on earth. Albert answered so many of my questions: Life and faith were profoundly embedded in day-to-day 'praxis' (practice) and the challenge to each of us was to DO!

This teaching demonstrated that both theology and justice could be used as verbs, and in doing so, Albert would help change the eyes with which to see reality. I was also introduced to the penetrating See–Judge–Act method of the Young Christian Students (YCS) which provided a comprehensive manner of reflection and analysis which opened my eyes to the complex articulation of faith, politics, social and economic justice and the need for action leading to change rooted in the wisdom of the Gospel.

Such an approach required openness to change in one's personal life and commitments. Personal piety also had its place but needed to be translated into action both in the world and in one's personal lifestyle choices and behaviours. It was not enough to have sympathy with the oppressed, the marginalised and the poor—rather, action founded in empathy, compassion and solidarity was required. The focus was on *doing things* which would result in some action or change that would bring us closer to the Kingdom of God.

As Dom Helder Camara, who was another of the pioneering figures of the Liberation Theology movement, wrote in 1964, while Vatican Council II was taking place: 'it is essential to begin, trustingly, a crescendo of dialogue. It would be a grave matter before the judgement of God and of history to withdraw oneself from the reconstruction of the world.'[1] Faith is 'a radical heart commitment to entrust myself and my life to God, that results in a radical change in the way that I live my life.'[2] Such a call for conversion was central to Albert's writing and preaching.

At the launch of the Institute for Contextual Theology (ICT) in June 1982, Albert outlined what such a theological approach meant in the context of Apartheid South Africa. He summed it up as follows:

> It wants to start from the fundamentally political character of life in South Africa; it wants to do theology quite explicitly and consciously from within the context of real oppression that exists in South Africa—racial oppression, the oppression of the working class and the oppression of women, and finally, it wants to start from the actual experience of the oppressed themselves.[3]

In Paul's letter to the Hebrews (11:1), it is stated that 'faith is confidence in what we hope for and assurance about what we do not see'. Anselm's maxim that 'theology is faith seeking understanding' is again a 'doing' process of discernment. Albert's approach to theology from the perspective of the poor and oppressed is in keeping with the *sensus fidelium*, that is the 'sense of the faithful'. Increasingly, it has come to be seen as a key concept in the development of Church doctrine and teaching. The Vatican International Theological Commission held in 2014 proclaimed that

---

1. Dom Helder Camara in 'Into Your Hands', written in 1964 on his installation as Archbishop of Olinda and Recife, Brazil.
2. 'What does the motto "faith seeking understanding" mean' at <https://www.gotquestions.org/faith-seeking-understanding.html>. Accessed February 2023.
3. *Inter Nos*, August. 1982:6

the faithful are not merely passive recipients of what the hierarchy teaches and theologians explain; rather, they are living and active subjects within the Church. In this context, it underscored the vital role played by all believers in the articulation and development of the faith.[4]

The *sensus fidelium* of each believer is important because 'in your lived experience, in your sense of what's good and true and faithful you have something to contribute to the church as a whole'.[5]

Albert did not see morality as something that could be easily divided into right or wrong. Rather it should be seen in terms of its consequences. He adopted a non-judgemental attitude to those with whom he engaged and he was judgemental of systems but not of individuals which made him such a powerful change agent. He clearly saw the complexity of the transgenerational transmission of trauma and prejudice that was a product of our country's violent colonial and Apartheid past. Albert understood that people have the capacity to change throughout their life cycle. He fundamentally believed in the agency of people to make good choices. He listened carefully, was open-minded and above all compassionate. He understood that many of the choices of action to follow or behaviour to change would be difficult and would take courage but that this would be facilitated by the gift of grace which can be understood as 'the dimension of God active within us, doing for us what we cannot do for ourselves. It is not static, but dynamic'.[6] Grace is most needed and best understood in the midst of sin, suffering, and brokenness and has the power to transform and enable the work for justice. Grace would become an important theme in the *Kairos Document*.

Albert believed that we all have the capacity to be part of the transformation of both the Church and of society and, as the Bishops' Conference of England and Wales wrote, should,

---

4. 'Sensus Fidei: In the Life of the Church' at <https://www.vatican.va/roman_curia/congregations/cfaith/cti_documents/rc_cti_20140610_sensus-fidei_en.html#Chapter_3>. Accessed February 2023.
5. '"Sensus fidelium": the sense of the faithful' at <https://catholiccourier.com/articles/sensus-fidelium-the-sense-of-the-faithful/>. Accessed February 2023.
6. Cecile S. Holmes, 'The Gift of Grace' at <https://www.resourceumc.org/en/content/the-gift-of-grace>. Accessed February 2023.

claim whatever rights and opportunities are available to us only in order to exercise an influence on behalf of whatever we believe to be true and good, especially in solidarity with people everywhere who are on low incomes, disabled, ill or infirm, homeless or poorly housed, in prison, refugees or who are otherwise vulnerable, powerless and at a disadvantage'.[7]

For Albert it could be summed up very simply by asking the question 'what is the most loving course of action to follow in this particular situation or context'?

Albert had an unwavering sense of hope. His life and ministry were a sign of the Kingdom of which Jesus spoke and that was his gift to all of us and his ongoing challenge to us. He opened our eyes to truly see the possibility of and hope for the realisation of the Kingdom of God.

Nobel Peace Prize laureate Adolfo Pérez Esquivel emphasised that

we also have to focus on the signs of hope that exist. As peoples, we cannot be mere spectators. We have to become the protagonists of our history. As peoples, we have to learn to unite in the building of a culture of solidarity and of hope ... But if we have hope, hope makes change possible. It makes it possible to think about and to achieve a new world, a more just world, and a more humane world. What will happen depends on what each of us will do. Each of us must decide.[8]

When Pope Francis stood alone at St Peter's Square on 27 March 2020, during the COVID-19 pandemic, he spoke words of hope to the world when he asked humanity 'to reawaken and put into practice that solidarity and hope capable of giving strength, support and meaning to these hours when everything seems to be floundering'.[9]

---

7. 'The Common Good', Statement of Catholic Bishops' Conference of England and Wales, 1996.

8. 'Adolfo Pérez Esquivel Acceptance Speech' at <https://www.nobelprize.org/prizes/peace/1980/esquivel/acceptance-speech/>. Accessed February 2023. Adolfo Pérez Esquivel Nobel acceptance speech, 1980. He was awarded was awarded the 1980 Nobel Peace Prize for his leadership and courageous defence of human rights and democracy for the people of Latin America and for serving as an inspiration to oppressed people all over the world

9. Stan Chu Ilo, 'Francis is asking the church to dream again. Why do so many oppose him?' at <https://www.ncronline.org/opinion/guest-voices/francis-asking-church-dream-again-why-do-so-many-oppose-him>. Accessed February 2023.

I chose St Teresa of Lisieux as my confirmation name, who wrote in her book *The Story of a Soul* that 'what matters in life is not great deeds, but great love'.[10] Her spirituality was one of doing the ordinary with extraordinary love. Albert's writings have been read by countless people all over the world and his contribution to theology is immense. He inspired a generation of Christian activists, but the life he led was one of simplicity, humility and full of great love for all he encountered.

In spite of his very busy schedule Albert was always on time and he always made time to listen and counsel. While working as a social worker for the then racially segregated Johannesburg Child Welfare Society I had a heartbreakingly difficult case which caused me extreme distress. As so many of us have done in times of difficulty I turned to Albert and found such gentleness and understanding as well as important and useful insights into my personality. He provided comfort and understanding in a manner that nobody else did. On another occasion I asked him to say mass for my much loved grandmother and he told me that he had already done so on hearing the news of her death. Albert was always kind, thoughtful and mindful to the needs of others.

I did not see Albert often after leaving Johannesburg but when I did, the warmth of recognition and the affection of his embrace were always a joy to be treasured. However, the resonance of his voice, the clarity of his vision and the conduct of his life have been with me down through the decades. It is my hope that it has informed the way that I interact with others wherever I have found myself; in the way I have parented the children in my life and cared for the frailty of my late mother as well as the research and writing that fill my days.

In speaking to other contributors to this collection the concern has been expressed that we are writing more about ourselves rather than about Albert. I think that is testament to the overwhelming impact that he had on our lives and on our attempts to practice what he preached!

---

10. "Story of a Soul" by Saint Thérèse of Lisieux' at <https://mycatholic.life/books/story-soul-saint-therese-lisieux/>. Accessed February 2023.

Albert, at the annual assembly of friars at La Verna receiving the solemn profession of Thomas Chuma in the presence of Mark James in 2002.

A Mentor and a friend

Peter Sadie

I first met Fr Albert Nolan as NCFS's national chaplain. As provincial of the Dominican priests in South Africa, he was responsible for deciding to sell the Order's large headquarters in Houghton and move them to a dilapidated building in Mayfair, where my mom was later employed as his administrator. At the first national conference I attended in 1979, Albert fed our hunger for reasons to hope as few others in the world could have done. His spirituality and insight offered us ways of confronting our anxiety about being conscripted into Apartheid's army and the despair about the increasingly violent oppression and exploitation that this army entrenched. He used his gift as a writer through *Jesus before Christianity* to encourage us to bridge the gap between the materialistic world we lived in and the Christian values we aspired to live with a spirit of transformative compassion.

Albert had a phenomenal ability to unravel the complex challenges we faced in ways that simplified the moral decisions we needed to help us make choices about our lives. He taught us to theologise by 'reading the signs of the times' and find a way to channel our youthful energy into working for justice. Albert explained that God's reign was not simply about 'a pie in the sky' afterlife; rather eternity begins right here and right now in our daily choices on earth.

Albert's life was a tangible witness of how Jesus called his followers to realise God's Kingdom in all aspects of our lives. By striving to live His values, we were challenged to transform our motives *and* fight against the political power structures of Apartheid that ruled us. As white university students, we were privileged to be on our way into professions which would provide financial security within a racially divided society. But like St Paul we were thrown from our horses, as we began to see how our narrow perspective blinded us from seeing what God called us to.

At our national YCS conferences, Albert listened intently to the reality of oppression as students, especially our members from the poorer rural and township regions, shared their experiences of repression. As one of the very few adults present at these conferences, he sometimes also found himself playing schoolmaster, scolding us to get some sleep when we continued partying, debating and making a racket into the early hours of the morning. With the invincibility of youth, we used to say we'd sleep when we died.

The reality of the 1980s was that South Africa was deeply divided racially. Black South Africans could barely move outside of crowded townships without a pass allowing them to work, and those same townships were out of bounds for whites unless they had a permit to work there. Police in uniform and in plain clothes stalked the streets of our cities and towns; army tanks filled with young white soldiers were rolled into townships at the slightest sign of protest. Conflict between the young conscripted white army and the black youth-led organisations of the oppressed smouldered and it felt as if it could ignite into a major bushfire at any moment.

It seems quite strange thinking back on it now, but spaces in which black and white youth were permitted to meet, talk, laugh, sing, eat, drink, pray and just spend time getting to know one another were exceptionally rare. YCS regional and national conferences made such encounters possible. Together with Albert, we shared the Eucharist and sang hymns and freedom songs to the heavens. We were imbued with a sense of hope that God was present, and would reinforce our efforts to resist Apartheid and build an alternative society based on the values of God's Kingdom. Albert clearly loved being present at these events—the loud bursts of his laughter regularly echoing through our ears made his joy at being with us clear for all to see.

Albert's clarity of thinking was enormously helpful to me when I was doing my Masters dissertation in the late 1980s on the different responses of youth to integrating their faith and political life. Albert's editing and publicising of the *Kairos Document* at this time clarified the Church's choices into three options: We could support the Apartheid regime through 'State Theology', We could sit on the fence while our country burned with 'Church Theology', or we could act as a 'Prophetic Church' in choosing to resist the evil of Apartheid. I have no doubt that the course of my life would have been quite ordinary but for the impact of Albert's witness of who Jesus truly is. A generation of our student community found ways to resist Apartheid as activists, building leaders in both legal and underground structures. The core of my own ANC underground unit, which effectively contributed towards South Africa's transformation, was led by YCS activists.

Later, as young professionals, this meant we all found ways to channel the skills we had gained at university into serving the poor. For some, it meant working in township and rural hospitals, education, workers unions, ending conscription, while a few of us focused on shifting our Church towards justice and peace by serving in the Southern African Catholic Bishops' Conference. We continued meeting weekly in review groups within the Christian Action Movement (CAM) where we strategised together on how we could transform our organisations to serve the interests of the poor and we celebrated Mass together monthly with Albert. He usually introduced the homily, but this too was shared by us as in the early Christian communities.

In 2006, a few of us ex-YCS members, including Chris Langefeld, a past chaplain, started a company focused on training leaders for the public and private sectors. Our original vision had been to focus on developing leadership among unemployed youth, yet none of our proposals with government met with success, and so we were forced to change tack. In 2012, our lay Dominican group initiated a process which led to the growth of Meriting Youth Development. We piloted a project of training unemployed youth in free learnerships in the Johannesburg city centre together. Two of our members, Mahlape and Tony Osei-Tutu, accommodated the classes in their school. Soon thereafter, Albert became the chaplain to our group and taught us the *lectio divina* method as a way of contemplating the Gospels. This enabled us to integrate our faith and our work and family lives in creative ways. Albert's contemplative approach nudged me to introduce meditation into Meriting focused on healing the spiritual trauma of the youth. They subsequently were able to choose learning goals to complete for themselves. These interventions had a positive impact and as the learners grew in self-confidence so too did their pass-rates. Meriting has grown to serve a few hundred unemployed youth in two other Catholic centres nationally.

In 2013 I joined a contemplative reading group that Albert initiated. Each week participants would summarise books they had read which would be shared within the group. Albert often facilitated this sharing with a keen eye for what benefits the group could focus on for our lives and work. In this way the contemplative group continued to inspire us in ways which I've missed since Albert passed on. My hope is that we continue by picking up the baton Albert so generously carried with us while he had spirit left in his frail body. He always teased us, 'Old age isn't for sissies'. Albert incarnated for me who Jesus was in ways which I found impossible to be indifferent to. I will forever be indebted to Albert as a prophet and a friend who I grew to love.

A Humble Servant of God

Mike Mailula

I joined the Struggle at a tender age of thirteen after witnessing the events of 1976 in the township of Pretoria called Mamelodi. In 1979 I was expelled from high school for participating in student political activities. I found a factory job at a pharmaceutical company towards the end of 1979. I had had to work because I came from a poor background.

I joined the Young Christian Students (YCS) through a friend, Chikane Chikane, whom I met at our drama group. He introduced me to Peter Manchidi, may his soul rest in peace. So, we put together a YCS group where we learnt the See–Judge–Act method. I believe this is a great method of analysis and action. We tried to find a venue for meetings at our local parish, St Raphael. However, the local priest would hear none of that. He knew somehow that YCS reflected on politics and Christianity and it was linked to Albert Nolan who wrote for various Catholic publications besides having written his world acclaimed book *Jesus before Christianity*. We met at various houses until Albert convinced a priest at St Mary's in Mamelodi West to accommodate us. During our meetings at this parish, the priest and the nuns looked after us very well, and they were discreet about our meetings at the parish. It should be mentioned that the South African Police's Security Branch had spies in the communities. Therefore it could not be assumed that all black people were rooting for the struggle for freedom in South Africa.

Although Chikane's elder brother, Moses Chikane, was an activist and was held many times in detention without trial, I never thought I would gain the unwanted attention of the Security Branch. At the time I was travelling regularly to Soshanguve to assist in organising

YCS groups and to Johannesburg to the YCS office which was based at the Dominican House in Mayfair. It was during this period that the Security Branch started harassing my family. They wanted to know whether my mother knew that I was conniving with the communists to bring down the South African government. This was quite a shock to her, but the fact that Albert was a priest put her at ease. My mother did not speak English but Afrikaans, learnt as a domestic worker in the white households of Pretoria. In Afrikaans, Albert managed to help her understand the antics of the police and that they would carry on with such tactics until the Apartheid system fell. True to fact, the harassment never stopped as my political activism grew, and my mother grew stronger in her resolve to fight Apartheid.

Through my interactions with Albert in YCS workshops or conferences I learnt how erudite and eloquent he was. He could break down any complex political or theological question to make it easy to understand. I knew him for his seminal sessions on servant leadership, religion and politics and on non-racialism. Albert was also well-known and respected in political and religious circles. He was held in high esteem by the Southern African Catholic Bishops' Conference as a distinguished theologian. In political circles he knew everybody who was important to know in South Africa and in exile. He was well respected by many South African leaders, such as erstwhile President Thabo Mbeki, Dr Beyers Naudé, Archbishop Desmond Tutu, and Reverend Frank Chikane. He was extensively consulted by South Africans on broad strategies and tactics of the struggle against 'Apartheid and the role of the Church in it'. He was also consulted by the academic world. He was a key editor of the *Kairos Document* which chartered the way to democracy in South Africa by giving direction to the role of the Church.

Throughout all this, Albert, remained a humble servant of God, living a simple lifestyle, in a humble house in Mayfair and generous to others with his resources. For as long as I knew him from the early 1980s, he always drove a Volkswagen Beetle which he shared with others without qualms. Albert used to be away for weeks on end and as activists we knew what he was doing because we were engaged in similar activities—organising people to join the struggle for freedom and building the underground movement. He always worked very hard, celebrating Masses as a priest, writing speeches, addressing meetings and conferences, writing academic papers, accommodating walk-ins, doing general pastoral work and travelling.

For those of us from the townships and rural areas, when we heard of the concept of *taking an option for the poor* in YCS we were full of consternation. We could not understand why we as oppressed, deprived and disadvantaged black people were called upon to taken an 'option for the poor'. How could we consider this option when we were poor ourselves? At almost every workshop or conference we struggled with this concept as new members attended. However, as we learnt along the way, the central issue is leadership of service on the side of the poor, and we were conflating *option for the poor* and *option to be poor*. As always, Albert broke down the concept for us to understand, spicing it up with his infectious laughter.

One of the major contributions to South Africa by YCS was the high-quality leadership that was produced for the society. YCS members played important and critical roles in the formation of trade unions, civic and student organisations, United Democratic Front, Theology Exchange Programme, Congress of South African Students and many others. And although many are not prominent, they continue to play important leadership roles in government, civil society, parastatals, higher education and the church.

Albert's role in enabling this to happen was indispensable through his continual presence, accompaniment and encouragement.

Fr Albert Nolan, National YCS Chaplain 1977-1984

Taming a Wild Cannon

Norman Malatjie

Introduction

It has indeed taken me a while to just plunge in and write my testimony of how I was influenced by the life and times of Fr Albert Nolan. In fact, truth be told, I was very anxious and procrastinated a lot. I was anxious because I did not want to take a scholarly approach in writing this, as I wanted to be as simple and humble as I could in telling my truth, and yet, with substance.

In this regard, the quality and inspirational teachings and books by Fr Albert inspired me also to express my thoughts without any inhibition, without any fear. This article is also inspired by a deepened faith, derived from the writings, mentorship and counsel of Fr Albert.

Joining the Young Christian Students'

When I joined the Young Christian Students (YCS) in 1982, I was immediately elected as the secretary of Soshanguve region near Pretoria. At that time, the group was very small and consisted of two cell groups. This way of operating was daunting for me at first, but I got accustomed to it in no time. Consequently, despite me being more of an introvert than an extrovert, my confidence level deepened, and I started believing in myself.

Unbeknown to me, the influence of Father Albert, who I met in the same year I joined, made me dig deeper into my life and recall my humble formative years as a child, from seven years of age in the rural farm settings in Naboomspruit (Mookgopong) and Potgietersrus (Mokopane). I was born in Boksburg but throughout most of my life as a child, a teenager and a youth, my parents moved from farm to farm, from one township to the other in search of better prospects—a nomadic lifestyle which had a major influence on how I would turn out to be. When I met Fr Albert in Magaliesberg in 1982, I was immediately influenced by his philosophy and outlook on life because of his simple lifestyle, humility, humanity, justice and passion for life.

From then on, his teachings and writings sharpened my focus, thoughts, analysis and judgement of different situations especially on how to use the See–Judge–Act method. This way of analysing situations was very useful to me, enabling me to summon information stored in my subconscious mind, particularly about my early life in the farm setting in Mokopane/Mookgopong, where the master-slave relationship between the farm owner and farm workers was a reality for decades. Armed with these tools, I was strongly capacitated to analyse, judge and evaluate from all angles the plight of the farm workers whose situation had not changed much, despite the land tenure act.

Personally, I am a victim of child labour from the early age of six years. My chores included being a shepherd and tilling the land before the planting season. As a result, my formal schooling was delayed until I was eleven years of age. I started my primary education in May 1974, in Mamelodi, Pretoria, and completed it in Soshanguve, Pretoria.

My situation as a working child without pay prompted me when I was at high school, to take a stand against Apartheid policies, and that is why I opted to join YCS in 1982.

Significantly, my conviction about and yearning for justice started from the day when I witnessed my uncle being beaten to a pulp by his farm boss for 'loafing' as he was not feeling well enough to go to work. This incident, and the 1976 uprisings in Mamelodi and across the country, shaped my political consciousness.

In November 1980, while in standard five at Mamashianoka Primary school, I was exposed to Black Consciousness by a fellow student, and from then onwards I never looked back. At that time there was a void left by the banning of the liberation movements in the country, and we began to see the heightened repression by the Apartheid regime in townships and at the work place.

After I was recruited to join YCS by a fellow comrade, Master Molokwane, in 1982, I was soon elected the Regional Secretary for

Soshanguve. My political consciousness and Christian faith took on meaningful shape and led me to being elected the Regional Coordinator in 1983. I was very fortunate in that I was groomed by Father Smangaliso Mkhatshwa, who was our chaplain in Soshanguve at that time. Father Albert Nolan was the national chaplain.

The YCS national conference in Magaliesberg in December 1982, was a watershed moment for me. Fr Albert's guidance and wisdom as national chaplain was invaluable to us as delegates. I was personally inspired by his tutelage and uplifting sermons, my understanding of spirituality was broadened and my faith was deepened as a result of his presence.

His way of relating and simple lifestyle was a clear testimony of his passion for humanity, justice and peace. He was national chaplain at a time of great volatility in the country as many young black militants were leaving in droves to go for military training in neighbouring countries. The mid-1980s was a *kairos* moment for everyone concerned with justice and peace, particularly the progressive religious faithful, and hence stalwarts like Fr Albert and other like-minded progressive religious leaders took a stand against Apartheid as a heinous crime against humanity and led from the front.

The mid–late 1980s proved to be a watershed moment for South Africa because during this period, a State of Emergency was declared a couple of times. Many activists were mysteriously disappearing without trace or being detained for long periods without trial. It was during this time that, at the initiative of Fr Albert and others, the ICT was established to counter the propaganda of the Apartheid regime.

Young people were continually taken to camps organised by the army for brainwashing purposes. Fr Albert and other religious leaders developed the *Kairos Document* that educated Christian activists and Christians in general about the true nature of spirituality and not the distorted one as propagated by the Apartheid regime. We attended a number of workshops, where we were taken through the *Kairos Document* step by step. This way of dissecting and analysing the document empowered me to also organise workshops in my township of Soshanguve, and so counter the military brainwashing camps organised by the regime. We also teamed up with other activists from Mamelodi and Atteridgeville to form the Pretoria Cultural Forum as a counter measure against the regime. This in a sense was a battle for the minds of the people who were apathetic to what was going on in the country. Fr Albert and others taught us how to make biblical studies relevant to the plight of the people and how to gain their trust in the process.

Under Father Albert's influence I grew to believe in my abilities and my self-confidence was boosted. This resulted in me being elected as the national coordinator of YCS in December 1985, immediately after completing my high school education. This led to me participating in the World Council of IYCS in 1986 at the University of Arenberg in Louvain, Belgium. The Council grappled with issues such as technology in developing countries, economies of scale in Third World countries and globalisation. This was a very enriching exposure as I was chosen as the scribe for the commission focusing on the impact of technology in Third World countries. Exchanging experiences with like-minded students from other countries greatly deepened my knowledge of the world order.

Inspired by the rich debates, analysis, and interaction within ICT, I did not hesitate when TEP nominated me as one of the two people who would eventually go to Costa Rica in 1990 to participate in a study of Liberation Theology in Latin American countries. Hosted by the Costa Rica Department of Education and Research, this was a breakthrough moment for me. The convergence of reports from all the Latin American countries highlighted the negative impact imperialism had on all of them. The debates emanating from the daily sessions for four months were eye opening, constructive and exposed the massive divide between the haves (developed countries) and have-nots (developing countries). These countries at the time all expressed the need for more inter-regional cooperation and a united front to face up to imperialism. Other deliberations focused on the need to repudiate the doctrine of discovery of countries that are developing (Third World countries) by western nations, using the Bible as a tool for nefarious intent and indoctrination, thereby demonising culture and tradition in developing countries.

The Latin Americans appreciate a 'Contextual Theology' that responds to their needs, and hence if, during Mass, the sermon was not relevant to their plight, after church they would converge under the trees to run an alternative service that spoke to their issues. The beauty about the alternative was that it was celebrated in the most electrifying and indigenous manner. The Latin American experience was a 'Damascus' chapter for me, and in fact, it was also my own *kai-*

ros moment, feeling the global inter-connectedness of the third world countries and the unity of purpose against the dominant capitalist and imperial powers.

To enhance my knowledge further, immediately after the formative training sessions in Costa Rica, I visited Nicaragua and Cuba as places of interest and study. Whilst in Nicaragua we met with the Cardenal brothers, Ernesto and Fernando, and Miguel d'Escoto, all priests, who served in the Sandinista government, which had been voted out of office and replaced by Violeta Chamorro's government. In our meeting with them, they explained that the setup was temporary, because the people of Nicaragua were tired of the prolonged war sponsored by the United States of America, which supported the counter revolutionaries (Contra rebels) in an effort to oust the legitimately elected government. The Cardenal brothers and Miguel d'Escoto were vilified by the hierarchy of the Catholic Church in Nicaragua, particularly by the archbishop, for participation in the Marxist-Leninist government. In their defence, they argued that Marxism offered the best way of solving people's problems.

On the other hand, the visit to Cuba was aimed at learning about the impact of the economic embargo imposed by the United States to frustrate Cuba's chosen economic path, socialism. Indeed, at the time, Cuba was adversely affected and economically devastated, particularly after the disintegration of the Soviet Union which was their major trading partner. However, the spirit of unity and patriotism stood the Cubans in good stead, despite all the odds.

Conclusion

When I joined YCS in Soshanguve in 1982, I was a very angry young man (acting more like a wild cannon) who wanted to change the *status quo*—like yesterday! However, from my interactions with Fr Albert in Magaliesberg, I began to know the value of discernment and what it meant to be an activist. I also learned how to deal with different situations in a calm and mature way.

Furthermore, the cultural immersion in the Latin American situation helped me to understand the geo-political regional dynamics of Central America, South America and North America. I learnt that, in fact, most Latin American countries loathe capitalism and the imperial power of the US.

These interactions, rich life experiences and challenges changed my paradigm, educated me, transformed me and rocked my comfort zone. In essence, the influence of Fr Albert in my early days at YCS deepened my understanding of the life of a true Christian, devoid of being a hypocrite in thoughts and deeds.

With a sense of international solidarity, my conviction and faith deepened in learning how to do good for humankind, whenever possible, wherever possible and however possible.

In summary, in truth, had I not interacted with Fr Albert, learned from his wisdom, and listened to his sound advice when I was a young militant person, my character would not have changed to what it is today. His influence enabled me to know how to discern, how to listen actively and how to act empathetically in the best interests of justice and peace. As a result of his influence, my demeanour and character have been shaped for the better and my interaction with other people has improved tremendously.

In the Footsteps of Jesus

Shepi Mati

When I was asked if I would care to contribute to a volume in honour of Fr Albert Nolan, I felt conflicted. On the one hand I felt I was way too far from the immediate circle of Fr Albert Nolan to be in a position to talk about him. And on the other hand, I felt an urge drawn from a sense of responsibility we each have to the other in the liberation community. For I can lay claim to being one of the young militants of the Young Christian Workers who derived inspiration and great spiritual strength from the work of that community of Dominicans of which Fr Albert Nolan was a member. Although he was a chaplain to our sister organisation, the Young Christian Students (YCS), his influence went way beyond YCS and even the Christian community.

So, after some soul searching, I arrived at a decision to talk about the influence of liberation theologians—including Fr Albert Nolan—on our generation as YCW militants. And how this somehow forged a social conscience, sensibility and ethical conduct which still sustains some of us in these difficult times.

Young Christian Workers—our circle expands

The first time I met Fr Albert Nolan was at the joint YCW-YCS office in Central Avenue just across from the railway station in Mayfair. Father Nolan belonged to a small community of priests who lived in this communal house-cum-office. This community of Dominicans counted amongst others, YCW chaplains, Fr Joe Falkiner and Fr Ben Mulder as well as Fr Emil Blaser, who founded Radio Veritas. They were following in the footsteps of Jesus Christ of Nazareth. And I was to learn later they were specifically continuing a tradition begun by Bartolomé de las Casas who, originally a slave-owner and landlord, later took the side of the oppressed and condemned the cruel treatment of indigenous people and Africans enslaved by the Spanish conquistadors in the Americas.

The YCW-YCS community and Fr Albert Nolan and the Dominican community lived by the following credo found in Matthew 25:35–36: 'For I was hungry and you gave me something to eat, I was thirsty and you gave me something to drink, I was a stranger and you invited me in, I needed clothes and you clothed me, I was sick and you looked after me, I was in prison and you came to visit me.'

When I reflect back on my own personal journey to a life committed to social justice, I can identify specific defining moments where the seeds of social solidarity and caring were sown. One such moment was at the knees of my great-grandfather Daniel Daniso Mati. I was brought up by my great-grand parents Daniso and Deliwe in an isolated homestead called KwaDingane near what the KhoiKhoi called eKhobonqaba—and the colonialists called Adelaide—in what is now called the Eastern Cape province. My great-grandfather often would send me to call back a stranger who was walking past our homestead on their way home to one of the many farms in the vicinity. Once I had delivered the stranger to him, my great-grandfather would engage in conversation with the stranger, offer them tea and *amasi* and, after an evening meal, even offer them a place to sleep until the morning when, rested and refreshed, they could resume their journey home.

Years later I was interviewing a Somali refugee—a man who held a master's degree in mathematics and was regarded as a national musician in his home country before the war. He told me a similar story growing up in Somalia where people lived a nomadic life and would travel great distances for trade often finding shelter overnight with strangers where they were fed and offered a warm bed and, in the morning, after saying *as-salaam-alaikum*,[1] they moved on to their destination.

Even today in our multiply-wounded and broken society (to use the words of Martha Cabrera[2]) when I see a stranger walking past, I am tempted to offer them water, tea and a chair to rest. Or when I drive past someone walking, I am tempted to offer them a lift to wherever they're going. It was this practice of the concept of *ubuntu*

---

1. A greeting in Arabic that means 'Peace be upon you'
2. Martha Cabrera (2002) available at https://www.medico.de/download/report26/ps_cabrera_en.pdf. Last accessed March 2023

that I found in YCW and in the community of Dominicans of which Fr Albert Nolan was a friar and a living embodiment of caring and communion.

Another defining moment in my life was when I used to take my grandmother to church in New Brighton, Gqeberha—then known as Port Elizabeth. We lived in Boast Village and she was blind as a result of diabetes. I would hold her by the hand all the way to eRhabe church in Malakane Street, eLundini. Our priest, who had baptized me, was the Reverend De Villiers Soga—a descendent of Reverend Tiyo Soga.[3] In church I used to overhear the kids, sitting on the pew just behind ours, gossiping in whispers about my appearance including my patched trousers. And so, in reaction to this, I developed a tendency to drop my grandmother at the church and then disappear until the Sunday service was over, then come back to pick her up. When she enquired about this, I was evasive. But as adults have a deep sense of wisdom to discern when something is amiss, she persisted until I told her the truth. She then reassured me that Jesus loved me as much, if not more than those little spoilt brats in church. When I joined YCW I found an even further affirmation of my worth and dignity. I was drawn to the words of Jesus of Nazareth, '. . . I tell you, whatever you did for one of the least of these brothers and sisters of mine, you did for me' (Matt 25:40).

We can safely say that Fr Albert Nolan, the Dominicans and the Liberation Theology community instilled in us not only this love of our fellow human beings, but also the love of reading as spiritual nourishment. Perhaps one of the most moving instances of personal sacrifice I read about then was of two priests who hailed from Latin America. One was Fr Camillo Torres of Colombia who, realising the limitations of ministering through Sunday sermons, decided to join the guerillas in the mountains and died fighting alongside them. The other was of the Bolivian priest and revolutionary Nestor Paz who died in similar conditions. I still remember the red-covered autobiographical account of his life entitled *My Life for My Friends: The Guerilla Journal of Nestor Paz, Christian*. Albert Nolan, too, epitomised this readiness, not only to identify with the poor but to be prepared to risk his skin to realise his convictions.

---

3. Tiyo Soga (1829–1871) was the first black South African to be ordained in an established Church, the Presbyterian Church.

Again, I do not want to forget the blazing trail of selfless service left behind by scores of Catholic nuns who devoted their lives to the caring for the sick, feeding the poor, and fighting alongside us for social justice. At this moment I would like to propose to you the reader to observe a minute of silence in tribute to all of them—especially Sr Áine Hardiman OP (who the community of Guguletu and Nyanga East called Sister Matswele using a phonetic approximation to 'onion') and Sr Claire-Marie Jeannotat HC who was deported and was living in Switzerland until she died recently.

The next defining moment for me was when I was detained in 1977 and kept in New Brighton Police Station for fourteen days under the General Law Amendment Act. I was literally thrown into a cell with common law detainees and perhaps the hope of the Special Branch was that these fellows would finish me off. But instead, as they enquired as to what brought me *edanyana* [township slang for prison], I raised my clenched fist and instantly won their respect and admiration. I had read the biography of Malcolm X and drawing from his experience, began to politicise my fellow detainees about how the source of their social and so-called criminal activities lay in the socio-economic conditions of inequality imposed on us by Apartheid.

In moments of self-doubt and temptation to falter, I would draw on that other story of the three believers who were persecuted for their beliefs and eventually were captured and thrown into a fire so hot that it burnt the men who carried and tossed them into it.[4] And in the darkest of times when circumstances seemed grim and trying, I would see Shadrach, Meshach and Abednego walking about inside the furnace but only this time joined by a fourth man. And in those times, I would know that we in the struggle for social justice were not alone. In times like this, you'd hear us humming a song *Zingadidakumbisi, iintlungu nokufa, sendiyibon intlalontle engunaphakade!* [Let pain and death not deter me, for I can see the eternal social justice on the horizon]. Albert and the Dominican friars became a living embodiment of these three believers as they faced persecution, vilification, harassment, torture, prison and the ever-present possibility of death at the hands of the Special Branch, Apartheid thugs and the Apartheid government and its ideological zealots.

---

4. See Daniel 3.

See, Judge and Act and the preferential option for the poor

YCW had converted us into young worker militants. And with its method of *See, Judge and Act* had brought about a revolution within the clergy who accompanied laypeople—worker lay preachers—in becoming militants committed not only to understand the world as it is but to seek to transform it into a world as it could be. These early militants were inspired by the founder of the movement, Belgian priest Fr Joseph Cardijn. Addressing the Second Vatican Council in 1965, Fr Cardijn said:

> I have shown confidence in young people's freedom in order to better educate that freedom. I helped them to see, judge and act by themselves, by undertaking social and cultural action themselves . . . in order to become adult witnesses of Christ and the Gospel, conscious of being responsible for their sisters and brothers in the whole world.[5]

The commitment of both the YCW and YCS to the *preferential option for the poor* meant a complete identification with what Eduardo Galeano calls 'the nobodies of this earth' and a commitment to fight for social justice and equality. One of the early adherents of liberation theology to which I was exposed was Dom Helder Camara. This Archbishop of Recife in Brazil is known to have uttered the words: 'when I give food to the poor, they call me a saint. When I ask why the poor have no food, they call me a communist'. YCW taught us to go beyond giving food to the poor by asking why the poor had no food. A YCS militant and comrade of mine, Vincent Williams, who worked closely with Fr Albert Nolan, used to remind us, 'Ask why until you die'.

Another source of inspiration in those days was a trade unionist by the name of Oscar Mpetha who lived in Nyanga East in Cape Town and was for many years banned. He used to say: *senza iijezi, kodwa asizinxibi [We make jerseys, but we cannot afford to wear them]*. And then he would issue a challenge to us young militants to figure this out and explain what it refers to: the source of the exploitation with which the system of capitalism is synonymous. While Karl Marx was a philosopher and thinker from which liberation theologians drew inspiration and who opened our eyes to how this capitalist system

---

5. See https://seejudgeact.org/see-judge-act-with-joseph-cardijn/ on the origins and development of the YCW. Last accessed March 2023.

works with his labour theory of value and on which he derived the theory of surplus value, we simply referred to him as *intshebe* (the bearded one). And later we learnt that the Cuban revolutionaries, some of whom descended from the Sierra Maestra[6] to join fellow revolutionaries in the urban underground, were also called the bearded ones. The story of one of them and how religion shaped his own thinking is aptly told by Brazilian Dominican liberation theologian, Frei Betto, in *Fidel and Religion: Conversations with Frei Betto* (1985).

Recently we hosted a launch of a biography of Jabulani Nobleman Nxumalo, otherwise known as Mzala, by Professor Mandla Radebe in conversation with another YCS militant and revolutionary intellectual, Thandeka Gqubule-Mbeki. It was held at Rhodes University in Makhanda. Mzala too was one of those militants of the liberation movement who drew inspiration from his own religious roots in the Seventh Day Adventist Church. I do not know if Mzala ever met Fr Albert Nolan, but of this I am certain—they met in a shared inspiration drawn from liberation theology and in a commitment to social justice and social solidarity. And, as his friend and contemporary, Vusi Mavimbela said in his opening address at the event, Mzala never saw a contradiction between his religious beliefs and his Marxism. It would appear that those who have their roots in liberation theology have more often than not been consistent in upholding ethics and values of deep commitment to social and ecological justice, and a personal conduct in constant dialogue with their commitment to social solidarity.

The regional office of YCW in the Eastern Cape was in Haupt Street in the white working-class suburb of North End otherwise known as eDasi in Gqeberha. One winter morning Zim Nondumo, Lulu Johnson, Cuan Stanley and I were arrested in this office. The Special Branch went through the place with a fine tooth-comb. Under the carpet under the bed and spread out so as not to attract attention, I had hidden copies of the journal of the South African Communist Party (SACP), the African Communist, the journal of the ANC, *Mayibuye*, and *Dawn*, the journal of Umkhonto Wesizwe (MK). Early the next morning a couple of uniformed policemen pounced on the house ostensibly to enquire about the sale of the property. And lo and behold they stumbled across a poster *Down with the Fascist Repub-*

---

6. A mountain range in Cuba

lic, Forward to a People's Republic which was hung up defiantly by one of the YCW militants—against every caution I preached. On discovering this poster, all I could hear them uttering nervously was '*Veiligsheid! Veiligsheid!*'.[7] The Special Branch arrived within minutes and, on searching the place, they not only found the literature under the carpet but also, behind the fridge, a big poster of Che Guevara, a cigar in his hand, wearing a bottle-green uniform and smiling. They asked me who this was, I replied, 'It's our chaplain Fr Dave Jones', to which each kept telling the others, '*Dis daai vark* David Jonas', as they mocked Father Jones after the Biblical Jonah. Only much later one of them dismissed the others saying, '*Nee, dis twak, dis daai vark Fidel Castro* [No, that's bull, it's that pig Fidel Castro]'. That was the closest they got to Che. All along, this photograph of the Jesus Christ of the Rio de la Plata[8] kept a constant smile, as if saying, in the words of that jazz giant 'barefoot boy from Queenstown', Mongezi Feza, 'you think you know me, but you'll never know me!'. We cherished moments like these, overcoming a personal fear of these thugs of Apartheid and celebrating a small victory even if only for a fleeting moment. I had never been so proud of leading those fascist thugs astray and watching how they entangled themselves in this.

After weeks in solitary confinement at Sanlam Building and St Albans Prison, they brought in our Port Elizabeth Diocesan Bishop, John Murphy, and a delegation of YCW clergy to impress upon them what these Young *Communist* Workers were busy with under their noses. Our mentor Roddy Nunes later told us the Bishop surveyed the literature for which we were detained, and turned back to the Special Branch, 'You've detained these young men for this? This literature is freely available in all the Sociology and Political Studies Departments of most liberal universities even in this country!'. If anything, these words from the mouth of Bishop Murphy endeared him even more to us. After the dawn of political democracy, I told this story to another priest who was in our company at the grimmest of times, Fr Richard 'Dick' O'Riordan, and he said to me, 'Bishop Murphy is from some village in Ireland and would never have abandoned you'. Bishop Murphy, Fr Albert Nolan and the Dominicans showed their commitment to Christ by never abandoning the weak and vulnerable

---

7. Reference to 'Security Police' in Afrikaans.
8. Che Guevara grew up in the area of the Rio de la Plata in Argentina.

in the hours of their greatest need. As students and young workers, we knew Fr Albert Nolan was standing with us as we faced the might of the police and their henchmen.

Continuing the journey

Over the years, the dawn of political democracy scattered us in different directions as we rolled up our sleeves to rebuild our country, and so I seldom met Fr Albert. I last met him by chance in Cape Town in the company of Professor Barney Pityana and Reverend Cedric Mayson while they were surely in deep reflection on this difficult moment in the history of our country and continent. And my last indirect connection with him took place recently when I was in Johannesburg staying with Leslie Dikeni while undergoing treatment for prostate cancer. Veteran activist, Jabu Ngwenya, came by and informed us that Fr Albert Nolan was not well. Jabu and Leslie resolved to go and see him and I was sad that I was not able to accompany them. Yet, perhaps our most profound monument to his memory is to continue the journey he inspired us to walk in the footsteps of Jesus Christ of Nazareth with informed and conscious indignation at the persisting injustice and indignity we are exposed to: every time an official treats us with contempt, every time we see a gaping pothole, every time we hear of someone looting public resources. With God on our side, we will eventually begin to construct a more just, humane and caring society for which many gave their lives.

Section Three
Mayfair

Mayfair Community in the 1980s. The building is in the centre with Benedict Mulder waving from the balcony. The railway station is on the left, out of view.

124 Central Avenue

Joseph Falkiner OP

When Albert's book *Jesus before Christianity* was published in South Africa in 1976, he dedicated it 'To the people of the Third World'. He devoted several chapters to topics like 'The Poor and the Oppressed' (chapter 5), 'The Kingdom and Money' (chapter 7), and 'The Kingdom and Solidarity' (chapter 9). The book reveals where Albert's heart lay. It was with the poor and oppressed anywhere in the third world. Their ethnic or racial group was irrelevant. Knowing this will help the reader to understand Albert's terminology. The reader may prefer to interpret this in the South African context as meaning mainly black people.

1976 was also the year of the Soweto uprising. Soweto is a huge residential area for the millions of black people working in Johannesburg. Coincidently, the very day that the uprising began, 16 June 1976, was also the day that Albert spent driving up to Johannesburg to assume his task as provincial of the South African Dominican Vicariate.

The uprising was not over in one day. For several months after that day black school students in town after town held demonstrations to show their solidarity with those who participated in the uprising. Some of these demonstrations resulted in damage to school property and led to further repressive measures by the police and security forces. During the 1980s the actions of the State security forces became extremely brutal.

All this forms part of the background for the initiatives that Albert was to take during his term as provincial. One of these initiatives was the establishment of a new Dominican community in a predominantly white working-class suburb of Johannesburg called Mayfair. Mayfair was a down-market mixed industrial and residential suburb of Johannesburg situated on the railway line linking Soweto to Johannesburg. Albert wanted the members of the community to live in solidarity with most of the people of Soweto who were poor. The brethren making up this community were all white, and therefore they could not actually live in Soweto.

Albert initiated this community very cautiously as he knew that there could well be opposition from some of the brethren on both political and spiritual grounds. He could not just propose it to his vicariate council, for it would likely have been rejected. This potential opposition from some of the brethren had its background in the historical division of the Dominican brethren of South Africa in three distinct groups. There were those missionaries who had been sent from England with the original aim in 1917 of establishing a province of the Order in South Africa and who by the 1970s had become heavily involved in staffing the national seminary for black seminarians in Hammanskraal, north of Pretoria. There were others who had come from the Dutch province in 1932 to be missionaries in the Orange Free State province of South Africa. Most of them were still working tremendously hard, building up the Diocese of Kroonstad. They kept themselves at the same standard of living as they had had in the Netherlands. They saw themselves departing back home to the Netherlands once the diocese was fully established with a full complement of local diocesan clergy. Finally, there was a small group of white South Africans including myself and Albert. Albert, as the new provincial, had to keep all three groups happy. The vicariate had been established by the Dominican Master of the Order, Anicetus Fernandez Alonso, in 1968 in order to unite these groups into one structure. But their interests were still diverse.

Albert's own interest was that the Church and also the Dominicans should develop a sense of solidarity with the 'poor and oppressed', and that any new Dominican community should have this as their project. If he could not propose this himself, how was he to achieve it? He worked out a strategy. In 1978 he called an informal meeting with four of us—Finbar Synnott, Benedict Mulder, Gregory Brooke and myself—to ask if we would be prepared to ask permission from him (Albert) and his council to engage in an experiment of setting up a new community in Mayfair. The purpose of the community was 'to make more contact with the youth of Soweto and learn why they approved of the uprising'. The four of us had a background of doing such youth work in the parishes of the East Rand, namely Payneville and Kwa Thema. The fact that Mayfair's real purpose would be to convert people away from a belief that the only way to achieve happiness was to become rich could not be mentioned in the petition. Nor could it be mentioned that it would entail, for those who took part, living on a salary no higher than that of a working-class family in Soweto. Nor could it be mentioned that the idea had come from Albert. That would have to be kept secret. Three of us (Finbar, Ben and I) agreed to start the new community. Gregory chose not to join.

Finbar was an elderly Englishman heavily engaged in promoting the Justice and Peace Commission of the Southern African Catholic Bishops' Conference (SACBC). He was also running what he called the *Self-tax movement* by which financially well-off people taxed themselves monthly for the sake of the poor. Finbar used their gifts to pay accommodation rents for a number of otherwise desperate Soweto widows. He could easily do all that in Mayfair. But his real reason for agreeing was, in his own words: 'When I joined the Order I took a vow of poverty, and I have never been allowed to live it. This new community will make that possible.'

Benedict was a white South African who had grown up in a racially mixed economically depressed part of Cape Town in the days before Apartheid was enforced there. He was an experienced parish priest who had worked mainly in black townships on the East Rand and was well aware of the poverty there. He had developed a loathing for the disparity in income between whites and blacks and wanted to identify more with the poor and oppressed.

I was by this time the regional chaplain for the Young Christian Workers (YCW) but had been based in our Springs community. There were YCW groups that I had to assist all over the diocese of Johannesburg. Moving to Mayfair would certainly help me. The YCW members mostly earned extremely poor salaries (seldom more than R10 per week at that time) and I felt that by living in this new community, I would better be able to appreciate their struggle to get decent working conditions and a living wage.

Our petition was accepted and approved 'as an experiment'. Now all we had to do was to find suitable premises to do what Albert had in mind.

It was Benedict who found the ideal place, an old complex of ten two-roomed flats that had been slightly vandalised and left very dirty before it had been completely shut down. It was owned by a widow who wanted to keep it safe in memory of her late husband. If we would clean it and protect it, she would let us move in for a purely nominal rent. It suited us as it was in the main shopping street running through Mayfair and opposite the railway station. This made it very easy for black people to visit us. In any case, hundreds if not thousands of young black clothing-factory workers alighted from trains there every morning and afternoon as they made their way to work and back.

The complex consisted of two blocks. The ground floor of the front block facing the street was still occupied by a few shops. Above them on the upstairs level were four of the flats together with a communal toilet and a shower. That was all we needed for the Dominican community to start with and we moved in. Behind that was a closed courtyard and then a second block of six flats, three of them at ground level and three on the upper level. These gradually became offices for the various organisations that we worked with, first the YCW of which I was regional chaplain; then the Young Christian Students (YCS), of which Albert was the chaplain, which included university and high school students. Then followed the Catholic Students Association (CASA) and the National Catholic Federation of Students (NCFS), who shared an office. Last of all, after some years, the Diocesan Justice and Peace Commission also took one of the flats for their offices with Dominican Emil Blaser after he became the episcopal vicar for Justice and Peace in 1985.

When we moved in in 1979, we had one bed for Finbar, and two camping stretcher beds for Benedict and myself. We also had a kitchen cupboard that Benedict had rescued from a rubbish dump, and a dining table that I begged from a convent that was closing down. We had a small paraffin stove on which to cook. That was all. Our first Mass was offered on top of a cardboard carton with us seated around it on the floor. We had no electricity for the first few years as the wiring throughout the complex, except in the shops, had been declared unsafe. We used paraffin lamps at night. So, in effect we were living as did many poor families in Soweto, making do with the little we had. Our lifestyle was to be similar to that of working-class labourers. Finbar even refused to ride in the one car we had, saying that the poor did not travel in privately owned cars. We restricted our eating of red meat and used soya and lentils as replacements.

What impression did this create? Priests and nuns, especially those connected with Justice and Peace and with the YCW, loved us and soon donated a table for an altar and simple benches and chairs for the chapel and dining room. A friendly family living nearby offered to do all our laundry in their washing machine. The YCWs from Soweto gave us a name: *Freedom Square!* This was to distinguish it from the notorious John Vorster Square which housed the security police and their prisoners. Some relatives of mine heard of the camp stretchers and arrived with proper beds for Benedict and myself. Albert looked in and was clearly happy. His idea was coming to fruition. In late 1979 he himself joined us. He did not want a private room and joined Ben and me in one room. We slept in what became known as the dormitory.

A few other brethren also joined us. The first was the elderly ex-vicar provincial, Peter Paul Feeny, who had accepted me as a novice when I joined the Order. In 1982, a candidate for the Order, Mark James, joined us and stayed for two and a half years. He was study-ing at Wits University and was involved in Cathsoc and later YCS. He became provincial himself many years later. He initially shared a room with a full-time worker for YCS—Peter Manchidi. We were also joined by Peter Hortop, who was returning to the Order after having been away for many years. In 1982, after a time in Mayfair, Peter was sent to Lesotho to do a second novitiate. When he returned in 1983 for a few months, before he went to work in Virginia in the diocese of Kroonstad, he was able to get the lights working again as he was a qualified electrician. After getting electricity, we did away with the paraffin lamps. A fridge was donated, and we got a TV. So ended the fun-filled nights of sitting around the dining room table play-ing Crazy Eights by lamplight. Instead, the new community pastime became watching the seven o'clock news on SABC. Emil Blaser also came to stay in Mayfair in 1983 to study Sociology at Wits. Albert wanted to prepare him for leadership and, in 1984, he indeed took over from Albert as provincial and moved in permanently.

In two successive years we also received postulants: Patrick Giddy and Brian Williams in 1983 and Stephen Lowry, Paul Shiel and Har-old Caledon in 1984. There was an elderly Dutch Dominican, Fr Charles Mendel, living in retirement in a convent of sisters in Johan-nesburg and he came in regularly on Sunday evenings to join our recreation. When he met these postulants along with the candidate, Mark, he said: 'Now I can die in peace, because the next generation is on its way in'.

These were the happiest four years of my life, but in 1983 I was chosen to be the YCW national chaplain and had to move to its Dur-ban headquarters. But while I was in Mayfair, I had begun to hear little snorts of deprecation from some brethren when Albert's name came up in conversation. That led me to realise that not all the brethren were happy about what had been taking place. Even though the house was full of superiors and ex-superiors, some brethren never came near the Mayfair community. While some Dominicans shunned the place and some Dominican Sisters accused us of staying in filth, we had many international visitors passing through. Among them were Ian Linden, the director of the Catholic Institute for International Relations (CIIR) and Fr Damian Byrne, the Master of the Order.

In 1979 towards the end of his first term of office as provincial, Albert made two structural changes in the vicariate. He raised the status of Mayfair from being an experimental house to what our constitutions refer to as a *domus*. This meant that it was no longer temporary but could continue. Then he sold the rather posh vicariate headquarters, a mansion bought by his predecessor in the rich suburb of Houghton, and he himself joined the Mayfair community. These changes did nothing to endear him to the group that disagreed with everything he did. Resentment against Albert grew. There were those who did not wish that Dominicans show their solidarity with the poor in this way. Yet, despite this opposition, in 1980 Albert was re-elected as provincial for another four-year period. During this term, in 1983, he was even elected to be Master of the Order, which he was allowed to decline in order to continue his work against Apartheid in South Africa. He was therefore able to continue to stay in Mayfair.

In 1992, Emil Blaser's second term of office came to an end and Carel Spruyt was elected as the new provincial. This was the death-nail for the Mayfair community as Carel was one of those who opposed its establishment. He closed down Mayfair immediately and the community moved to another block of flats in Troyeville on the eastern side of Johannesburg, far away from the black townships, but closer to the airport.

In the year 2000, Albert was again elected to serve four more years as provincial and it was decided to buy a convent in Mondeor from the Holy Cross Sisters. Troyeville was sold to Radio Veritas, a project of Fr Emil Blaser and the community moved to Mondeor. Although this convent was not far from Soweto, it was not an area frequented by Soweto people and did not have the same attraction as Mayfair did. It is now merely our provincial headquarters and serves as a house of formation from time to time. Albert's project for Dominican solidarity with the poor thus came to an end.

Outward Going, Yet a Haven

Ian Linden

Many will remember Albert Nolan OP as a hero of the struggle against Apartheid, a humble Dominican priest and theologian awarded the national Order of Luthuli by President Thabo Mbeki in 2003. Many more will know his name and have read his 1976 best-seller *Jesus before Christianity* about the historical Jesus. But I also remember him personally as an inspiration and spiritual guide when I worked as Southern Africa Desk Officer at the UK based Catholic Institute of International Relations (CIIR) during the 1980s when both civil resistance and state repression peaked in South Africa.

After Albert became provincial for Southern Africa in 1980, the Johannesburg Dominicans abandoned their priory in the leafy suburb of Houghton, for a decrepit building in—for a Londoner—the ill-named Mayfair, opposite the station on Central Avenue, home to down-and-out whites and surprisingly multi-racial. I first met Albert before the move when I would stay, alongside intermittent black activists on the run, in the Houghton provincial house. Benedict Mulder OP was tasked with finding somewhere to live more in keeping with the province's solidarity with the poor. The estate agent couldn't believe his luck when he was given a description of the building the Dominicans were seeking. I imagined him at the golf club describing his encounter with Ben; how he sold the unsaleable, the worst property on his books, to this odd walk-in.

I was acting at the time as a conduit for funding from the Swedish government to the internal movement of the ANC. Leading up to and into the State of Emergency in South Africa (1985–1990), this was a time of massive repression and mass resistance by the United Democratic Front (UDF), drawing together African National Congress

(ANC) front-organisations, Church institutions and independent civic bodies. Sweden had concluded that leaving support for the ANC solely in the hands of the Communist Party of the Soviet Union and East German Stasi boded ill for the future and was secretly getting money into South Africa to boost non-violent forms of resistance.

Between visits we'd communicate via callboxes, Albert from Johannesburg usually in Garden City Clinic, me in a post office near Trafalgar Square. The Mayfair priory was the ideal bolthole and Albert the ideal adviser on funding priorities. He was a key member of a clandestine Christian group that included the indomitable dissident Dutch Reformed Church *dominee*, Reverend Beyers Naudé, the charismatic Pastor Frank Chikane, later Chef de Cabinet for President Thabo Mbeki, along with Fr Smangaliso Mkhatshwa, then Secretary-General of the Catholic Bishops Conference. They performed the invaluable role within South Africa of guiding this stream of funding to the internal movement of the ANC—whose base was outside South Africa in Lusaka, Zambia and to a lesser degree in Maputo, Mozambique.

To give an example of one of the major requests of this 'Christian ANC' group was money to rebuild and strengthen leadership among black youth. Arrests of the young leaders of the Congress of South African Students (COSAS), the secondary student organisation, was decapitating the youth movement and creating anarchy in the townships; 'necklacing', that is, killing suspected collaborators with flaming tyres around the neck, was becoming disturbingly prevalent.

I was one of many who valued Albert's counsel. Most notable were youth seeking how to live in an unjust and divided society and wanting to explore how to harmonise their faith and a political commitment to justice. The need to 'take sides' and the development of a spirituality of struggle describes Albert's approach in these critical years. Though under surveillance from security police, he was able to share his thinking with theological counterparts around the world, notably in Peru, with fellow priest Gustavo Gutiérrez, the father of Liberation Theology and Spirituality and later a Dominican.

Albert nurtured in Mayfair a group of young Catholics committed to the liberation struggle. He listened to their difficulties, to their fears about the consequences of imminent arrest, their doubts about having children, their problems in handling the violence of the State and their undercover work. He was able to articulate a spirituality that both discerned with them the signs of the times and helped them develop a fitting moral framework within which they could actively resist Apartheid. At the Mayfair priory, praying the Magnificat became almost a bidding prayer as each attending, in their different ways, was in the business of 'pulling down the mighty from their thrones'.

For Albert, Apartheid was 'sin made visible'. I can hear him saying it now in his strong Cape Town accent. For him, and particularly in this unique context, the religious and political task dovetailed. I can also hear his gentle humour coming through hair-raising stories of things nearly going wrong.

One of the immediately pressing things that could go wrong at Mayfair was the security police apprehending fugitives passing through the priory. The peril was increased by the lovable, but eccentric Father Finbar Synnott OP. Finbar was a staunch opponent of Apartheid but with an unusual conviction: lying was *always* wrong. Surveying political leadership around the world today, he had a point. But it meant that if the security police rang up asking if a particular activist they were trying to find was staying in the priory, he would feel obliged to the tell the truth. As a result, when the phone rang with Finbar in the room, there was the surprising sight of one of the brethren leaping across the room to the handset.

Looking back, the Mayfair priory under Albert's leadership housed a foundational expression of Christian community. It was outward looking yet a haven. Albert never stopped seeking what a religious order dedicated to preaching should look, sound and act like in the midst of the gross injustice of Apartheid. For whom should the Dominican community exist? And the answer that informed all his writing and preaching, and applied beyond South Africa, was 'for the poor and oppressed'. It was a theology profoundly influenced by Thomas Aquinas' greatest theological theme in his *Summa Theologica*: justice.

The 1985 *Kairos Document*, workshopped and put together in response to South Africa's political crisis by the Institute for Contextual Theology (ICT) of which he was a prominent member, was a tangible expression of that vision, radical and accessible. It was, as its subtitle had it, 'a Challenge to the Churches' taking their leaderships way beyond their comfort zone by rejecting the 'Church Theology' that put reconciliation before justice. And three years later he and Ed de la Torre, the Filipino activist and theologian, were the prime movers in taking their 'doing theology' global with the *Road to Damascus* document, engaging with Central American theologians in comparable revolutionary situations, denouncing the persecution of Christians working for justice.

Albert saw the movement against Apartheid bringing together the different races and Christian denominations as a glimpse of the 'Kingdom of Heaven'. He saw no conflict between faith and political commitment to work for justice. There was something 'right and fitting' about the way he and those around him lived out that integrated vision. We should learn from him.

Declining Election as Master of the Order

Nicholas Punch OP

I was fortunate enough to attend the August 1983 General Chapter of the Dominican Order, witnessing the election of two Masters of the Order. It was at this General Chapter in Rome that Albert Nolan was elected. This was a very unique election, however, as he was allowed to decline his election by the Chapter, and then Damian Byrne of Ireland was elected. They were close friends!

First, I would like to describe democracy within the Dominican Order. The Dominican Order is a democratic institution; all our leaders are elected. The Catholic Church is not highly regarded for democracy. Hierarchy would be a word that would normally come to mind! But going back to the thirteenth century, St Dominic decided that all superiors—from local community leaders to the Master General[1]—should be elected. Not only that, but the normal business of each community should be decided by the community as a whole.

While democracy is a good name and many countries in more recent times have aspired to it, it is hardly a reality in the world. Even democratic countries act undemocratically and do not always live what they profess to be. Among many religious orders too, democracy has not been a desirable system. It was generally thought that elections would produce poor quality institutions, people seeking leaders who would do the bidding of weaker members, not providing leadership by example! I have been a leader in a number of communities, and know it has been easier as a superior to give in to people doing what they want: 'Don't challenge people too much!' is a truism today!

---

1. Originally the international leader of the Dominican friars was known as the Master General until 1968 at the River Forest chapter in Chicago when the name of the office was changed to Master of the Order.

South Africa was a country that was not fully democratic. Only whites could vote and so there was little chance for minorities to find fairness in that society. There was rampant racism, sexism and poverty. Education was the province of the wealthy. Black women were at the bottom of the heap in gaining access to it. If you wanted a good education you needed the means to pay for it. Due to Apartheid policies black children did not get the same quality of education as whites. The government tried to take over all schools for black children to ensure that they would have an inferior education and would remain as unskilled labourers.

Albert Nolan had an advantage in joining the Dominican Order; he was a white man and so more advantaged racially. He was selected for leadership and became leader of the Dominican Order in South Africa, which meant he was elected to go to the General Chapter in 1983. When the Chapter was looking at possible Masters of the Order, his name was mentioned. He thought he could withdraw his name from the election process but this was not possible. His name went forward and consequently he was elected as Master. He declined his election but was told that, because he was already elected, the whole Chapter had to vote again to see if they accepted his reasons for declining. After Albert had expressed his reasons—that he was needed back in South Africa to fight Apartheid—another vote was taken which voted in favour of Albert declining his election.

So we had to go through the process of electing again! It did not take long for the Irish provincial Damian Byrne to be elected. However, Damian travelled lightly and did not bring his habit, so he was sworn into office in someone else's habit! Damian added something though. He promised obedience not only to the Order and to the pope, but to Albert Nolan. That received a standing ovation!

I dare say this was probably the most unusual election in the history of the Dominican Order!

Before he submitted his request to be allowed to decline the election, Albert Nolan told us something else that was hard to hear. He told us that because of his reputation and the political unrest in South Africa, he could very well be killed for his stand against Apartheid! I have never feared anything like this in my life, so to hear this simple statement gave me a profound shock. It also made me well aware we were living through brutal times. I do not think those times have changed! Living now in the USA myself, I am very aware that our society is violent. Society does not spare us just because we are members of a religious order or priests. If we challenge people through our preaching, we can face death! That is the reality of the world today! Jesus on the cross made a plea to God, 'Father, forgive them; they know not what they do!' We all have to learn to forgive those who would kill us!

During the Chapter, we had asked Albert to talk about social justice. He addressed a full hall one evening. He spoke about the evil of Apartheid. He told us that none of us can demand attention because of who we are. No one is more important than anyone else. The evil of Apartheid is racial; none of us has rights because we are British or American or Catholic or Muslim. All we can say is that we are God's children! And we respect each other because we recognise this fact. We cannot claim superiority because of wealth or colour. He said that Apartheid had a fundamental flaw, that it claimed superiority for some over others based on colour. White supremacy is an evil! This is the teaching of St Paul whose words I will paraphrase: There is neither Jew nor Greek, slave nor free, male nor female, white nor black. We are all one in Christ! Paul was speaking the mind of Jesus.

I believe Albert Nolan's most famous book was *Jesus before Christianity*. It was one of the most significant theological books I have read in my life and I revered it immensely. Through this book I rediscovered Jesus and this was very exciting to me. It helped me, and I suspect so many others, to give purpose to my Christian faith. What an outstanding contribution he has made to spirituality of our day!

Albert died in 2022. I believe he is one of our modern saints!

Visit of Damian Byrne OP, Master of the Order to South Africa in 1984. Albert concelebrating with Damian Byrne and Emil Blaser.

A Man with Whom I Could Engage

Neil Mitchell OP

I first met Albert Nolan in 1978 at the 'freshers' conference' of the Students' Catholic Society of the University of the Witwatersrand. New students had been invited for a weekend away to be welcomed to Cathsoc and introduced to its activities. Albert was one of the speakers. As it happened, I got a lift back with him. On the journey, he asked me about myself. One of the things I told him about, with evangelical fervour, was my involvement in the Catholic charismatic renewal. I asked him, wouldn't he like to come to one of our prayer meetings? Without passing any comment on the charismatic movement, he politely declined.

I went on to become so involved in the Catholic student movement that my university studies were sometimes in danger of taking second place. What I was discovering, and the formation I was receiving through contact with people like Albert Nolan, seemed more important and relevant than what I was learning in the lecture halls. I still have my typewritten roneo copies of Albert's talks. In one of them, he spoke about 'verticalists' and 'horizontalists'. Verticalists emphasise love of God and prayer, whereas horizontalists emphasise love of neighbour and action. While the two aspects needed to be integrated, a caveat Albert made was that the vertical is not our love for God, but God's love for us. 'As we cannot love God directly, we return God's love by loving our neighbour', he explained.

Through my earlier involvement in Catholic charismatic renewal, the vertical aspect of my faith was flourishing. As for the horizontal aspect, it was not entirely undeveloped. At the Dominican primary school I went to, the Sisters taught us to respect all people. And so, as a child growing up in Apartheid South Africa, I wondered why the black people sat at the back of the church and why, at our local post office, there were separate entrances and a wall down the middle inside that kept black and white people apart. I was still at school when the 1976 Soweto uprising broke out. For some reason, I kept the front-page *Rand Daily Mail* news reports of those events. What was happening seemed somehow very significant.

Now, in Cathsoc, where the social gospel was emphasised, we were grappling with what our faith was telling us about the injustices of Apartheid. The national Catholic student movement was split along racial lines. The black students felt they could not consort with white students, the beneficiaries of Apartheid, as long as we showed no commitment to changing things.

People in Cathsoc were reading Albert's book, *Jesus before Christianity*. I got hold of a copy and devoured it avidly, feeling that I was crossing a frontier into a whole new world of insight into what faith in Jesus entailed. I was active in Cathsoc's 'Social Action Group', which exposed me to some of the realities of South African society. We were involved with two communities, Tamatievlei and Heavenly Valley, in Kliptown, south-west of Johannesburg. Kliptown was where the Freedom Charter was signed. My university classes were not entirely irrelevant, as I was learning about such things in History. I wrote an essay on the ANC's liberation struggle, for which I had access to the banned books section of the university library. It astounded me that this was a struggle we were not supposed to know anything about, as if it could be obliterated from the country's history.

The Social Action Group did things like assisting people to get the births of their children registered. When a landlord was extorting some residents, we accompanied them to seek justice from the lawyers in Johannesburg who administered the row of dilapidated houses in which they lived. Other Cathsoc members said what we were doing was racist paternalism. We were tinkering with the symptoms, while they apparently were addressing the real causes of the problems. Maybe, but we persisted nevertheless. The people of Tamatievlei and Heavenly Valley were never anything but warm and welcoming.

Once I had left university, I continued visiting the Dominican community in Mayfair where Albert lived and where Cathsoc students were welcome. I got to meet people like Finbar Synnott, whose simplicity and poverty were inspiring. Whenever I visited, Emil Blaser, the provincial at the time, would challenge me, 'So, when are you joining us?' But there was another challenge I first had to face: conscription. The South African Defence Force (SADF), to which all white South African males were called up for 'national service', was being used by the Apartheid State to suppress black resistance. I became involved in Church circles where we discussed these things intensely. We met at the home of Rob Robertson, a pacifist Presbyterian minister, anti-Apartheid activist and doyen to people considering conscientious objection. I was challenged by the peace witness of the Quakers in the group. I did some serious thinking about how Jesus responded to violence and injustice. A conviction grew in me that I could not be part of any armed force anywhere, not only the SADF, even if the law required it. After all this deliberation, refusal was a no-brainer. In July 1982, after a court martial, I was imprisoned for ten months, initially in the military detention barracks in Voortrekkerhoogte, Pretoria, and later in Pretoria Central Prison. I was given a 'dishonourable discharge' from the SADF, which pleased me no end: to me it was a badge of honour. Conscientious objection, and the associated anti-militarisation movement, which grew into the End Conscription Campaign in the 1980s, were appropriate ways for white people to resist Apartheid and to challenge other whites to think about the role they were playing in upholding it.

I found myself at odds, however, with aspects of Albert's theology in *Jesus before Christianity*. The book had brilliant chapters on the Kingdom of God and money, the Kingdom and prestige, the Kingdom and solidarity, and the Kingdom and power. With Albert's permission, which he granted readily, I had used these chapters as the basis for religious education lessons when I was teaching in Catholic schools. However, I felt that the chapter on 'The Temptation to Violence' introduced a false dichotomy. Albert argued that Jesus was not a pacifist in principle but rejected violence out of pragmatism and realism. In other circumstances Jesus' compassion for the poor and oppressed might have overflowed temporarily into taking up the sword.

To my mind, if Jesus resorted to violence, it would have undone everything he ever worked for. He kept his means consistent with his ends. He absorbed the violence and hatred of those who vilified him, transformed it, and gave it back to them as love. The Gospels present Jesus' peace-making as a unified, sustained and consistent narrative, at the heart of his mission. Just as it was necessary to witness to what Jesus taught about money, prestige, solidarity and power, so it was necessary, I believed, to witness to what he taught about violence.

Years later, when I finally heeded Emil Blaser's challenge and joined the Dominicans, I had robust debates with Albert on violence and pacifism. I wondered sometimes whether Albert said what he said about Jesus and violence because he did not want to be seen as critical of armed struggle. But to imagine that, for Albert, it was a matter of expedience or something he did not agonise over would be a grave injustice to him. In his discussion of the struggle and violence in *God in South Africa*, it is clear that his compassion for the poor and oppressed is what motivated him to argue that in extreme circumstances, not out of a desire for revenge but to prevent far worse violence and to end intolerable suffering, people may resort to armed struggle. The gospel, he argued, was about more than ethical debates. Albert was scathing of a system responsible for so much bloodshed and suffering, self-righteously condemning a peace-loving people for resorting to violence.

In 1985, when the victims of Apartheid had tried just about everything against a violent oppressor who showed no sign of retreating from its brutal Apartheid policies, the *Kairos Document* was a timely and necessary mobilisation of the Churches in South Africa to act decisively against the Apartheid state. I do not know the extent of Albert's involvement in the document, but his style and thinking are evident in its pages. The document dealt extensively with violence, both institutionalised state violence and the violence of those who defend themselves against it. It also commented on how we change our terminology (violence becomes 'legitimate force') depending on which side we are on.

The document also dealt with nonviolence, categorising it as 'Church Theology . . . superficial theology which ignores social, political and economic structures.' There is, however, another view that understands nonviolence as an organised programme of activism that employs civil disobedience to bring change. Some activists use nonviolence tactically and pragmatically (as Albert claimed about Jesus), while others are committed to nonviolence as a spiritual pathway that unifies means and ends (as I claimed about Jesus). Nonviolence is anything but superficial. Because it did not take the trouble to understand nonviolence properly, the *Kairos Document* ended up caricaturing nonviolence, based on how some Churches were condemning as violence, for example, the actions of youth burning down buildings or throwing petrol bombs, but describing the actions of the police who killed some of the youth as peacekeeping. Ironically and disingenuously, at its very end, the *Kairos Document* advocates nonviolence (the proper form of it), but without naming it as nonviolence.

Linked to the *Kairos Document*'s belittling of nonviolence was its advocacy of 'just war'. At a time when the 'just war' position was increasingly being seen as untenable, unconscionable and obsolete, it did so almost triumphalistically, categorising (by implication) 'just war' as 'Prophetic Theology'. To my mind, nonviolence is authentic 'Prophetic Theology', while 'just war' is classic 'State Theology', to use the document's own categorisation.

When I was a Dominican novice, I was privileged to have Albert as my novice master. In many discussions with him about violence, he restated his difficulty with doing things 'on principle'. This made idols of abstract principles. To try and understand his view, I offered the example of Rob Robertson, who as I mentioned before impressed me as a highly principled person. For their eventual retirement, Rob had purchased for himself and his wife Gert a flat in Cape Town. In the meantime, he was letting the flat, but *on principle* he would not let it to any unmarried couple who were 'shacking up' together. Albert said, yes, that's exactly what he meant: this was putting an abstract principle before people. I didn't quite agree, but I understood him better.

There were four of us in our novitiate group. Albert wanted us to understand Jesus well. He was giving us so much input on Jesus, he explained, because we wouldn't get it later in our seminary training. We've got a long way to go to catch up to Jesus, he always used to say. Albert had published *Jesus Today* some years before, after the dismantling of Apartheid, and much of what he taught us came from that work. In *Jesus Today* he explains how the feminist perspective had opened his eyes to many things, and how the new cosmology has given us a new vision of God's grandeur and creativity. At the same time, he said, we were witnessing the destruction of the environment. We accompanied Albert to presentations he gave on the theology of creation. He explained that until about sixty years ago, theologians didn't think there was much more to say as far as creation was concerned. The theology of creation had been eclipsed by the theology of redemption. We now know that that has been disastrous for the earth and for all God's creatures on the earth, he said.

In keeping with his concern for contextualisation, Albert began *Jesus Today* with his usual reflection on the signs of our times. Ecological breakdown was one he identified. Others were the hunger for spirituality, the crisis of individualism that is producing worship of the ego, the global divide between rich and poor and new developments in science that are revealing how little we know about the ever-expanding universe. We may have been liberated from the social sin of Apartheid, but we need personal liberation too, he wrote, from our own egos and personal selfishness, otherwise we are in danger of repeating the very things against which we fought. Dare I say that, in reading the signs of the times, Albert saw the time had arrived to give greater prominence to the vertical dimension of faith, to use his old terminology from Cathsoc days.

Jesus Today delves into Jesus' profound spirituality and asks what we must do to make it relevant for our time. Jesus, a prophet and a prayerful contemplative mystic, instituted a social revolution that subverted almost everything his contemporaries took for granted. With his experience of God as his *abba*, serving as the source of his wisdom and radical freedom, Jesus' revolution was aimed at bringing people into the Kingdom of God. Jesus was a healer: his assurances to suffering people that God loves and forgives them unconditionally healed them not only in body but in spirit too.

Imbibing Jesus' spirituality involves getting to know who we really are, and understanding how the machinations of the ego hide our true selves. We have to learn to recognise our compulsions and obsessions, so that our true selves can emerge and we can live with gratitude and childlike trust in God. Ultimately, personal transformation can only happen when we learn detachment: letting go of whatever enslaves us, whether it be money and possessions, our reputation, an ideology, or even things like punctuality and tidiness. Radical inner freedom is the result of a growing experience of oneness with God, with oneself, with others, and with all of creation.

A prominent theme in Albert's spirituality is *mystery* and *uncertainty*. This starts with God himself. The apophatic tradition in Christian mysticism tells us we can know only what God is not. God is not an object or a thing that can be compared to other objects, nor is God one mystery among others, but *the* mystery. What matters is whether God is real to us or not, for God, although mysterious, is closer to us than we are to ourselves. Similarly, science has made us aware of how mysterious the universe is. We hardly understand the atom. We hardly understand the relativity of space and time. We are not sure whether light is a wave or a particle. We are even a mystery to ourselves. Consciousness is so basic that we have nothing to compare it to. How our brains remember everything is completely mysterious.

For people who want the certainty of definite explanations, this is a let-down. We have to have the humility to accept that we are mere human beings, not God. Hubris has made humanity think we know it all and that we are above all other creatures that inhabit this planet with us. 'We must know our place', Albert says.

Around the time of Albert's death, there were many obituaries and tributes recounting his activism against Apartheid. The spirituality of radical freedom that he offers as the fruit of his contemplation is less well known. It is a profound part of Albert's wisdom that awaits fuller discovery.

When Albert retired to Marian House in Boksburg, I visited him as often as I could. He so enjoyed going out for lunch and having a good chat. He was interested in the progress I was making on my PhD thesis on salvation, in which I was looking at how Jesus' peace-making Gospel, with peace extended beyond human beings to all of creation, could respond to traditional atonement theology. The narrative of an atonement theology is that Jesus offered himself as an atoning blood sacrifice in our place on the cross for the propitiation of God's wrath and the expiation of our sins. Albert encouraged me, saying this was the kind of theology we Dominicans ought to be doing. After reading my proposal, he commented,

> If the meaning of salvation is the revelation of God's unconditional love and forgiveness and the effect that this has on our lives when we believe it, then Jesus saves us by being this revelation, by being the Word of God, by embodying all that is meant by God, the Incarnation.

This is talking about salvation without the mythology or magic associated with atonement and other similar theories.

Albert invited me to talk about my project at his contemplative book club. I was nervous. Most of the members were serious academics and intellectuals and I thought I would be out of my depth. My fears were unfounded. They were receptive and affirming, and I went on to become a regular member of the book club. I looked forward immensely to the rich and fruitful monthly discussions, as did all the members, including Albert, who was the mainstay of the group. He was getting old and weary now—'Old age is not for sissies', he would often joke—but the book club was one of the few activities he kept up.

One thing so refreshing and attractive about Albert was his complete lack of malice towards anybody. Whatever he may have thought about armed struggle and violence, his own spirit was serene, joyful and nonviolent. He was so at peace with himself because he was assured of God's unconditional love for him. What he taught us back in those heady Cathsoc days, about the 'vertical' and the 'horizontal', was completely integrated in him.

At Albert's funeral, with a lump in my throat, I watched as his ashes were interred in the soil of the grave of his brother novice from their Stellenbosch days, Gregory Brooke, deeply grateful that this remarkable saintly man, who I had come to know as a dear friend, had shown so many of us, mostly by his own example, how to integrate faith and life in the context of our time. He truly mastered his vocation.

'What I do is Me'

Ann Wigley OP

'Each mortal thing does one thing and the same:
Deals out that being indoors each one dwells;
Selves—goes itself; myself it speaks and spells,
Crying *What I do is me: for that I came.'*
Gerard Manley Hopkins: As Kingfishers catch Fire.[1]

When I was reflecting on Albert, these lines from Hopkins came to mind. Since I have known him, Albert has spoken his word clearly through his life, his words, his writings, his way of being towards others. At all times he showed respect for the dignity of the other, even when the other disagreed with him.

> I am concerned about people, the daily sufferings of so many millions of people, and the prospect of much greater suffering in the near future. My purpose is to find out what can be done about it.[2]

These are Albert's own words regarding his purpose for writing *Jesus before Christianity*. They epitomise for me the kernel of Albert's desire for the world and his involvement in the struggle for justice in the Church and in South Africa.

Albert's courage and willingness to think and to speak outside of the box impressed me before I ever met him. He was both an inspiration and a challenge. He, together with other Dominican brothers, spoke out against the rigidity of the encyclical of Pope Paul VI,

---

1. GM Hopkins, *Poems and Prose* (London: Penguin Books, 1953).
2. Albert Nolan, *Jesus before Christianity* (Cape Town: David Phillip, 1976), 1.

Humanae Vitae which showed little understanding of the struggle of millions of people across the world. The English translation stated that artificial contraception was intrinsically wrong, meaning wrong under every imaginable circumstance. While an encyclical is not deemed to be infallible, our brothers were aware that for the ordinary person, especially those living in impoverished conditions, the Church teaching is clear and forbids the use of artificial contraception. Many women I have spoken with are using different artificial methods of birth control and they feel guilty, but know no other way as the Billings method has not worked for them and they are teased about their 'Billings' babies. Some have the inner freedom to make choices at variance with the Church's official position, but many do not. It is for these women that Albert and the other brothers were speaking. Already in 1968, he showed his concern for the people who suffered because they could not do what the Church seemed to be asking and yet wanted to be faithful to Church teaching. To many this criticism of Church teaching seemed to be a disloyalty to the Church, but to me and to many others it showed rather his true love for the Church. To Albert, as to Jesus, people were always more important than the law. Thus, already as a young man Albert was willing to push the boundaries of Church teaching. Through this brave and prophetic action, Albert and his brothers gave us the gift of knowing that changing times demand new and different responses and that true loyalty to the Church includes pushing boundaries and promoting the evolution of Church teaching in accord with new levels of consciousness.

A number of years after this initial impact of Albert on my life, I met him in person. He continued to be both an inspiration and a challenge to me in a variety of ways. His interest in the collaboration among the Dominican Family in South Africa and his continued call to us to be engaged in promoting justice and peace in any way we could, affected us profoundly. His collaboration was not limited to the Dominican Family or the Catholic Church. He worked for many years in the Institute for Contextual Theology (ICT) with people belonging to other denominations. The *Kairos Document*, which emerged from this collaboration, had a huge effect on the Christian community in South Africa. The *Challenge* magazine, which was initiated by Albert, was also a consequence of this work. We cannot measure the effect of this collaboration. Besides the value of the written word, seeds were sown for the unity among the Christian Churches that so many long for.

When Albert was provincial of the South African general vicariate, he supported his brothers in their desire to live more simply among the poor. Three of them moved to a simple dwelling in Mayfair in a fairly run down area where people of all ethnic groups lived at the time. Later Albert left his posh residence in Houghton, which was then exclusively occupied by wealthy white people, and joined them. I visited him in Mayfair and was impressed by the simplicity of their lives. They were indeed living the gospel simplicity which they preached. This time in Mayfair is for me an example of Albert's singleness of purpose and real desire to live the gospel radically. His sense of humour and lack of defensiveness while living in Houghton also impressed me. One of his visitors greeted him as 'King of the castle'. Without missing a beat Albert replied, 'That makes you the dirty rascal!'

I was fortunate in being at the General Chapter of the Dominican Order at the Angelicum in Rome in 1983. It was indeed a privilege to be in a space influencing so much of Dominican life. A few Sisters were chosen by the brothers to be present. Our role was not clear. When we were asked to report on behalf of the Sisters, I realised we could not, as we had not been chosen by the Sisters. It highlighted the fact that only if there were a united body of Dominican Sisters could we relate on an equal level with the brothers. This planted the seeds for the eventual establishment, at a meeting of English-speaking Dominican women in 1989 in Rome, of an organisation of Dominican Sisters International (DSI), which continues to flourish to this day. It was at this Chapter that Albert was elected as Master of the Order. He declined on the grounds that he was needed in South Africa, which was at the peak of the struggle for justice at the time. This was accepted by the Chapter and he was able to return to the very volatile situation in South Africa. This, too, was an illustration of Albert's desire, not only to find out what could be done about the situation of injustice in South Africa, but to continue walking with all of us through whatever needed to be done. As Malusi Mpumlwana says in the foreword to Albert's book *God in South Africa*, through this action and so many others, Albert 'throws a beam of light on the narrow path for all to see.'[3]

---

3. Albert Nolan, *God in South Africa: The Challenge of the Gospel* (Grand Rapids: Eerdmans, 1988), vii.

Albert's courage to speak the truth as he understood it and to collaborate with so many others who held his vision of a united and just South Africa and Church enriched our lives in many ways. Hopefully in death he will continue to inspire many to speak their word in the world in order to help to create the opportunity that all can have the basic necessities and live in harmony.

Each mortal thing does one thing and the same:
Crying: *What I do is me, for that I came.*
Gerard Manley Hopkins

More than a Colleague

Celia Smit OP

For almost forty years Albert has been my friend, mentor, spiritual director, colleague—always like a brother to me. The epitome of hope, he was uncomplicated, interested in everyone and everything.

On a retreat with Albert in Lesotho, he gave me a draft of his book *God in South Africa* and invited my comment. I felt humbled and honoured but this was Albert—he believed everyone had a contribution to make and he was always open to expand his own ideas by listening to the opinions of others.

I used to go to Mayfair for Mass when the brethren lived there, and sometimes took visitors or friends with me. Once, I took Ronnie Kasrils. Ronnie was a member of the ANC and was in hiding from the South African government. His background is Jewish. We had a wonderful shared homily on the readings of the day and Ronnie was very taken by Albert's inclusive welcome and his openness to listen to every opinion.

During the time I worked as personal assistant to Smangaliso Mkhatshwa at both the Southern African Catholic Bishops' Conference (SACBC) and later at the Institute for Contextual Theology (ICT), Albert was a great support to me. He could always see beyond a situation, suggest new possibilities, have reasons to remain positive and never give up hope. Albert once said: 'Our hope does not depend on success; our hope is that God will act through us' and this about says it all.

While Albert was extremely supportive of the SACBC initiative to begin the publication of *The New Nation* newspaper in 1986 and of his confrere Emil Blaser's vision of a Catholic radio station, he dreamt of a magazine that would address the issues of the ordinary people, educate, expand and give hope. I remember having some heated debates with him around this. He was so convinced that his idea could work that he pursued it with all his energy and became the first editor of *Challenge* magazine.

For a number of years Albert and I belonged to a group which represented the different Dominican congregations in South Africa called the Federation of Dominicans in Southern Africa (FEDOSA). We organised the FEDOSA days which were held in January, in April around the feast of St Catherine, and in August, the feast of St Dominic, for all Dominicans in the area and anyone else who was interested. Albert believed in collaboration, communication, and networking. As the true Dominican that he was, he took every opportunity to preach the Good News of the gospel. Albert was a real teacher and had the ability to impart knowledge in a simple way that still held depth and meaning. He also had the ability to challenge one's thinking and behaviour without alienating or judging in any way.

In 1997 I was on a three-month sabbatical course at Siena Spirituality Centre, Watermill NY run by the Amityville Dominican Sisters. During this time the Sister director of the Centre asked me if I knew Fr Albert Nolan in South Africa. He had written asking if he could stay at the Centre during the coming year for some time out to research another book. When I told her that I not only knew him but that he was also a friend and colleague of mine, she was stunned. I realised by her reaction that she and many of the Dominican Sisters in the USA held Albert in such high esteem that they put him on a pedestal. She showed me the space they would offer him asking if it was suitable. She asked if I knew his likes and dislikes. I explained that Albert was totally uncomplicated and down-to-earth and would rather be treated as a brother than a high-ranking official.

Albert was once asked how he viewed or felt about the public criticism aimed at him and his theology in *The Southern Cross* by a Franciscan friar. His response was very simple: 'He defends the faith, I spread it'.

Long before Pope Francis wrote *Laudato Si*[1] Albert began to see the connectedness of all of life in a very real way and acquired a pas-

---

1. Pope Francis, Encyclical letter *Laudato si'* 2015. [Vatican City] https://www.vatican.va/content/francesco/en/encyclicals/documents/papa-francesco_20150524_enciclica-laudato-si.html. Last accessed April 2023.

sion for earth spirituality. This awareness crept into all his conversations integrating it with his passion for the gospel message of justice, equity and respect for all.

Gustavo Gutiérrez OP is deemed to have said: 'The preferential option for the poor is ultimately a question of friendship. When we become friends with the poor, their presence leaves an indelible imprint on our lives, and we are much more likely to remain committed'. This speaks powerfully to me of Albert, his experience and his commitment.

Albert as part of the choir in Stellenbosch community church.
Albert is the celebrant and so not wearing his habit and cappa.

A Theology Rooted in Dominican Life

John O'Leary

Albert Nolan was chaplain to the South African National Catholic Federation of Students (NCFS) when I met him just over forty years ago. What first caught my attention was his voice, a curious blend of the sonorous and nasal that was instantly easy to listen to, especially when his infectious laugh punctuated his speaking. He was interesting but also interested, and it struck me at the time how he was always ready to speak his mind, but equally ready to meet individual students and hear their stories without ever leaving anyone feeling 'less than'. He had the ability to take people seriously even if he disagreed with what they were saying or doing (which he frequently did).

Those early encounters have remained inspirational for me ever since. In paying tribute to him, I would like to emphasise his Dominican life, partly because that has also been a shared life-long inspiration. More importantly, because his profound influence on so many people in discerning a theology which read the gospel in the context of the struggle against Apartheid in South Africa (and oppression and injustice wherever it is found) was rooted in his Dominican life. That life, simply put, consists of four key elements: Community, Study, Prayer and Mission.

Community

Albert had a great commitment as a Dominican friar. Being a brother was core to his calling, it seemed to me. He also had many other roles, some of which were priest, teacher, leader, activist, challenger, mentor and spiritual director. He had a great gift for solidarity with marginalised people, and a great gift for friendship. Even in the last of his eighty-eight years he loved hearing from friends, asked all about what was going on in their lives and worlds, always with that ready laugh, radiant smile and dark shine in his eyes. The last time I saw him he said he was generally in good health, apart from some *kwale*, an Afrikaans word for ailments—nothing too serious, but enough to slow one down a bit. And then that laugh again.

Study

Albert was a passionate scholar in and of the world. He was an avid reader and keen analyst of anything he read. A constant student and critical reader. About ten years ago I felt unsure about a draft of a talk on hope that I had prepared for an adult faith enquiry group in my parish. I sent it to him asking for any critical comment. He would already have turned seventy-eight by then and I diffidently wrote that it was not urgent and that any comment would be appreciated. Two days later a detailed two-page response arrived, affirming the value of the project in a short introductory paragraph, and suggesting many improvements—all of which seemed obviously correct as soon as I read them.

This capacity for critical reading is so important today. We live in times when so many people cannot be bothered to read more than 140 characters and, before they have even finished reading those, are already firing off an attack in response (after blocking the other person first, of course). In an age of narcissism and cancellation culture, dialogue rooted in critical study of how we and others are reading the signs of the times has never been more important.

Truth matters. It mattered for Albert, and I hope his life and work inspire a renewed dedication to truth-seeking in all walks of life. I also hope that the grief we feel at Albert's death will be transformed quickly into energy for lively attentive listening, and incisive, questioning conversations in our relationships with God, each other and globally.

Prayer

In those early days when he was a student chaplain, much of Albert's focus had to be on working with students who saw prayer and action as mutually exclusive alternatives. Part of Albert's genius was to show, in very direct and simple language, that prayer is not an alternative to mission. He showed how the Bible is the living story of noticing and paying attention to the movements within us, our communities and in all of creation. I imagine that Albert's prayer was profound and private, probably a space in which he could allow the anxieties he must have felt about life in the world and the church to surface and settle. Increasingly as he got older, Albert discerned the need to encourage people not to lose hope in a time of despair. I was blessed to spend about a week in the Dominican community at Mayfair in Johannesburg in the early 1980s. The very, very slow reading of the psalms in the very, very simple rooms of the flats have stayed with me always as a metaphor for living simply with steadfast hope.

Mission

Sometimes referred to as one's 'apostolate'; basically, it is 'what we do' or 'our faith in action'. For Albert, carrying to others the fruits of his contemplation was his mission: preaching the Kingdom of God and helping people to discern how they contribute to discovering the Kingdom of God and how they help to make it visible and tangible, whether they used that language about what they are doing or not.

Albert carried out this mission with passion and dedication, often in the face of criticism within the church and threats from the state. In the many spaces where tribute has been paid since Albert's death, it has been wonderful to hear so many people say how much they are grateful to Albert for inspiring their own life choices. Clearly his mission was accomplished!

Albert's life challenges us and inspires us to read our own lives and be open to community, study, prayer and action ourselves, because these are not four elements of Dominican life in any exclusive sense: they are elements of Dominican life because they are universally important for every single person and community.

Albert with Gregory Brooke OP January 2014.

A Sound Sounding Board

Michael Lewis SJ

Albert Nolan has always been part of the landscape of the Catholic Church in South Africa. I found him the kind of person one could approach with a problem or difficult situation who would not try to solve the issue for you but help you to deal with it oneself.

Soon after he completed his stint as provincial of the Dominican friars in South Africa in 1984, I was appointed to a similar job. I went to ask him how to do the work. While he was sympathetic and aware of what appeared to be a daunting prospect, he was also a mine of information about the Church and the South African political landscape during Grand Apartheid times. However, he was careful not to tell me how to do the work, which of course showed his wisdom.

The best piece of advice Albert gave me then was to work closely with Emil Blaser, who was also just taking on the leadership of the Dominicans in South Africa. In fact, Emil and I worked well and often closely together during the 1980s when the political atmosphere was horrible with much violence and political manoeuvring. It was said among the more irreverent that South Africa was one of the few places where Jesuits and Dominicans got on together, which had not been the case previously. Often we had to take decisions which were neither popular nor obviously the way forward. We would decide whether or not to attend political demonstrations and whether we would sign the *Kairos Document*, among other things. We tried to balance our primary concern for the welfare and safety of our members on the ground with a need to witness in the last years of Apartheid.

Meanwhile, Albert was organising the *Kairos Document* which neither Emil or I signed after long and difficult discussions as to whether it would be good for our constituent bodies. Albert was always accepting of individual decisions whether he agreed with them or not. At the time he was deeply involved in many areas of activism against Apartheid, mostly unheeded and with no fanfare. He was not shy to ask for help and cooperation from other religious for activists, such as Frank Chikane, who were in trouble, needing a secluded place to live or to be brought across a border. He also encouraged me and others to join the Christian Action Movement (CAM) which provided support and information for those of us who were wanting to see the fall of Apartheid and some of us who were ministering in pastoral situations of parishes, prisons and universities.

He was at his best talking to groups of students and clergy. In 1986, I invited him to talk to all the Jesuits meeting in Victory Park at our annual gathering. We ranged from solidly conservative to marginally radical. He was careful to identify with us and told us much of his own background before presenting what was an adapted contextual theology for our particular situation. To a large degree he was able to convert some of us and at least relieve some of the fears of others. Above all he was charming and sociable in a group of widely differing views and opinions.

He was greatly valued as an integral part of the Church and certainly was considered for the episcopate on occasion. However, if he was able to persuade his brethren to relieve him of the burden to be the Master of the Dominicans it is highly unlikely that he would have accepted a bishopric. He certainly did much for many of us who were not at the centre of ecclesiastical circles.

The Struggle *Ad Intra* and *Ad Extra*

Kevin Dowling CSsR

Memories, experiences, stories—sharing these are the stuff of life! This is particularly so when one reflects on someone whose path in life touched or even shaped one's own life.

For me, this was/still is true of Father Albert Nolan OP. As a young priest I worked in three Cape Flats townships in Cape Town from January 1970 to April 1975, encountering poverty and injustices which led me to challenge the political authorities and respond as best I could to the needs of the people. After that period, I was elected into leadership of my congregation, the Redemptorists, in South Africa and Zimbabwe—a position I held for eleven years from April 1975 until December 1985.

It was during that period that I personally encountered Albert for the first time when we both served as congregational leaders and met together at meetings of the Conference of Major Religious Superiors in South Africa.

But in November 1985 I was elected to the General Council of the Redemptorists. I moved to Rome and worked internationally until I was appointed Bishop of the Diocese of Rustenburg on 3 December 1990. I returned to South Africa early in January 1991.

As we know, Albert was elected to leadership of the worldwide Dominican Order, not just as a member of the Council as I was, but as Master of the Order. But he declined, taking a prophetic stance to stay in South Africa in solidarity with the millions of oppressed people under the Apartheid regime. Others will share more about that prophetic choice of Albert which I admire greatly.

But even in those earlier years of the 1970s and 1980s when we were congregational leaders at the local level in South Africa, I already experienced Albert's warmth as a human being and his great intellectual and theological gifts. Subsequently, my experience widened in recognition of his ability to analyse situations from the perspective of the suffering poor in the light of the person and witness of Jesus and the values of the gospel, and therefore the challenge to discern relevant options or directions to follow, especially for churches and faith communities.

In all that I read or heard about Albert over the years, I sensed always his faithfulness to Jesus as he understood him and his mission in the world. He became a living example for us as he got ever more deeply involved in what was termed 'The Struggle' in South Africa. An example of this was his working with others in the ecumenical movement to create the *Kairos Document*. He inspired and enabled the faith communities to participate meaningfully in the quest to overthrow the Apartheid system.

All this was instructive and formative for me in my own journey and personal analysis of the socio-political-cultural issues and pathologies in the political and community domain, at first in South Africa, and later on elsewhere. This was true especially after I was immediately confronted after ordination as a bishop in January 1991 with the 'Struggle' in the Bophuthatswana homeland which occupied me almost on a daily basis from then until the 1994 elections.

This awareness subsequently expanded through my involvement for many years in the Justice and Peace Commission of the Bishops' Conference on local justice issues, and then in several countries in Africa from 1997 onwards, especially in North and South Sudan. I also served for fifteen years on the Board of Pax Christi International (PCI), and as Co-President for nine years. I was engaged in the worldwide PCI quest for just peace through nonviolence, for 'Transitional Justice' after war, atrocities and violence—in the former Balkans for example—and in other aspects of peace work.

Albert was and still is a mentor to me together with two other pastor-mentors in my life as a bishop for the past more than thirty-two years—Archbishop Denis Hurley and Archbishop Oscar Romero. They enabled me to reflect on my personal memories, experiences and stories of my calling, life, mission and ministry in the Church and world in a critical and holistic way. This led me to discern responses which I felt called to make. Sometimes such options or decisions come with a cost.

For Archbishop Romero the cost was indeed huge. It was because he lived a preferential option for the poor by fearlessly denouncing the oppression of his people by a brutal military regime that he paid the ultimate price—assassination by a sniper's bullet on 24 March 1980. I was privileged to participate in a week-long conference in El Salvador to mark the twenty-fifth anniversary of the assassination, and I was so inspired by other prophetic Church leaders there, like the two great liberation theologians Gustavo Gutiérrez OP and Jon Sobrino SJ, who shared a platform of reflection to rapturous applause. The theology of Albert, I think, was in line with theirs. It was/is people like them that honed or refined my understanding of what we as Church should be, and the witness we should give in a world of suffering, marginalisation and exclusion in all their forms.

But not only in that socio-political domain. I felt drawn also to apply the same process of analysis and discernment to issues relating to the witness and mission of the Church, and particularly of the institutional church and its hierarchical leadership. It was through this that I sensed that a 'site of struggle' could also be found or experienced in different ways in the institutional church if it did not reflect the Jesus of the Gospels in the context of the life experience of people, especially of those who feel oppressed or excluded in any way in the Church itself. It is this that I will come back to as a particular focus in this reflection on the Church and the Struggle.

Evangelisation, in addition to the *ad intra* dimensions of church life and practice, has to seek to transform at the same time every form of injustice and suffering, everything which diminishes and degrades the infinite dignity of every human person on this earth, and by extension what degrades and destroys our 'common home', the environment.

I sense there will always be a tension between our focus on the *ad intra* dimension of internal Church life and practice with its multiple dimensions, and the *ad extra* focus of the Church's mission and response to the multiple examples of oppression, injustice, poverty, inequality, violence and vulnerability that exclude millions of people from a life that is worthy of them as human beings.

Where then do we as institutional Church place our primary focus in terms of time and resources? How committed are we as institutional church to integrate exponentially the *ad intra* and *ad extra* missions of the Church not as something good to achieve, but as absolutely essential to the mission of evangelisation and to transforming the experience of the 'little ones' in both society and the Church?

And so, I come back to my reflection on Albert in terms of the 'Church and the Struggle'. This began for me with the arrival of his seminal book *Jesus before Christianity*, published in 1976, very early for me in my journey of discernment. What does that title say to anyone, even before reading the book?

That title always fascinated me. After all, should Christianity, manifested as Church communities, not flow seamlessly from the life and witness of Jesus, his preaching of the Good News to the poor, his setting free of the downtrodden, and so on (*cf* Lk 4) into the actual life and practice of those communities? Is Christianity not a 'way of life' in which we become ever more truly disciples of Jesus who follow his way, truth, and life in the actual context in which we live so that his promise, 'I have come that there may be life and life to the full' (Jn 10:10) can be fulfilled, especially for the downtrodden of the world?

This challenge for me was summed up by Albert in the final chapter of this book, entitled 'Faith in Jesus'. The first lines of that chapter read as follows:

> Jesus did not found an organisation; he inspired a movement. It was inevitable that the movement would quite soon become an organisation but in the beginning there were simply people, scattered individuals and groups, who had been inspired by Jesus.

In the second paragraph, Albert wrote:

> Each remembered Jesus in his own way or had been struck by a particular aspect of what they had heard about him. There were at first no doctrines and no dogmas, no universally accepted way of following him or believing in him.[1]

What the title of this book, and that final chapter in summary, says to me is that 'Christianity' can become institutionalised to the extent that the Jesus, who should be the inspiration and model for everything we are and do as 'Christians', can become weakened or obscured—in our witness, the way we actually live our faith in real life, in the way the Church as an organisation is perceived or experienced, and in the way hierarchical leadership and authority is exercised *vis a vis*

---

1. Albert Nolan, *Jesus before Christianity* (Cape Town: David Philip, 1976).

people–people as they are and where they are in life. This weakening can happen if a particular church community or diocese anywhere, particularly in its leadership, while professing to embrace 'Christianity', focuses more on structural dimensions, or on power, authority and control in the community, rather than on promoting the essential spirit and witness of Jesus and the Gospels, a Jesus who came to reveal a God of compassion and mercy as the only true God.

Many reflections are being written about Pope Francis at this time of his tenth anniversary as pontif, the Pope who so often speaks of 'mercy' as the defining characteristic of God. This should be at least *the* major defining characteristic of the Church in the face of a world of suffering and danger, a world which could be moving towards a 'catastrophe' through wars, poverty and violence precipitating an exodus of migrants and refugees in their millions, environmental degradation and climate change destroying our common home and its future capacity to feed the world, and so forth.

In his book, Albert highlighted 'catastrophe' as the expectation of the people of Jesus' time—the catastrophe which actually occurred finally with the destruction of Jerusalem in AD 70. This is why it is so important to understand who Jesus was for that time, and who he is for our time, and what this should mean for a 'church in mission' as it faces a potential catastrophe in our world in the future if crucial issues endangering the future are not dealt with now.

The editorial in *The Tablet* of 11 March 2023, just before Pope Francis' tenth anniversary, was headed, 'The world in crisis—10 years that shook the Church'. It said:

> The agenda of the Francis papacy is the Gospel. The Second Vatican Council ended nearly 60 years ago but it remains the touchstone for the expression and application of the teaching of the Church in the modern world, even if many of the conditions the Council addressed have since grown more intractable and new critical challenges have appeared. Mass migration, climate change and environmental degradation, wars within and between states, gross economic inequality, abiding racism, injustice to women and other groups suffering discrimination—these all cry out for moral leadership in a world in a permanent state of crisis. Yet at this precise moment the moral credibility of the Catholic Church lies battered. It has been devastated by the shameful abuse of children

by thousands of priests and the covering up of their crimes by the Church's leaders. The scandal has revealed the Church's weakest point—its tendency to reserve power and authority to an elite brotherhood of priests and bishops, answerable to virtually no one.

It was certainly with this in mind that Pope Francis in 2021 initiated the process of synodality to provide a space for bishops, clergy, religious and laity all over the world to reflect on all these issues, to articulate the kind of Church community we should strive to be for today's situation in different contexts, and to highlight the issues and needs which require attention if we are to become that kind of church community.

In this process, the 'blocks' in the Church that have been named many times in the past years have been re-stated, such as clericalism, autocracy, bureaucracy, use of power and control with the absence of due process and accountability, and so on. My personal knowledge of a great moral theologian and ethicist, Fr Charles Curran, illustrates this. When I was in Rome in the 80s, the professors at the Alphonsian Academy there, specialising in moral theology and ethics, told me that his defence of his doctoral thesis, 'Invincible ignorance and natural law according to St Alphonsus', under Father Bernard Haring was the most brilliant they had experienced for many years. Later he lectured at a Catholic University in the USA, obtained 'tenure', but then in 1986 he fell afoul of the Congregation for the Doctrine of the Faith under its Prefect, Cardinal Joseph Ratzinger. He was forbidden to teach in any Catholic University or Institution.

As far as I know, Albert did not face censure by the Congregation for the Doctrine of the Faith except that, in 1990, the Holy See would not allow the University of Fribourg in Switzerland to give him and Archbishop Rembert Weakland from the USA an honorary doctorate. Nevertheless, for me, even this use of power is a blight on the Church and the way it should deal with issues. Thinking people really question this, and are even scandalised by it. There surely has to be another way to deal with theological differences of opinion or even disputes rather than secret investigations of theologians, or worse still, 'silencing' them. We surely cannot ever return to an 'Inquisition' model to find common ground between the Vatican authorities and theologians who, by their very calling, should continuously be pushing boundaries, as it were, to assist the development of doctrine as the Church grapples with complex issues in real life situations which are constantly evolving. Cardinal John Henry Newman was a prophet in the Church in the nineteenth century with his theological position that there is, or should be, *development* in doctrine. St Anselm of Canterbury visualised theology as 'faith seeking understanding'. So, the purpose of theology and the calling of theologians everywhere is to deepen our understanding of what faith is, and the understanding of the mysteries of faith.

An example of development in theological understanding occurred during a landmark conference in Rome in April 2016, co-hosted by PCI and the Dicastery for Promoting Integral Human Development. I was privileged to participate as Co-President of PCI, to listen to and share in the insights of theologians from various disciplines, and the experiences of grassroots peace activists working in situations of war and unspeakable violence. This resulted in a critique of the prevailing Just War Theory, and a counter proposal that the Church should be at the forefront of promoting 'Nonviolence as the way to Just Peace'. Pope Francis affirmed this new thinking in his World Peace Day Message on 1 January 2017, entitled: 'Nonviolence: a style of politics for peace'.

Among all Albert's writings and addresses, we as Church can be enlightened in a special way by his conclusion to *Jesus before Christianity*, where he says,

> We have seen what Jesus was like. If we now wish to treat him as our God, we would have to conclude that our God does not want to be served by us, he wants to serve us; he does not want to be given the highest possible rank and status in our society; he wants to take the lowest place and to be without any rank and status; he does not want to be feared and obeyed, he wants to be recognised in the sufferings of the poor and the weak; he is not supremely indifferent and detached, he is irrevocably committed to the liberation of humankind.[2]

That is my understanding, succinctly, of the call to leadership in the Church—no hint of any use of power, privilege, position, and control, only an 'authority' of compassionate service as found in Jesus.

---

2. Albert Nolan, *Jesus before Christianity,* 137–138.

This understanding of Jesus, I believe, is what Pope Francis has been promoting as the basis for the synodal path for the Church of today and the future. The question for all of us, and above all for the clerical leadership in the Church of today is: is this the model of Church today that we want to be lived out at local parish level, community level, diocesan level, national level and global level going into the future? The Church, in my understanding of evangelisation and mission, should follow the model articulated so well by Pope Francis, namely that leadership in the Church, the bishops in particular, but also the priests, should be shepherds who 'smell like the sheep', and who inspire and create a 'field hospital' model of Church which is present at the 'peripheries' of life and people's experience—to use the celebrated phrases of Pope Francis.

To sum up: What Albert revealed to me through his life and theology was that theology must speak to and be done in the actual socio-political-cultural context as it changes and develops. This contextual theology model, breathing the spirit of the Jesus of the Gospels, must inform the model of Church which is called for today and into the future. It is a model of communion, participation and mission founded on listening, encounter and co-responsibility between all the members of the Church, and which must be actively promoted by all bishops. Perhaps the synodal path is another *kairos* moment for the Church, and Albert's theology and indeed witness have much to contribute to this moment. Pope Francis speaks of Jesus knocking at the door of the Church wanting to be 'let out' so that he can reach and heal every form of suffering in the real world 'out there'—and that is the vision of Church I experienced in Albert.

An Evangelical Discovering Contextual Theology

Moss Ntlha

Albert lived and practiced his craft as a theologian, activist and priest in the context of a South Africa caught in the throes of a revolutionary mass struggle that eventually triumphed over Apartheid. He lived to see the new South Africa being born and witnessed its faltering steps as she tried to reinvent herself as a new democratic, non-racial society.

Albert brought his incredible theological skills to bear in the service of the country both before and after the momentous 1994 transition, in which Apartheid gave way to a democratic order of non-racialism. He had a rare ability to bring a sharp, scholarly and disciplined mind to the service of the community and the poor. This meant simplifying complex theological concepts and making them accessible to people who never had the privilege and benefit of theological studies, even though they lived and breathed in a predominantly 'Christian' society. The word 'Christian' is in inverted commas because a) the South African society is, according to official censuses, upward of seventy per cent Christian, and b) it is a form of Christianity that itself needed to be set free from its ideological captivity to Apartheid. Otherwise, it would hold no good news to the beneficiaries of Apartheid nor the victims of Apartheid. Both needed emancipation from such an idolatrous religion.

Albert was a warrior who brought his sharp theological sword to the battle against the theology of Apartheid. In this war, he was as fierce as he was humble. True to his Master's charge, he was as 'wise as a serpent and harmless as a dove'. It was his commitment to serve the process rather than the often-imperfect personalities that tend to take away from the essentials of a revolutionary process aimed at setting the captives free. It is this amazing gift that endeared him to the present author, a committed evangelical. It took a Dominican Catholic priest to open my mind to the gifts that God, in His wisdom, placed in different parts of His body, for the mutual benefit of all His children. Albert's ecumenical contribution was immense, as this volume will show.

When I met him, Albert worked at the Institute for Contextual Theology (ICT). This was at the height of the successive States of Emergency imposed by the Apartheid government on the people of South Africa, aimed at giving the security machinery of the regime all the cover they needed to defend Apartheid by any means possible. Along with other theologian activists who worked with him at ICT, he introduced me to the theological method of Contextual Theology. I was a lay Christian at the time, working in secular employment but wanting to take Jesus seriously. Needless to say, Contextual Theology was a refreshing novelty to my evangelical mind whose theological method tended to be neo-fundamentalist.

My learning from Albert, processed through my evangelical mind, can be summarised thus: *Read the signs of the time. Hear God. Do Jesus.* Let me explain.

Read the signs of the time

This was a favourite phrase Albert used to connote the idea that context was important in understanding both what the Bible taught in its day and what it might mean for us in ours. This task, Albert would explain, required social analysis. He was quick to add that this is to be done as much by ordinary people as well as professionals who approached the task as an academic discipline. This was helpful to those of us who felt intimidated by the highbrow label of 'social analysis'. It gave us permission to on-ramp into the world of critical theology and its prophetic relevance to our times. For the task at hand, which was to read the signs of the times during the intense and deadly conflict between the Apartheid government and the people of South Africa, social analysis could be done by simply asking a series of questions until you got a satisfactory answer, beyond which no further enquiry mattered. The questions were, in any given situation a) who benefits from this arrangement? b) Who pays the price for its sustenance? c) Who suffers?

Answering these questions in group conversations made for a rich experience of community learning and change. The voice of each participant mattered, and everyone felt they contributed to the definition of the problem. It demystified systemic evil and helped break it into its constituent parts, making it easy for people to figure out for themselves how to even begin the journey to bring a stop to their misery.

In this way, 'reading the signs of the times' helped to build a foundation for a more revolutionary spirituality, giving participants the confidence to become subjects in the process of history-making and not merely objects in the process of history-making by others. It fostered thoughtful agency in the democratic process and struggle.

Hear God

My Pentecostal evangelical tribe has a different take on hearing God that often excludes community and context. It is often done in an ahistorical manner and is susceptible to co-option by the powerful. To hear God with the benefit of community social analysis makes it possible to escape the domestication of God in an individual believer, which renders the faith irrelevant to current human predicaments.

For Albert, it went further. It relativised the assumptions of popular struggles to a superior and transcendent reference point. To admit God into the daily struggles of the people is to be as critical of structural injustice perpetrated by the enemy out there, as one is of the propensities towards materialism and greed that lay deep inside our selves and our group. Albert returned to this in his later works, *Jesus Today: A Spirituality of Radical Freedom* (2006) and *Hope in an Age of Despair* (2009), which focused on the importance of values in a post-Apartheid society. These two books appeared well into the post-Apartheid South Africa in which those formerly oppressed were now in political power but lacked a spirituality to sustain the transformation programme that their political manifestos committed them to.

Do Jesus

This is shorthand for the importance of incarnation, which is the way God chose to reveal Godself in the world. Contextual Theology, as Albert taught and modelled it, is done, and not only theorised. It was for this reason that the ICT regularly held workshops in which Christian activists and theologians, each coming from different contexts of struggle, gathered to share learnings and insights about how they saw God at work in their everyday struggles in civil society—be this as the labour movement, academics, women, churches, muslims, youth or any other manner of social sector. The agenda was to 'do Jesus' in the struggles for life and personhood in the fight against Apartheid.

It is easy to see how faith could become a powerful weapon in the struggle for justice. The miracle in this is the fact that, for over 300 years before 1994, the Christian faith was weaponised against the oppressed both by colonists who preceded the Apartheid regime as well as the Apartheid regime itself. The theological task that Albert and others like him undertook culminated in the reclamation of the Bible and its saving message from the cold grip of Apartheid power and mischief, and correctly located it firmly in the terrain to which it belongs: the poor and the oppressed. As an ancient prophet, quoted by Jesus put it:

> The Spirit of the Lord is on me, because he has anointed me to proclaim good news to the poor. He has sent me to proclaim freedom for the prisoners and recovery of sight for the blind, to set the oppressed free, to proclaim the year of the Lord's favour (Lk 4 18–19 NIV).

Albert went further. Believing as he did in the necessary agency of the poor in reflecting and acting as subjects of their own liberation, he bemoaned the scarcity of theological texts written by the poor themselves. What made the problem worse is that African people in South Africa—and I suspect elsewhere on the continent—are a more oral culture than their Caucasian counterparts. When they do finally succumb and take to the pen, it is often in self-defence. It is for this reason that many texts written on them are often written by others rather than themselves. 'Until the lion learns how to write, every story will glorify the hunter' said novelist Chinua Achebe in his 1958 classic *Things Fall Apart*.

To mitigate against this unfair treatment of the king of the jungle, Albert took the bull by the horns. He ran a writing school for aspirant writers who lacked the requisite skills for the craft. That had impact. Being a beneficiary of that writing school, I have slowly crossed the boundaries of orality, as evidenced by this present essay. It is my little contribution to honouring one of our nation's finest theologians.

A Significant Impact on Evangelical Movements

Aaron Mokabane

Introduction

Our country recently lost one of her beloved sons who was well-known and admired in ecumenical circles and also a great hero of our anti-apartheid struggle—Fr Albert Nolan. This has left us all very much poorer and we will miss his presence. He has left an indelible mark that is not only captured in many books and articles but is deeply in the hearts of most of us who knew and were impacted by his life and ministry. In this short contribution I will try to capture my encounters and journey with our beloved Fr Albert, my reflection on his legacy and the lessons that he has left for all of us.

My encounters with Fr Albert

Fr Albert was a towering figure in the churches' anti-apartheid struggle in the eighties and early nineties. It is commonly known that his activism started from his days as a chaplain amongst Catholic university students, then later developed when he became the head of research at the Institute for Contextual Theology (ICT) and the editor of *Challenge* magazine. His books and, later through Challenge, his writings informed and shaped many church social justice activists of the era.

I first came across Fr Albert and his writings in the late eighties when I was a university student at Wits University in Braamfontein. He was based at the Institute for Contextual Theology (ICT) in Jorissen Street, Braamfontein. He had already authored two famous books that were widely read in both theological and church activist circles—*Jesus before Christianity* and *God in South Africa*. It was also common knowledge that he played a key role in editing the famous *Kairos Document*.

As a young evangelical student who grew up in rural Limpopo and now bewildered as a student at an urban university I had lots of questions about my faith and the pertinent political questions that were confronting us at the time. We devoured any literature that came into our hands including political and theological literature. There was not much literature available to assist in wrestling with all of the political questions that impacted on our faith at the time. The only relevant evangelical literature which was produced locally and spoke to most of the issues that were confronting us as young evangelical activists was the Evangelical Witness in South Africa (EWISA) document.[1] This document was an evangelical response to the *Kairos Document* and the deepening political crisis of the time. The other related and relevant documents for the evangelical audience were books and articles written by American evangelical theologians and activists including James Cone[2], J Deotis Roberts[3], Jim Wallis[4], Ron Sider[5] and others.

I had the benefit of attending a Catholic High School in Polokwane—Pax High School in Ga Mashashane, Limpopo between 1983 and 1985. This gave me a good understanding and respect for the Catholic faith and its core teachings and settled any uneasiness I had with it. Thus I had little apprehension in reading and embracing what Fr Albert had written. Furthermore, during my studies, first at Wits and later at Turfloop, I was actively involved and part of the leadership of the Student Union for Christian Action (SUCA).[6] SUCA had a presence in many universities and some colleges. It sought to disciple and involve students in practical actions for justice, peace and social

---

1. The Evangelical Witness in South Africa (EWISA) document was released by a group of concerned evangelicals in 1986 and gave birth to an organisation that was working to catalyse renewal among evangelicals called Concerned Evangelicals (CE).
2. James Cone is a famous African American theologian who has written a lot on black theology.
3. J Deotis Robert is a famous African American professor of Philosophical Theology who was for a long time based at Eastern University.
4. Jim Wallis was the founder and leader of Sojourners based in Washington DC and now the Director of Faith & Justice at Georgetown University.
5. Ron Sider was the founder and president of Evangelicals for Social Action based in Philadelphia, US and also professor of Theology & Culture at Eastern University. He passed away in 2022.
6. SUCA was formed after the 1979 South African Christian Leadership Assembly (SACLA) to respond to the socio-political challenges of the time from our faith.

transformation on tertiary campuses. We had the benefit of having Fr Albert to speak at most of our annual national congresses. Later, the material he produced in *Challenge* magazine was used as a resource in our biblical reflections.

Impact of Fr Albert's life and ministry

I now wish to reflect briefly on two notable impacts that Fr Albert's ministry has had on many Christians, student leaders and the ecumenical movement in our country.

Discipling student leaders in the biblical imperative of justice and peace

The eighties was a tumultuous time in our country for everyone. Many students and young people were searching for direction and answers amidst the political turmoil. A number of organisations mushroomed to fill the space and offer direction to our youth and students. I am thinking of organisations like Young Christian Students (YCS), SUCA and Cathsocs.

I can safely say that Fr Albert, through his speaking engagements, books and other writings, helped greatly to disciple and answer intractable questions that many students and youth were confronting at the time. This enabled many of them to continue contributing to the struggle against apartheid as Christians and later playing their part in building the new post-apartheid society. They owe their sustenance and growth in faith amidst the tumult of the time to unsung heroes, pastors and theologians like Fr Albert. He taught and empowered us with key tools for doing theology like See-Judge-Act and the Hermeneutical Cycle.

Organic scholarship

There is a famous quote that is attributed to Karl Marx, 'Philosophers have defined the world in many ways, the point is to change it'. Fr Albert was a scholar and generated a lot of original work that shaped much of church and Christian activism, thought and practice in the anti-apartheid struggle. His books, two of which are mentioned above—*Jesus before Christianity* and *God in South Africa*—became famous and were not only read widely in academia but also in church activist circles.

Lessons from Fr Albert's life

Finally, I wish to reflect on two important principles from Fr Albert's life that provide invaluable lessons for each of us: consistency and simplicity.

Consistency

Many church activists like Fr Albert are teaching us through their lives and work the importance of consistency and running one's race till the finish line. They were not involved in the struggle for positions but as a practical outworking of their faith and convictions.

Sadly some activists have been caught in some shameful unethical acts of abuse of power and public funds. This has unfortunately soiled the rich history of courageous and ethical struggles for justice and peace in our country.

The life and ministry of Fr Albert Nolan is an admirable testimony to the virtue of 'consistency in one's life and ministry'. He was very consistent in living out his faith and calling in pursuit of the cause of justice and peace in church and society.

Simplicity

Fr Albert lived a simple life without any frills and was forever approachable. He was very much loved, respected and adored as a fountain of thought in 'doing theology'. Many of his peers from the anti-apartheid struggle moved into cushy public positions with the advent of the democratic dispensation. He, however, stuck to his primary calling as a priest and also as a member of his religious order within the Catholic Church.

He was always approachable and friendly. This simple and yet approachable life is something that we need to recover amongst many activists who have now grown accustomed to power, positions and wealth.

Conclusion

Fr Albert Nolan has now passed on to glory and has left behind an admirable legacy that is worthy to be emulated. The memory of his simple and yet impactful life will remain a dear possession in the hearts of those of us who knew and were influenced by his teachings and writings. He joins the monument of heroes and heroines who have played a key role in our anti-apartheid struggle and delivered a democratic dispensation.

For those of us who remain on this side of life, as we continue to journey ahead in the quest for the ideal non-racial, non-sexist democratic society, his life and teachings will remain a source of encouragement. Like him we aspire one day to reach the finish line as good and faithful servants.

Albert concelebrating Mass at the NCFS National Conference, July 1974 at Hekpoort with Michael Austin SJ and Jan Haen CSsR.

Section Four

Theologising in the Midst of the Struggle

Frank Chikane speaking at launch of the United Democratic Front (UDF) in Cape Town, 20 August, 1983.

On Context in Context

James R Cochrane

Albert Nolan's name is irrevocably linked with what came to be known as 'Contextual Theology' in South Africa. Besides his influential writings in this field,[1] he was also an original and vital member of the staff of the Institute for Contextual Theology (ICT). Founded in Johannesburg in 1981, ICT was a significant exemplar of Christian resistance to Apartheid, perhaps best known for its influential publication, the *Kairos Document: Challenge to the Churches*.[2] Not so well known is how this humble man came to ICT in the first place. It says something significant about his character, so it is worth sharing.

The idea for ICT emerged after the banning (declared illegal, outlawed) of the Christian Institute of Southern Africa (CI) in October 1977, whose activities in faith-based resistance had become increasingly troublesome for the Apartheid State and system. The CI had also been a key source of information and solidarity for many others outside of the country. The banning of the CI left a vacuum—not least for the Ecumenical Association of Third World Theologians (EAT-WOT), which brought liberation theologians of one kind or another into global relationships of solidarity, and for which the CI had been a key link.

---

1. Albert Nolan, *Jesus before Christianity* (Maryknoll, NY: Orbis Books, 1992), 197; *Taking Sides* (London: Catholic Institute for International Relations, 1984); *God in South Africa: The Challenge of the Gospel* (Cape Town: David Philip, 1988); *Hope in an Age of Despair: And Other Talks and Writings* (Maryknoll, NY: Orbis Books, 2009).
2. *The Kairos document: Challenge to the Church* (Braamfontein: Skotaville, 1986, 2nd edition).

EATWOT leaders in its New York office began pressing Allan Boesak to help establish some new entity to which they could relate. Allan, in turn, asked me to assist. With his backing and three others, we spent two years developing a constitution and negotiating the establishment of an institute under the protection of the University of Cape Town, with the full support of the then Vice-Chancellor, Stuart Sanders. In the end, the negotiations failed, largely because the relevant faculty insisted that one of its members must be the director of the proposed institute, a move that would take away control from those who established it and inevitably change its fundamental *modus operandi*.

Disappointed, we turned to Beyers Naudé, with whom we had been consulting all along (though he was a banned person). He now persuaded Reverend Elia Thema to help launch the Institute in Johannesburg as part-time Acting Director until a full-time Director could be found (that would be Frank Chikane). What was needed most, however, was someone to work full-time on setting up the Institute and helping shape its theological direction. Boesak was on the Board, as was Bonganjalo Goba, another Black Theologian, but they were in no position to shift roles at that point. Beyers knew exactly who could help: Albert Nolan.

Albert quickly saw the need, agreed to take on the role, and invested himself into the task, giving up as much of his time and energy as he could to help bring the Institute into being. Absolutely vital to his role, however, was his self-understanding of his place in the mix. He knew that the others around him, not him ultimately, were crucial to its success. He never claimed anything for himself, never undermined the leadership of those like Elia or Frank whom he knew had to lead, never did anything but give of the very best of his theology and the very best of his commitment to those who suffered the yoke of oppression, and never asked for any thanks or honour on the way. He saw his role as serving, not in being served.

This is perhaps clearest in what was without doubt ICT's most renowned, fabled output, the *Kairos Document*, published as a *Challenge to the Church* but also radically undermining the legitimacy of the Apartheid state. First issued in 1985 and revised in 1986, with dozens of prominent signatories, it challenged the complicity of 'Church Theology' (even denominations that officially condemned Apartheid all too often were timid or overly cautious about offending especially white members or were themselves racially divided at local level) and called for a 'prophetic theology'. Its impact was felt not only in South Africa but in several other parts of the world, giving rise to groups or movements in Europe, the USA, the Middle East and the Philippines that took on the term *Kairos* as definitive for their own struggle against systemic injustice.

Albert played a critical role in its production and made several crucial contributions to its theological formulations. However, by a long way, he was not its author. It began, as the *Document* itself declares, with a group of black clergy and theologians who were under considerable stress, occasioned by a declaration of a State of Emergency by the Apartheid State as it ramped up its attempt to control black resistance. The pastors experienced the consequences on the ground, virtually on a daily basis, both personally and often because of its direct impact on their congregants. They felt a pressing need to write a joint pastoral letter to their congregations and Churches in this context.

The idea was for ICT to publish it and distribute it as widely as possible, but before that happened, it was shown to Beyers Naudé. Reading what had been written, he immediately saw from his own history and struggle against the Apartheid State, particularly in the Christian Institute that he had co-founded (now banned along with him), that its content went far beyond the scope of local congregations. To him it was clear: it should be addressed to the Church at large and to the nation.

And so, it was. But first it had to be shared more widely across the country, as clandestinely as possible (this process had to be protected from the state's security police). Comments were requested from many others and incorporated where necessary into an increasingly large document. Here is where Albert's theological and writing skills came into their own.

To the formulations of what now became the *Kairos Document*, Albert made a fundamental contribution, not least in articulating the charge against the nominally Christian Apartheid state as guilty not just of heresy, a distortion of the faith—an accusation already made by the South African Council of Churches and the Christian Institute in 1968 in their *Message to the People of South Africa*—but of tyranny, in effect a betrayal of the faith, apostasy in short. The *Message* had called for reform, for a return to the roots of the faith the government also professed along with the Churches that supported it.[3] However,

---

3. It is noteworthy that at one stage one of the Vorster brothers was head of the South African State (BJ), the other (Koot) head of the Dutch Reformed Church (Nederduitse Gereformeerde Kerk, or NGK), the oldest Church in South Africa.

to declare its rule as tyranny and those who supported it on Christian grounds as apostates was a far more radical stance with serious implications. It was, in effect, a call to the Churches to reject the authority of an illegitimate state.

The *Kairos Document* was an expression of what ICT meant by Contextual Theology. But what, after all, is 'Contextual Theology'? The term at the time was contested, and it is in any case imprecise: Contested because some black theologians, who had shaped much theological discourse in the 1970s and early 1980s, felt that the term, whether intentionally or by default, effectively sidelined or silenced Black Theology; imprecise because many others, including white Afrikaner theologians who traced their own heritage back to Boer resistance to British colonisers, could claim that theirs, too, was a contextual theology.

Let me then pick up on this question (on which I have already written in a book published in Albert's honour in 2001).[4] There, besides describing how ICT got its name and noting the criticism from some black theologians of the term (several were members of the Board and staff of the ICT), I argued that Contextual Theology 'does *not* mean theology arising from a particular context and speaking to that context. All theology does that if it is worthy of the name . . .' Instead, I believed, voice is the key issue, specifically, the voice of the other. Not just any 'other', however, but those whose voice is subjugated, silenced, who are marginalised from centres of power and wealth, and whose interests are usually treated as secondary, if at all. This binds Contextual Theology to other theological projects that seek to give voice, and space, to women, the poor, the disabled, the excluded, the aged and so on.

Here we are speaking of no abstract other but of particular persons, not just of them as individuals but as affected directly and indirectly by entrenched self-interests reflected in harmful structures of polity and economy. This is what the *Kairos Document* defined as 'prophetic theology', the preferred term for the contextual theology that arose in South Africa and with which Albert Nolan was identified. It is not something of the past. The impulses that guided Contextual Theology

---

4. James R Cochrane, 'Questioning Contextual Theology', in *Towards an Agenda for Contextual Theology: Essays in Honour of Albert Nolan*, edited by MT Speckman and LT Kaufmann (Pietermaritzburg: Cluster Publications, 2001), 67–86.

under the Apartheid regime are not chaff blowing in the wind, but signs of the enduring gospel by whatever name we call it.

In *Circles of Dignity* I suggested that contextual theology 'begins with an emancipatory interest grounded in the real material conditions of oppressed local communities, groups or persons' and linked it to a congruent understanding of salvation (*salus* = health, well-being) as 'an overcoming of the conditions that enslave, dehumanise, marginalise, and alienate us from neighbour, our self and God . . . in the name of the comprehensive well-being of all.'[5] It does not matter if one uses other words than 'contextual' to articulate this fundamental orientation and, in fact, that term may even be misleading because of its fuzziness. But, however named, the orientation is the point.

Two points remain muted in these earlier formulations that I later added in an address to the Ujamaa Institute.[6] One is our intimate bondedness with nature, with the earth, and the struggle for ecological justice that I believe is part and parcel of any contextual or prophetic theology properly understood. Another, present in African understandings of the ancestor, is the importance of intergenerational blessing—of what we have gained from those who have gone before us whom we are called on to honour in our own life and action. To these points I would now add a third: a concern that the notion of 'the other', inevitably opposed to 'the self', does not introduce a binary notion that tends to reify both the self and the other when, in fact, relationships between human beings are more complicated than that, more fluid, more knotted than we like, with complicities in injustice and struggles for dignity dynamically interlinked with one another.[7]

So, what does all of this mean today? Post-Apartheid South Africa, in some respects a galaxy away from the horror of what preceded it (at least in respect of its foundational norms and aspirational Constitution), is nevertheless full of deeply disturbing inequities and experiences that challenge and sometimes shame us (because of a failure to rise to the early hopes of a more just and healed society).

---

5. James R Cochrane, *Circles of Dignity: Community Wisdom and Theological Reflection* (Minneapolis: Fortress Press, 1999), 56.
6. James R Chochrane, 'On Contextual Theology in a Post-Apartheid Era' at <https://www.academia.edu/437343/On_Contextual_Theology_Today>. Accessed April 2023.
7. For this point, I thank Tobias Müller, who also commented on other aspects of the chapter.

Building a new society on the back of the past, it was clear from the outset, would be a grave challenge, intimidating in the face of the potentially crushing effects of the past on the debilitation of human capital through Apartheid education policies whose generational impact is still felt, and because of the iniquitous distribution of resources and institutional capacities that had to be rectified (still a major challenge not yet adequately met). This is not even to consider the systemic damage done to human relations through migratory labour policies destructive of family life and through a long history of systemic racism.

Yet the past cannot rule us, and in South Africa, a post-Apartheid reality is now nearly a third of a century old. Old inequities and injustices have not disappeared, racism is not eradicated, economic imbalances have grown if anything, the excessive accumulation of capital among a very small part of the population can (and should be) considered obscene, discrimination in educational and other opportunities remains extreme (and more). Global realities have also shifted substantially, not least in the highly dubious post-Cold War 'triumph' of neo-liberal economic theories that have excoriated the public or common good, in heightened awareness of climate threats and diversity loss, and in more recent renewed contestation around the post-World War II international order and norms.

To this may be added the rise of autocracies and of international criminal syndicates enamoured of what Misha Glenny called 'state capture,'[8] the two things not infrequently bound up with each other. Technological developments have also profoundly compressed time and space, altering our communications for better and worse, with more to come in the radical possibilities of artificial intelligence, which will not only impact on whole political economies but include what its creators themselves call 'risky emergent behaviour' that they cannot fully foresee or perhaps control.[9]

One could go on, but the point is this: It is not entirely clear—if one steps back from any ideological framework that claims to understand it all—what the future holds or how it will unfold. Prediction, as the renowned Danish physicist Niels Bohr said, is very difficult,

---

8. Misha Glenny, *McMafia: Seriously Organized Crime* (London: Vintage Books, 2009).
9. Open AI, 'GPT-4 System Card' at <https://cdn.openai.com/papers/gpt-4-system-card.pdf>. Accessed 2 April 2023.

especially about the future. We don't know fully the nature of what we are living through, and we cannot see its end. This should, if nothing else, caution us about any fixed, rigid claims to truth and any actions devoid of humility. It should alert us to our own unmerited certainties and arrogances, in this sense call us to 'fear and trembling' in the face of the sacred.[10]

What I mean by this can be misunderstood. It is *not* a call to passivity. On the contrary, not unlike Gandhi's *satyagraha*, it is a call to enjoin the pursuit of justice and liberation in full awareness that we do not carry the mantle of God, that is, to acknowledge the paradox that our faith, however well meant, is accompanied by our own hypocrisies or complicities. This is what protects us from further injustice or violence to others now carried out by ourselves in the name of the divine.

What contextual or prophetic theology means under these circumstances, in practice rather than theory, is an open question. It cannot be discarded if its basic insights hold, and there are good reasons to believe they do. What is clear is that any contextual or prophetic theology—or any other kind of theology, for that matter—certain of its truth falls short in the test of humility. Because it thereby substitutes itself and the person who espouses it for God, it is a dangerous theology, potentially or actually tyrannical, a source of death rather than life.

This is what Albert Nolan, in his own way and time, saw clearly and lived out of. Never claiming much for himself, either materially, politically or even spiritually, he sought love and justice—'love writ large'—and he did so for all. Wherever it was thwarted, he spoke out. Wherever it was diminished, he cried out. Wherever love and justice were alive, he sought to support it. In word and deed, his vision was always wholly inclusive. The preferential option for the poor, the oppressed and the marginalised, for him was never in the name of exclusion but always for the sake of all. No mere political rhetoric, it was a call from the heart of the Gospel he proclaimed, a demand that the dignity and freedom due any and all human beings, no matter any differences between them, be respected and met.

---

10. I draw my interpretation of this phrase from Søren Kierkegaard, in *Fear and Trembling and Repetition* (Princeton: Princeton University Press, 1983).

His vision echoed a pivotal writing by Steve Biko, whom Albert greatly admired and by whom he was influenced. In it, Biko declares that the ultimate goal of Black Consciousness, as he understood it, is not a racially defined (or any other specific identity) reality, but 'the quest for true humanity'.[11]

That was also Albert's quest. In remembering and honouring him, it becomes ours too.

---

11. Steve Biko, 'Black Consciousness and the Quest for a True Humanity', in *I Write What I Like: Steve Biko—A Selection of His Writings*, edited by A Stubbs (Oxford: Heinemann, 1987), 87–98.

Hope Against Hope!

Frank Chikane

I cannot provide a specific time or date for my first meeting with Fr Albert Nolan, as that is not how Albert operated. He never imposed himself or demanded attention. Rather, he entered every situation, every 'context', with a genuine desire to listen, to accompany and to build true solidarity. This approach meant that, in the end, his work not only spoke for itself, but also did so with far more power and impact than his presence at a particular event or any sermon could ever have achieved. So, while I knew Albert and his activist 'disciples' in the Young Christian Students (YCS) well before the formation of the Institute for Contextual Theology (ICT), my five years or so of employment at the Institute, where I worked closely with Albert, were highly enriching. What's more, the Institute and its community of activists also provided me and my family with a semblance of security during what was an especially insecure period.

Although I had been ordained as a minister of the Apostolic Faith Mission of South Africa (AFM) in 1980, I was forced to stop ministering to my Kagiso Assembly congregation in Krugersdorp (now Mogale City) in August 1981, after I was suspended for my involvement in 'politics'. The suspension was meant to last for a year, but endured for far longer, and I spent most of the initial period of the suspension in detention (November 1981–July 1982), during which time my family was evicted from the church in Kagiso and forced to relocate to Soweto.

While my own Church was throwing me and my family out, activists and leaders from other Churches were opening their doors and offering to help. As my wife Kagiso pointed out in a chapter of my biography, the Institute and other friends helped us to get a new house. Ahead of my detention in November 1981, the ICT had promised me a temporary job. After I was detained, Kagiso approached the Institute for help when the AFM West Rand district committee leaders refused to extend the two-month deadline that had been set for her and my children to vacate the manse. The Institute stepped in to offer my family their full backing and even wrote an affidavit to the building society indicating that the ICT would make the repayments for the mortgage bond. Kagiso got the keys for our Pimville house on the last day of April 1982, providing us with shelter during a tumultuous period.

I was employed by the Institute full-time in September 1982 and was appointed ICT General-Secretary in 1983. The Institute was just the right place for me to further systematise and develop my theological understanding of my Christian pastoral praxis. Throughout my life there was never any question of a systematised theory coming before experience or praxis, but it was always a struggle at a particular time, faced with a particular reality, to determine what role one had to play as a Christian.

Here, Albert Nolan's theological perspective and support proved pivotal. In fact, he was also the one who encouraged me to write my biography whilst I was operating from underground at a time when the Apartheid Security Police detained many of our leaders and kept them in what was called 'preventative detention'. Albert managed the scripts as I produced them from underground and he smuggled them out of the country to the Catholic Institute for International Relations (CIIR), which published the manuscript in the UK in 1988 entitled, *No Life of My Own*. My life at that time was indeed not a 'life of my own'.

During that period, Albert also used his Catholic network to keep me, as far as possible, out of the hands of the South African Security Police, by spiriting me away to safe houses that were often the homes of religious communities. At one point while on the run, I even spent three months with the Jesuits in Jules Street, Johannesburg where I was welcomed as a full member of their community, participating completely in their Masses and community life. At one time, Albert arranged for me to meet my wife and my children underground in a convent in Johannesburg. Even when I spent some time in exile, that network (this time under the leadership of Ian Linden of CIIR) helped house me and keep me safe. And when I decided I needed to return to South Africa, that network was used not only to undertake a reconnaissance mission to confirm the safest route back into the country, but to give me safe haven during that potentially treacherous journey. Various nuns and priests helped me every step of the way, including navigating the Botswana-South Africa border crossing. That crossing would have posed a significant risk had the reconnaissance mission not discovered that the border gate they took me through was a fully manual border, which meant it would take longer for the Security Police to realise that I had entered South Africa than would have been the case at a more sophisticated post.

From the way he helped manage my life underground, including my return to the country, it is clear that Albert's acts of solidarity with the oppressed went further than many realised. As was confirmed after his death on 17 October 2022, Albert was also active in the underground struggle, and was part of a secret underground network that managed logistics, including the transportation and movement of activists, providing safe houses and a means of communication while in South Africa. Horst Kleinschmidt, who operated from exile at that time, has revealed that Albert was part of a group of more than twenty operatives who smuggled communication out of South Africa to the then exiled African National Congress (ANC) and returned with messages from Oliver Tambo and Thabo Mbeki to activists inside the country. Kleinschmidt confirmed that Albert was known as 'Operative 42' and the numbers '4' and '2' were scrambled into texts and figures—and the Security Branch never found the key to this messaging. The long-running operation involved the smuggling of letters, none of which were ever intercepted, as well as call-box to call-box communications that changed location each week, and the swapping of money that made any tracing of bank records impossible.

From pastoral and theological perspectives, too, my time at the Institute and my time with Albert helped me as I struggled with the question of how one should minister in a context of injustice and conflict. In the course of this struggle, I was forced to look into past and contemporary theological models of life and pastoral work in a variety of situations of conflict, throughout the history of the Christian faith. My involvement with the Institute made this reading task easier. I was able to look at Black Theology in South Africa and in the USA, at African Theology, and I also looked at Liberation Theology and its development in Latin America. Through the Ecumenical Association of Third World Theologians, I was also exposed to Asian theologies. Albert also had networks into Latin America and Asia, particularly the Philippines, which enabled us to exchange views and share our experiences. This enriched our theological perspectives enormously. He also got funding for the work of the Institute from Catholic agencies internationally.

This theological development continued in parallel to my disrupted efforts to consolidate my position through academic studies. For Albert, however, academic qualifications and titles were secondary in his Christian journey. Remember, this is a man who decided not to publish his own doctoral thesis, a prerequisite for securing the title of doctor, on the basis of it being 'too expensive' to do so. His view was that this money could instead be used to help the poor or support their struggles for liberation. Albert's humility was particularly striking when they wanted me to take up the position of General-Secretary and then Director of the ICT. While he was more qualified, he took up the position of 'research officer' saying he is 'here to help'. I drew on this help for my ongoing theological development, not only in the broader South African struggle but even in my struggles within my own Church.

In fact, I leaned on this theological development, and on Albert's own writings, in my ongoing battle with the AFM at the time. In a submission to the AFM leadership in 1982 regarding my continued suspension for my political involvement, I told them that I believed that 'I am called to proclaim His Kingdom on earth, as Fr A Nolan says, to make humanity "adopt the lifestyle of the future Kingdom on earth". I told the AFM leadership that, whereas I believed that a person had to be saved as an individual, and that every person is and will be responsible before God as an individual, I also believed that national sin starts from individual sins. A sinful nation consists of sinful individuals. I thus argued that the change that the gospel effects on a sinful individual must result in a change of the structural sins of the nation.

One of those structural sins was the ongoing violence of the Apartheid State, which was led by those who claimed to be Christian. I became involved in the Ministry in a Conflict Situation Project, which involved ministers in the Pretoria–Witwatersrand–Vaal area (now Gauteng). This group of ministers met once a month for some three years and helped me reflect on and share experiences with other pastors on our situation. Most of these ministers were themselves detained either for short or long periods, and in some instances also tortured by the police. Others were subjected to one form of harassment or another. All because of their contact with victims of the Apartheid system and their ministry to them.

My own experience was typical of what they were going through. After long periods of reflection and sharing we reached a consensus: that the traditional and dominant position that looked at reality and understood our faith from the point of view of the powerful and dominant forces in society and their 'ideology-theology' was not compatible with the demands of the gospel.

As I reflected in my biography, as we surveyed and analysed the history of the Church since Constantine, we concluded in the 1980s that the Church had taken sides, in the main, with the dominant classes of society which were responsible for the pain, suffering, misery and even death of many, especially the weak, poor, and powerless. Since Constantine the Church had shifted from being a persecuted Church to being the Church of the persecutors. In the early Christian Church, it had cost the lives of many just to confess that Jesus was Christ and to be baptised into the Christian faith. After Constantine, not being a Christian put one at risk. The Church was elevated to a position of power, had tasted power, and articulated its faith from that position. Therefore, the Church often failed to see the injustices perpetrated by the powerful and rich against the powerless and the poor. One needs only to look at the conduct of the Church during the period of colonisation and in relation to the struggles of the 'Third World' (I use 'Third World' as it was used then), colonised peoples against colonial powers. The Church tended to take sides with the colonial powers against those who resisted them. To us, this amounted to collaboration with the forces of evil. In the light of this analysis, our group, which became known as MUCCOR, or the Ministers United for Christian Co-responsibility, opted for taking sides with the victims of Apartheid and for justice.

Both the MUCCOR and the 1983 ICT conference on this topic were very useful to me in clarifying our theology of taking sides with the oppressed and the marginalised. Our option was in line with the theological models of the Confessing Church in Nazi Germany and manifested concretely in the life of Dietrich Bonhoeffer. It was also in line with many of the Third World theological models emerging from Latin America, Africa, and Asia, including that of the black theologians in North America. As we took this decision, we were conscious that we were called to minister to all in the world, both oppressors and oppressed, white and black. The mission of the Church is directed to the whole world, as much as Jesus died for all.

Taking sides with the victims of society in our situation, we concluded, meant taking sides with the ideals of the Kingdom or Reign of God proclaimed by Jesus. This is a governance of justice, righteousness, and peace where goodness will always prevail. Some saw a contradiction in this position, but there was none. What we were doing was calling both oppressor and oppressed, rich and poor, black and white, to repentance and, in line with the ideals of God's Reign, to take sides with justice and against the injustice perpetrated by the oppressors.

During the struggle of the 1980s, this meant taking the side of black South Africans against the heresy of white racism. We concluded that the question of justice, which is an inherent characteristic of the Reign of God, went beyond the question of the so-called group interests or the colour of particular people. For me the best way to understand what justice is about is what Jesus himself said, that we should do to others what we would that they do to us (Mt 7:12). In this regard, God's justice was justice for all humanity. In trying to explain this position I often said to my black colleagues and comrades that if they took over this country and practised injustices against their white compatriots, or racism in reverse, they would also have to detain me. I would just have to go back to prison, to the same cell in John Vorster Square, but this time it will be under the control of black authorities.

This is a position I could take only because of my contact with white activists such as Albert and Dr Beyers Naudé. Many of us had been brutalised at the hands of whites and tortured by white security policemen. Our natural inclination would have been one of great bitterness towards, and hatred of whites. However, Albert and other white activists who took sides with black South Africans 'humanised' us and helped us not to think about the struggle against Apartheid only in racial terms. It allowed us to begin talking about the ideals of the Reign of God together, with people like Albert accompanying us in those theological reflections in true solidarity. It also allowed us to embrace the name Institute for Contextual Theology at a time when some theologians felt strongly that we should be emphasising black or African theology. A 'contextual' approach for some felt like a liberal approach. For the institute, a contextual approach was more inclusive of all the liberation theologies globally, including Black and African theologies. Our reflections brought to the fore the importance of 'context, context, context' as Albert would say and how a 'Contextual Theology' could be transcendent in helping us to discern how to deal with all the contradictions of our contexts, including race, class and gender.

As we looked at the life of Jesus together, there could be no doubt about the spirit of Jesus' ministry. The favourite text of many theologians of liberation sums up what Jesus perceived as his mission in the world:

> The spirit of the Lord is upon me, because He has anointed me. He has sent me to preach good news to the poor, to proclaim release to captives, and the recovery of sight to the blind, to set at liberty those who are oppressed, to proclaim the acceptable year of the Lord (Lk 4:18–19).

As we analysed and developed our theology, I agreed more and more with Albert that Jesus was wrongly associated with all the things he denounced and rejected. He is associated with kings and lords, with the powerful and important people in society. He is seen as a friend of the upper classes. But did not the 'historical Jesus' (as Albert Nolan would say) refuse to be a king? Did he not choose to identify and live with the poor, the blind, the sick and the hungry, deliberately associating with a rejected class of people in the society of His time? Did he not rebuke the Pharisees, the chief priests, and the Scribes? Did He not warn the rich that it was easier to pass through the eye of a needle than enter the Kingdom of Heaven? Albert Nolan in his book *Jesus before Christianity* depicts Jesus' attitudes very clearly. Christians cannot just ignore this practice of the Lord Jesus Christ.

The *Kairos Document* grew out of this Christian struggle, but took it a step forward theologically by stating clearly that the two opposed forces are irreconcilable. You cannot reconcile God and the devil, it says. What Christians need to do is remove the evil, fight the devil, and join the forces of good and righteousness in their march into God's Reign. It was strongly critical of concepts of reconciliation that suggest injustice can remain while oppressor and oppressed are reconciled cheaply and superficially.

Albert's role in the development and writing of the *Kairos Document* was immense, even though he tried to downplay it. One should know that it was never meant to be a document at all. We, as ministers in a conflict situation, were reflecting on how best to make sense of the position we found ourselves in. Albert participated in these discussions, sometimes at great personal risk, as meetings in the townships were often raided by security police. He collected our thoughts and wrote them up. He then used his underground skills to distribute drafts to other Christian activists around the country, who reflected on and added to the document to the point where it made sense to be published. Those efforts were accelerated after one of our comrades, who was in possession of a draft, was arrested in the Eastern Cape. The security police obviously did not grasp the significance of what they had in their hands. We certainly did. So, we hastened our publication efforts and distributed it to activists countrywide lest they were thwarted by the regime.

In the context of the development of the *Kairos Document*, for me, the language of 'tyranny' in the document was powerful in clarifying my own theological understanding, and that language emerged largely from a non-Pentecostal perspective. It arose primarily from those Church denominations that understood law and power relations and that the struggle against tyranny could be a long one. Small victories needed to be celebrated and consolidated if the struggle was to prevail and tyranny overthrown.

In many ways that is also the lesson for today. The struggle is not over and if we are to pay tribute to people like Albert, we need to recognise that and take up the mantle from them. That was my message to Albert the last time I saw him before his death. While physically frail, he was not just deeply troubled by the state of the country, but he was also in deep pain. In my last visits to Sister Bernard Ncube and Archbishop Desmond Tutu before their deaths, I witnessed the same pain of being equally traumatised about what had become of the South Africa for which they had sacrificed and risked their lives. They were all deeply wounded by seeing their comrades (their family) collaborating with tyranny, choosing sides with the rich and powerful and turning their backs on the poor and oppressed. To truly honour those who gave us hope and meaning during the struggle against

Apartheid, we need to recommit ourselves to choosing sides with the poor and oppressed. This is as true for South Africa as it is for the unfolding geo-political reality, where countries are striving to sustain or build power relations based on dehumanising inequality.

The theological construct that has been bequeathed to us by Albert and other Christian activists must give us hope. It tells us not to give up and to have, as Paul puts it, 'Hope against hope' (Rom 4:18).

Albert at a launch of the United Democratic Front (UDF) Million Signature Campaign against the Tricameral Parliament constitutional amendment January 1984.

The Story of the *Kairos Document*

Molefe Tsele

It may be stating the obvious to say context matters. To say context matters is more than an acknowledgement that all theology is contextual. The context that gave rise to the *Kairos Document* was essentially the struggle for the affirmation of the faith of the Gospels, in a context of an oppressive system that equally claimed its progeny in the faith of the Bible. In that sense, Contextual Theology is a genre of theology drawing from the same wells of the liberation tradition, along with Black Theology, feminist theologies, and liberation theologies of the South and Third World. It was in that tradition of Contextual Theology, that we must locate Fr Albert Nolan. He saw himself as a practitioner located within that context, being formed by it, and, in turn, engaging and shaping it. Our starting point, therefore, is the struggle context that gave birth to the *Kairos Document*,[1] because this was from the perspective of the faith of the gospels, no ordinary context.

The date is 14 June 1985, and Operation Plecksy[2] undertaken by the then South African Defence Force (SADF) unleashes a deadly cross-border raid in Gaborone, Botswana, claiming twelve lives, killing Botswana citizens and exiled members of the African National Congress (ANC) including, among the victims, women and children. The brutality and deadly effect of this incident removes any doubt in our minds that we are engaged with a system that is intrinsically evil.

---

1. The *Kairos Document* (Braamfontein: Skotaville, 1986, 2nd edition), is a product of the work of the Institute for Contextual Theology, which was then headed by Reverend Frank Chikane, and Fr Albert was head of Research, with Reverend Tsele as junior researcher and editor of ICT News, the Institute's quarterly publication.
2. South African History Archives and Truth and Reconciliation Commission Report.

A month later, on 20 July 1985, in response to mass protests against the rule of the Apartheid government, PW Botha declared a State of Emergency.[3] The State of Emergency paved the way and provided the justification for the introduction of draconian laws and regulations which paved the way for a complete clamp-down on protests, the curtailment of media and civil rights, the mass detentions and house arrest of hundreds of anti-Apartheid activists, and the introduction of the Internal Security Act, under which security forces became a law unto themselves.

As oppression intensified and more and more resisted, so many died. It became clear that this was not a normal context. This unique context, characterised by a cycle of resistance followed by even harsher retaliation, created a new reality of daily deaths and funerals.

It was in this context and in seeking to respond to this new reality of death and dying, that a group of theologians and clergy met one winter morning at St Paul's Anglican Church's Ipelegeng Community Centre, in Crossroads, Jabavu, Soweto,[4] to reflect on these unfolding events and the nature of the situation, and to question the relevance or meaning of these events for our faith. The critical question posed was: As those who profess the living faith of the gospel, how can we characterise this moment and how should we respond to it? What was clear from the onset was that this was a situation of extreme vulnerability and of the real presence of death. After intense deliberation on the nature of the crisis in which the Church finds itself, the group came to the conclusion that our fundamental problem is not the Apartheid state, but the Church itself, and the liberal theology underpinning its responses. As one of the participants remarked, the events of midnight did not change the content of the sermons of the following morning, which were prepared a few days earlier. The reflection sought to understand the nature and character of the crisis and give it a name.

---

3. Consult South African History Online: Towards a people's history: State of Emergency – 1985 Produced 21 July 2015.

4. Amongst those attending the first meeting, (that is, in addition to the ICT staff of Reverend Chikane, Fr Nolan and Reverend Tsele) were Dr Beyers Naudé, Dr Wolfram Kistner, Dr Bonganjalo Goba, Fr Lebamang Sebidi, Fr Xolile Keteyi and Reverend Elia Tema.

In one of the reflection sessions, Reverend Frank Chikane shared a personal testimony of how, during one of his many detentions and interrogations, he came to discover that the security policeman interrogating him was an elder in his own denomination. We reflected on that irony and lamented that: 'There we sit in the same church while outside Christian policemen and soldiers are beating up and killing Christian children or torturing Christian prisoners to death while yet other Christians stand by and weakly plead for peace.'[5] As the reflection went deeper into the reality of the context we were in, our conviction grew that the cardinal threat for the confession of the Christian faith was not the Apartheid state, but a Church that had become complicit through its silence and passivity. It was Fr Nolan who gave a name to the moment and said, 'the current crisis is a moment of truth for the Church'.

The point of departure for the *Kairos Document* was no longer that Apartheid is a heresy, or that it is evil. There was no debate that the Apartheid State is the antithesis of the faith of the gospel message. The prime concern was with those who claimed to profess the tenets of the gospel, and yet at best, failed to stand against the system of Apartheid, or at worst, gave it tacit endorsement and legitimacy. And so, the target of the *Kairos Document* became not so much the proponents of Apartheid, but the liberal Churches. It was the complicity and hypocrisy of these liberal Churches, that was indicted. The question for the Church was, 'What are you doing when hundreds of your members are thrown into prisons and some are murdered by agents of the state?'. This was the *Kairos Document*'s question.

The initial working title for the document was: *A Theological Comment on the Political Crisis in South Africa*. Significantly, the reflection group did not commence its work with an output of the *Kairos Document* in mind. It was not as if we gathered and decided to write the *Kairos Document*. The document was a product of intense reflection on the prevailing political crisis, the study of the scriptures, prayer, introspection on our roles, and the confession of our failure to live up to the demands of our faith. As the reflection deepened, especially our being outraged by the growing conviction of the culpability of the Church in this crisis, a new realisation began to emerge that our

---

5. *The Kairos Document*, 1985, 2.

primary problem was not so much a 'political' crisis but a theological crisis. We became more and more convinced that this was the moment of judgment for the Church and its theology. This new radical insight was captured by Fr Nolan's words that 'the moment of truth has arrived', the moment of truth for the Church and for theology itself. As this was so precarious a moment for the very being and future of the Church, it became imperative that we speak boldly and clearly about the real significance of this moment and how there can no longer be a place to hide or to sit on the fence.

Largely due to Fr Albert's clear articulation of the notion of *kairos* in the Bible, we adopted a new approach that this was a moment that simultaneously came as a judgment but also provided us a new opportunity to become true to our faith. A realisation grew that confronting us was a situation that was too critical to fail to speak out against and to denounce, but it was also a 'favourable time in which God issues a challenge to decisive action, thus a new opportunity for the Church to become the true Church of the gospel'. It was Fr Nolan who provided us with those prophetic insights that called on us not to fail to see this moment as God's time, *KAIROS*—for the Church to choose the path of the truth of the gospel. Thus, the title for the document was born, *The Kairos Document: Challenge to the Church.*

At this point, it may be necessary to make an observation about one of the factors that also contributed to the final form and content of the *Kairos Document*, namely, the *kairos* process, or the methodology of compiling the document. Having come to a consensus that a document challenging the Churches needed to be released, the follow up questions were: How should such a document be prepared? How should we avoid the risk of it being just another academic denunciation of Apartheid? How can we ensure that the document is a product of an inclusive consultative process that will be owned by those who attach their names to it?[6] The participants were mindful that by participating in the *kairos* process, they were exposing themselves to arrest by the State or even harassment by their Churches. Noting

---

6. To address these matters of methodology, the secretariat was tasked to prepare a discussion document and the draft document had to be circulated far and wide, at seminaries, at various provincial study groups, and amongst other like-minded church activists, students, and clergy, academics. Although originating out of the Institute for Contextual Theology offices, the document became the people's document.

the risk of association with the document, it was debated whether it should be published anonymously or with the signatures of the authors. The decision was that, regardless of the risks of arrest and harassment, the document must be published with names attached.

The existential threat of such a methodology, working and writing under the State of Emergency, necessitated that we conduct these broad discussions in secret, under disguise or even underground. Thus, in some areas, discussion meetings met under the pretence of Bible Study.

Even as we acknowledge the plurality of authors in the drafting process, it fell on the hand of one author to reduce this plurality of inputs through a reductive process, into a single document. This was a difficult process that needed an author who would not only faithfully capture these diverse comments, inputs and views, some of them even contradictory, but also listen to others and through a disciplined writing process, craft a coherent single document. The hand that did the miracle was the hand of Fr Albert. He collated all the comments, viewpoints, debates, big and small, and produced a document which everyone could own as their document. The end product was that it was collectively owned, whilst there was a single hand that reduced it to paper. In that way, it satisfied the original intention of the reflection group, which was to produce a people's document that could be owned by the people and could 'stand the test of biblical faith and Christian experience in South Africa'.

The ultimate objective of the project, what we called the real agenda, was not so much critique or analysis, but to wake up the faith and conscience of the Church—a call to action. Very few of the reflection group members needed convincing that Apartheid was unjust, unchristian and thus a heresy. The critical question was, what does the gospel require of us at this moment? However, even as we were focused on action, we were compelled by several events to challenge the prevailing theologies of the moment.

The starting point was to demonstrate that Apartheid was not only an ideological system about which one could hold a difference of views or debates, but that it was a theological dogma with its own view of God and the Bible, and thus was idolatrous. It became necessary to mount a challenge to this false Apartheid theology.

Another event that brought the Apartheid theology into sharp focus was the uprising in the Vaal Triangle townships starting on 3

September 1984, led by the Vaal Civic Association, an affiliate of the United Democratic Front (UDF). The uprising was brutally repressed by the State, resulting in many deaths and imprisonment of the entire leadership of the Vaal Triangle, including the entire leadership of UDF. It was in the midst of this uprising that the State distributed biblical tracts in the community, featuring the Romans 13:1–7 text which called on residents 'to obey authorities, since all government comes from God, and civil authorities were appointed by God'.

It was due to this blasphemous use of the Christian scriptures to justify the evil of Apartheid that the reflection group chose to focus on the prevalence of State Theology in the Church. The task group that worked on State Theology, focusing mainly on the misuse of the Bible to justify the Apartheid repression, as well as the appeal to the notion of peace, law and order to justify the State of Emergency, sought to expose how the State was misusing the Bible and what the real biblical tradition of resistance to tyranny meant.

From the onset, it was clear that our task was not simply to analyse the situation and expose its ills, neither was it to repeat the trite condemnations of Apartheid Theology; more than anything, we were conscious of the enormous task of developing an alternative theological model, informed by the liberating tradition of the gospels. The opening words of the Chapter 'Towards a Prophetic Theology' succinctly capture that task in saying:

> Our present crisis calls for a response from Christians that is biblical, spiritual, pastoral, and above all, prophetic. What is it then that would make our response truly prophetic? What would be the characteristics of a prophetic theology? The theology of the prophets is not vague or generalised, it speaks to the particular circumstances of a particular time and place.[7]
> – *Kairos* (1985:17).

In developing an alternative theological model, which we named Prophetic Theology, we benefitted immensely from Fr Albert's rich scholarship of the Old and New Testament teachings on the prophets. It was out of this tradition that he cautioned that:

---

7. *Kairos Document,* 1985, 17.

> To be truly prophetic, our response would have to be, in the first place, solidly grounded in the Bible. Our *KAIROS* impels us to return to the Bible and to search the Word of God for a message that is relevant to what we are experiencing in South Africa today.[8]

What was unique, was an insistence on the link between prophetic theology and context. It was in dealing with that nexus between theology and context that the model of 'Theology of the Signs of the Times' began to take shape.[9] Fr Albert was later to articulate with great clarity this nexus when he expounded: 'The starting point for prophetic theology will be our experience of oppression and tyranny, our experience of conflict, crisis and struggle, our experience of trying to be Christians in this situation'.[10]

Prophetic theology should, above all, equip us with the eye to see the situation for what it really is, not what it is superficially, which means it must unmask reality, expose the lies, and call evil by its name. It must talk to the core issues, to the heart of the matter. It must name the sin. It was in that context that the characterisation of the crisis moved from being an analysis of diverse political models or differences on how society should be structured, or even divergent views on race and class stratification, to the real issue of a system whose currency is the shedding of the blood of its victims. Once we began to link Apartheid with its maintenance costs as measured in the human dignity of persons it was destroying and the lives it was claiming, it became clear that we were being challenged to respond to a radically different enemy. Again, it took Fr Albert's theological insights to assist us in naming this enemy.

'The situation we are dealing with here is one of tyranny and oppression'.[11] When Apartheid is characterised as tyranny, and the Apartheid god as an idol, this lays the ground for a response that can only be prophetic. When seen as tyranny, it becomes a system that must be opposed by any means necessary, including the taking up of

---

8. *Kairos Document*, 1985, 17.
9. 'A prophetic response and a prophetic theology would include a faithful reading of the signs of the times', *Kairos Document*, 1985, 17.
10. *Kairos Document*, 1985, 17.
11. *Kairos Document*, 1985, 21.

arms. It becomes a situation where, even those who choose not to be involved, are by omission, involved. There is no room for neutrality or compromise[12].

The enduring challenge for the Church should be heard in the concluding text of the document where Fr Albert summarised the thinking of the group with these words:

> The Church should challenge, inspire and motivate people. It has a message of the cross that inspires us to make sacrifices for justice and liberation. It has a message of hope that challenges us to wake up and to act with hope and confidence.[13]

---

12. 'There are two conflicting projects here and no compromise is possible.' *Kairos Document*, 1985, 22.
13. *Kairos Document*, 1985, 30.

Common Ground for the Common Good

Smangaliso Mkhatshwa

Prior to meeting Albert Nolan, whom I initially came to know when I was seconded to the Southern African Catholic Bishops' Conference (SACBC) in the 1970s, I had already become aware of this supposed progressive Dominican priest working with university students in Cape Town. However, my theological and political consciousness at the time was governed by the networks I had developed at the St Peter's Seminary, first in Pevensey and later in Hammanskraal, in the 1960s, as well as the Black Consciousness Movement. The St Peter's Old Boys Association (SPOBA), which was made up mainly of black Catholic priests, had developed close relations with leaders such as Steve Biko and Barney Pityana and our spirituality and theology was heavily influenced by Black Theology which had become very popular in the country, as well as by some of the progressive developments arising from the Second Vatican Council. We were militant and were regarded with some uneasiness by some Catholic authorities.

My promotion to the SACBC was heavily debated within SPOBA at the time. There were concerns that it could weaken our militancy which, while at times an embarrassment to the Catholic authorities, had played a significant role in conscientising many black Catholics. Some previously 'compliant' black Catholics began to question the obvious racial inequalities that had penetrated not only society under Apartheid but also within the Church structures. For example, after my ordination in 1965 for the diocese of Witbank, I had been appointed assistant parish priest in Sacred Heart parish in Ackerville, where I was also to live. However, I was told by the government officials that I could only live there on condition that the white parish priest employed me effectively as a domestic worker. These, as well as many other contradictions, started to be questioned more openly following the emergence of structures such as SPOBA, whose ranks later swelled, and it assumed the name of the Black Priests Solidarity Group. The Black Priests' Manifesto which was handed over to a shocked gathering of SACBC members in January 1970 caused a lot of consternation. Led by five black priests and supported by hundreds of lay people, it sparked considerable controversy. The Manifesto decried racist practices in the Church, especially the exclusion of black priests and religious from leadership in the SACBC, including in parishes (both in white and black congregations), theological training institutions, and religious congregations. Such practices, the Manifesto asserted, compromised the official anti-apartheid stance of the SACBC.

Arguably, our militancy was somewhat diluted after my appointment at the SACBC, where I eventually stayed for eighteen years in total, eight of which were as Secretary-General. The appointment included a three-year stint at the University of Leuven, a Catholic University in Belgium, where I studied theology and philosophy. On my return, SPOBA had undergone some changes of leadership and strategy. Nevertheless, the fact that black South African priests were playing a leadership role in the Church was welcomed by many, and also played an important role in ensuring that the Catholic Church's voice in opposition to Apartheid and the injustices associated with it, was amplified. As things turned out, my new position in the SACBC also opened up new opportunities for the Black Priests Solidarity Group that emerged after the 1970 march. It enabled these formations to extend their engagements to a wider audience inside and outside the Catholic Church, including students, youth organisations, political formations, ecumenical and educational organisations. It was also at the SACBC that I began drawing on the intellectual and diplomatic muscle of Albert, who became a valuable resource. Interestingly, he was also widely respected by black theologians and members of the Black Consciousness Movement, who soon recognised his genuine commitment to fighting oppression in all forms, but especially racial oppression. I remember some of the leaders even light heartedly quipping: 'This is a black man in a white skin!'

At the SACBC, I was initially tasked with matters of justice and peace and engagements with the ecumenical movement. Here, Albert and I joined forces and I regularly turned to him not only as a bright and progressive theologian, which he was, but as someone who was also able to skilfully navigate Church politics. One of the significant roles Albert played at the SACBC was to champion the teachings of the Second Vatican Council (1962–1965) within the structures of the local Church. Announced by Pope John XXIII in 1959, its main aim was to bring the Church into the modern world, kicking and screaming as it were. In other words, to make the Church's message and teachings relevant in order to communicate the gospel more meaningfully. The Second Vatican Council documents became Albert's tool to revolutionise the pastoral work of the Church. In South Africa, that translated into a Church that was non-racial, outward looking and one that took seriously the empowerment of the local clergy and religious, as well as bringing black and white youth organisations to see themselves as one ecclesial force that was refreshing and innovative. I, too, was heavily influenced and inspired by the Second Vatican Council, the significance of which I came to fully appreciate with the help of the Dominican Fathers that lectured me at St Peters Seminary in the 1960s.

Albert had a tremendous gift for listening to all perspectives and for finding common ground. Yet he also had a way of gently shifting perspectives, albeit in a non-threatening way, towards an outcome rooted in social justice. He was able to convince people to choose to side with the oppressed, or those on the margins. Part of this came down to his intellect, which was immense; and part to his experience in working with people, including angry youth activists, and helping them to act strategically to ensure they were effective. However, I believe he also had deep and profound spiritual reserves that enabled him not only to understand the human condition, but to respond to it with great empathy and gentleness. Although he must have been angry sometimes, I can genuinely never remember seeing Albert lose his temper, even during the most stressful periods. Likewise, I don't remember him displaying any hint of intellectual arrogance and he always strove to elevate the argument or positions of the humblest participants in a meeting.

It was this humble and trustworthy presence that also made Albert such a respected and well-liked member of political formations outside of the Church, including the United Democratic Front. It was also what probably made him such an effective underground activist—a dangerous role he played with tremendous discretion and to great effect. While I was myself not able to escape arrest, imprisonment and torture, including six months in solitary confinement when I was charged with high treason by the then Ciskei government, church activists such as Albert offered, or facilitated, sanctuary for many others who were on the run from the authorities in the 1980s.

One of Albert's greatest gifts, however, was his ability to absorb, distil and analyse not only what intellectuals and theologians were saying about the brutality of apartheid, but also the thoughts and words of ordinary activists. He had an ability to listen to and interpret the humble contributions of ordinary people and translate these into a language acceptable even to the intellectuals among us. Nobody was left behind. He was also able to convert these thoughts into a coherent, yet highly accessible, written form.

While I was fully aware of his writing abilities from my time at the SACBC and from some of his books, including the international best-seller *Jesus before Christianity*, I came to appreciate it again while at the Institute for Contextual Theology (ICT), where I worked with Albert for several years after leaving the SACBC. His ability to capture the thoughts of Church activists and theologians came to the fore in the run-up to the publication of the *Kairos Document*. At the time, there was a group of what we then called progressive theologians, very much in the mould of the liberation theologians of Latin America. We had a method of doing theology—drawn from the See–Judge– Act method of the Young Christian Workers and Young Christian Students—and we were also in constant contact with political activists, students, trade unionists and church parishioners. We developed this 'Contextual Theology', which was distinct from the mainstream theology of the time. At a certain point, we decided that we should consider publishing a document to highlight the 'prophetic' stance that we felt the Church should adopt with regard to Apartheid. This should also be compared and contrasted with the compromised position of the Churches that were aligned to the ideology of Apartheid, as well as the half-hearted response of many of the other mainstream and independent Churches.

We did a thorough analysis, arrived at certain conclusions, and, after several discussions, we agreed to publish our theological intervention. After reaching that position, we realised we needed someone to put it together and, almost unanimously, all fingers pointed to Albert. It was partly because we knew he was a good technical writer, but more importantly for us, we knew that Albert could write the *Kairos Document* in a way that would make it accessible to most people.

In other words, there were other gifted academics and theological writers amongst us, but we knew they would crowd out the message with technical language. By contrast, Albert's writing would be technically perfect, but also understandable to many, many more people. So, we requested him to finalise the draft and come back to us with regular progress reports. Once the final draft was presented, it did not take long before it was adopted and the next step was all about securing as many endorsements as possible, including from high-profile church figures. Some readily signed, others held back for strategic reasons, or because they disagreed. In my view, the document had a profound impact on the Church and increased opposition to apartheid. It also stimulated greater contact with the liberation movements in exile, leading to direct contact between Church leaders and the African National Congress in Lusaka, Zambia.

The *Kairos Document* became so popular and in such demand that it was soon translated into several different languages, locally and internationally. In 1990, I led a group of theologians to Nicaragua and Cuba to engage liberation theologians as well as those involved in their own socialist struggles. We popularised the *Kairos Document* and our Contextual Theology methodology. At the end of that trip, Albert was once again the one chosen to compile a report on our findings. On a lighter note, much as Albert actively participated in struggle and cultural activities, I do not recall him singing struggle songs. The same applies to his proficiency in speaking an African language. Having lived and grown up in Cape Town, I assumed he might have learnt *isiXhosa*. This may have been because English became the unofficial official language of communication among the youth and social justice activists. It was appreciated largely because it soon became a language of protest and rebellion against Afrikaans.

I continued to work closely with Albert at ICT, where he was far more than the Research Officer his official title suggested. He built up a team of writers around him that produced various documents and theological reflections. His approach to theology was foundational. It was not based on research centres or academia, but rather it was about people, about real life. Ultimately, Albert suggested that we produce a popular magazine through which the prophetic vision and theology that we had developed at the institute could be shared with a wider audience. As a result, we launched the magazine *Challenge*, with Albert as editor. It proved to be an extremely popular medium and played a critical role for those Christians having to adjust to the profound changes that were taking place in the run-up to and in the aftermath of the 1994 democratic elections in South Africa. It was also a time when Church activists and clergy were having to come to terms with their new roles as South Africa transitioned from minority rule to democratic governance. There were many difficult decisions to be made and challenging conversations, as some of us decided to take up an active role in the African National Congress, or other liberation parties, and the unfolding political dispensation. I personally decided that I should join government and was appointed Deputy Minister of Education by President Nelson Mandela in 1996 and later Executive Mayor of the City of Tshwane in 2000.

In those early days after liberation, we were convinced that we would be able to transform South Africa in a way that was fully aligned with the values that we fought for and promoted during the struggle: a non-racial, non-sexist, and just society. None of us, including Albert, would have ever expected that dream to have been betrayed as profoundly as it has been. We would never have anticipated that the model of selfless, servant leadership promoted and implemented during the struggle would have so quickly been usurped by self-serving individuals, focused almost entirely on enriching themselves and their relatives. It was typical of Albert not to have broadcast his disappointment, but I have no doubt that he was deeply disappointed and hurt by developments. He would have been horrified by the corruption and also the violence of post-Apartheid South Africa, particularly the shocking gender-based violence that is perpetrated daily.

That said, Albert also believed deeply in the capacity of human beings to change and to change the world. He believed profoundly in the youth and the ability of young people to overcome injustice. To do so, however, they should be organised, and I think he would, thus, be praying for a revival of youth formations that could fight for social and environmental justice. Such formations made a real difference in the fight against Apartheid and would make a real difference today, especially if they could build leaders that would prioritise the 'common good' and who would choose sides with those on the margins: the poor, the unemployed and all those on the periphery. Given his deep spiritual reserves and exceptional theological insight, Albert would ultimately have died as he lived: knowing that evil can never prevail in the end. It will be defeated!

In Hiding

Brigid Rose Tiernan SNDdeN

In mid-1985, resistance to the Apartheid regime in South Africa had gathered momentum. The Apartheid government, under PW Botha, responded by declaring a partial State of Emergency in July, applicable to thirty-six magisterial districts in the Eastern Cape and in the Pretoria-Johannesburg-Vereeniging area. The following year the Act was applied nationally. We Sisters of Notre Dame, living in a community house in Melville, Johannesburg, had known Albert Nolan for over a decade. Some of us had lived and worked in the Archdiocese of Cape Town more than a decade earlier and had met him on a number of occasions and in different roles, like when he was prior of Stellenbosch. In Johannesburg, we had contact with some of our former students studying at Wits university, and through them we were aware of his strong formative influence on them as chaplain to the National Catholic Federation of Students (NCFS). After they had completed their university courses and moved into the world of work, Albert formed the Christian Action Movement (CAM) with them, using the See-Judge-Act methodology to continue engaging them in reflecting on their lives and the context in which they were living in the light of their faith. Some of us religious women (and men) were invited to join these CAM review groups and for a time I was blessed to be in one with Albert himself.

One of our SND sisters was working in the SACBC Justice and Peace Commission in Pretoria and knew Albert to be a strong reference point for all things concerned with Justice. His book, *Jesus before Christianity*, published in 1976 was read by many of us, and was a good source for us as we continued to deepen the Vatican ll call to all religious congregations to renew themselves and to read the signs of the times as we did so. His approach to gospel or evangelical poverty, as we name the vow we make at our religious profession, was something that touched and challenged us deeply. Albert had already given workshops on much of the content of this book so, after it was published, we could discard our workshop notes and have all this challenging material in one book.

When Albert approached us in the Melville, Johannesburg community, in mid-1985 and asked us if he could come and live in our community for security reasons, we didn't ask too many questions and made the necessary arrangements for this to be possible. Our house in Melville was an ordinary three-bedroomed house, with an 'annex', which provided several more bedrooms. One of us moved out of her room in the main house into the 'annex', so as to give him easier access to the ablution facilities, and a key to the back door so that he could come and go as needed. He drove a small blue car, which he managed to snuggle into a corner of our back drive-way, enabling both him and us to come and go as required.

Albert melded into our small community with great ease. Nearly each day he celebrated the Eucharist with us in our small chapel, a highlight of which was the shared reflections following the Gospel. We grew in appreciation of his familiarity with the Jesus of the New Testament. Perhaps he was writing his next book, *God in South Africa* at the time, and his original way of presenting Jesus, in the context in which we found ourselves, was challenging and inspiring.

He came and went during the day, getting to know good places in Melville to meet with a variety of people who were also involved in resistance to Apartheid. We had no idea at the time who these people were or how involved he was with the members of the banned African National Congress (ANC). For the most part he joined us for our community meal in the evening where the conversation was never dull. His simplicity was tangible. He joined in the clearing up after the meal and the washing of the supper dishes, just as we did. Whoever happened to be in our kitchen in the course of the day learnt to keep looking out of the window for any suspicious vehicles or individuals, which could have been an indication that his whereabouts had become known to the Special Branch. This was the age before cell phones and we became accustomed in time to the click when our landline was answered, an indication that our telephone was being tapped. After some weeks it seemed that Albert's whereabouts had been discovered by the Security Branch, and it was time to move on to another safe house. We had noticed a rather well-dressed individual, regularly sitting on the pavement opposite the house, who could see Albert's small blue car and presumably give information about its movement in and out of the driveway. This was enough of a hint that Albert needed to move on to another 'safe place' for his own security.

Before he left us, Albert asked us a favour. He was in regular contact with Reverend Frank Chikane, who was also in hiding at the time. He knew that Frank's wife and two small boys were missing their father enormously. Frank's birthday was coming up. Albert asked if we would be willing to arrange a small celebratory birthday party for Frank in our annex in the evening of the birthday. Frank would come to this, and would be joined by his wife and sons from Soweto. We had great joy in preparing for this event, in planning a meal that would be good for the two boys and their parents. We decorated the space appropriately to give it a festive appearance and when the family arrived, served the meal and left the family to enjoy a few hours together. We knew from the laughter that emanated from the annex that this was indeed happening. The family celebration didn't last late into the night as Frank's wife and sons had to return to Soweto. Mrs Chikane told us that she hadn't told the boys where they were going when they left home, in case they were stopped by any Security Officials or roadblocks on the way. The short, joyful family reunion was an indication of Albert's thoughtfulness and his sense of what was important to a small family, even while engaged with the serious business of bringing an end to Apartheid.

Albert's stay with us was the first of many such in the years to come, and in various ways his short sojourn among us prepared us for the kind of service that we as a small community of sisters could offer—a safe house for meetings and for hiding people on the run from security officials. Our house had the gift of not being a pretentious one. It was a 'convent' in the post–Vatican ll tradition. Its members learnt with Albert how to be a community 'at the service of humanity'. Our communal life was enriched by his presence among us, an enrichment that we hope was mutual.

A Different Way of Doing Theology

Larry Kaufmann CSsR

Writing about Albert Nolan is not, nor should it be, an academic exercise. Albert was a great theologian, there's no doubt, but he shunned the idea of a theology that did not touch the lives of people; indeed, a theology that was not 'Good News', that was not gospel, that was not deeply rooted in Jesus himself and Jesus in the life of people. So, I am not going to attempt a clear systematic analysis of Albert as a contextual theologian at the Institute for Contextual Theology (ICT), where I worked with him for many years. Besides, I have already done that in my doctoral dissertation on 'Contextual Theology in South Africa: An Analysis of the Institute for Contextual Theology'. My interest here is to sit quietly, to watch and observe Albert anew, albeit through memory. Perhaps from that I will be able to draw out some of the innumerable lessons that we can learn from Albert's extraordinary legacy.

When I joined ICT at the beginning of 1990 it was situated in an old building in Braamfontein, Johannesburg. Cramped space was shared by several members of staff. Albert and I were tucked into a small dark office facing the huge brick wall of the building behind us—we would have struggled with South Africa's current load-shedding problem to get any work done. That's not entirely true. Albert did not work with a PC; he did all his work with pencil, paper and rubber in his neat, clear handwriting. He said writing with a pencil helped him to think; and the rubber helped him to change his mind if necessary. Once he had finished a document or whatever he was working on at the time, Albert would take it to one of the secretaries for typing.

Less than a year after I joined ICT, Nelson Mandela was released from prison. Albert was excited and said we would have to publish something. 'This is a new sign of the times', he said, 'and it requires a theological reflection. I have to be away for a week, so you make a start. Write a draft and when I get back we will work on it together'. He suggested two things. First, that I ask as many people as possible what they thought about this historic event, particularly in the rural areas where I ministered at weekends in the Rustenburg area, and also that I was to read up as many news items as possible and pay attention to reports of what ordinary people were saying. The second thing I was to do was trawl the Scriptures for any light they could throw on this historic event in our country.

Biblical references and reflection were easy for me, a synch really, because I had done something that I never normally do and have never done since. During my own detention of a mere two weeks in prison in 1986—a drop in the ocean compared to Mandela's twenty-seven years—I underlined in my bible any verse that had a reference to arrest, detention, interrogation and the like, beginning with the story of Jesus himself, but then going on to references to the imprisonment of the early disciples in the Acts of the Apostles and in the writings of Paul himself. I had done that as an encouragement to myself in prison, but now I was able at a glance to return to an abundance of relevant verses for a contextual theological reflection on the release of Nelson Mandela.

The following week, feeling chuffed with myself, I presented Albert with my first draft of my first project at ICT. He took hold of it and got no further than the opening line when he said, 'No, this won't do. This won't capture anyone's attention. This is too academic, starting off with such an inane phrase as "the Bible has many things to say about imprisonment". Much too boring! But let me see what else you've written, we might find a sentence there that will capture people's attention as an opening line.' As Albert continued reading what I had written he kept saying that this is not Contextual Theology, this does not speak to people. Fortunately, he affirmed my collection of Scripture texts, which would save time researching it. Duly put in my place, I gradually came to see what Albert was getting at. I can say that that's when my training began, working with this brilliant theologian, but most of all seeing how the theology he was writing was true to people, to their struggles, to their language and also true to the vision and purpose of ICT. All this 'true to . . .' would be contained in the booklet that we published, *The Release of Nelson Mandela: Reading the Signs of the Times.*

It is perhaps appropriate at this juncture to say more about ICT's vision and purpose. For that we need to go back to the watershed year in South Africa's history: 16 June 1976, and the Soweto schoolchildren uprising. In the wake of that event, in some Church and theological circles questions began to be asked. What is the role of the Church in this crisis? Does theology have any contribution to make in putting an end to the evil and oppressive system of Apartheid? How can committed Christians minister to people of the black townships whose daily bread is the bullets of the police?

It was these soul-searching questions that brought together a group of South African theologians (Allan Boesak, Walter Gill, James Cochrane, Renate Cochrane and Tony Saddington) in Cape Town in 1980, advocating a theology that would respond to a situation of conflict and oppression. The suggestion was made that an institute be founded specifically for this purpose. One year later, ICT was launched in Johannesburg, with Elia Tema as Acting Director, Cedric Mayson as Publications Officer and Frank Chikane as Research Assistant. Gradually, others became involved, not least Albert Nolan, who brought with him the experience of his involvement with YCS (Young Christian Students) and its See–Judge–Act method of theological reflection.

They must have been doing something right. Within two months, two of the staff members were detained by the South African Security Forces: Frank Chikane, arrested on 20 November 1981 and held for 231 days without charge or trial, and Cedric Mayson, detained on 23 November 1981 and only brought to trial in February 1983, more than a year later.

Meanwhile, others continued to implement the vision. ICT was firmly established, taking theology out of the university and the academy and finding a *locus theologicus* within the context of the daily struggles of ordinary people, particularly the victims of Apartheid.

There can be no denying the key role Albert played. He was passionate about developing a theology that arose from and spoke to the hopes and dreams, fears and challenges, of ordinary people. But before ICT could speak, it had to learn to listen. Albert, truly a Dominican committed to his Order's motto, *Veritas–Truth*, was convinced that the Spirit of Truth moved through the faith questions which ordinary people were asking. He often, jokingly, spoke about the rigorous scholastic theology he studied on the road to ordination as a priest, 'that was answering questions people were not even asking!'

I had had the same Catholic seminary training. However, working with Albert for three years as a member of ICT's staff was a delightful conversion experience; delightful first by being in his jovial company, and delightful because the weight of my own theological baggage was increasingly lightened as I sought, like Albert, to 'listen to what the Spirit is saying to the Churches' and to heed the warning of Jesus: 'You know what the weather is doing, but you do not know how to read the signs of the times'.

Contextual Theology takes seriously the notion that the lived, contextual experiences of history are a *locus theologicus*. It was so for the prophets. And it was so for Jesus. How many of Jesus' teachings emerge from acute observation of people and events? One of my favourite examples is the story of the widow's mite, Mark 12:41–44.

> Jesus sat down opposite the place where the offerings were put and watched the crowd putting their money into the temple treasury. Many rich people threw in large amounts. But a poor widow came and put in two very small copper coins, worth only a few cents.
>
> Calling his disciples to him, Jesus said, 'Truly I tell you; this poor widow has put more into the treasury than all the others. They all gave out of their wealth; but she, out of her poverty, put in everything—all she had to live on.'

Voila! See–Judge–Act! Jesus *sees* what happens, *judges* it, and *acts* by teaching his disciples the lesson it gives. Albert lived this method—in himself and in his work at ICT.

There is a word one finds constantly in Albert's writing: 'challenge'. It is a word found in the title of one of his books, *God in South Africa: The Challenge of the Gospel*. It is a word found in the titles of two of ICT's publications, *The Kairos Document: Challenge to the Church*, and a lesser-known sequel, *Violence, the New Kairos: Challenge to the Churches*. Albert always saw the signs of the times as challenging, and he also saw the Gospel of Jesus Christ as challenging (as did Dietrich Bonhoeffer, who spoke of the 'cost' of discipleship).

It is no surprise therefore, that Albert, for the title of the popular magazine that he started and which ICT launched in 1992, chose *Challenge: Church and People*. Ever passionate about involving people in theological reflection, Albert initiated a feasibility study in which he involved communications experts to explore the best medium for popular theology. The study indicated that an affordable magazine would be the way to go. This was a few years shy of the IT explosion and social media.

I was still on the staff of ICT then and worked closely with Albert in preparation for the launch of the magazine, and worked with him once it got going. He left it in my care for three months as acting editor with Andrew Johnson as manager while he went away on sabbatical, doing research for what was to become his next book, *Jesus Today*.

Challenge: Church and People had a relatively short life, and it is hard to judge its impact. I know pastors who used it with their congregations, especially for the Bible studies and other reflective items it contained, and I know a pastor of a wealthy white parish who told me that the minute it arrived he tossed it in the nearest bin!

After a hiatus of some years, during which I was away writing my dissertation on the history, method and contribution of ICT, Albert and I next resumed contact in KwaZulu-Natal, where Albert was based at the Dominican student house in Pietermaritzburg and where I was teaching, first at St Joseph's Theological Institute and later at UKZN. Albert asked me to be resonator as he wrote *Jesus Today: A Spirituality of Radical Freedom*. Reading the signs of the times (yet again!) of the widespread quest for spirituality, Albert—typically—applied it to the person of Jesus, wondering what Jesus' own spirituality might have been.

What I remember about the process while creating his book is that every bit of wall space in Albert's study was covered with newsprint full of headings, sub-headings, arrows linking sections, or question marks indicating a doubt about including something. As soon as Albert had completed a chapter he sent it to me for comment, corrections, or suggestions. I kept asking myself, who am I to be working thus with such a world-renowned theologian? But my come-uppance day finally arrived when Albert sent a certain chapter (Recall the way he dismantled my first writing effort at ICT on the release of Nelson Mandela).

The piece was, as always, well written, clear and inspiring. But the tone was different; somehow it did not harmonise with all the previous chapters I had worked on with Albert. I took it to him and, with a mischievous twinkle in the eye, asked him where he had published this piece before as it read like something that could stand on its own. With his infectious laugh, he admitted to being caught out and immediately set to work writing another piece on the same theme, but within the tenor of the book as a whole.

As an aside, I want to suggest that this experience in itself highlights the importance of the way context shapes meaning. Out of context, that piece did not work as a chapter in *Jesus Today*. But in the context of the book, I think it is one of the best. And no, I am not going to reveal which one it was!

Working with Albert with an eye to exploring the spirituality of Jesus was, for me, most providential. It was during that time that I was stripped by the Archbishop of Durban of my faculties (license) to preside and preach as a Catholic priest. Albert counselled one thing only: Practice the silence of Jesus before Pilate and the High Priests.

If I may venture a final word on Albert the people's theologian in the sense that I hope I have described above, namely of theology as a community exercise best done through dialogue than in the isolation of a library or an academic ivory tower. By this time, we were both living in Johannesburg. Albert started a spiritual reading book club. We met regularly at the Dominican house in Mondeor. I remember the first book we pored over together, Martin Laird's *Into the Silent Land*. Once again, Albert's humility and ability to value the contribution of each participant shone through. His own insights, were, of course, profound and I soon came to realise that Albert had moved into a more intentional contemplative phase of his life. But that too was contextual—his own.

Conclusion

After Albert died there was a mass outpouring of grief, sadness, loss, gratitude, tribute, memories and more. I say 'mass' not massive, because of its closer association with 'the masses'. The outpouring was positive proof that Albert had served people in great numbers and had served theology as a right and privilege of 'the people' (another of his favourite phrases).

My own debt to Albert is enormous. He taught me to write with ordinary people in mind, to write with attention to simplicity of style, to be accessible yet not without challenge. He taught me to read the Scriptures in a new way. He taught me to laugh at myself and, in appropriate ways, at the follies of others. He taught me amazing qualities of friendship. He gave me a renewed commitment to contemplative spirituality.

Most of all, more than anything else, Albert taught Jesus: Jesus before Christianity, Jesus before institutional religion, Jesus of the Gospels, Jesus radically free by being immersed in the Love of the Father and driven by the Love of the Spirit. In a word, the *Veritas* of Jesus.

Albert giving a talk at a Justice and Peace conference, Diocese of Johannesburg C 1986–1988 Koinonia Retreat Centre.

Prophetic Ecumenism

Edwin Arrison

A letter to Albert Nolan

Preface

On 26 November 2022, a memorial service was held in Cape Town for Albert Nolan. This was on a Saturday before the beginning of the Advent Season. This memorial service was attended by his sister and some other family members and other Cape Town-based friends and colleagues of Albert.

Because I knew Albert and worked with him on a few things from the early 1980s, I was asked to speak at the memorial service on the topic of 'Albert's ecumenism'. I was travelling in the USA when I was asked to do this, and so I contemplated—on train journeys and flights—on what I would say and also, what genre I would use. I decided that a 'Letter to Albert Nolan' would be the most creative way for me to express what I would have wanted to say to him, and also to those who might read the letter.

As an Anglican priest, I knew how Albert respected me and my own activism and reflection. With him, there was never any sense of superiority and I was in fact surprised when he published some articles I had written for Challenge *magazine. Not only did he publish an article I wrote on the Good Samaritan in the South African context, he also found a cartoonist to do a set of drawings about the article!*

I knew about his work with the African-Initiated Churches and whilst I did not understand everything, I deeply respected that work. Because I am deeply involved in ecumenical work, and head up an Ecumenical Youth Leadership Training programme (see https://volmoedyouth.org.za)—and because this memorial service was being held in the Western Cape—I could bring some key ecumenical figures into the letter, such as the Moravian Khoi evangelist, Vehettge and the Xhosa woman who helped to take the Good News to the Xhosa people, Wilhelmina Stompjes. I knew that Albert would have appreciated this bit of contextual missiology and he would particularly have appreciated the fact that I brought the voices of two key African women into the conversation.

Albert was way ahead of his time. One of the things I do not mention in the letter, was when he published an article I had written in 1993 about Bishop Samir Kafity, the Palestinian Anglican Bishop of Jerusalem. In 2009, I gave Albert a draft copy of the Palestine Kairos *document. After reading it, his comment to me was: 'This is so much better than our* Kairos Document!*'. I mentioned this to the Palestinian Christians who drafted their* Kairos *document, and they were overwhelmed by this comment.*

I dedicate the letter below to the memory of Albert and also to all those who are marginalised.

Dear Albert

Ever since I heard of your passing, I have been thinking so much about you, re-reading and reflecting on some of your writings: how crystal clear you always were! How patient you were. How you would laugh at things you found either absurd or funny. Actually, how uncomplicated you were.

I think it was you who explained to me about the Order of Preachers, the Dominicans, and I was almost always in awe of your preaching ability. I remember you saying that preaching should really be the fruit of deep contemplation.

But your humility is probably the thing I will remember most. You would explain things so patiently and would untie theological knots so easily. While some theologians wanted to make theology as complicated as possible, you moved in the opposite direction and even freely gave the title of 'theologian' to all those who reflected on God and faith. You wanted the *Challenge* magazine to be a magazine of theological reflection that was accessible to everyone and even to be read on taxis! I really wonder if there is another theologian who equally shared your passion and longing for the practice of 'people's theology'. For you it was not only a theory to be explained or expounded upon; you practised it and did everything possible to make it a reality.

I remember saying: 'one day when I grow up, I want to be like Albert!' So, thank you and thank God for the gift of you.

I want to reflect on your ecumenism, but I think I cannot really do that without briefly reflecting on your Roman Catholic-ness. Fortunately, I come from an Anglo-Catholic or Tractarian background—something you would have appreciated as these tracts were written for lay Christians—so Roman Catholicism is a relatively easy jump for me. But of course, as I also explained to you, there is a certain kind of Roman Catholic-ness that I find difficult, especially the kind that mostly tries to exclude me and others and makes us feel that we are not quite Christian enough. So, thank God for Pope Francis today! But long before Pope Francis, you showed me that there is another kind of Roman Catholicness, for lack of a better word a truly 'Catholic' Roman Catholic-ness, or even an ecumenical Roman Catholic-ness, but certainly a welcoming, open Roman Catholic-ness. Perhaps if this was the approach of the first Portuguese when they landed here, the Khoi people might have welcomed them here at Salt River and most of us might be Roman Catholic today! But like most colonists, they came to plunder and steal, and so they were sent packing only to be replaced by the Dutch and the English and we know what happened then. But you would have been proud of the work of the great Khoi women and Moravian evangelists at Genadendal: Vehettge (who was baptised Magdalena) and of course Wilhelmina Stompjes, who was so moved by the Good News that she wanted it to be taken to her people, the Xhosa people. Besides calling them evangelists and pioneers, you would have given them the title of 'theologian', the first to experience Dutch Reformed Church oppression and engage in the 'Church Struggle' in South Africa.

You made it your life's work to experiment with, to produce and introduce a theological vaccine against the viruses of colonial theology, the strongest of which was *kairos* theology! But as you would have taught us and as we still know, the Church is and remains a site of struggle (and our primary site of struggle).

Since meeting you, I have been fortunate to meet many other Roman Catholics like you and long for, look forward to and urge the coming of the day when we can truly be the one, holy, Catholic and apostolic Church. Albert, pray for us as we strive towards this. Pray for us as we long for this. Pray that this may become part of our Advent longing.

Your ecumenism was rooted in your catholicity and for that reason, many of us could embrace both and use these words interchangeably. But the spirit and substance of your ecumenism was not 'Church ecumenism', but 'prophetic ecumenism'. What would be the point of ecumenism if it was to preserve the unity of Empire theology and Church structures rooted in patriarchy? And so, you told us that prophecy is about 'afflicting the comfortable and comforting the afflicted'. It was this spirit and substance that led you towards the poor, the suffering, the marginalised.

If catholicity and ecumenism were to mean anything, it had to serve them, make sense to them, liberate them, otherwise it would simply be empty church words. You therefore gave a special substance to these words. You saw God in the faces and the lives of the poorest and did not practice social distancing with them, but unity.

For you, Church unity would not make sense if it did not privilege and centre and liberate the poor and if it did not privilege and centre and liberate those who are most excluded. Towards the end of your life, you taught us about the importance of seeing our interconnectedness with all of creation and our need to speak up against the destruction of the environment. This message has become ever more urgent.

I remember that you had a special concern for the African Initiated Churches. You spent a lot of time with some of their leadership, particularly the ones among them that were the most progressive, as you knew that that is where the majority of Christians in this country were located. In 1988, you asked Malusi Mpumlwana of the Order of Ethiopia to write the foreword to your book, *God in South Africa*, thereby signalling the need for his and other voices to be heard.

You and I had several conversations about *kairos* theology and you even gave me your last copy of your *Kairos Document*. The only thing that is underlined is the following:

> *Kairos* theology is an attempt by concerned Christians in South Africa to reflect on the situation of death in our country. It is a critique of the current theological models that determine the type of activities the Church engages in to try to resolve the problems of the country. It is an attempt to develop, out of this perplexing situation, an alternative biblical and theological model that will in turn lead to forms of activity that will make a real difference in the future of our country.

This is still worth reflecting on today as we continue to face a situation of death in our country and as we still need to develop alternative biblical and theological models that are rooted not amongst the elite, but amongst the poor.

The last time you spoke at a *Kairos* event was when we celebrated the thirtieth anniversary of *Kairos* in 2015. You were very happy with that gathering and I remember Zach Mokgoebo coming to me with tears in his eyes and thanking us for bringing everyone together!

You once suggested that perhaps we need a *Kairos* Foundation. We even speculated about a *Kairos* Order and what that might look like. We did not get very far with these conversations, but perhaps all you wanted to do was plant a seed.

Albert, as we enter a new liturgical year, pray for us. Pray that we may be guided by God's Holy Spirit to hear what God is saying at this moment in the midst of our current challenges and to be faithful to that.

We thank God for you.

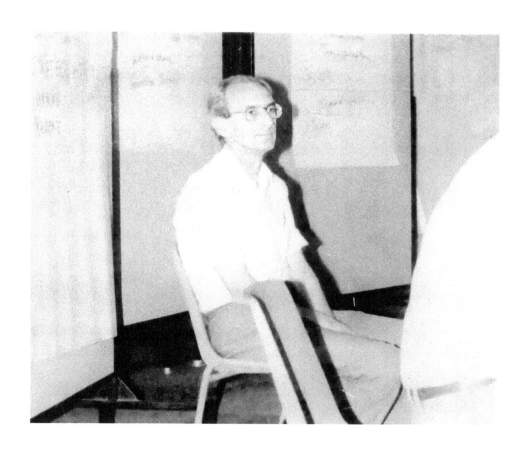

A Grounded Intellectual

Leslie Dikeni

Introduction

Writing this note about Albert Nolan gives me an apparent contradictory sense of fulfilment and being distraught. Fulfilment because of the opportunity I had to encounter a man with such intellectual integrity. Distraught because it is not easy to part with a spiritual intellectual who has become part of one's social intellectual life. It was only after his death that I realised that the encounters I had with him embodied a journey through a multitude of conversations, situations and events while being an activist in South Africa.

I have had many different social encounters with this activist, priest, intellectual and pedagogical theologian. My first encounter was during my formative years (in the early 1980s) as a member of the Young Christian Students (YCS).

During this period, the late Chris Langefeld (another great scholar and theologian) was the national chaplain and Norman Malatjie the National Coordinator. The other members of the National Team were Mike Mailula (national organiser), Luke Connell (national publications Rep), Nhlanhla Makhathini (national secretary) and Charles Mabaso (national treasurer). In short, I developed in YCS from being a regional coordinator and afterwards joined the national team as the national organiser and later national coordinator.

It will be very difficult and laborious here (for reasons of time and space) to offer a detailed account of all these different experiences that I have gained over the years in these encounters with Albert. Instead, I offer a thumbnail sketch of the debates that used to take place during that period; in other words, to sketch a picture of the many situations that shaped those debates.

These were debating moments in workshops, the writing of texts in offices, meetings of YCS and even sometimes in restaurants where the relationship between theory and praxis, and how these relate to our faith and generally to societal problems, was questioned. Albert's contribution emphasised that theory, faith and empirical practice are all interrelated and mutually dependent. Hence, the popularly known method 'See-Judge-Act' served as a guiding approach to those problems.

My other prominent encounters with the author and activist were outside YCS. Key to those was when I was a steering committee member of the Institute for Contextual Theology (ICT) and later was working for the Cape Town-based Theology Exchange Programme (TEP).

During these encounters Albert was always there for consultation, to advise on how to deal with these most complex and difficult organisational problems. He would even go to an extent of offering his advice and time for my own personal and social life problems.

In this regard, I offer a few examples of the type of interventions Albert made that helped me be a better activist and person.

Activist and organisational experiences

During this turbulent time, I was working for the Young Christian Students (YCS) and also serving on the steering committee of the Institute for Contextual Theology (ICT). Of importance here is that I was also an underground member of the then banned African National Congress (ANC). In the underground of ANC, I was a member of its military wing, Umkhonto we Sizwe (MK), and served the military force in various capacities.

I was offered an opportunity by *New Nation* (a progressive prominent weekly newspaper) to be interviewed on the 'state of the country' and how these political events relate to religious faith, the Church as an institution, society at large and the organisations I was serving and working for.

Amongst many different social inputs I gave to the journalist was the following particular social analysis:

> . . . We are in a situation of increased repression by the State on the South African society at large and the use of police, soldiers and other security apparatuses to brutally suppress dissent by anyone in the country. There is the general banning

> of civil society organisations, progressive organisations, the detention of political activists and prominent people of faith and the killing of citizens in the townships and elsewhere.
>
> Indeed, at this time the bombing of the offices of the South African Council of Churches is one of the most direct attacks on religious institutions by the state. All these draconian actions by the state and its security apparatus require us to consider banning a police presence in the places of worship (they must be banned from churches and other religious institutions). Henceforth, people of faith can no longer and should not worship with the same 'killers'.

Unbeknown to me the interview with the journalist reached many ears within the public domain including those of Albert. Soon afterwards, I was invited by Albert for a discussion on the interview. He briefly acknowledged the relevance of my interview with the journalist from *New Nation*. However, he questioned my thinking and the statement I made at the time. He suggested: 'Would it not have been better to rather have the police attending religious places of worship (church, synagogue, etc) and be ministered to by the clergy which might help them to change their consciousness and behaviour instead of isolating them from these places of worship?'

I interpreted this to mean that places of worship are 'sites of struggle' similar to a factory, a university, school and other community-based institutions. In these sites of struggle, different social groups and/or individuals compete for power, ideas and resources. They are also where dominant and less dominant religious and ideological social actors exist and compete over ideas. In other words, these are places where 'progressive' and 'reactionary' forces operate. Hence, our primary goal (among others) within these spaces is to socially transform them in order for them to serve society better. Through this process, different social actors operating in these various institutions will gradually become more socially conscious.

Another informative encounter with Albert took place while I was working for TEP as a field worker with the role to facilitate dialogue between South African and Latin American social activists, religious groups, trade unions, members of different political parties and liberation movements. Key to this process was to facilitate and create social platforms for different social movements from these countries to share organisational experiences and engage in discourse on experiences of struggle in their different countries.

During one of my field work travels in South Africa, I had to accompany a prominent Nicaraguan scholar and activist from the Sandinista movement, Alejandro Bendaña. My assignment was to organise 'face-to-face' meetings for him with various organisations in South Africa to interact with and share experiences on the process of negotiations here and on the transitional political process in Nicaragua after the Sandinistas had re-taken power under the leadership of Daniel Ortega. These included meetings with trade union organisations, faith-based organisations, different members of the (then unbanned) liberation movements, civic organisations, community-based organisations, non-governmental organisations (NGOs), academic institutions and different individual prominent South African leaders.

Several of these various meetings included Albert and his colleagues. During this process, Albert was one of the people with whom I chose to review my work programme and content thereof on an ongoing basis.

In one of the reviews, I discussed with him how the programme was unfolding and raised concerns about the cultural and social differences observed as a host during my travels with my visiting scholar. The important issue I wanted to understand was how to aesthetically treat him socially and culturally. For example, do I place him in some township house or place him in affluent suburbs and/ or hotels, taking into account that he was an activist and needed to experience the culture of the South African 'oppressed' in its fullness?

His response to my ignorant and naive questions was very swift and clear: 'Different people, different tastes, different cultures and different lifestyle behaviours must be respected and tolerated. Thus, we cannot impose our cultural tastes and lifestyles on others. Also, the programme is very intense and your visitor needs to be afforded the necessary comfort and space to rest.'

Knowledge and pedagogy

In many of my conversations with Albert during those years, what came out was his concern for serious study and research. In this regard, he meant reading widely, and to be constantly prepared to learn new things from people from all walks of life. Hence his emphasis: 'Read religious books, literature, scientific books, books on music, learn from everyday life experiences and constantly read the signs of the times and be informed by them.' This meant, amongst other things, to avoid dogma and refuse to be deterministic.

I came to realise that knowledge was not something esoteric—as others I had encountered during that period (and now) have assumed. Rather, in my view and observations it was a 'social construct' where social actors through their 'everyday' life struggles and experiences interact and through this process 'construct' and 'deconstruct' knowledge and shape society in different ways.

This was demonstrated to me through my working with him in different situations. While he was working for ICT, for example (as editor of *Challenge*), I would occasionally be asked to contribute pieces for the magazine. The themes requested would derive from previous discussions we had had over intense conversations or remarks I had made in a workshop, meeting, conference or social event. I would also on occasion be asked to read manuscripts and offer commentary when necessary. He would do the same for me and I received the best pedagogical advice for my texts on various subjects.

In many different ways Albert contributed immensely to my educational and intellectual life as an activist. He did so both materially and in helping to shape my theoretical and conceptual analytical framework of society.

Materially he supported me by organising and writing letters of support to funders for me to further my studies and research projects. He also maintained contact with me while I was pursuing my studies in Europe and Scandinavia (mainly Norway, the Netherlands and France) by offering encouragement, advice and constantly engaging theoretically and conceptually with me from a distance.

He did this during his own travels and through writing and communicating with me telephonically. He always encouraged me to think harder, develop patience in debates, maintain discipline in writing, think independently and finally think with the other.

He was indirectly a sounding board for ideas during my underground operative days as an activist during that turbulent period in South Africa. He did the same when I was working for the unbanned ANC by encouraging me to always distinguish between 'subjectivity' and 'objectivity'. Most importantly, on approaching research work he would emphasise the need to not overlook people whom others treat as oddballs, but rather to treat them as research subjects that are knowledgeable and capable. 'These subjects may reveal other factors relevant to your research that are often taken for granted by many researchers', he would say.

The theologian: intellectual and activist

Concerning the role of the intellectual, Albert says it all:

> The intellectual life is not a job or a profession. It is a way of life that provides a service to one's community or society. The intellectual is often equated with the academic, the writer or the professional speaker. These may be some of the ways that the intellectual communicates with his or her society, but the professional academic writer is not always a committed intellectual. The intellectual is someone who serves others by dedicating his or her life to the pursuit of truth. My contention will be that one cannot do this effectively without some measure of what we generally call 'spirituality'.[1]

Albert Nolan was elected Master of the worldwide Dominican Order in 1983 and he declined the election in order to continue his work against Apartheid in South Africa. When interviewed about his reasons for declining he had the following to say:

> I did not accept the offer, because I wanted to continue my work of activism and doing theology in South Africa. I did this because the Apartheid regime used Christian theology to justify their policies. It therefore seemed more important to fight this bad theology than to take up a prestigious international position in the Church . . . However, I have now [in the democratic South Africa] an Albert Luthuli presidential award for doing theology in South Africa . . . [Laughs].[2]

Paraphrasing Diarmuid O'Murchu, the theologian intellectual, Albert further elucidates his contentions and convictions.

---

1. In *The Povery of Ideas: South African Democracy and the Retreat of the Intellectuals*, edited by Leslie Dikeni and William Gumede (Johannesburg: Jacana Media, 2010), 57.
2. *The Povery of Ideas*, 66.

> O'Murchu, among others, argues that while spirituality has been with us from the beginning, religion was introduced 5000 years ago, and today spirituality is flourishing outside the great world religions. Thus, when I speak of the life of the intellectual, I do not mean that the intellectual must become a member of a religious institution attending services in a church, mosque, synagogue or temple, though for some this may seem invaluable.
>
> In a similar way, spirituality very often includes belief in God, but there are forms of spirituality that may refer to the transcendent in some other way and in that sense do not include a belief in a personal god. In my own spirituality, belief in God is absolutely fundamental, but in this essay, I will speak about spirituality without reference to God . . .[3]

Hence, as we can see above, Albert does not treat intellectual thinking, spirituality and his theological convictions as separate different entities. For him they are different and yet interrelated and interwoven. Indeed, it is almost unthinkable to separate them.

Nolan was, in his own distinctive and sometimes idiosyncratic way, a formidable intellectual who shaped the contours of world theology, but still would spare time for the young activist that I was.

Many of us who were and are thinking with him and are attempting to think beyond him will remember him for the See–Judge–Act method that he contextualised, deepened and introduced to us and South African society. In a nutshell, a method (in my own interpretation thereof) that seeks to constantly connect knowledge, theory and praxis.

His views on politics, theology, philosophy, world history and relations among different religions will always be an issue for debate. But the standing Albert Nolan will eventually retain can only result from the relevance of his thinking for all societies in the world at large.

He was indeed a true intellectual giant who did not seek to gain face nor fear to lose face. Yet he had many different faces. He was a man who truly lived a public life and was accessible to all in society.

For many of us he held a lighted candle that guided us when we could not see. However, even when the wax from that candle burned his hand, he kept it burning for us in South Africa and for others in the world.

---

3. *The Povery of Ideas*, 57.

Albert at wedding of Benita Pavlicevic and Mike Roussos (with Sr Brigid Flanagan Hf) 1984.

The Christian Action Movement

Benita Pavlicevic and Peter Stewart

The Christian Action Movement (CAM) was set up in the first half of the 1980s in Johannesburg by people who had been involved in university Young Christian Students (YCS) and some who were not ever in YCS but were part of review groups of post-university people. Many of these were graduates who had participated in the National Catholic Federation of Students (NCFS) and YCS and lived in Christian simple-lifestyle communities, characterised by shared values and activism, collective decision-making, sharing of chores and, in some communities, sharing of money and resources. There was also an ethic of affirmation of responsible intimacy and sexuality. This lifestyle was a direct result of the influence of Albert in our time at university in Catholic societies and YCS. These communities were the roots of CAM.

The idea of CAM was to have a post-university See–Judge–Act movement for middle-class people who, given the realities of South Africa at the time, were mostly white. CAM included lay people, sisters and priests, all of whom were involved in the struggle against Apartheid in a variety of ways—both underground and above ground—in society and in the Church. CAM members were involved in underground African National Congress (ANC) political work, the Umkhonto weSizwe (MK) military struggle and the South African Communist Party (SACP). Above-ground work included involvement in the United Democratic Front (UDF) and its affiliates, such as the Federation of Transvaal Women, UDF education structures, and the Johannesburg Democratic Action Committee (JODAC). CAM members were involved in the End Conscription Campaign (ECC), in the trade unions and in education struggles. In the Church,

CAM members participated in Justice and Peace groups, in the laity and youth councils of the SACBC, working to pressure the bishops to speak out against Apartheid and conscription, and in support of the struggles in Namibia and South Africa. We participated in the Institute for Contextual Theology (ICT), of which Albert was a leading member, and in ecumenical work.

The core of CAM was a series of review groups (numbering eight groups at one point and comprising between four and eight people in a group) which used the See–Judge–Act method to reflect on life choices, including work and activism, in the light of our faith, interpreted through liberation and contextual theology. During the 1980s and early 1990s, CAM members came together in general meetings, typically bringing together twenty–thirty members, in somewhat festive and hardworking sessions, dealing with the national context and Church issues from a broadly liberation theology perspective. These meetings were more or less regular, depending on the context at the time. The second half of the 1980s was characterised by states of emergency and mass detentions, including of CAM members, and so general meetings were less frequent as many of our members lived in hiding. However, the review group structure meant that CAM continued to exist and its members continued to review their involvement in the struggle during these times. The early 1990s was a time of looking forward to a post-Apartheid South Africa, of understanding ANC as a potential government and discerning how to participate in and support the transition to democracy. By the time of the first democratic elections, CAM had run its course, although some of the review groups continue meeting to this day.

What did Albert have to do with all of this and what impact did he have on us?

We remember Albert bringing together groups of people in the Dominican house in Houghton (Johannesburg) in the late 1970s to encourage them to start review groups. He was totally committed to the See–Judge–Act method and believed that it should be used by 'adults' as well as school and university students. Meanwhile, as YCS chaplain, Albert was also in a review group with post-university ex-YCS people and out of this the idea of CAM was born. Many of us who became part of CAM were strongly influenced by Albert during our student days when he gave a series of talks about Jesus (the precursor to his book, *Jesus before Christianity*) and when he introduced us to Liberation Theology and connected us to liberation theologians across the world.

His emphasis on Contextual Theology, and his understanding that theology was something that ordinary people *did* every day, meant that we, in our review groups and in CAM general meetings, were doing theology. Albert and Chris Langefeld were instrumental in developing and contextualising theology in CAM, while we used the Dynamic Model (borrowed from *Training for Transformation*[1]) to analyse the context and identify where our activism could best be targeted.

For many of us, this allowed our faith to develop in concert with our deepening political analysis and involvement since our faith was what informed and animated our involvement. We were politically involved because of the conditions in South Africa and the emerging mass struggle and also because we were Christian and our faith demanded it of us.

An important development at the time was the recognition that the Church itself was a site of struggle and that as Christian activists we had a role to play in ensuring that the Church spoke out on the side of justice. We engaged with the bishops on issues like the South African occupation of Namibia, the youth and the End Conscription Campaign. This was not always easy and we sometimes angered the hierarchy by the way we challenged them, but we were effective and the Church did produce statements and took stances that they might not otherwise have taken.

Albert was a master diplomat. He delivered his message by pointing to what Jesus did and what the gospel demanded of us in that context, he shared his analysis of the context, he challenged people's understanding of faith—and then expected them to come to the realisation that their practice and their lives had to change. Unlike we, who were wont to lecture and debate vigorously and annoy people, Albert used soft persuasion, which resulted in many nuns and some priests recognising that their faith had to have a justice component and they had to support the liberation of the oppressed. We would watch his impact with fascination and sometimes with impatience. Why could he not be more challenging and more forceful? But that

---

1. Anne Hope and Sally Timmel, *Training for Transformation: A Handbook for Community Workers* (Harare: Mambo Press, 1984).

was not his way! His personality was such that he could talk to anyone and meet them where they were at, and then transform their understanding of their faith and their praxis. He was the least prejudiced person we knew. He was seldom sexist, he could talk to people of any class or race or status, and they would feel he understood them and was talking directly to their reality. His message sometimes made them uncomfortable, but they never felt disrespected.

He exhibited a very different kind of leadership to what we typically saw in the struggle. He was not a prominent leader who appeared on public platforms and was cheered by crowds of people, but he nevertheless had a deep and lasting impact on many people, both those he met with and those he influenced through his writings. His impact was such that even left-wing activists who were determined atheists, were influenced by him, by his analysis and his way of working. To this day, such activists reflect on his impact, and recognise that faith and theology are important in all struggles.

Within CAM, much of our emphasis was on the struggle and politics. We sometimes discussed leadership styles and issues of domination, and we were (nominally at least) committed to feminism. But the personal aspects of our lives tended to be neglected, and later in life, Albert regretted that we had not spent more time reflecting on this and that he had not challenged us more on the personal choices and actions we took.

Albert had a very direct and lasting effect on CAM members—on our faith, lives and commitment to the dismantling of Apartheid. CAM itself, co-initiated by Albert, was a largely original structure which, for a few years, seemed to connect resonantly with that moment of history, in the intersection of the Church and faith with the broader struggle. This was not least in the affirmation it gave to its members in their activism in different sites. We will remember him for developing our commitment to liberation theology and linking our faith to our everyday struggles against Apartheid and capitalism. Today we continue to reflect on the context, the shockingly unequal structure of the economy, corruption centred in ANC, the poor governance and environmental degradation we experience daily. We look for ways to continue to struggle against these different forms of injustice. Perhaps there is a need now for similarly innovative organisations which are rooted in today's context.

Co-conspirator for God's Reign of Justice

Roxane Jordaan

Long before I met him in person, Albert Nolan touched my life in a most paradoxical way, through an encounter that was humiliating, yet ultimately lifegiving. It happened like this.

I had entered the Federal Theological Seminary (Fedsem) in Imbali, Pietermaritzburg. One of my lecturers was the late Dr Bonganjalo Goba, who taught a course on 'Church and Society'. He gave us first years an assignment exploring whether the Church reflects the elements of the Kingdom (Reign) of God. It was a good topic and I rose to the challenge. Here was I, full of first fervour, rooted in my own Church and all set to become one of its ordained ministers. Despite inevitable insecurities in one's first year, I was proud that I could 'think outside the box' as I waxed eloquent about a Jesus who cared dearly for those on the margins of society. I wrote about Jesus crossing the alienating boundaries of race, class and gender. By way of contrast, I tried to show how the Church, as I had so often experienced, manifested tendencies of racism, classism and sexism, except for the few times that it protested against the Apartheid regime. I put forward the idea that Church and society were so entangled that it was difficult to see Christianity as an organised religion in any way reflecting the values of the Reign of God. The Church had departed from the witness of Jesus in the Gospels.

Feeling pretty self-assured, so clever, so relevant, I handed in my assignment, certain that Dr Goba would be proud of me. A few days later he called me to his office, and I confidently sat down. Dr Goba asked me why I had not cited Albert Nolan's *Jesus before Christianity* (1976) in my bibliography because clearly, he said, I had used his ideas. Irony of ironies, I had not. Sure, I felt humiliated, yet there and then I 'met' Albert Nolan!

And so began a journey in which I came to know Albert's writings, his easy, accessible theology and his amazing ability to bring heart and mind together. I got to know an Albert who was a prophetic force *in* the Church and *to* the Church, and who put doctrines and sacraments in their historical context, pointing out deviations from the message of Jesus. Page after page reading Albert my eyes opened, my vision cleared, and my heart soared. It was not only Albert whom I met—it was Jesus. I wanted to be a part of his liberating message. I wanted to become his co-conspirator in working for justice, peace and the integrity of creation. I wanted to become part of a Church that would be a living memory of Christ, that embodied values of God's Reign as proclaimed by Jesus. Thank you, Bonganjalo Goba, for introducing me to Albert Nolan in such a paradoxical way!

In the mid 1980s, I finally met Albert in person. I was in awe of this unassuming man who trode lightly upon the earth, whose laughter made the space around him reverberate. He was serious about his mission to make real in the world the values of God's Reign. One of those values is joy. Albert's humour was witness to that. He spoke with ease about his love for God and his expectation that our unbinding of Jesus, wrapped and suffocated by the bands of our Church-made laws and structures, would make us participants in the unfolding of a 'Brave New World Order' (to use the title of Jack Nelson-Pallmeyer's book). For Albert, the Reign of God was not heaven-after-we-die, but something to be incarnated on earth.

But that demands, as it did for Jesus, a preferential option for the poor.

As a Dominican friar, Albert made a religious profession to follow Jesus in poverty. For him, the poverty of Jesus meant *kenosis*, self-emptying, even choosing to be powerless—paradoxically making the choice to have few choices, as the poor know too well. This insight has remained with me. Jesus' option for the poor—or as Albert liked to say, for 'the cause of the poor'—was radical. And so should it be for his true followers. To choose the poor is to choose like Jesus; indeed, it is to choose Jesus. It is the 'act' part of See–Judge–Act, the method we followed in doing contextual theology.

Some may recall the various conferences we had about 'making poverty history'. Hopes that the new political dispensation of 1994 in South Africa would have had the makings of a radical reduction in poverty have not been realised; if anything, the call to radical discipleship of Jesus is louder. During Apartheid we read Albert's writings against that backdrop. We need to read him again and again in every evolving context and to rise to his challenges, like this one from *Jesus Today*:

> Childish trust in God is also sometimes used as an excuse for not doing what we can and ought to do ourselves. I am thinking in particular of people who do not get involved in struggles for justice where they could do so, because they believe that all one needs to do is pray and then let 'God take care of it'.[1]

We need the spirituality of Jesus, ' . . . the experience and attitudes behind what he said and did, what fired and inspired him'.[2] Albert was inspired by this kind of spirituality. He was aflame with it, but not in a disembodied way. Albert was all of being human, a simple one at that. He stood squarely on the side of anyone, any form of life, that was denied a full life. The Reign of God kept unfolding as day after day Albert made his preferential option for the poor.

This is his legacy to us. He lived what he wrote, he embodied what he preached, he incarnated what he taught. May his spirit hover over us to realise in our daily lives too, that which Albert fulfilled in his mission here with us. His mission was inspired by his understanding of the values of the Reign of God proclaimed by Jesus. To paraphrase the letter to the Hebrews, with such a witness as Albert, ' . . . we should keep running steadily in the race we have started, and not lose sight of Jesus who leads us in our faith and brings it to perfection' (Heb 12:1–2a).

---

1. Albert Nolan, *Jesus Today: A Spirituality of Radical Freedom* (Maryknoll, NY: Orbis Books, 2006), 127.
2. *Jesus Today*, xviii.

Albert Nolan
GOD IN SOUTH AFRICA

The challenge of the gospel

God in South Africa: Then–and Now

Anthony Egan SJ

Introduction

This little contribution to honouring the memory of Albert Nolan—known to friends, confreres and generations of students as Albert, and hence called as such in this essay—explores one of his books, *God in South Africa: The Challenge of the Gospel,*[1] a text that has been (to my mind somewhat unfairly) eclipsed by his classic work *Jesus before Christianity*. While the latter has had a greater impact on the global theological scene, I will contend that Albert's theological reflection on the South African struggle was a major contribution to understanding a Christian response to a revolutionary situation, one that although its context has changed, its content remains potentially useful in new situations.

The book is divided into a series of sections: the situation in which it was written; Nolan's analysis of that situation; Nolan's creative theological adaptations of 3 S's—Sin, Suffering, Salvation; and his call to action. (If the latter three sections sound familiar, they might be summed up as a variation of Cardijn's classical See–Judge–Act method, wholly appropriate I think, given Albert's many years of work with the Young Christian Students (YCS). Finally, I shall suggest how *God in South Africa* can still speak to us today in South Africa and elsewhere.

---

1. Albert Nolan, *God in South Africa: The Challenge of the Gospel* (Cape Town & Johannesburg: David Philip, 1988) [Simultaneously published with CIIR in London, Eerdmans in Grand Rapids, and Mambo Press in Gweru, Zimbabwe]. Citations from this book will be in the text.

The *Sitz im Leben* of *God In South Africa*

God in South Africa was written somewhere between the release of the *Kairos Document* in 1985 and 1988. It coincides with the two States of Emergency imposed by the Apartheid State–the 1985 partial State of Emergency, followed by the 1986 national State of Emergency that officially ended on 2 February 1990. The present South African context is bad: rampant corruption, the slow unravelling of the African National Congress (ANC), populism, persistent power outages and a declining economy. Though perhaps less apparent to the presently privileged, the historically amnesiac or those born after 1994, the 1980s was worse: systematic Apartheid, the erosion of the rule of law under a state that used brutal force against its opponents: assassinations, torture, detention without trial—and mounting levels of guerrilla activity and township vigilantism that rendered life terrifying. During part of this period, Albert Nolan was in hiding, evading the State Security Police who sought to detain him without trial. This is obliquely alluded to in the book where he acknowledges the assistance of friends and colleagues 'who did such a good job in difficult circumstances' (xiii).

For Albert, the 1980s was a busy time. Having been elected Master of the Dominican Order in 1983, he was allowed by the General Chapter to step aside at his request to continue his work with the Institute for Contextual Theology (ICT) in South Africa, which he had helped to found. At ICT he was part of the reflection process that led to the *Kairos Document* in 1985 that issued a challenge to the Christian Church to move beyond neutrality or a 'compromise' form of reconciliation. *Kairos*, and Nolan (who though considered radical by some bishops was still an advisor to the Southern African Catholic Bishops Conference), called for a new, prophetic Church that in its daily, liturgical and preaching practice actively and openly supported the struggle for the end of Apartheid and the establishment of non-racial democracy. In many ways, *God in South Africa* is Albert's commentary on the *Kairos Document*.

Although *Kairos* had a mixed reception from established Churches, including the Catholic Church that found fault with its critique of what it had called 'Church Theology', in practice these institutions, notably the SACBC, offered safe public spaces for religious activists to work above ground, while some were also doing underground work, mainly as ANC operatives.[2] During this time, Albert himself was involved in secret work with the ANC. His friend, ANC and Communist Party activist Raymond Suttner has noted:

> [Albert] was part of an underground network that managed logistics, including the transportation and movement of activists, providing safe houses and a means of communication while in South Africa.

He added:

> The full extent of his role in these networks is not known, since much of the work was done on a disciplined 'need-to-know' basis.[3]

This information, communicated after Albert's death, confirmed that Albert was not just a theologian and chaplain to Christian youth and student movements that by the late 1980s had made a more or less explicit commitment to the broad alliance of opposition movements aligned to the ANC.[4] He was, like a small but significant group of clergy and Church workers during that period, actively involved in underground work. If I may borrow a phrase from Fyodor Dostoyevsky, *God in South Africa* may perhaps then be called Albert's 'Notes from the Underground'.

Analysis of the situation

God in South Africa focuses on the situation in the 1980s, commonly seen as the endgame decade of the Struggle against Apartheid. Apart from describing the situation—mass resistance, mostly nonviolent,

---

2. For one example see: Peter Sadie, *Faith in Our Struggle: A Memoir of Hope* (Johannesburg: Staging Post/Jacana, 2022).

3. Raymond Suttner, 'Father Albert Nolan – a non-believer remembers' at <https://www.dailymaverick.co.za/article/2022-10-19-albert-nolan-a-non-believer-remembers/>. Accessed April 2023.

4. Jeremy Seekings, *The UDF: A History of the United Democratic Front in South Africa, 1983–1991* (Athens, OH: Ohio University Press, 2000); Ineke Van Kessel, *'Beyond Our Wildest Dreams': The United Democratic Front and the Transformation of South Africa* (Charlottesville, VA: University Press of Virginia, 2000); Raymond Suttner, 'The UDF Period and its Meaning for Contemporary South Africa', in *Journal of Southern African Studies,* 30 (3): 691–702.

met by high level state violence—and its effects upon the people of South Africa, ranging from black rage to white paranoia about communism, Albert situates his analysis within a term he calls 'internal colonialism' (chapter 4, especially 70–74). For those in broadly ANC circles, or those familiar with the movement's history, this is deeply significant since it defines Albert's clear political position.

The term 'internal colonialism' was first coined by Leo Marquard, a member of the South African Liberal Party in 1957.[5] South Africa, he argued, was a kind of microcosm of colonialism, with a European colonial power (white South Africa) exerting domination over the black (colonised) majority. Later expanded by Marxist theorist Immanuel Wallerstein into a 'world system' theory, where the Global North and its elite allies dominated the Global South,[6] the theory got its wider South African application when it was adopted by the South African Communist Party and later the ANC under the title 'Colonialism of a Special Type'.[7] That Albert used this analysis (albeit couched in the more neutral terminology reminiscent of Marquard) is unsurprising, given his political commitment and its pervasiveness among people in the struggle during the period; that he used it in a book published in South Africa at the time, and aimed at a mass market as opposed to an intellectual elite, was remarkable. It was in effect a declaration of where he stood personally, an act of brutal honesty that could have had potentially bad consequences.

Then again, as I have noted, Albert was already on the State security apparatus' hit list. That he was able to surface in 1988 again, around the time of the book's publication, was more of a measure of the desperation of the security system's situation—who were perhaps facing bigger fish to fry than Albert—or its incompetence. Signifi-

---

5. Leo Marquard, *South Africa's Colonial Policy*, (Johannesburg: South African Institute of Race Relations, 1957).

6. *Cf* Immanuel Wallerstein, *The Modern World-System,* Volume I: Capitalist Agriculture and the Origins of the European World-Economy in the Sixteenth Century (New York, NY: Academic Press, 1974), *The Modern World-System,* Volume II: Mercantilism and the Consolidation of the European World-Economy, 1600–1750 (New York, NY: Academic Press, 1980), *The Modern World-System,* Volume III: The Second Great Expansion of the Capitalist World-Economy, 1730–1840s (San Diego, CA: Academic Press, 1989).

7. See: South African Communist Party, 'The Road to South African Freedom' at <https://www.marxists.org/history/international/comintern/sections/sacp/1962/road-freedom.htm>. Accessed April 2023.

cantly, too, though *God in South Africa* contained content thoroughly inimical to the Apartheid social order, it was never formally banned.[8]

'Systematising' a revolution

God in South Africa is not so much a systematic and moral theology of and for the South African revolution as it is prophetic proclamation, an attempt to proclaim the gospel in a particular time and place. Albert notes that 'when we ask about the gospel in South Africa today, we are asking about *the role of God (and therefore Christ and the Spirit) in our present situation of crisis and conflict*' (29; his italics). He juxtaposes his political analysis with the moral category of Sin, noting that:

> The Bible does not make a distinction between two kinds of sin, personal sin and social sin . . . The personal and the social are two dimensions that are present in every sin . . . all sins have a social dimension because sins have social consequences (they affect other people), sins become institutionalised and systematised in the structures, laws and customs of a society, and sins are committed in a particular society that shapes and influences the sinner (43–44).

A second dimension to Albert's thinking is Suffering, where Sin becomes visible. In South Africa and other countries this is manifested in unjust systems of power and domination, exploitation and inequality rooted in categories of race and class that Albert calls 'internal colonialism'. The black majority he calls a crucified people, evoking the logical analogy of suffering and mass struggle with the person of Christ (Here he draws on biblical scholarship that associates Jesus with social movements[9] challenging the political-religious establishment of first century Palestine).

---

8. If I may speculate, based on my experience as a regular book reviewer at the time, there seems to have been a minor collapse in the rigour of censorship after about 1987. Overt materials (posters, ANC and Communist Party publications, etc.) continued to be banned, but books considered academic or of limited interest were not. This, in hindsight, may coincide with the growing number of secret negotiations between the Apartheid government and the liberation movements.
9. In particular: *The Bible and Liberation: Political and Social Hermeneutics,* edited by Norman K Gottwald (Maryknoll, NY: Orbis Books, 1983); RA Horsley and JS Hanson, *Bandits, Prophets and Messiahs* (New York, NY: Seabury Press, 1985).

The third S in Albert's account is Salvation. Drawing on the biblical notion of Salvation from Sin in all its dimensions (108), he states that 'The most serious heresy of European Christianity, especially in the last few centuries, has been the reduction of the gospel to little more than the salvation of souls' (108). A true biblical notion of Salvation makes no such distinction. Salvation in 1980s South Africa is political and economic liberation, achieved by those who struggle.

The struggle itself becomes therefore part of God's own work, God working in and through the national liberation movements that are in themselves and their activities (for example, protests, strikes, alternative education, community organising) signs of hope. This is the privileged site where God is to be found in South Africa. And for Albert, it is essential that the Church, to be faithful to Christ and his liberating mission, should be integral to this struggle.

Given this claim, Albert cannot but address the problem of violence. Violence marked the Apartheid regime in all its dimensions—physical force, enforced poverty, psychological humiliation . . . But what of the violence of those who struggle? *God in South Africa* has to steer a careful path between condemning all violence (and those 'equalising' State and Struggle violence) and justifying or even advocating struggle violence. Noting the disproportionate level of State violence as opposed to the limited, often spontaneous violence of the oppressed, he notes:

> It is simply intolerable that a system which has been responsible for so much violence and bloodshed should self-righteously condemn a peace-loving people for now resorting to violence. I am not saying there isn't a problem here. There is and we need to be very sensitive to it. But when the upholders of the system rant and rave about 'necklace murders' and refuse to talk to people until they give up all violence, we must know that we are dealing with downright hypocrisy (167).

A dodge perhaps, but necessary at the time. Even an academic colloquium[10] on theology and violence—which studiously covered both classical Just War Theory and pacifism—avoided taking a direct posi-

---

10. *Theology and Violence: The South African Debate*, edited by Charles Villa-Vicencio (Johannesburg: Skotaville Press, 1987).

tion on whether armed resistance to Apartheid was legitimate. Such reflections could only be possible after liberation[11].

A call to action

Beyond the theological and moral analysis of the South African struggle, *God in South Africa* explicitly does what the *Kairos Document* did—it calls the Church to action. By situating the threefold Sin-Suffering-Salvation in the country, and not in the Church, Albert calls on the Church to 'relocate' itself to the context. Sin is not about individual personal action/inaction but social action or inaction; suffering takes on a historical, political form; and salvation can only be found in the world, a very disturbing concept for those who see it as salvation from the latter. The message to the Church comes out clearly: take a stand or become irrelevant!

From the start of his reflection on the role of the Church (chapter 11, 209–220), he insists that the Church's role is more than just preaching and sacraments, it is about its witness. This is complicated by the dividedness of the Church, in how it responded to Apartheid. The Church was itself a site of Struggle, 'a place in society where, in one form or another, the struggle for liberation takes places' (215). For those of us who came of religious age in South Africa in the 1980s, his observation resonates: issues of doctrine and worship style paled into relative insignificance compared to how sectors of the Church addressed the fundamental moral problem of the time, Apartheid.[12]

Albert ends the book hopefully:

> South Africa is remarkably different. God is doing a new thing here. We who are privileged to be South Africans, painful as it may be at the moment, have a calling or vocation that is of historical significance for Africa and indeed for the whole world. One day we shall be a united nation that is thoroughly non-racial, democratic at every level, liberated from political oppression and economically independent, a nation that

---

11. For example, Anna Floerke Scheid, *Just Revolution: A Christian Ethic of Political Resistance and Social Transformation* (Lanham, MD: Lexington Books, 2015).

12. Interestingly, as I studied the history of Christianity in Nazi Germany, I found echoes of the same issue. Unsurprisingly, people like Dietrich Bonhoeffer, Martin Niemoller, Rupert Mayer SJ and Alfred Delp SJ were spiritual kin of many in South Africa during the 1980s.

develops new forms of economic justice, new cultural values, new forms of music and so forth . . . God has called us to be the Church of Jesus Christ at this time and in this place. If we can measure up to the challenge, we can make a significant contribution to Christian practice and Christian theology in the world of tomorrow (220).

Did we?

Reading *God in South Africa* today

Did we? For a time, it seemed like it. But history and circumstance and the reality of human Sin seems to have dampened the hope (or optimism?) of Albert's vision of *God in South Africa*.[13]

Many works, including theology written in the heat of political and social crises, do not age well. They appear as texts of their time, works that do not stand up to the judgment of the present. Then again, there are works that still speak to us, like Dietrich Bonhoeffer's *Letters and Papers from Prison*,[14] that still say something that the Church, the Academy and Society ignore at their peril. *God in South Africa* falls between the two extremes of being a 'tract for the time' and having profound relevance.

Much of the book feels dated, generating a feeling of nostalgia for a possible future that never happened. Did we really believe that with liberation, and specifically the victory of the ANC, we would see the coming of a New Jerusalem, a socialist utopia that would end racism and vampire capitalism? Yes, we did, or at least spurred on by a kind of Christian optimism, we imagined that it was possible. Instead, we have seen a movement we once idolised turn into a greed-driven, corrupt parody. Albert's idealism seems tragically misplaced today.

But . . .

At the same time much of what he has said holds true. The poor are still with us. Injustice still exists, albeit less crass and brutal than the 1980s. The Church must still take its part in the struggle for human wellbeing—it needs new voices and a new theology in which

---

13. In some ways reflection on the new global realities are found in: Albert Nolan, *Jesus Today: A Spirituality of Radical Freedom* (Maryknoll, NY: Orbis Books 2006), and in *Hope in an Age of Despair* (Maryknoll, NY: Orbis 2009).

14. Dietrich Bonhoeffer, *Letters and Papers from Prison* (revised edition) (London: SCM Press, 1971).

to articulate the message of Jesus. The Kingdom may be postponed, but it has not been cancelled. It may have to take a different shape, may have to be more incremental in its evolution, but that is not all bad. One of the great mistakes we all made perhaps was to imagine that the Kingdom would come in its fullness in our lives, in our times.

A personal conclusion

Some books, like some people, become part of your life. Though I have read the more famous *Jesus before Christianity* many more times, have taught theology students with it, assigned it in exams, etc, this book is more significant for me personally. *God in South Africa* was a book that spoke to me in the 1980s, as my political and religious consciousness was developing. I read it at a time when I was discerning what to do with my life. I was trying to keep my conscription into the South African Defence Force at bay, considering variously an academic career in history or in law, while struggling against the possibility that I had a religious vocation. Somewhere in the 1980s, I also got to know Albert Nolan himself. When we first met, we discovered we had a common connection: an aunt of mine had worked with the young Dennis Nolan in a bank in Cape Town before he became a Dominican. Though our paths moved differently (I became a Jesuit, after all), we would meet occasionally, at conferences, clergy meetings, or on occasions when I visited his community. He was always warm and wise, a major theologian yet above all, a pastor.

I will miss him. Rest in Peace, Albert.

Brothers of the Vicariate General of South Africa at La Verna for an annual meeting in the 1970s. Includes both English and Dutch Dominicans in the amalgamated vicariate. The meeting where Albert was elected Vicar General in 1976. Back row Left to Right: Damian Magrath, Joseph Falkiner, Emil Blaser, Jan Jansen, Gregory Brooke, Hans Brenninkmeijer, Pieter Dielwart, Kees Keijsper, Do Lansen, Reginald Dellaert, Francis Middlewick, Ninian McManus. Kneeling: Charles Mendel, Oliver Clark, Carel Spruyt, Jan Versantvoort, Lambert Cartens, Harry Penninx Seated: Benedict Mulder, Albert Nolan and Peter Paul Feeny.

Operative 42

Horst Kleinschmidt

It happened in 1950, in 1960 and again in 1977. There were other times too but never were there the same far-reaching consequences. In 1950 the Communist Party, in 1960 the African National Congress (ANC) and the Pan Africanist Congress (PAC), and in 1977 eighteen Black Consciousness Movement (BCM) organisations, two newspapers and also the ecumenical Christian Institute (CI) and its magazine *Pro Veritate* were 'banned' (outlawed). In 1977 additionally, seventy BCM leaders were detained under the Terrorism Act and five white men were banned—a form of house arrest for named individuals.

After each of the repressive actions by the Apartheid rulers, resistance and the formation of secret underground operations ensued. When authoritarian rule curtails freedom of speech and freedom of organisation, it provokes—even demands—unconventional, secretive and often violent reaction. The obvious corollary is that as long as a democracy allows the voice of dissent, secretive underground or violent resistance can never be justified. But it is not that simple.

The perilous development of South Africa's 'negotiated revolution' since 1994 nudges those who believe in equality and justice to revisit the choices they made to form, join or support the underground struggle after the fateful 19 October 1977. What can we learn from Albert Nolan and his cohort of faith leaders who crossed the line into the underground? None other tested their faith to the core as they did.

They came from both the oppressed and the perpetrator class; they were black and some were white. After 1977, Fr Albert Nolan, with Drs Beyers Naudé, Steve Biko, Professor Barney Pityana, Reverend Theo Kotze, Archbishop Desmond Tutu, Reverend Cedric Mayson, Fr Smangaliso Mkhatshwa, Fr Cosmas Desmond, Reverend Frank

Chikane, Dr Wolfram Kistner, Fr Michael Laspley and Fr John Osmers conducted debates that go to the heart of our being. In previous epochs they included Chief Albert Luthuli, Nelson Mandela, Robert Sobukwe and Bram Fischer. And there was the influence of Dom Helder Camara, Canon John Collins, Archbishop Trevor Huddleston and others. They acted whatever the risk to themselves. But it is the ethics that circumscribed their actions that demands our attention.

In each epoch of repression there are also those who reluctantly accept their silencing, who remain morally opposed and those who went into exile to fight from abroad. And there were those who went into hiding or who deceived their persecutors by doing one thing in the open and public eye but simultaneously served an underground resistance. When they got caught—and they did in many instances— the worst wrath of the tyrant and his agents was visited on them. It is those who pursued the cause of liberty and justice when all other avenues were shut that need our attention, our study and our celebration! It is they whose thinking and writing teaches and inspires us—anywhere in the world—when the dark force of tyranny and authoritarian rule imposes itself. It is appropriate that we locate Albert Nolan in the latter context.

Those who constructed and re-constituted the struggle in secret were invariably not trained for the new roles they chose; they lacked preparation and were ill-equipped without the tools of secret communication and organisation. The history of resistance to Nazi occupied Holland, France and countries throughout Europe serve as one yardstick of what sacrifices people made, what underground plans were hatched but often failed. None of it dashed the hope of the majority populations they acted for and whose pride and identity they helped build. Similar examples in other parts of the world abound.

Steve Biko's monumental contribution to the struggle predates 1977. His contribution to liberate the mind of the colonised, of the victim, went together with re-building mass resistance after the political drought years that following the banning of ANC and PAC in 1960. He and his associates quenched a thirst and were so successful that the regime's 1977 bannings followed. Importantly, Steve and his colleagues also had a key influence on the minds of that generation of white South Africans serious about bringing an end to autocratic and minority rule. The University Christian Movement (UCM) stands out in this regard. The National Union of South African Students (NUSAS) became, despite its main liberal support base, an ally of those who sought to rid us of the tyrant rather than reform him. This new white radicalism helped build a new trade union movement. And, a late-comer for some, amongst this small group of white radical dissent was the Christian Institute. The Catholic-based Young Christian Students (YCS) and Young Christian Workers (YCW) equally were key to the shape of the politics that shaped resistance in the aftermath of the bannings. As one student activist from that period remarked: 'Albert and those from YCS and YCW engaged in class analyses that ultimately had to prevail over those who saw no further than a struggle between black and white.' Huge credit has to go to Steve Biko who pushed well-meaning whites to re-think their role. They came to re-define solidarity with the majority in the South African context.

This author's link to the internal resurgence, taking on a distinctive form from 1979 onwards, was from exile in London. From the time of the banning until 1990, a secret communications link was built between him and his colleagues inside South Africa. Beyers Naudé (Oom Bey) was the link for a remarkable group, mostly based in Soweto and in Mamelodi, that guided and acted and led the struggle against Apartheid in the late 1970s and throughout the 1980s. This group included Moss and Reverend Frank Chikane, Fr Smangaliso Mkhatshwa, trade unionist Rita Ndzanga, Reverend Castro Mayathula, the indefatigable revolutionary Jabu Ngwenya and some twenty others. Fr Albert Nolan was among them. For nearly eleven years they smuggled communications to the movement outside of South Africa and in turn, we sent messages inside from Oliver Tambo and Thabo Mbeki through a direct connection to Oom Bey. It contributed to re-building the broken linkage between the external ANC and the budding new internal resistance. Contrary to false narratives this was not to recruit internal resisters to become ANC, SACP or Umkhonto we Sizwe (MK) members, but instead to break the wall the Apartheid enforcers had built between the external capacity and the post 1977 revival inside. A principal task was to be able to service the new resistance funds in ways the enemy could not detect or stop. With Beyers, an unbroken linkage that was not intercepted contributed to the fall of Apartheid in the late 1980s. Letters, micro-film, call-box communication and the provision of funds were the tools of the trade that the Special Branch (SBs) suspected were there but which until the end of

Apartheid they never got their hands on; had they, the consequences for those involved can only be imagined.[1] This author had no direct responsibility for Albert Nolan, but in as far as Beyers Naudé needed to make reference to him, Albert was known as 'C4' until the end of 1980. After that his code was '42', a number always used with a different number preceding 42 and another number after it. The codes served as a further layer of disguise in the secret communication, in case letters or micro-film were detected, often hidden on the bodies of foreign clergy visiting South Africa and the SBs never found the key to this messaging.

Beyers was humble and when we met again when it was all over, unhesitatingly he insisted that he was not the theological pillar behind the many decisions and choices he faced post the banning. He pointed to Albert Nolan and Dr Wolfram Kistner as his theological anchors.

Beyers' initial attempt (started in secret one week after he was banned) to build an underground Confessing Community to succeed the Christian Institute foundered by late 1978. By the end of 1979 he, with his trusted friends, interacted with a group mostly based in Soweto and Mamelodi. This was important. The initiative to act came from the oppressed community who were offered solidarity from outside, from men and women from the privileged class.

Beyers' motivation, as much as of those whom he trusted in this period, was based on Christian principle and experience, constantly testing how what they did was in concert, or not, with those whom they met in the trenches of struggle: African Nationalists, Socialists and Communists. Commonalities had to be tested and in some cases borders drawn about matters they could not countenance.

One important bridge into the secret world they constructed was the influence of black theologians who had shaped black theology prior to the bannings. No-one stands out more prominently here than the Reverend Alan Boesak. They had built on the traditions of black theology espoused in the USA, and liberation theology developed by Catholic priests from South America. White activists were confronting an additional burden: that of the class they came from, that of coming from the perpetrator class.

---

1. The 750 pages of SB files on Beyers Naudé and interviews with SB policemen who testified at the TRC confirm this view.

The significant shift about the way to prosecute the struggle happened in mid-1978 when the detained BCM leaders were gradually released from detention at Modderbee prison. Broadly they had divided into one group which, once free, would seek to prosecute the struggle through an independent Azapo. The other group, the group Beyers and his close associates decided to support, was represented by Reverend Mashwabada Mayathula and the Reverend Drake Tshenkeng. This group had decided in prison that once free, the best way to advance the struggle henceforth would be by seeking 'a strategic alliance' with the exiled ANC. Mayathula had his roots in the ANC Youth League in the 1940s and until the banning had worked at the Christian Institute. The white and committed clergy in this period had not only chosen to identify with this new underground, they had also heeded the message first enunciated by Steve Biko and by now represented by persons like the Reverend Frank Chikane who said to white supporters: 'Are you ready to commit class suicide?' This was no easy slogan. It had profound implications.

The German dissident pastor, Dietrich Bonhoeffer, grappled with the role and responsibility of the perpetrator class. His reflections on what limits but also what challenges such individuals, was instructive. In Nazi Germany he defined the act of solidarity with the persecuted as follows: Solidarity demands accountability to yourself, by accepting the same risk and penalty meted out to the persecuted or the victim. Bonhoeffer said in his own instance this meant assisting Jewish people to flee to Switzerland. The Beyers and Albert associates in the 1980s acted by accepting that their solidarity actions, if found out, would result in punishment akin to that meted out to the oppressed person.

For Bonhoeffer this was only the first of three actions that were required. The second was 'to speak truth', even when the tyrant silences you for what you say. This had already happened by the time the bannings took place and press censorship was widely imposed. Beyers and others were silenced by banning them, but they continued to send their 'truth telling' messages to Europe and North America, countries that were the huge enablers of Apartheid. Being white and having clerical status, they influenced the debate in the different northern hemisphere confessions so successfully that churches eventually played a major role in persuading their governments to isolate Apartheid, to weaken it through sanctions and to stop arms sales to it.[2] Without knowing its content, this author facilitated a meeting between Albert Nolan and Oliver Tambo after Nolan had paid a visit to the Vatican. Without doubt Albert's visit to Rome at that time had a purpose beyond his role functions within his Order.

Bonhoeffer's third challenge concerned the use of violence against the tyrant to end his rule. For his contributory acts to have Hitler assassinated he was sentenced to death four months before the end of World War II. However, Beyers stated that he would not pick up arms to prosecute the struggle. He, along with all who helped to build the biggest challenge to Apartheid, the United Democratic Front (UDF), saw their role in building collective mass action across the country such that the Apartheid state had to lose its control over ever growing swathes of the land. Albert, through the help of the Catholic Institute of International Relations (CIIR) in London, supported this final assault on Apartheid. Beyers too smuggled funds from primarily Dutch and German Churches into the country to enable the hands that built a massive civic movement. The funders abroad, too, went an extra mile to ensure that Apartheid's friends in Europe would not prejudice the delicate nature of what was being built. The SB files reveal their frustration at not finding the evidence to break these links.

The Bonhoeffer theses tie in with what Steve Biko demanded: 'if you, the whites, want to liberate South Africa, go and liberate the white minds imbued with their arrogant sense of superiority'. 'Black man you are on your own' was a strategic measure but not a denial of a greater and universal common humanity. Steve Biko along with Robert Sobukwe was not racist. His was a necessary response to 'liberate the colonised mind' and in the South Africa of the day, to oust the prevailing do-gooderism, the charity, the reform, the acting on behalf of the persons of colour, that stunted the black cause, black self-expression and hence their very liberation. Many whites did not understand him. Student friends at the time thought that Steve was playing into the Apartheid ideology of separation or separate development. They were wrong. They could not see the need to liberate the black mind as a pre-condition for overthrowing the Apartheid system

---

2. This writer has not had access to the Nolan Security Police (known as SB) files, but the seven-hundred page file on Beyers Naudé proves just how and what these South African clerics' part was in moving the ex- and neo-colonial powers to finally take action against white rule in Southern Africa.

and not simply reforming it; they did not recognise the privileged class they came from and defended; and they did not recognise how patronising they were toward people of a colour complexion other than their own.

In the last decades of Apartheid, whites who understood that Black Consciousness was a necessary strategy at that stage of the struggle would be found in the UCM before it disbanded, in NUSAS after it shook off its liberal mantle, in sections of the all-women Black Sash, amongst trade unionists and others broadly known as radical or socialist. The Special Branch (Security Police) at one stage had a special section to focus on these white people. Former SB cop Paul Erasmus told me in 2021 that they celebrated every time a white activist went into exile. Their pathetic view was that the blacks were perfectly happy people but it was the white left who instigated them to rebel.

Those like Albert, who moved into and out of the secret world of the underground, confronted many decisions, nearly all of which tested their ethical or spiritual foundation. They supported an underground movement rather than functioned as individuals. Having grasped Steve Biko's message, this further entailed acting in solidarity without being in a leading role. It was the acceptance that the oppressed determined and led the struggle.

Albert, although interpreted here in large measure through his associate and comrade Beyers, broke through the barriers of race and class and in this way advanced the quest for true *égalité* under the conditions Apartheid imposed. But his vision goes far beyond what 1994 promised or delivered. Albert's challenge rings clear now: 'Demand ethical rule and never forget that the unparalleled inequality we live in demands our active engagement!'

Albert with Raymond Suttner.

Converging Journeys Towards the 'Sacred'

Raymond Suttner

I first met Albert Nolan when I emerged from prison in 1983. I was then a communist, although it was illegal to be one and I did not admit that in public or in private. And I was an atheist. It was not compulsory to be an atheist in the Communist Party. There were many members who were believers in Christianity and other belief systems. But I was not one of those. I was an atheist, and I did not then understand how much I could learn from someone like Albert Nolan. I would not then have expected to be contributing to a book on Albert, not realising then how much I shared morally and ethically with him and other believers.

Atheism is not a belief system in the sense that it conducts missionary activities or actively propagates its denial of the existence of a Superior Being like a religious or political doctrine. In my case, I simply did not believe and my atheism only needed to be articulated when I was asked to swear an oath and chose to 'affirm'. It is just how I understood that aspect of my life.

I grew up in a Jewish household, which was not very devout, and I did not know very much about Judaism or any other religion.

Until late in life, I did not understand what a disadvantage I was at in not drawing on the insights of a range of religions, especially in the developments that had been occurring during the twentieth century with the emergence of liberation and feminist theologies.

In fact, it is only in the twenty-first century that I have come to grapple with some of the insights that I have derived from these teachings and also the great Jewish scholar and companion/comrade of Martin Luther King Jr, Rabbi Abraham Joshua Heschel.

I was fortunate in this journey to benefit from discussions with Albert Nolan and the late Chris Langefeld, with both of whom I formed close relationships which were based on shared understandings and values.

Chris Langefeld was a Catholic priest who once ministered to the Phiri parish in Soweto and was the YCS national chaplain for many years. He left the Catholic priesthood in 1996 after falling in love with Barbara Gillbee whom he married in 1998. He died in 2017. Although Chris regularly preached in the Anglican Church, he never relinquished his links to the Catholic Church, and he and Albert remained very close.

Reading the signs of the times

Our discussions—with Albert or together with or separately with Chris—also related to our analysis of the situation in the country, what non-believers, perhaps especially Marxists would call the 'current conjuncture', and what Albert, Chris and other believers would call 'reading the signs of the times', in relation to prophecy. As Albert put it:

> Prophets are typically people who can foretell the future, not as fortune-tellers, but as people who have learned to read the signs of their times. It is by focusing their attention on, and becoming fully aware of, the political, social, economic, military, and religious tendencies of their time that prophets are able to see where it is all heading.
>
> Reading the signs of his times would have been an integral part of Jesus' spirituality.[1]

A lot of my discussions with Albert and Chris were related to such analysis.

When I first met Albert it was at a distance, because although we had a cordial relationship, I was not engaging theological or spiritual questions and I did not appreciate what I had to gain from such works.

---

1. Albert Nolan, *Jesus Today: A Spirituality of Radical Freedom* (Cape Town: Double Story Books. 2006), 63–64.

And I did not know that Albert was one of the foremost liberation theologians, or theologians in general, in the world. He was, as I saw it, simply a comrade who was a priest.

Equally, when I spoke to other priests or pastors about the Freedom Charter, I had not yet developed adequate respect for their specific belief systems nor learnt what I had to gain from them. I simply wanted to harness their support for the Freedom Charter as members of a constituency that carried weight in a time of contestation with other political trends.

Albert's book *Jesus before Christianity* has been repeatedly reprinted since its first publication in 1976.[2] As a theologian, he was a best-selling author and this work was prescribed in a range of educational institutions, not only Catholic ones. I had no understanding of this. I did not appreciate that he was not simply a conventional priest, university pastor or something of that kind.

What I also understand from my discussions with both Albert and Chris is that the period that both spent studying in Rome was a very broad foundation of knowledge and understanding, both being familiar with a much wider range of philosophers and other thinkers than most other people that I have encountered. They were open to everything. And this openness contrasts with the idea that many have of the Roman Catholic Church being dogmatic.

It may have its dogmas and dogmatists, but within the ranks of the priests, it had people like Albert and Chris and they were extremely open to reading and engaging with a range of belief systems, including other religions like Islam, Judaism and Buddhism, and approaches drawing on Marxism, post-modernism and a range of other methodologies for understanding social issues.

I was also unaware that Albert completed his doctoral studies at the Pontifical University of Saint Thomas Aquinas, the Angelicum, in Rome. But it was a requirement that he have it published. He considered that a waste of money and the degree was never awarded.

---

2. Albert Nolan, *Jesus before Christianity* (Claremont: David Philip, 1976). It has just been republished as a theological classic. (Maryknoll, NY: Orbis Books, 2022).

Albert's prophetic role

In the course of meeting Albert, I did not discuss theological matters initially, but when I was underground, in the first State of Emergency of the 1980s, from mid-1985–mid-1986, Albert asked to meet and it related to the *Kairos Document*.[3] I was very surprised to be consulted on this document that was a theological intervention, albeit on the crisis of repression and resistance in the mid-1980s. Why did he want my input? In compiling this prophetic document, there was agreement that it had to be a result of a consultative process, not simply intellectual work. Albert and the other editors of what would become the *Kairos Document* took consultations very seriously.

That is why he found it necessary to consult with someone like me, who was not a believer. That surprised me, though I did not really dwell on it at the time. As I recall, I was not pressed to make any statement related to religious doctrine and had a general discussion of how we understood Apartheid and the character of the freedom we wanted to see emerge in the future. And on this our views converged.

I went back to prison again in the 1986–1990 State of Emergency and Albert, I later learnt, had to go underground in that period.

When I came out of detention, I was under house arrest and this made it difficult to see people like Albert, who were also being monitored by the security police. After that I only saw Albert from time to time in the 1990s. His book, *God in South Africa*, had come out in 1988.[4]

I only really got to appreciate the significance of this work and his later work *Jesus Today* when I undertook research on Chief Albert Luthuli, about ten years later. I had to understand Luthuli's theology because I recognised that Luthuli's Christianity and his political actions and belief systems were intertwined.

Much of Luthuli's life was prophetic. Even the title of his book, *Let My People Go*,[5] which is the Mosaic call to Pharaoh to free the people of Israel, is part of a range of prophetic allusions in Luthuli's work that I had to understand. And in reading Albert Nolan's writings, much of which is preoccupied with the prophetic, I felt I got somewhere in my understanding.

---

3. *The Kairos Document: Challenge to the Church: A Theological Comment on the Political Crisis in South Africa*, revised second edition (Braamfontein: Skotaville, 1986, 2017).
4. Albert Nolan, *God in South Africa* (Cape Town: David Philip, 1988).
5. Albert Luthuli, *Let My People Go* (Cape Town: Kwela Books, 2017).

Albert Nolan and the struggle for liberation

Underground

It appears that it was his practising of 'theology from below', notably in contributing to the process leading to the *Kairos Document*, that evoked security police attention.[6]

It has been revealed since his death that Albert was an underground operative. That is a dramatic demonstration of the extent of his commitment to the struggle, that he was willing to link his ministry with the struggle of the oppressed, even including illegal work that risked his freedom and could potentially have led to torture and death.

But Albert's involvement was not an *ad hoc* engagement. Only since his death has it been revealed that he was a fully-fledged underground operative, charged with carrying out dangerous tasks that entailed real danger for him. His work entailed logistical support and transportation of other illegal cadres, among other work.[7]

Release after election as Master of Dominican Order

Less dramatic but perhaps an early indication of his single-minded devotion to the oppressed people of South Africa was his request to be released from the position of Master of the Dominican Order, to which he had been elected in 1983. It is the most senior position in the Dominican Order—with broad and direct authority over every brother, priory and province, and every nun and monastery. This may have been the first such request recorded and acceded to in 750 years of the Order, after Dominic himself declined the office in 1221, after serving from 1216.

When Albert asked to be allowed to return to South Africa, he was indicating—in line with his life work—that honours or high office meant nothing to him when measured against his duties in advancing

---

6. Terence Creamer 'Obituary. Father Albert Nolan–priest, anti-apartheid activist, author and renowned theologian' at <https://www.dailymaverick.co.za/article/2022-10-18-obituary-father-albert-nolan-anti-apartheid-activist-renowned-theologian/>. Accessed 10 March 2023.
7. Horst Kleinschmidt, 'Tribute. Albert Nolan—truth-teller, visionary, underground operative and revolutionary' at <https://www.dailymaverick.co.za/article/2022-10-23-albert-nolan-truth-teller-visionary-underground-operative-and-revolutionary/>. Accessed 10 March 2023.

the cause of those who experienced Apartheid oppression. To perform this ministry, he had to be located not at the periphery but in the primary site of struggle in South Africa.

My communism and Albert's Christianity

Why did I, who was a communist in most of this period, find kindred spirits in Albert Nolan and Chris Langefeld?

To understand this, I return to why I joined the Communist Party around 1969/1970 and how I understood my commitment to the struggle to defeat the Apartheid regime.

When I joined the Communist Party, I regarded it as something 'sacred' to become a member.[8] By that I mean it was an extraordinary commitment that I was making, that it had a significance that elevated it above other undertakings that I'd made to serve one or other cause. It was not sacred in the religious sense but similar in the importance I attached to the decision.

This was because it was part of a struggle that involved some of the most significant heroic figures in South African history. It had a purpose that was honourable and was respected by all freedom-loving people.

I feared that I would not be worthy of this task as I understood it, that I would not be ready 'to undertake what was required of me to adequately serve this struggle' that I honoured so greatly.

Some people may smirk and laugh and think that I was extremely naïve in seeing joining the Communist Party as having a sacred quality. Although the word sacred is generally associated with the religious and contrasted with the profane, it is also used more widely to refer to what is often secular, but viewed with great respect and reverence.

Whether or not I was naïve, I understood my commitment as entailing considerable sacrifice and requiring me to prepare myself adequately in the light of the life that I had lived before, to be able to act in accordance with what I believed was required of a communist undertaking a dangerous path to secure freedom for all. It was especially important to be prepared to demand as much of myself as black

---

8. Raymond Suttner, *Inside Apartheid's Prison* (Auckland Park: Jacana Media, second edition, 2017), xiii.

comrades did, in the light of my deriving from the privileged white community. I had to demonstrate that I took on the struggle of the oppressed as my own, as my life's 'calling'.

I had seen how some had betrayed the struggle when they had been arrested, and others had done so even before being arrested, sometimes deserting while in exile and joining forces hostile to the struggle.

I knew I would not betray the struggle in situations where I confronted those who disagreed on a conventional basis, as in debate. But I had to prepare myself for the likelihood, which did happen, of confronting the unleashing of terror against me, being arrested and tortured. I had to be ready for this and to handle myself in an honourable manner, disclosing as little as possible and refusing to betray the organisation and other individuals.

Beyond that, I conducted some level of self-examination at the point when I entered the world of the Communist Party. This was my own doing, and may have been conditioned by my not having had discussions with many people before seeking membership, because membership was secret.

I looked at my own life and asked myself whether I was living in a manner that was worthy of the grave responsibilities that I attributed to membership of the Communist Party. And I tried to learn new ways of acting, to listen carefully to other people, to hear all the details of what they said in order to understand all the dimensions that a statement might have contained. I also had to act with modesty and humility.

Some of these qualities I may have already acquired to some extent and this may have derived from values transmitted to me by my parents as a child, where I was instructed to act unselfishly and with integrity.

Looking back on the use of the word *sacred* to describe this moment of commitment, I think I had in mind something akin to the vows undertaken by Catholic religious—vows of poverty and chastity—when they presumably had to prepare themselves to renounce significant pleasures.

I was not undertaking those vows, but I did undertake to offer my life in the service of the people of South Africa, to undertake to do nothing that would undermine their wellbeing and to do everything within my power to remove the shackles of oppression that weighed on the oppressed.

Consequently, the way I understood this new path was not simply an intellectual commitment to a particular doctrine, in my case that of Marxist-Leninism and that of the broader liberation movement led by the ANC.

It is similar to the question which must arise for Christians and priests in other religions, whether their religious affiliation is purely a question of doctrine and disputation as to the meaning of words and passages of biblical and other religious texts. Albert Nolan writes:

> Faith is not primarily a way of thinking; it is a way of living. We talk about the practice of our faith, but in a very important sense this practice *is* our faith. It implies certain convictions or beliefs. What people really believe cannot be ascertained, with any degree of certainty, by listening to what they profess to believe. You can see without doubt what they really believe by observing what they do in practice. You judge a tree by its fruit. Faith, then, is a particular kind of practice.[9]

For such Christians or other religious adherents, their religious calling must also have had to be connected with the type of life they had to lead in relation to other people, especially those who formed part of their congregation or parish or ministry. The issue does not arise so much in thinking about the commitment, but in working in the context within which one has to live it out.

What I realise in retrospect is that there was something that drew me to Albert Nolan and Chris Langefeld that was not simply because we agreed on condemning Apartheid, or on the *Kairos Document* with which they were both involved and which bore strong similarities to documents of the liberation movement. It was more than that.

Just as they had taken vows which committed themselves to a particular life of service, my joining the Communist Party, as I understood it then, entailed similar undertakings, not just for a short term, not just for what I would write as an academic, but for how my life would unfold from then onwards.

While I had undertaken this commitment before meeting them or reading Albert's work, they enriched my understanding of its meanings and implications.

---

9. *God in South Africa*, 177 (See 177–179).

Albert's legacies

Albert made a range of choices in his life and these related to how he believed he needed to act out his Christianity.

He often wrote on and debated theological doctrine, but, as we have seen, believed that practice is key. From Albert's life, we learn the need to sometimes make decisions resulting in not seeking or holding high office.

The choices that he made, the way he lived out his choices, have lessons for all of us. His choices strengthened mine, despite our distinct doctrinal affiliations. Our lives were joined because we converged on how we confronted what we regarded as fundamental.

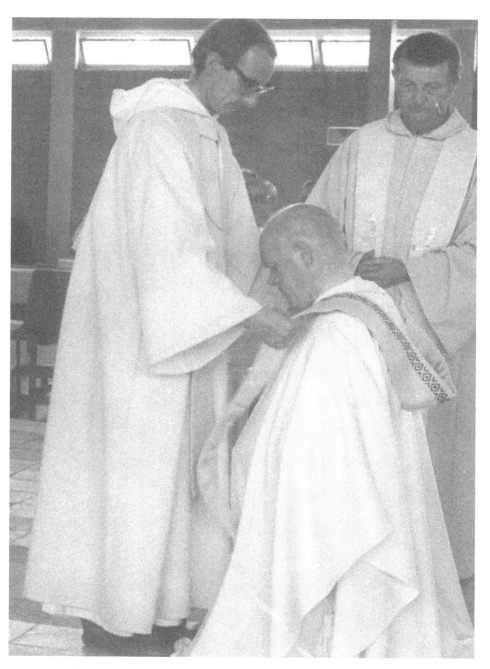

Albert clothing Martin Roden OP with his priest' stole at his ordination in 1980.

Section Five

Opening Space for Debate

The 'Option for the Poor' Debate

McGlory Speckman

It is an honour to be invited to participate in a volume that is being compiled to honour the late Fr Albert Nolan. I wish to focus on an area of his life that is usually taken for granted. Until his untimely demise in October 2022, Nolan elected not only to be on the side of the poor and oppressed, but to literally be where the lowly, the babies and other categories of marginalised people, which he had identified in Luke's gospel.[1] This characterised his ministry throughout his life as a priest. We may think of it as an 'option for the poor'. The actual phrase that is used by the Roman Catholic Church (RCC), which Nolan popularised in the South African circles of Liberation Theology, is 'preferential option for the poor' (Puebla 1979).[2] I believe that while Albert used the framework of the Puebla formulation, he actually lived in the spirit of Medellin,[3] reflecting honestly and theologically on the state of South African society and living out the theology of liberation he espoused, in response to the 'option for the poor' challenge. I will demonstrate this below.

The discussion in this short piece takes place under the following headings: i) A brief location of Nolan in the context of the struggle for justice for the poor and oppressed; ii) a critical appraisal of the 'pref-

---

1. In *Jesus before Christianity* (Maryknoll, NY: Orbis Books, 1976), 21.
2. The Puebla (1979) conference of Catholic bishops confirmed the position on 'Option for the Poor' which was taken at the Medellin conference in 1969. The Puebla conference, however, came with what appears to be a final version of 'Preferential Option for the Poor' (*New York Times*, 14 February 1979).
3. Most Latin American liberation theologians did, in fact, live in the uncompromising spirit of Medellin.

erential option for the poor' notion; iii) the challenge of the 'option for the poor' to proponents; and iv) a synergy between Nolan's theology and praxis. The last section comprises a brief conclusion.

A brief location of Nolan in Contextual Theology

Albert Nolan joined the Dominican Order of the RCC in 1954, six years before the banning of the African National Congress (ANC) and the Pan Africanist Congress (PAC). The banning left the Church and its theologians with the task of keeping the hopes of the poor and oppressed alive. Nolan found a niche in Liberation Theology, first settling for the branding 'Contextual Theology', later honing it and adopting the term 'Liberation Theology'.[4] He focused in particular on the poor and oppressed, as it is clear in his *Jesus before Christianity*, which he first published about three years before the Puebla affirmation of the 'preferential option for the poor'.

The latter book, consisting of Nolan's lectures on Jesus, may even be regarded as the South African counterpart of Gutiérrez's *A Theology of Liberation*.[5] Reading it with a mental picture of Nolan's personality and conduct reveals how well he understood the historical Jesus' mission and how much he sought to imitate him in his own life. His priority concern, among other concerns he had, was the Church's role in giving hope to the marginalised. In his article, 'The option for the poor', published in 1986, Nolan again raises the issue and he looks at the place of the poor beyond Apartheid. His next major publication, *God in South Africa*, published in 1988, also takes up this theme. Here he looks at structural violence and collective sin in South Africa, and his approach might as well be labelled a 'theology from the side of the oppressed'. He believed that the 'option for the poor' was about choosing sides with—and for—the oppressed, especially where the latter were unable to do so for themselves.

As was the case with Jesus, the establishment of God's Kingdom was always before Nolan's eyes and on his lips. For that he freed himself of earthly attachments, including privilege as a white person, living a fancy lifestyle, having worldly titles, wealth and positions of

---

4. Contextual Theology is an overarching term for several strands, while liberation theology refers to a particular strand.
5. Gustavo Gutiérrez, *A Theology of Liberation* (Maryknoll, NY: Orbis Books, 1971).

power. A good understanding of the 'option for the poor' will show that his was a 'kenotic ministry'.[6] I reflect on that below.

Preferential option for the poor: a critical appraisal

This phrase was discussed in its short and long forms before it was eventually adopted by the Latin American bishops at the respective conferences of Medellin (1968) and Puebla (1979). It appears that apart from a focus on basic human conditions, especially in Medellin, the 'thorny' theological issue was the difficulty to reconcile the preaching concerning God's 'universal charity' and the proclamation of a God who is 'exclusively for the poor'. With that, the authors of the 'option for the poor' concept intended to place the poor and suffering at the centre of the Church's theology and ministry. However, there are slight differences in emphases and interpretations of the principle after Puebla. Some theologians, Latin American liberation theologians in particular, retained the spirit of Medellin. Below I focus on the respective views of Gustavo Gutiérrez and Jon Sobrino.[7]

There appears to be a consensus between the above two theologians (and perhaps many others) about the meaning of the phrase 'option for the poor'. It has to do with the dignity of the human person, encouraging justice for those whose dignity is ignored or overlooked. The report of the Birmingham Diocesan Justice and Peace Commission (no date) states that this is 'a principle which gives priority to the needs and rights of those who are economically disadvantaged and consequently suffer oppression and powerlessness'.[8] As it is clear, the poor and suffering are at the centre. It is to these most vulnerable people that Pope Francis (2013) claims the Church exists to bring the Good News of the gospel.[9] This Good News, according to the Pope, is about the coming Kingdom of love, justice, dignity and peace.

---

6. *Kenotic*, from the Greek term *kenosis*, refers to 'emptying of oneself' as the Letter to the Philippians describes Jesus (Phil 2:7).

7. This may sound limited and narrow. My point is to find a specific theological emphasis of Albert Nolan's 'option for the poor'. A lot has been written about the 'preferential option for the poor' since the 1980s, but that is not my concern in this short tribute to Nolan.

8. Birmingham Diocesan Peace and Justice Commission, n.d. at <https://www.birminghamjndp.org.uk> Accessed April 2023.

9. Pope Francis, 'Lenten Message, *Evangeli Gaudium*, 2013' at <https://w2vatican.va/content/francesco/messages/lent/documents/papa-francesco20131226 messaggio-quaresima2014html>. Accessed April 2023.

In his 1971 book, *A Theology of Liberation*, Gutiérrez acknowledges God's bias towards the poor. However, he deems it necessary to address the issue of the place of the universal charity of God whom he portrays as loving and wanting everyone to experience love. How is it then possible to proclaim a God who opts for a particular social class? Gutiérrez is aware of the overwhelming scriptural evidence to the effect that in all cases, God invariably sides with the poor and oppressed. This notwithstanding, the Church has both poor and rich, oppressed and oppressor in its ranks. It appears that the 'preferential option' notion was born through the interstices of this wrestling at Puebla.[10] The Birmingham Diocesan Justice and Peace report suggests that the Puebla formulation was in opposition to the idea of an 'exclusive option for the poor'. Working within the framework of the RCC's pastoral teaching, Pope Francis (2013) affirms the preferential option when he writes:

> without the preferential option for the poor, the proclamation of the Gospel, which is itself the prime form of charity, risks being misunderstood or submerged by the ocean of words which daily engulfs us in today's society of mass communications (*Evangelii Gaudium*, 169).

This neither denies nor captures the sharpness of the scriptural evidence in this regard. It therefore does not affirm the radical theologians who only understand Jesus to be exclusively with and for the poor.

Gutiérrez, according to John Dear,[11] reminds us of our own need to side with the poor and oppressed in their struggle for justice. Christ, he argues, is present among the poor and oppressed, especially in their struggle to end poverty and oppression. An 'option for the poor' is an 'option for Jesus'. He understood poverty in a materialistic rather than in a spiritual sense. He elaborates thus:

> to be poor means to die of hunger, to be illiterate, to be exploited by others, not to know that you are being exploited, not to know that you are a person.[12]

---

10. See Hyer, 1979 *Washington Post*.
11. John Dear, 'Gustavo Gutiérrez and the Preferential Option for the Poor', in *National Catholic Reporter* (8 November 2011) é
12. Gutiérrez, *A Theology of Liberation*, 289.

Voluntary poverty is a response to this, that is, as a choice to live with the materially poor and as a protest against the injustices committed against them. This echoes the sentiments of the Medellin conference.

In *Jesus the Liberator*, Jon Sobrino asserts that Christology is not merely about Jesus Christ but also the entire body of Christ.[13] This echoes Takatso Mofokeng's *The Crucified among the Crossbearers*[14] and Jürgen Moltmann's *The Crucified God: The Cross of Christ as the Foundation and Criticism of Christian Theology*.[15] God suffered on the cross on behalf of the body, the Church. Therefore, on the cross, it was the entire body that was crucified. Like Gutiérrez, Sobrino lists a number of relevant Old and New Testament passages in support of his view that since Old Testament times, God has always been understood to be on the side of the poor and suffering. God always confronted suffering and oppression. It is for this reason that Sobrino (2008) could not but conclude that God cannot be understood apart from his '*partial* (my emphasis) compassion and concern for the poor'.

I promised above to substantiate my choice of the 'option for the poor' as opposed to the 'preferential option for the poor'. The above discussion of Sobrino's views hints at a firmer assertion than Gutiérrez's 'firm commitment'. Sobrino is not apologetic about God's relationship with the poor and suffering. God is partial or biased towards the poor. That is his message. There is no consideration of the implications thereof for the Church's teaching on God's universal charity. Thus, he takes the argument beyond what he regards as Gutiérrez's 'dilemma', namely wrestling with the notion of God's 'universal charity' in relation to the 'option for the poor'. He correctly argues that the gospel speaks *to* the poor and *of* the poor.[16] Citing Luke 4:18, he asserts that Jesus specifically offers salvation to the poor, the lame, the downtrodden, etc. It is good news *specifically* for these categories of people.[17] Given what the scriptures teach about God's intervention, Jesus cannot be on the side of both the oppressor and the oppressed, the exploiter and the exploited. This would be more appreciated at

---

13. Jon Sobrino, *Jesus the Liberator* (Maryknoll, NY: Orbis Books, 2001), 26.
14. TA Mofokeng, *The Crucified among the Crossbearers: Towards a Black Christology* (Kampen: Uitgevermaatschappij JH Kok, 1983).
15. Jürgen Moltmann (Minneapolis, MN: Fortress Press, 1993).
16. Sobrino, *Jesus the Liberator*.
17. The synoptic gospels in particular follow the ministry of Jesus from Galilee to Jerusalem, moving among the poor and marginalised, this confirming that he was always found among the poor.

Medellin where, according to Gutiérrez,[18] statements such as 'there are rich people because there are poor people, and there are poor people because there are rich people' were occasionally heard.

My view is that it makes better sense to see Jesus on the side of the poor, beckoning the oppressor and exploiter with Zacchaeus' conscience (*cf* Lk 19:1–9) to 'come over' to him. Accordingly, I align myself fully with Sobrino's approach on the grounds that the scriptures are unambiguous about God's role and place in the struggle against poverty and suffering. If Jesus had watered down his message, he might have escaped death, but his message of the Kingdom would have been insignificant.

The 'option for the poor' principle was embraced by both formal Church structures and para-Church activist groups during the struggle for liberation in South Africa. It had implications for their individual conduct. Below I look at the challenge it sets for its proponents.

The challenge of the 'option for the poor'

Is it possible to espouse the notion of the 'option for the poor'—whether in its shorter or longer form, without leading by example? Put differently, is it possible to alter the consistent biblical message about God's bias towards the poor in order to accommodate the powerful? Gutiérrez's emphasis on the 'preferential option' tempers the sharpness of the message of Jesus despite him arguing that it is a 'firm commitment' to the cause of the poor. Entry into Jesus' 'presence' or fellowship with him was not unconditional. The new/aspiring recruit had to convert and turn over a new leaf if they wanted to walk Jesus' Way.

Some of those who heard the message of Jesus but did not act may have been motivated by their refusal to detach themselves from the things that held them back (for example the rich young ruler in Lk 18:18–23) or they had rejected the message of Jesus outright (for example the Pharisees in Lk 16:14, Mt 12:14, 22:15). The gospel message cannot be adjusted. They are clearly refusing to heed the message of their salvation. This is the challenge of the 'option for the poor'. Choosing the side of the poor means working against themselves and ending their dominance. This might mean 'committing class suicide'.[19]

---

18. Gutiérrez, *A Theology of Liberation*, 289.
19. Amílcar Cabral, *Revolution in Guinea: An African People's Struggle, Selected Texts* (London: Stage 1 Publisher, 1969).

However, it is possible to espouse the idea without practicing it. Contemporary empirical research might even suggest that most proponents of the 'preferential option for the poor' are by virtue of their academic qualifications and their income levels located in lower and upper middle-class groups. There is nothing wrong with this. It is, however, not clear how many of these have totally emptied themselves of concomitant aspirations and possessions as required by their preferred theological stance. Observations from the empirical situation show that most have since sloganised the 'preferential option for the poor' principle by shouting 'solidarity' from the comfort of their security and opulence.[20] It probably soothes their consciences. However, they continue to live life as they wish, away from the discomfort of situations that demand a total commitment.

This has not always been the case. There were individuals in the 1980s who had made sacrifices for the sake of the poor. In some cases, there was a total *'kenosis'* (at least, in the public eye) and in others, a 'trickle-down', that is, a sharing of their possessions in a piecemeal manner. Hence, Gerald West, still in the spirit of the 1980s, could boldly and confidently allude to a fundamental difference based on the social location of an engaged reader.[21] For him the fundamental difference lay in the respective methodological approaches of those located in the 'First World' and those in the 'Third World'. A drop in such standards of accountability and value systems is indicative of the materialistic society South Africans have become used to after the 1994 transition to democracy. This is regression rather than progress, a reflection of a mind shift from a socialist orientation to capitalist aspirations. Meanwhile, the legacy of inequality remains intact, while the poor are being multiplied daily. If the 'option for the poor' is understood in the spirit of Medellin, as in the Latin American liberation brand of theology which had influenced South Africans in the 1980s and 1990s, actions must follow the words.

This is possible. I will demonstrate it below with Nolan's theology and praxis.

---

20. I count myself among these by virtue of my income level and priorities with it.

21. Gerald West, 'The Bible and the Poor: A New Way of Doing Theology', in *Bible in Mission. Regnum Edinburgh Centenary Series.* Volume 18 edited by Pauline Hoggarth, Fergus Macdonald, Bill Mitchell and Knud Jorgensen, at <https://www.researchgate.net/publication/291294338>. Accessed April 2023.

Nolan's theology and praxis

Viewed in light of the above discussion, Nolan's theology and praxis have been consistent throughout. He used the framework of the Puebla formulation, but the extent of his involvement in the struggles of the poor and oppressed puts him in line with the theologians who never shrugged-off the Medellin spirit. Elements of both Gutiérrez and Sobrino can be discerned in his theology and praxis. There is no space to go into that here save to make the following comments.

He remained the same until his death in October 2022. The sale of the fancy house of his religious community in Houghton when he took over the reigns as the Dominican provincial and settling for a modest building in Mayfair, Johannesburg, signalled his seriousness about living out the theology he believed in.[22] His concerns successfully rubbed off onto his brothers in the Mayfair Dominican house.

Nolan's publications, which made him world famous, did not overtake his theological and social cause. They were simply his vehicles for teaching and disseminating ideas rather than a means for recognition, amassing power and upward mobility. When he was nominated to the position of Master of the Dominican Order in 1983, he quietly requested to be released from the post, ostensibly because it would have removed him from the struggles of the poor and oppressed back in South Africa.[23] The Rome based position was prestigious and it could have been an entry point to higher positions. Nolan did not make an issue of this. It was others who did because the position had apparently never been declined by anyone before, many coveted it instead.

It is important to acknowledge that all the above stems from a theological base. While Nolan was not a slave to 'orthodoxy',[24] he worked within the framework of the RCC's principles and teachings. Vatican II pronouncements and pontifical messages to the body meant much to him. These are reflected in his publications and teaching notes. He questioned some of his Church's teaching if it was in conflict with his idea of the 'option for the poor' and suffering.

---

22. Terence Creamer, 'Albert Nolan: Priest, Activist, Author and Renowned Theologian' at <m.polity.org.za>. Accessed April 2023.
23. Raymond Suttner, 'Albert Nolan- "Memories of a non-believer"' at <m.polity.org.za>. Accessed April 2023.
24. Albert Nolan, RF Broderick, *To Nourish Our Faith. The Theology of Liberation in Southern Africa* (Hilton: The Order of Preachers, 1987).

However, I take issue with Nolan's lowering of the biblical bar on God's relationship with the poor. As Nolan himself admits, the phrase is extra-biblical, but it is predicated on a biblical principle.[25] When Nolan asserts that the phrase has nothing to do with the individual's handling of material possessions, but with their stance in relation to structural violence against the poor, he is watering down the sharp and unambiguous message to the Rich Young Rulers and Pharisees of this world. He might have been influenced by the diversity of sympathisers with the struggle of the poor at the time, an issue similar to that which Gutiérrez wrestled with. His own life and theology suggest that he lived out what he believed to be God's option and emptied himself as did his Lord Jesus.

Conclusion

The 'preferential option for the poor' was not only controversial (Nolan, Buffel),[26] but it created the impression in some that they could choose how to sympathise with the poor or intervene on their behalf. God on the other hand, is always with the poor and is beckoning those on the other side to fight alongside the poor against injustice, manifesting in exploitation and oppression. Jesus and his early followers demonstrated that the guarantee for full participation required a personal *kenotic* process first. Albert accepted the challenge and organised his life accordingly.

---

25. Albert Nolan, 'The Option for the Poor', in *South African Cross Currents*, 36/1 (1986): 17–27.
26. Olehile Buffel. 'Bringing the Crucified Down from the Cross: Preferential Option for the Poor in the South African Context of Poverty', in *Missionalia* 43/3 (2015): 349–364 and Albert Nolan, 'The Option for the Poor', in *South African Cross Currents*, 36/1 (1986): 17–27.

Albert making a presentation on The Impact on Africa of Dominican Formation at an international congress on Dominican Formation held at the Angelicum in Rome in November, 1994 on the occasion of the beatification of the former Master of the Order, Hyacinthe-Marie Cormier.

Eschatology for Urgent Times

Paul B Decock OMI

God in South Africa is one of Fr Albert Nolan's major theological works.[1] Judging by the attention it received in the reviews in different journals in South Africa and worldwide, it was a significant book for that time. *For that time* already indicates the thrust of Nolan's work. He did not aim to theologise for all time and all places, but for South Africa at that particular *kairos* (crucial moment). He was one of the major contributors to the *Kairos Document*[2] and he was therefore well qualified to articulate the understanding of eschatology in that document in an article in *Missionalia,* the prominent journal of the *Missiological Society of Southern Africa.*[3] In this document, the words of the Gospel, 'the time [*kairos*] is fulfilled and the Kingdom of God has come near; repent and believe in the good news' (Mk 1:15), were concretised and understood in terms of the South African context at that time. The *Document* speaks of the *'kairos',* 'the moment of truth (. . .) the moment of grace and opportunity, the favourable time in which God issues a challenge to decisive action . . .'.[4] The opportune time at that moment was the crisis in the political situation and in the conviction that Apartheid's days were numbered. However, it is not

---

1. Albert Nolan, *God in South Africa: The Challenge of the Gospel* (Cape Town: David Philip, 1988). This is not to underestimate the famous earlier work, *Jesus before Christianity* (1976), and the more recent, *Jesus Today: A Spirituality of Radical Freedom* (2006).
2. *Kairos Document: Challenge to the Church* (Johannesburg: Institute for Contextual Theology, 1985).
3. Albert Nolan, 'The Eschatology of the Kairos Document', in *Missionalia,* 15 (1987): 61–9.
4. *Kairos Document*, 1.

only 'good news', but also a challenge to repent and to be ready to act. A *kairos* is, therefore, both opportunity and challenge.

It was in this context that *God in South Africa* appeared. Soon after, in 1990, the local journal, *Grace & Truth*, produced an issue examining this work.[5] In replying to the different comments and criticism of his work, Fr Nolan also further articulated his own contextual and pastoral approach to theology.

The primary focus in this article is an exploration of the ways in which he has been inspired by biblical scholarship and the ways in which he has appropriated their interpretations. In all of this his focus is on the 'world in front of the text', what it means in our context. His own main focus is not to enter into dialogue with scholars but with the people of South Africa.

Albert Nolan's general approach to theology

Nolan[6] situates his own approach in a much wider context of developments in theology and other disciplines and he points to this development as 'the paradigm shift'. This explains the title of his response to the articles in the 1990 issue of *Grace & Truth*. He summarises this shift for his own work as follows:

> In the simplest and most general terms I would like to describe the paradigm shift in theology as a transition from theology as the study of revelation (Word of God, Bible, tradition, doctrine, ideas, etc) to theology as a reflection upon experience in the light of traditional Christian symbols.[7]

He views the epistemology of traditional theology as defective, in that:

> the acquiring of knowledge is not a purely disinterested or objective pursuit, that it serves particular interests and concerns (good or bad) and that ideas are not neutral, absolute and eternal but conditioned by the material circumstances, the context that gave rise to them.[8]

---

5. *Grace & Truth*, 10/2 (September 1990).
6. Albert Nolan, 'The Paradigm Shift', in *Grace & Truth*, 10/2 (September 1990): 97.
7. Nolan, 'The Paradigm Shift', 97.
8. Nolan, 'The Paradigm Shift', 97–98.

We recognise a variety of related influences here: the See–Judge–Act approach of the Young Christian Workers (YCW), the South American Liberation Theology with their materialist and contextual approaches. Besides the importance of knowing his exegetical sources, it is also revealing to see how he appropriates these for the South African context of the time of the approaching end of Apartheid.

Among the different approaches used in the study of the Scriptures, his approach is focused, not on 'the world behind the text', that is, how the Scriptures came about. He does not even want to get absorbed in the pursuit of the scholarly details of 'the world of the text', but he wants to grasp the core of 'the world of the text' and let it become a transformative message for Christian life in the present context. His real concern was the transition from the 'world of the text' to the 'world in front of the text', in other words, the meaning of the text in our context, the contextualisation of the gospel. He aimed at making the reading of the text a 'useful' experience for contemporary Christian readers. This was in line with the ancient approach to the Scriptures, but while this approach focused on the personal 'transformation of the individual believers' in a comprehensive way, Fr Nolan focused on the transformation of the social commitments of the Christian. His concern was to liberate Christians from a kind of 'Apocalyptic Christianity' which turned their focus on the 'Last Judgment' or the nearness of the 'End of the World' while neglecting responsibility for the present state of the world:

> Domination or liberation, wealth or poverty, dictatorship, slavery, war and peace, all this is of no importance, of no account; all this is overshadowed by the only important consideration: we have a soul which is urgently in need of salvation. There is no time to think of anything else.[9]

He recalled this traditional language of the ascent from the Letter to the Spirit, but he proposed instead to think in terms of a 'translation' of the gospel from the time of Jesus into its meaning for the present South African context. While the *shape* remains (the quality of Good News), the *content* is determined by the experience of the readers. The good news of liberation in the context of Roman

---

9. Nolan, 'The Paradigm Shift', 100; quotation from Joseph Comblin, 'The Current Debate on Christian Universality', in *Concilium* (May 1980): 81–82.

imperial domination now corresponds to liberation in the context and experience of Apartheid society.[10] In response to Mueller's evaluation of his proposal,[11] Nolan replied, that in other contexts these proposals may be appropriate, 'but in the South Africa today we have more urgent matters to deal with, related to our particular conditions, needs and problems'.[12] Nolan is driven by the urgency of the situation. He reminds us again, referring to the influential North American theologian, David Tracy,[13] that all theological work does, in fact, take place in a particular and limited context and that Western theologies cannot lay claim to universal validity and as norm for all local theologies.[14]

This sense of focus on the concrete context is further illustrated in Nolan's comments on the contribution by Brian Gaybba,[15] where he points out that a theology of 'the people' should assess and challenge the ways in which the term is used in the South African political debates, and not remain on the level of abstract, universal or even historical considerations of the idea of 'the people'.[16] Similarly, with regard to the question of the power of faith, Nolan makes the significant remark that Contextual Theology must focus on the question: who in the South African context 'benefits from the cry: *Amandla* (power)? And what kind of power or use of power is it opposed to?'[17]

Nolan's understanding of eschatology for South Africa

With regard to eschatology, Nolan wants to understand it as touching our own situation in the here and now and not as some event in the distant future, so far away that it is no longer part of our horizon and becomes insignificant for our daily lives. His concern is not with 'universal eschatology' or with Apocalyptic in the abstract in the minds

---

10. Albert Nolan, *God in South Africa: The Challenge of the Gospel* (Cape Town: David Philip, 1988), 7–30.
11. JJ Mueller, 1990. 'A Critical & Methodological Extension: Where Do We Go from here?', in *Grace & Truth* 10/2 (1990): 85–86.
12. Nolan, 'The Paradigm Shift', 102.
13. David Tracy, 'On Naming the Present', in *Concilium*,(1990): 81–82.
14. Nolan, 'The Paradigm Shift', 102–104.
15. Bernard Connor, 'Faith in Power and the Power of Faith', in *Grace & Truth,* 10/2 (1990): 85–86.
16. Nolan, 'The Paradigm Shift', 98–99.
17. Nolan, 'The Paradigm Shift', 99.

of Scripture scholars, but with the minds of the Christians in South Africa whose minds are distorted by 'Apocalyptic Christianity'.[18] He is particularly critical of an understanding of eschatology which moves it far away, to the end of time (*chronos*) instead of seeing it as a challenge in the present, calling for the work of human hands:

> But the *eschaton* or last day is still [that is, for modern eschatology] thought of as the end of *all* history for *all* people for *all* times. The result of this universalising tendency is that it still removes the day of salvation from particular struggles and postpones it until the end of time, far out of the reach of particular peoples who are struggling with particular manifestations of sin and evil in particular places at particular times. In short, it makes the day of the salvation or the reign of God irrelevant.[19]

We will examine here how he draws insights from prominent biblical scholars in order to articulate his own approach.

First of all, he has drawn from Joseph Comblin[20] with his experience of the Brazilian context and the other-worldliness of the various churches there. Comblin has called this 'Apocalyptic Christianity'. In South Africa, Nolan finds a variety of this otherworldliness in conservative Catholics, fundamentalists, born again Christians, Dispensationalists and Millenarianists of the various kinds. Either the Parousia preoccupies them to such an extent that nothing of this world counts anymore, or else the ongoing course of world history is seen as irrelevant to the salvation of the individual soul and the salvation of the soul has nothing to do with universal and cosmic salvation. Comblin maintains that this form of 'Apocalyptic Christianity' is the cause of the widespread otherworldliness among Christians and of the excessive preoccupation with predictions of the date of the Parousia.[21] Nolan is determined to correct this distortion of the faith of so many and attempts to inspire them to care for justice and peace in South Africa precisely in view of the *kairos*.

---

18. Nolan, 'The Paradigm Shift', 100.
19. Nolan, *God in South Africa*, 132.
20. Comblin, 'The Current Debate on Christian Universality', 70–80.
21. Nolan, 'The Paradigm Shift', 100–102.

Furthermore, Fr Nolan was enlightened by Gerhard Von Rad's work on the prophets. Von Rad's[22] discussion on the eschatology of the prophets drew Nolan's attention to the difference between the Western and the Hebrew understanding of time. It was for him a way of extricating the message about the *'kairos'* from the idea that it was tied to the end of time (*chronos*). Von Rad points out that the prophets, and even the Apocalyptic texts, envisage 'the continuation of time and history after the historical consummation'.[23] Different from Modern Western time, 'Israel was not capable of thinking of time in the abstract, divorced from specific events'.[24] Eventually, they realised that their faith was based not only on one event, the Exodus, but on a string of events, from the promises to the patriarchs to the settlement in the land. In this way Israel moved away from a view of cultic actualisation to a 'linear and chronological view of history'.[25]

Fr Nolan, however, retains from all this that we should not imagine that the *eschata* are 'events which will happen only at the end of time'.[26] In this light the crisis in South Africa at the approaching end of Apartheid could be seen as an eschaton, one of the many opportunities offered by God in the course of time. Nolan does not want us to see the meaning of the word *'eschaton'* as related to *'chronos'* in the quantitative sense as 'last', but in the qualitative sense as a crisis laden with divine potential, an opportunity offered by God, a challenge put before us by God to See, to Judge and to Act. He sees the *'kairos'* as being upon us, not in the sense of 'Apocalyptic Christianity', where people get excited about the date of the end of the world, about the course of the events of the end, the coming of millennium, about the afterlife. He does not deny that there will be an end, a last judgment and an after-life.[27] Rather, he wants to move the focus of the Good News to the here and now with its hopes and its particular challenges. He wants to get away from the great danger of 'supernaturalism' with its divine magical interventions as well as from the other extreme, of 'some kind of iron law of social determinism'.[28] Both 'Apocalyptic

---

22. Gerhard Von Rad, *The Message of the Prophets*. (London: SCM Press, 1968), 89–4.
23. Von Rad, *The Message of the Prophets*, 90–91.
24. Von Rad, *The Message of the Prophets*, 78.
25. Von Rad, *The Message of the Prophets*, 82–85.
26. Nolan, 'The Eschatology of the Kairos Document', 67.
27. Nolan, *God in South Africa*, 119.
28. Nolan, *God in South Africa*, 155.

Christianity' and Marxian theories tend to take away human responsibility for the course of history.

With regard to the Bible, Nolan blames apocalypticism for the corruption of the prophetic tradition. The prophets proclaim a particular message for a particular situation, while the idea of a universal eschatology is an Apocalyptic innovation that 'divorces salvation from any particular time and place and people'.[29]

This is then also the reason why Fr Nolan argues that Jesus was not an apocalyptist, but continued the tradition of the ancient prophets: 'Jesus was not an apocalyptic dreamer'.[30] The issue has been much debated since the time of rationalism. However, since the publications of Johannes Weiss and Albert Schweitzer, it had become very difficult to ignore the fact that Jesus' message of the Kingdom had its roots in Apocalyptic and displayed many of the characteristics of an Apocalyptic understanding of the Kingdom. Klaus Koch[31] has exhaustively explored the history of what he has called the attempts 'to save Jesus from Apocalyptic'. Since then, James Dunn[32] came to the cautious conclusion that 'it is difficult to avoid the conclusion that Jesus' expectation of the future Kingdom was apocalyptic in character.' Nevertheless, Nolan remains convinced of his prophetic view of Jesus.

Another scholar who inspired Nolan was Rudolph Bultmann. Nolan[33] agrees with Bultmann in making the *kairos* an experience in the present detached from the idea of the end of *chronos*. He also agrees that the Scriptures do not proclaim universal truth but are concerned with the particular. However, Nolan disagrees on many points. The particular for Bultmann is a very personal, private experience, a *kairos* without any visibility in the socio-historical realm of events, while for Nolan the particular is a socio-political, visible situation. Furthermore, Nolan does not see the problem in the apocalyptic *language*, but in its supernaturalism, in the sense that it excludes the work of human hands.[34]

---

29. Nolan, *God in South Africa*, 122, also 132.
30. Nolan, *God in South Africa*, 123–125.
31. Klaus Koch, *The Re-Discovery of Apocalyptic* (London: SCM Press, 1972), 57–97.
32. James DG Dunn, *Unity and Diversity in the New Testament: An Inquiry into the Character of Early Christianity* (London: SCM Press, 1977), 321.
33. Albert Nolan, 'The Eschatology of the Kairos Document', in *Missionalia*, 15 (1987): 76.
34. Nolan, *God in South Africa*, 132.

> What all the theories [about eschatology] seem to have over-looked is that the Bible is not dealing with general religious truths. The message of the Bible is timebound, not in the sense that it reveals something about chronological times and dates, but in the sense that it records the quality of previous times in order to bring us face to face in our time. We need to be clear about the meaning of time as a quality (. . .) the exodus from Egypt and the exodus from Babylon was qualitatively the same event. Thus events that are chronologically different but have the same quality of finality and ultimateness are one and the same eschaton for the people who experience them as such. They are all the death and resurrection of Jesus fore-shadowed or made present again.[35]

For Nolan, the *eschaton* is something which happens again and again within our history as God's offer and challenge and our response to situations of crisis.

Of course, he does not deny the universal eschatology, but his concern is that for many people in South Africa the excitement over the universal eschatology is sterile and produces no fruit in the present. Nolan intended make people aware of the misplaced focus at the centre of their attention and turn people away from a fruitless emotionalism, but also from a merely individualist morality, and especially from the idea that it all depended on God with no human contribution in shaping that future, from that kind of 'Apocalyptic Christianity', which he saw as 'distorting the faith of so many Christians in South Africa today'.[36]

Conclusion

Fr Albert Nolan's views on eschatology were driven by his sense of urgency; his concern at that time was to awaken Christians to the *kairos*, the great opportunities which the end of Apartheid was fore-shadowing with its great challenges. He wanted to awaken people to their great opportunity to realise God's Kingdom in the here and now as God's trusted collaborators. This challenge remains in the present situation in new ways.

---

35. Nolan, 'The Eschatology of the Kairos Document', 77–78.
36. Nolan, 'The Paradigm Shift', 100.

With regard to his approach to exegesis, his focus is on the 'world in front of the text'. In South Africa, this was not the time to remain involved in the insoluble questions of the 'world behind the text', it was not the time to remain caught up in the 'world of the text'. His aim is to search and proclaim what the text means for us now, a search which means learning by putting it into practice, hearing and doing. His views are supported by aspects of the interpretations of a number of important exegetes, but he does not enter into a discussion with them. He rather selects what he judges to be true and must be done in the here and now, based on his own understanding of Jesus. For instance, he will not enter into the disputed questions about apocalyptic and prophecy, or in the question about the place of *chronos* and *kairos,* or about Bultmann's demythologising program. The time was seen as too urgent for academic disputes about all of these.

Albert, with the Master of the Order, Carlos Aspiroz Costa OP and the Socius for Africa, Roger Houngbedji OP during their visit to South Africa, c. 2002, listening to Sr Alison Munro in a meeting with the Dominican Family.

Biblical Interpretation as Prophetic Process

Gerald O West

Introduction

In the last volume of the *Journal of Theology for Southern Africa* (JTSA) for 2022, a volume which celebrates the fiftieth anniversary of JTSA, we also celebrated the legacy of Albert Nolan. We honoured Albert Nolan by republishing two of his seminal articles: 'The Option for the Poor in South Africa', and 'A Workers Theology'.[1] We chose these two regularly republished articles because they exemplify the biblical and theological praxis of Albert Nolan.

In this essay I reflect on more than three decades of 'contextual' biblical and theological work alongside Albert Nolan, using these two articles of his as a lens through which to document biblical interpretation as prophetic process. Specifically, I will analyse the conceptual contribution Albert Nolan has made to the 'Contextual Bible Study' (CBS) praxis of the Ujamaa Centre for Community Development and

---

1. Albert Nolan, 'The Option for the Poor in South Africa', in *Resistance and Hope: South African Essays in honour of Beyers Naudé*, edited by Charles Villa-Vicencio and John W De Gruchy (Cape Town and Grand Rapids: David Philip and Eerdmans, 1985); Albert Nolan, 'The Option for the Poor in South Africa', in *CrossCurrents* 36/1 (1986); Albert Nolan, 'The Option for the Poor in South Africa', *Journal of Theology for Southern Africa* 174 (2022); Albert Nolan, 'A Workers' Theology', in *The Threefold Cord: Theology, Work and Labour*, edited by James R Cochrane and Gerald O West (Pietermaritzburg: Cluster Publications, 1991); Albert Nolan, 'Work, the Bible, Workers, and Theologians: Elements of a Workers' Theology', in *Semeia* 73 (1996); Albert Nolan, 'Work, the Bible, Workers, and Theologians: Elements of a Workers' Theology', in *Journal of Theology for Southern Africa*, 174 (2022).

Research.[2] Albert Nolan 'shaped' not only my own work, being cited on the very first page of my published PhD,[3] but also the work of the Ujamaa Centre (then the Institute for the Study of the Bible), being inspirational in the formation of the praxis of CBS and endorsing the first attempt to analyse it.[4]

More significantly, Albert Nolan shaped my life, mentoring me in the discipline of Contextual-Liberation Theology from the late 1980s until his death in 2022. I remember him with deep gratitude.

The option for the poor

Drawing on the full array of Third World reflection on emerging forms of liberation theology, including the work of Nolan, Per Frostin identifies a decisive shift in the formation and characterisation of 'liberation' theologies. The key shift is to ask the question, 'Who are the interlocutors of theology?' or, 'Who are asking the questions that theologians are trying to answer?'[5] Decisively, Frostin goes on to assert, the question of the interlocutors of theology is given a specific answer by liberation theologies: 'a preferential option for the poor.'[6] Frostin goes further, stating that according to theologians of liberation, 'solidarity with the poor also has consequences for the perception of the social reality, as seen in the phrase "the epistemological privilege of the poor"'. 'This startling expression suggests', continues Frostin, 'that cognizance of the experience of the those defined as poor is a necessary condition for theological reflection.'[7] An option for the poor, which Nolan's article clearly articulates, is more than an ethical relationship, it is an epistemological relationship.[8] Theolo-

---

2. For a more general history see Gerald O West, 'Contextual Bible Study as a Form of Contextual Theology: An Early Conceptual History', in *Studia Historiae Ecclesiasticae,* 48/2 (2022).

3. Gerald O West, *Biblical Hermeneutics of Liberation: Modes of Reading the Bible in the South African Context* (Pietermaritzburg: Cluster Publications, 1991), 2.

4. Gerald O West, *Contextual Bible Study* (Pietermaritzburg: Cluster Publications, 1993).

5. Per Frostin, *Liberation Theology in Tanzania and South Africa: A First World Interpretation* (Lund: Lund University Press, 1988), 6.

6. Frostin, *Liberation Theology in Tanzania and South Africa,* 6.

7. Frostin, *Liberation Theology in Tanzania and South Africa,* 6.

8. Frostin, *Liberation Theology in Tanzania and South Africa,* 6; Nolan, 'The Option for the Poor in South Africa', 5.

gians need 'to learn from those who are oppressed'.[9] What the Good News is—the gospel—is shaped by our primary interlocutors and their (organised)[10] knowledge and understanding of reality.[11]

Collaboration with the embodied presence and the knowledge of actual communities of the economic poor is the fulcrum of Nolan's Contextual-Liberation Theology. Nolan refuses metaphorical notions of 'the poor', whether in the contemporary South Africa context or the ancient contexts of the Bible, insisting on economic poverty as the distinctive feature of 'the poor'.[12]

Doing theology with the poor

In his article 'The Option for the Poor in South Africa', Nolan is cognisant not only of the poor but also of those who will read his article and who will need to be persuaded. The tone is pastoral and didactic. The tone of the second article republished in JTSA, 'Work, the Bible, Workers, and Theologians: Elements of a Workers' Theology' is quite different. Here Nolan is talking among comrades. The article took form as part of the Institute for Contextual Theology's (ICT) 'Church and Labour Research Group', and was presented at the 'Theology, Work, and Labour Conference' in Pietermaritzburg in 1989.[13]

This article is about doing theology. Hearing Nolan present his paper at this conference was an inspiration. My PhD work on the biblical hermeneutics of liberation struggles had regularly read the claim to 'an option for the poor',[14] but I saw little evidence of what 'the epistemological privilege of the poor' would mean for biblical interpretive method. While not dealing specifically with biblical studies method, Nolan engaged directly with theological method. Nolan asserts: 'a genuine theology of work will have to be a worker's theology, that is to say, a theology constructed by workers and for

---

9. Nolan, 'The Option for the Poor in South Africa', 14.
10. Nolan makes it clear that this is not about the individual poor, but all the poor and oppressed in Nolan, 'The Option for the Poor in South Africa', 12–13.
11. Nolan, 'The Option for the Poor in South Africa', 5.
12. Nolan, 'The Option for the Poor in South Africa', 7.
13. James R Cochrane and Gerald O West, *The Three-fold Cord: Theology, Work and Labour* (Pietermaritzburg: Cluster Publications, 1991).
14. Gerald O West, 'Biblical Interpretation in Theologies of Liberation: Modes of Reading the Bible in the South African Context of Liberation' (Thesis University of Sheffield, 1990).

workers—a theological reflection of workers upon their experience of work and their experience of struggle'.[15] Here is the epistemological privilege of workers writ large! Nolan then goes to make it clear that '[t]his does not mean that the professional theologian, biblical scholar, or pastor will have no role to play in the construction of a theology of work, but that they will have a subordinate role to play'.[16] The socially engaged biblical scholar, theologian, and pastor should *serve* the struggle of the economically poor.

> The ideal situation for constructing a theology of work is not that the professional theology makes use of the insights of workers, but that workers make use of the expertise and technical knowledge of academics, so that it is, and remains, in fact, a worker's theology. In practice this means that we, the trained theologians and clergy, have to learn the skill of being used, of putting our expertise into the hands of the working class as a service to them, what Jesus called 'learning to serve rather than to be served'.[17]

As Nolan goes on to state astutely, 'As academics, intellectuals, or biblical scholars we are more accustomed to making use of the insights of others than allowing ourselves to be made use of'.[18] A form of conversion is required, being 'born again from below', as we say in the Ujamaa Centre. In Nolan's words: 'It requires a conscious and concerted effort to do more than just listen to what workers have to say.' 'In fact,' he continues, 'it requires a confident and militant group of workers who will dictate their needs and interests to us and correct us whenever we begin to determine the pace and the requirements.'[19]

This article of Nolan's has become something of a manifesto for me and for the work of the Institute for the Study of the Bible (ISB), the House of Studies for Worker Ministry, and the Ujamaa Centre (which reconstitutes both). Here is a theologian grappling with what it means to serve the organised poor with biblical, theological, and pastoral resources in order to enable them to articulate their theology. Nolan is clear that '[t]o say that a genuine theology of work must be

---

15. Nolan, 'Work, the Bible, Workers, and Theologians', 15.
16. Nolan, 'Work, the Bible, Workers, and Theologians', 15.
17. Nolan, 'The Option for the Poor in South Africa', 19.
18. Nolan, 'The Option for the Poor in South Africa', 19.
19. Nolan, 'The Option for the Poor in South Africa', 19–20.

constructed by Christian workers and not expert theologians raises a host of questions', questions which have beset liberation theologies from the outset.[20]

These questions have shaped my own contribution to the work of the Ujamaa Centre for more than thirty years. In the early years of the ISB I regularly attended ICT workshops and consulted directly with Nolan in his work with the ICT.[21] We were trying to forge a biblical hermeneutic praxis modelled on Nolan's theological praxis outlined in 'A Worker's Theology', and in the *Kairos Document*.

From peoples' theology to prophetic theology

The *Kairos Document* was another formative discourse in my life. Not only did it explain my own pastoral experience within the Church, having been asked to leave my Pentecostal Church in 1983, like so many others,[22] it also provided a glimpse into theological process. While the first edition (1985)[23] says too little about the process which generated the document,[24] the second revised edition (1986) includes an illuminating footnote, which I will cite in full:

> Many readers of the first edition suggested that the meaning of prophetic theology should be spelt out more clearly. The characteristics of prophetic theology that have been included in this second edition are a summary of discussions among the *Kairos Document* theologians both before and immediately after the publication of the first edition.
> It should also be noted that there is a subtle difference between prophetic theology and people's theology. The *Kairos Document* itself, signed by theologians, ministers and other Church workers, and addressed to all who bear the name Christian is a prophetic statement. But the process that led to the produc-

---

20. See for example Juan Luis Segundo, 'The Shift Within Latin American Theology', in *Journal of Theology for Southern Africa,* 52 (1985).
21. ISB, *Annual Report*, Bible (Pietermaritzburg: Institute for the Study of the, 1990).
22. Frank Chikane, *No Life of My Own: An Autobiography* (Maryknoll, NY: Orbis Books, 1988).
23. Kairos Theologians, *Challenge to the Church: A Theological Comment on the Political Crisis in South Africa: the Kairos Document* (Braamfontein: The Kairos Theologians, 1985).
24. But see Philippe Denis, 'The Authorship and Composition Circumstances of the *Kairos Document*', in *Journal of Theology for Southern Africa,* 158 (2017).

tion of the document, the process of theological reflection and action in groups, the involvement of many different people in doing theology was an exercise in people's theology. The document is therefore pointing out two things: that our present *Kairos* challenges Church leaders and other Christians to speak out prophetically and that our present *kairos* is challenging all of us to do theology together reflecting upon our experiences in working for justice and peace in South Africa and thereby developing a better theological understanding of our *Kairos*. The method that was used to produce the *Kairos Document* shows that theology is not the preserve of professional theologians, ministers and priests. Ordinary Christians can participate in theological reflection and should be encouraged to do so. When this people's theology is proclaimed to others to challenge and inspire them, it takes on the character of a prophetic theology.

This formulation of theological praxis has proved particularly useful in my own work and the work of the Ujamaa Centre,[25] as has the eloquent elaboration of this kind of theological movement from the 'incipient' theology of the poor to public theology found in Jim Cochrane's *Circles of Dignity: Community Wisdom and Theological Reflection*.[26] But as I have said, biblical studies has been my terrain and the discipline of biblical studies had a far from clear account of what 'working with'[27] the poor might include by way of process. Given the centrality of the Bible to the South African poor and workers,[28] my life's work, shaped by Nolan's example, has been on what Nolan's theological praxis would look like within a *biblical* hermeneutics of liberation.

---

25. Gerald O West, 'People's Theology, Prophetic Theology, and Public Theology in Post-Liberation South Africa', in *The Bible and Sociological Contours: Some African Perspectives. Festschrift for Professor Halvor Moxnes*, edited by Zorodzai Dube, Loreen Maseno-Ouma, and Elia Shabani Mligo (New York: Peter Lang, 2018).

26. James R Cochrane, *Circles of Dignity: Community Wisdom and Theological Reflection* (Minneapolis: Fortress, 1999).

27. *Reading Other-Wise: Socially Engaged Biblical Scholars Reading with their Local Communities*, Semeia Studies 62, edited by Gerald O West (Atlanta and Leiden: Society of Biblical Literature and EJ Brill, 2007).

28. ICT, 'Workers, the Church, and the Alienation of Religious Life', in *The Threefold Cord: Theology, Work, and Labour*, edited by James R Cochrane and Gerald O West (Pietermaritzburg: Cluster Publications, 1991).

The Bible as a site of struggle

Somewhat strangely, the *Kairos Document* does not embrace South African Black Theology's argument that the Bible itself—intrinsically—is a site of struggle.[29] The *Kairos Document* accepts that society, the Church, theology, and biblical interpretation are sites of struggle, but not the Bible.[30] Nolan's work itself, though it tends to foreground the liberation axis of the Bible,[31] acknowledges ideological contestation within the Bible. In his section on 'The Bible and Work', Nolan proposes that 'it is workers who must re-read the Bible from the point of view of their experience of work', not only because they might 'notice the frequent references to work or labour in the Bible which we the experts might overlook because we are not workers', but because 'workers would notice something of their own experience in texts that do not make use of the word "work" at all'.[32] He then goes on to give an example of 'something that we *might* overlook and a worker *might* notice', being quick to acknowledge, 'of course, I am now guessing just to illustrate my point'. The example he gives is from the creation story in Genesis 1, where he identifies 'two strands' within the same source text (P), one where 'God acts like a "boss", a manager, a Lord, or king. God issues commands: "Let the earth produce vegetation", etc. And this is followed each time by the statement: "And it was so"'.[33] The second strand, he explains, 'follows immediately after the first on almost all the days of creation'. Here,

> God acts like a worker and not like a boss. Here God is said to have made or created or fashioned the vault, the two great lights, the great sea-monsters, the animals, and the first human beings. The vault or firmament, the sky, is pictured as a huge inverted bowl of hammered metal. In verse 7 God is not said to have created this, but to have made it or manufactured it,

---

29. Takatso Mofokeng, 'Black Christians, the Bible and Liberation', in *Journal of Black Theology,* 2/1 (1988); Itumeleng J Mosala, *Biblical Hermeneutics and Black Theology in South Africa* (Grand Rapids: Eerdmans, 1989).

30. Gerald O West, 'Kairos 2000: Moving Beyond Church Theology', in *Journal of Theology for Southern Africa,* 108 (2000).

31. See for example J Severino Croatto, 'Biblical Hermeneutics in Theologies of Liberation', in *Irruption of the Third World: Challenge to Theology*, edited by Virginia Fabella and Sergio Torres (Maryknoll NY: Orbis Books, 1983).

32. Nolan, 'Work, the Bible, Workers, and Theologians', 17.

33. Nolan, 'Work, the Bible, Workers, and Theologians', 17.

which suggests a picture of God hammering out the sky like a metalworker. Also like a worker, God can stand back from the product of his/her hands and show appreciation and satisfaction by seeing it as good. And finally, like a worker, God rests on the seventh day because God is tired: 'God rested on the seventh day after all the work God had been doing.' This strand in the story of creation provides us with an image of God that must have come originally and immediately from workers of some kind. It is an image of God as the great worker.[34]

Unfortunately, this kind of attentiveness to the ideological detail and dimension of an internally contested Scripture does not find expression in the *Kairos Document*, but it has become a core value of the Ujamaa Centre's CBS praxis.[35] The Ujamaa Centre has drawn deeply on Takatso Mofokeng's and Itumeleng Mosala's cogent arguments for a sacred text that is itself fraught with ideological contestation, not only between different 'books' but also within any particular book. Indeed, we argue that post-Apartheid there is an even greater danger of 'State Theology'-type and 'Church Theology'-type biblical ideologies becoming the dominant understandings of 'what the Bible says'.[36]

CBS praxis

I will not reiterate in detail here CBS praxis, what has been the labour of more than three decades. There is now a substantial literature, from within the Ujamaa Centre and without,[37] of our praxis. However, it may be useful to share a recent formulation of how we understand our work. Drawing from James Maxey's work on biblical translation studies, we have adopted his heuristic notion of 'translation as

---

34. Nolan, 'Work, the Bible, Workers, and Theologians', 17–18.
35. Gerald O West, 'Reading the Bible with the Marginalised: The Value/s of Contextual Bible Reading', in *Stellenbosch Theological Journal,* 1/2 (2015).
36. Gerald O West, 'Scripture as a Site of Struggle: Literary and Socio-Historical Resources for Prophetic Theology in Post-Colonial, Post-Apartheid (neo-colonial?) South Africa', in *Scripture and Resistance,* edited by Jione Havea (New York and London: Lexington/Fortress Academic, 2019).
37. See for example John Riches *et al, What is Contextual Bible Study? A Practical Guide with Group Studies for Advent and Lent* (London: SPCK, 2010); Simon Mainwaring, *Mark, Mutuality, and Mental Health: Encounters with Jesus* (Atlanta: SBL Press, 2014); Tiffany Webster, 'When the Bible meets the Black Stuff: A Contextual Bible Study Experiment' (PhD University of Sheffield, 2017).

hospitality towards the strange(r)',[38] adapting it for an understanding of CBS as community-based hospitality biblical hermeneutics. Community-based hospitality biblical hermeneutics embraces both the strangeness of biblical text itself (its internal difference and ideological contestation) and the strangers we encounter within biblical text (excluded, like Tamar (2 Sam 13:1–22), from our lectionaries) through interpretive practices which are participatory, dialogical, and inclusive.

We will not abandon Black Theology's formulation of biblical hermeneutics as 'a site of struggle', but Nolan reminds us of the relationships of hospitality that constitute the collaborative project of socially engaged biblical scholars and theologians working with the poor as we collaborate in re-reading an ambiguous Bible for social transformation, so that all 'may have life and have it abundantly' (Jn 10:10). Nolan certainly embodied this hospitality in his collaboration with me personally and with the Ujamaa Centre. The struggle and its hospitality of solidarity with the poor continues!

---

38. James A Maxey, 'Alternative Evaluative Concepts to the Trinity of Bible Translation', in *Translating Values: Evaluative Concepts in Translation*, edited by Piotr Blumczynski and John Gillespie (London: Palgrave Macmillan, 2016), 58.

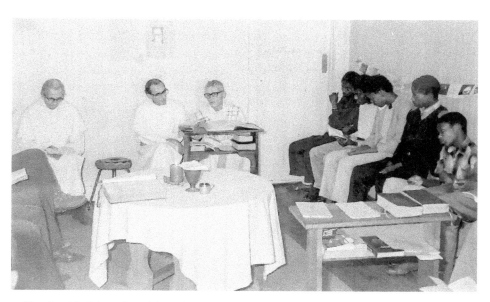

Vocations Workshop of candidates from Virginia in the Orange Free State, in Mayfair chapel (1980s), L-R: Finbar Synnott OP, Albert Nolan OP, Thomas Heath OP and with candidates.

The Known and Unknown God

Charles Villa-Vicencio

I recall a particular in-depth discussion with Albert Nolan on the nature of Christianity shortly after the first democratic elections, at a restaurant close to the Dominican provincial house where he lived in Mondeor, Johannesburg. We discussed the new age of democracy and the problems of the world (which we commonly did). Our conversation next drifted into the past and current history of the Christian Church. This included discussion on the history of the Dominican Order, as well as the birth of Methodism, and other mission-based Churches in South Africa in the nineteenth century. We discussed the mutating notions of heresy that included the Dominican attack on the Cathar heretics in the thirteenth century, and the definitive 'Apartheid is a heresy' declaration by the World Alliance of the Reformed Churches (WARC) in 1982.

It was a long and rambling conversation (which we should have recorded). What stays with me is Albert's anticipation of things yet to unfold in South Africa. I recall his reflection on different ways of reading the Bible in history, and the clarity of his understanding of belief and the limits of the Christian faith. He spoke of the distortions of biblical literalism, often used to promote different political ideologies, and the dangers of post-Apartheid Liberal Theology, as well as the (inevitable) presence of race-based ideologies in the Churches. Our conversation emphasised the need to (re)define 'Prophetic Theology' to meet the contextual needs of each new age. This led to a discussion on the use of scripture in his book, *Jesus before Christianity*,[1] and in the *Kairos Document*.[2]

---

1. Albert Nolan, *Jesus before Christianity* (Maryknoll, NY: Orbis Books, 1972).
2. *Challenge to the Church: Kairos Document* (Johannesburg: Institute for Contextual Theology, 1985).

Ultimately the way in which the Bible is understood by ordinary people in South Africa is probably more influential in society than all the sophisticated doctrines of the Church. The task of theologians and teachers is to play a constructive role in the production of popular religion.

On reading the Bible

More people live in an interregnum between science, political change and religious belief in the contemporary world than is often recognised. Many people have moved beyond the reassurances of the faith within which they were raised, while some, having adopted an empirical or scientific outlook on life, continue to be conscious of a sense of transcendence, in nature, history and literature, as well as in the unknowns of science, art, solitude and more. Others find meaning and purpose of life in the confines of empiricism alone. The discoveries of science and political change have disturbed the *status quo* in South Africa and elsewhere in the world. Gender and classist myths in the Bible are increasingly questioned in the modern world, while popular scriptural teachings on governance have left many believers confused about the authority of the state. This begs the question of the relationship between God and the Bible.

Similar questions have been faced throughout the Judeo-Christian tradition, and notably at the time of the destruction of Jerusalem and the second temple by imperial Rome in 70 CE, which provoked the early followers of Jesus to predict the imminent dawn of the Kingdom of God. Breaking away from institutional Judaism, Jesus' disciples struggled to understand the nature of his person, with the Church eventually declaring him to be the Son of God, 'truly God and truly man' at the Council of Nicaea in 325. Subsequent years saw theological debate shift towards philosophical debate on the union of Christ's humanity and divinity in one person, which lessened the focus on the humanity of Jesus in mainstream theology. This is what made Nolan's *Jesus before Christianity* such a powerful intervention at the height of the struggle against Apartheid, with the State insisting that believers ought to refrain from engaging in politics, arguing that this be left to the government. Sadly, this response was at times supported by mainline Churches that preferred to remain aloof from controversial political concerns. The debate intensified, posing the question whether the dominant interpretation of the person of Jesus by the state and some institutional Churches was an accurate version of the gospel record.

Origen of Alexandria (185–253 CE), perhaps the most reliable and systematic theological and biblical scholar in the early Church, wrote of the Bible being read in different ways: literally, as moral insight, through allegorical interpretation, and mystically.[3] The reading of the Bible was at the time largely confined to monasteries, requiring the study of separate manuscripts rather than a single volume of the Bible as it would later come to be known. The *lectio divina* (divine reading) was an integral part of prayer in monastic disciplines, which produced a framework within which the doctrine of the early Church emerged. Origen and others examined the historic origins and syntax of texts, while accepting the literal (denotational) meaning of scripture through meditation and metaphorical application. This led to the assimilation of critical exegesis and the contemplative art of imaginative understanding of scripture in different schools of theological teaching in the Christian tradition.

In the thirteenth century the Dominicans (the Order of Preachers) engaged the text in a related way, merging the *lectio divina* with a scholarly (Aristotelian) approach. They argued that the truth or spiritual meaning of the text was not to be found beyond or above the text (in a Platonic sense), but within the historical and literal meaning of the actual words of the Bible. God's Word was discovered through a disciplined, methodical approach to reading the Bible. This suggests that God's Word was made known in the Bible, *as understood by believers*. Differently stated, biblical texts convey God's Word, as understood in the context of the time and place within which human authors wrote. As God was seen (by Aristotle) as the First Mover of the cosmos, God is arguably the First Author of the Bible, conveyed through secondary and subsequent movers. As such, Dominican hermeneutics communicates a middle course between literalism and rationalism. This (I suggest) made Nolan a 'good' Dominican, living a simple life, preaching the gospel, and prioritising the needs of the poor. Rejecting a literalist-fundamentalist interpretation of Scripture, he lived and preached (communicated) in a manner that attracted believers across a range of people who were committed to the imple-

---

3. Karen Armstrong, *The Bible, The Biography* (London: Atlantic Books, 2007), 127.

mentation of the spiritual and ethical message of Jesus, as well as the law and prophets in the Hebrew Bible. In terms of Marcus Borg's distinction between a 'literal-factual' reading of the Bible and a 'historical-metaphorical' reading, for Nolan, the litmus test of true belief was the life of Jesus that the New Testament portrays as service to the poor, politically oppressed women, culturally excluded people, and other outliers of society. This interpretation, argues Johann Metz, was the 'dangerous memory' of the life of Jesus that continues to disturb the politically complacent members in the Churches.[4]

Throughout history, institutional Churches have been inclined to use popular literalism to bolster ideological ideas, including racism and sexual abuse, to promote dogmatic brands of theology as manifest in the Christian crusades, the Inquisition and religious wars in the wake of the Protestant and Catholic Counter-Reformation. Contemporary brands of this hermeneutic continue to be practised in right-wing fundamentalist and conservative evangelical Churches today, fuelling not only ecclesial conflict, but aggression in supporting western forms of nationalism and militarism against Marxist-Leninist Communism and perceived atheistic forces in China, Russia and elsewhere.

Chastened by these and related events, notable theologians in the Catholic and Protestant traditions have positively dismissed these and related varieties of literalistic readings of Scripture and dogmatic religion. Karl Rahner, a Jesuit priest and one of the foremost Catholic theologians of the twentieth century, promoted a philosophic understanding of God as the existential fulfilment of humanity that transcends class and creeds. The great Reformed theologian, Karl Barth, suggested that Christians ought to read with the Bible in one hand and the daily newspaper in the other. In his *Epistle to the Romans,* Barth wrote of the need to reject both State authoritarianism and left-wing anarchy. He defined 'God's revolution' as the corrective to both ethical quietism and anarchy, while suggesting that the gospel 'displays a certain inclination to side with those who are . . . ready for revolution'.[5] In parallel, the *Kairos Document* referred to Jesus' call to 'read the signs of the times' (Mt 16:3; Lk 12:56), providing an

---

4.   Johan Baptist Metz, *Faith in History and Society: Towards a Practical Fundamental Theology* (New York: Seabury 1980), 88–89.
5.   Karl Barth, *Epistle to the Romans* (London: Oxford University Press, 1960), 463.

understanding of revolutionary violence in response to state tyranny. This is a theology which challenges the state order in each new state that promotes authoritarian control and dictatorship, as well as more subtle forms of support for a particular racial, gender, cultural and/or religious group over others. Among these disparities are a range of chauvinistic, economic and nationalistic ideologies incorporated into different right-wing trends across Europe, the Americas, Africa and other third world countries.

Nationalism

There is often an affinity between religions committed to social transformation and the State government. This can be both for the good, and to the detriment, of government and religion. Despite the attempt to inject theological ethics into government praxis, the danger is that the power of the state can manipulate and appropriate the church to serve its own ends. The ideas of society are seldom other than the rules of the ruling class that find existential meaning and purpose in both Church and State. The overt appropriation of the Dutch Reformed Church and other Churches, in different ways by the Apartheid State, is a case in point.

Christian nationalism was the heartbeat of Apartheid, recognising that the stranglehold of Afrikaner nationalism was a slow and gradual one, and not unique to South Africa. Noting the dangers of extrapolation, there are several examples of recurring practices in history that are important to explore. The headline story concerning the appropriation of the Orthodox Church in Russia as the inner soul of Russian President Vladmir Putin's imperialism is but one such warning that suggests the affinity between religion and politics in nation-building endeavours. Add the benefits of material greed, social privilege, ethnicity, racism and gender prejudice to nationalism and the bomb explodes.

Fuelled by the pursuit of political power, land grabs and nationalist aggression, the origins of the Russian Orthodox Church emerged in the wake of the Great Ecclesial Schism of 1054. The Roman Catholic Pope excommunicated the Patriarch of Constantinople (currently Istanbul), who responded by excommunicating the Pope! The Constantinian Orthodox Church established Orthodoxy in Kyiv in Ukraine, until its prominence shifted to Moscow in 1921, in the wake of the Russian Revolution. This lasted until the Russian invasion of Crimea in 2014, when a group of Churches in Ukraine established the independent Orthodox Church of Ukraine (OCU), declaring loyalty to the Ecumenical Patriarch in Constantinople. Today approximately seventy-five per cent of Russians claim cultural allegiance to the Russian Orthodox Church, and seventy per cent of Ukrainians are OCU adherents. The Patriarch of the Russian Church promotes Vladimir Putin's invasion of Ukraine war as a legitimate form of resistance to Western aggression and secular values. In contrast, the OCU views the invasion as an act of theological fratricide.

The Churches in South Africa suggest the possibility of a similar political divide that could escalate into the kind of tensions that gave rise to the divide between Orthodoxy in Russia and in Ukraine. The Protestant Churches in South Africa were the backbone of colonial subjugation and white domination. In the nineteenth century this led the breakaway by the African Independent Churches from Churches established by the colonial missionaries. The *Kairos Document* was published by politically aware, mostly black Christians, in 1985. It embraced participants across the spectrum of Churches, with Nolan being 'one of the leading theologians' involved in the process. The signatories to the *Document* committed themselves to support for the poor, committing themselves to acts of civil disobedience, while calling on the West to support economic boycotts and disinvestment campaigns. Groups within and outside the South African Church that supported the *Kairos Document* became involved in initiatives to make the country ungovernable, calling on people to pray for the government's downfall. Not without its limitations and exclusions, as a product of its time, it embarrassingly failed to give attention to gender and sexual orientations. A prophetic statement now at the present time would clearly need to identify gender and sexuality, as well as racism and economic transformation, as *l* moments.

Despite the present façade of non-racism and wider inclusivity in the South African Churches, arguably most white believers are hesitant about decisive forms of economic and political transformation, and supportive of the primarily white Democratic Alliance and Freedom Front Plus, while most black believers are conceivably supportive of the ANC, the EFF and black-majority political parties. The spiritual and existential divide in the Churches is clear to be seen.

The challenge of Prophetic Theology includes the need to question the existing form of God-talk that all too often lends itself to the anthropomorphic reduction of God to tribal, patriarchal, and self-centred theologies. A wise person once said that we can safely assume that we've created God in our own image when it turns out that God opposes and supports all the same people and things we do. God is surely, by definition, more than our comprehension of the divine: God is made known in history, but more than history—an unknown God, a not-yet-known God.

Rethinking God

The evolution of theological ideas and ethical values is a slow (and tedious) process, invariably accompanied by resistance, influenced perhaps more by emotions than by rational thought. The rational critique of dominant thinking has, however, relentlessly challenged prevailing ideas in each age and underpins theological debate. The unknown God is nowhere more powerfully portrayed than in the Genesis story of Moses and the burning-bush (Ex 3:1–17). God is here portrayed as the transcendent and the Unknown God: 'I am who I am' is a message that must interrogate any of the nationalistic understandings of the God of Abraham, Isaac and Jacob and the partisan God of Israel.

And, to provoke our complacency! The cultural critic and satirist, HL Mencken, disturbs our nationalistic and theological fervour in his classic list of 'dead Gods' in his essay, 'Memorial Service for Dead Gods'.[6] Mencken suggests that not even a deferential and respectful believer could find the 'tombs in which they [these Gods] are lost' in an endeavour to pay his or her respects. The existence of powerful Gods he suggests, 'doubted only by barbarians and traitors', was destroyed by the dogma and dictates of their most loyal emissaries and foot soldiers, who brought mutual destruction on themselves, their enemies, and their Gods, that include Jupiter, Venus, Zeus, Thor, Baal and other war Gods. Life could simply no longer sustain them. King Ahab dismissed the prophet Elijah as a 'troublemaker', but he too died as kings and Gods before him (1 Kgs 18:22). Elijah, John the Baptist, Jesus, Muhammad, their apostles, companions, and followers

---

6. *The Vintage Mencken* (New York: Vintage Books, 1955), 47.

(women and men) offered new life to the self-indulgent Abrahamic communities. Branded as deviant and apostate, they did more to save theology from self-defeat than most conformist sages and apologists in the Church.

Albert Nolan was a prophet, and a critical scholar of the Church. When some over the years walked away from Catholic religious orders, and others exited Protestant denominations, he remained a loyal and troublesome priest. He trod further than many others have trod and decidedly further than this partner in conversation has trod. I continue to listen to Nolan's testimony, being mindful of his witness. He reminds me that there is One God, omnipresent, inimitable, inconceivable, without form, transcendent and eternal. My rejoinder: I believe in a nameless essence, silent, beyond understanding, yet strangely present in the person of Jesus as the fulfillment of the prophets in the Judeo-Christian and other traditions, and revealed in the reality of the mystery of the solar system, the planet earth, plants, animals of the field and all humanity. My awareness of transcendence is in silence, using cautious metaphors. Albert Nolan went further. He was a preacher, a devout believer and mentor to the end.

Hamba kakuhle tata.

God the Stranger

Michael Worsnip

I don't remember Albert Nolan preaching very much. Possibly because of the different Church settings in which he and I moved. And it is certainly true that Albert was, personality-wise, more of a listener than a speaker. It seemed to me to be a position he preferred. When you spoke to him, whether it was an opinion or an observation or an analysis—or a story—Albert would listen intently. And one would often find what one had been telling him reappearing in a later discussion. It had been through the processing mincer that was Albert's brain, Albert's vast knowledge, Albert's quite extraordinary, critical and analytical ability.

And there would be the little idea you had shared with him, burnished, re-moulded, re-imagined and magnificent. It would all happen without any hint of superiority. There was never a desire to show off the vastness of his intellect, or any other aspect of his extraordinary vision. It was just what happened when Albert was around.

He looked a bit like a banker to me, only far less judgemental. He habitually wore a grey suit. A white shirt, without a tie. His spectacle lenses made his eyes seem bigger than they were and gave his face a slightly hawkish look. But Albert could blend easily into any crowd, anywhere. And that went with his personality. He never sought the limelight. He wasn't one to look for praise and accolade. He was a true revolutionary.

But on one occasion I do remember him preaching. I don't remember what occasion it might have been, but Albert was standing in the pulpit of a church which had a large crucifix. The corpus was fairly western and fairly standard. The longish brown, straight hair, the look of agony on the face, the boldness of colour of the bleeding wounds.

Albert started his sermon by drawing the attention of his audience to the crucifix. He said:

> Images and models like this are fairly common in some of our Churches. Even if we don't come from a particular tradition that uses crucifixes, probably nobody would be surprised to see one in a church.

'But', he went on,

> if one were to walk into a building somewhere and see this not as a model or an image, but actually happening—a real person nailed to a real cross—it would be something which undoubtedly would affect us very deeply!
>
> We would be shocked and horrified! We would leap into action! We would call for help. We would try to help the person in any way we could. We would do whatever might be needed to end the suffering. We wouldn't discuss it. We wouldn't pray about it. We wouldn't schedule a meeting. We would (and we should!) take immediate action—whether or not we were a doctor or a nurse; whether or not we had the right tools or the right height of stepladder. We would just do whatever we could to help the person nailed to the cross and to end the suffering taking place. That would be the normal response.

As it happens, I can't remember where Albert was going with this start to his sermon, but it is one of those moments in my life where my view of what was normal changed dramatically and forever. Because it is perfectly true that the horror of the crucifixion can simply become something normalised. Washed over by centuries of hymns and incantation; made commonplace by cheap reproduction and commercialism; inured by familiarity. And so, it is that something so fundamentally ghastly, dehumanising and violent, can become an ornament between two shapely breasts.

So, the place I would like to start is a place in my own life. To do this, I need to say a little about my life journey that brought me to the point where the story I am going to tell you starts.

I grew up in Apartheid South Africa. I grew up white, with all the benefits which the system of Apartheid ensured would come my way, because of the colour of my skin. I grew up in a quiet suburb of Johannesburg. Around our house, on every side, were white people, also reaping the benefits of the system of exclusion. I went to white schools. If I got sick, I could go to a white hospital. If I rode on a bus, it would be one reserved for the use of white people. If I went to see a movie on a Saturday afternoon, it would be at a place reserved for white people. If my father took us to have Sunday lunch at the local hotel, we could reserve places, only if we were white.

My local Anglican parish church was white, though not explicitly so. There was a service held on Sunday afternoons 'in the vernacular', which meant that black people went to that service and not to ours in the mornings. And though I was not, by any means, politically educated or exposed, something about going to that church, Sunday by Sunday—something about the chanting of those Psalms, something about Cranmer's hieratic language in the Prayer Book, taught me about justice and what was right.

There was, of course, a payment which needed to be made for this peace and security which white people in Apartheid South Africa enjoyed. Every white male child, on reaching the age of eighteen needed to join the military structures which, by dint of force, kept the structures in place in the society. That was the price. You could postpone doing so, for one reason or another, but in the end, your service would be required.

And so, there I was. I had run out of options. I had to decide whether I was going to defend Apartheid with my body or whether I was not. And whether the motivation was cowardice, or principle (or cowardice dressed up as principle) or whether it was pure, I decided that I would not do it.

My options then, were very few indeed. I could either declare myself and be sent to jail, or I could flee the country as a war resister. After much planning and subterfuge, I chose the latter and my then wife and I fled to Lesotho in 1979, a tiny land-locked independent former British protectorate. My rector and my bishop in Johannesburg were furious that they had not been informed of my intentions to do so beforehand. Because I was at that stage a postulant in preparation for training for the priesthood, and they somehow felt that they had rights over the decisions I made.

But I decided not to consult with them on my intentions and eventually my decision, because of the fact that there was some possibility that it would implicate them. Also because this was a personal decision, not an ecclesiastical one. The then Bishop of Lesotho, Phillip Mokuku, saw the point and based on my academic qualifications, as well as my good standing, decided to ordain me without much further ado and without me attending seminary before he did. I have no doubt that he wasn't thanked for doing so by my former bishop.

I decided to join the underground structures of the African National Congress (ANC) after encountering Anglican priests such as Fr Michael Lapsley SSM and Fr John Osmers—both of whom were deeply and publicly involved in the struggle for liberation in South Africa. But it wasn't with them that I was to be trained. My controller (even though, at the time, I had no idea that he was that) was a young student called Tito Mboweni. One day, Tito was to rise to the ranks of Minister of Labour and Governor of the Reserve Bank in the new democratic state. But for then, he was just Tito. My new friend. The first black friend I had really ever had.

I would teach Tito how to drive in my rather elderly, but functional VolksWagen Beetle. And on the other hand, Tito would educate me about stuff I had absolutely no idea about, in relation to our home country. Because we had lived in completely different worlds. We had experienced entirely different realities, all of our lives. In Lesotho, I learned about my own whiteness. I learned about a struggle I knew only vaguely—and from books. Tito taught me what no set of lectures could. He gave me perspective and insight and must have assessed that I was not, in fact, a spy. Because gradually, I was brought to the point of enlistment into the people's struggle. I was taught that this was not a struggle that white people could lead. I remain hugely indebted to that insight.

One day, as he and I sat talking in that VW Beetle, I told him that there was something I needed to tell him. I told him that I was gay. I told him that the woman I was married to knew I was gay when she married me, so that was not particularly the issue. But what might be the issue was—and this was the case that I put to him—what would be the consequences be for the Movement, if I were one day arrested for struggle activities—and the Boers would publicise the fact that that a White, Gay, Married Anglican Priest had been arrested for subversive activities, who claimed membership of the ANC?

Tito was certainly shocked. He said he needed a minute or two to think about it. And then he said this:

> When you have been in the struggle for as long as I have, you have experienced many terrible things. You have experienced people being shot. You have experienced 'necklacing' (the mob-justice meted out to suspected informers—of putting a petrol-soaked tyre around their necks and burning them to death}. You would have experienced torture at the hands of the police and the army. 'And so', he continued, 'hearing that someone is gay, is a very small thing indeed'.

I cannot describe how important—how affirming and significant—those words were to me. In one sentence, he had placed this profound uncertainty of mine in context. It was and would remain, comparatively, 'a very small thing'. This is to say nothing about its own importance. Or about its importance as essential to my substance and being. But it gave it perspective.

What I didn't know at the time was that our conversation was then, as it needed to be, reported up the ANC structures. Apparently the matter went right to the top of the ANC asking the question 'Do we have any policy on this issue, of gay and lesbian people in the organisation?' The answer came back down: 'You need a policy on gay people in the ANC'. And so, Tito drafted a policy which said, simply, that what we now know as LGBTQIA+ people, were exactly the same as any other ANC member. That duly became official ANC policy and that was the policy which was subsequently placed on the table at CODESA and the policy which would eventually form the basis for the inclusion of the 'sexual orientation' clause in the Bill of Rights, Chapter 2 paragraph 9 (3), as one of the critically flagged conditions where no unfair discrimination could take place in a future South Africa. I was unaware of this extraordinary journey until relatively recently, when Tito contacted me, looking for a blog I had written some years ago, mentioning the conversation that we had in Lesotho, all those years ago. I am still quite overwhelmed by the information.

As is well known, queer people are included in the South African Constitution. And they can rely on more than just inclusion, they can expect protection because of that inclusion. I am married to a man who I have been with for the past twenty-five years. We have two adopted children, who are now in their twenties. We have led an ordinary, normal life, as a family, thanks to the protection provided to us by the Constitution of the country.

But, needless to say, my position in the Church is far less clear. If I were to have lied, down the years, and maintained that I am gay but celibate, I might conceivably have been able to retain a licence to officiate. But I would have needed to maintain a fiction in order to do so. There are indeed many priests who are forced into this unenviable deceit.

The Anglican Church of South Africa has been unable to come to a position of unqualified acceptance of LGBTIQIA+ priests within its midst, despite many years of discussion, contemplation, prayer and seeking guidance. It has been easier for laypeople, but the Church is still unable to recognise their relationships and seems deeply uncomfortable with anything beyond heteronormative sexual expression.

The Church is, as I write, in discussion about what sort of prayers could be used to bless the houses in which queer people live and whether or not baptism can be offered to their children. We were fortunate, twenty years ago, to have found a priest in Pretoria, where we lived at the time, who was entirely open to our full inclusion. When we brought our children for baptism, it was simply done with other children being brought for baptism. On the baptismal certificate, the word 'Mother' was crossed out and an additional 'Father' written in its place. In the beginning, he and his wife made the effort to welcome us at the door to the church, just so that everyone knew that 'Father approves'. It was easy and it was uncomplicated. There was no fuss and there were no fraught discussions. We all just got on with the business of being human.

Down the years, I have asked many bishops for a licence. Even the gay ones have not been able to give me one. Not because I am lacking in 'good standing' but because I am determined not to hide my sexuality, or my marriage, or the children of this same-sex marriage. And so I have lived, for the past thirty years or so, in this strange contradiction: in a country where my rights as a gay person are enshrined and protected—and in a Church where, as a priest, I am unable to function with a licence.

Marcella Althaus-Reid, in her ground-breaking book *The Queer God* writes as follows:

> Queer Christians seemed to be condemned to be outside the gates of the Church and away from the presence of God, while in reality they know . . . that they can claim not victim-hood

> but agency in their praxis. Queer dissidents in search of paths of holiness through social practises of justice in sexual, religious and political areas of their lives, might well be reducing the hetero-God to impotency. It is not the church which has forgotten us: the truth is, we do not know that Church. In this sense Queer spirituality is an affirmation of agency and a de-colonization process in itself. It can claim that God the Stranger amongst our community of strangers may have declared us, made us, irredeemably lost in the eyes of the church and Christian ethics, yet it is not we who are lost.[1]

Now, it would be trite to speak of the colonial role which the Anglican Church has played, not only in the world, but also in my home country. And it is also perfectly clear that this coloniser role has never stopped. There has never been any sense of guilt or contrition; any public apology; any acknowledgement of complicity. And yes, it is true that there have been dissidents within the Church who have spoken up against the insanity of Apartheid (but—it must be said—much less to the role the Church played in colonial conquest and suppression). One can think of such luminaries in leadership roles as Trevor Huddleston, Michael Scott, Ambrose Reeves, Gonville ffrench-Beytagh, Colin Winter in Namibia and quintessentially, Desmond Tutu. But the near complete silence which this Church has maintained in the democratic era has certainly been notable and alarming, as has the rather obvious retreat into 'being the Church'. The inclusion, acceptance and celebrating of queer people has been something which is almost entirely absent. It is perhaps enough to note that the now celebrated Archbishop Desmond Tutu's own lesbian daughter Mpho, who is a married priest, would not be given a licence to operate. This same Church with a despicable colonial history, continues, seemingly unashamed in its colonial concept of God—a colonial concept which demands hegemony and commands obedience, submission and subservience. If those are not offered, the punishment is death, in the form of banishment and exclusion.

A tour of the Castle of Good Hope, which I went on some years back, led by a local tour guide, Lucelle Campbell, was undoubtedly one of those moments in life which changed my thinking forever. The castle is usually showcased as having been built by the Dutch trader

---

1. Marcella Althaus-Reid, *The Queer God* (London: Routledge, 2003), 165.

Jan van Riebeeck, and is one of the oldest surviving colonial buildings in Cape Town. Lucelle, as our tour guide, took us to the imposing gate of the castle and then led us to one side of it. She said 'This is as far as my people got, with this Castle. Either here, or in one of the jails inside it. Our experience has always been that of outsiders'.

And she spoke with a depth and a meaning that I only ever before experienced in a visit to Auschwitz. She spoke of colonial othering, categorising, domination, exclusion, control. This was her experience of the Castle of Good Hope. It was, for her, the Castle of Suffering. A castle symbolising colonial brutality, pain and dehumanisation. No words, no handshakes, no smiles would ever make it anything else. And I can remember thinking then of the parallel with queer people and the colonial God, worshipped in the colonial Church.

Marcella Althaus-Reid makes the bracing point that the colonial God is, in fact, quite obviously demonic. It is the outsiders—specifically in this regard the queer outsiders—who stand at the gate of hegemonic theology, and reveal God the Stranger, despised and rejected.

Albert Nolan's point of his sermon which I referred to in the beginning, was simple. The normal reaction to seeing torture and persecution would be immediately to launch into action. To do something–whatever it took—to stop the suffering. That would be the normal reaction.

The God who Dignifies and Humanises Us

Trevor Peter Amafu Ntlhola

Fr Nolan is gone! Indeed, he has gone forever—he's passed on. It is sad. It is also comforting! We, the previously exploited and sinned-against oppressed who were privileged to meet Fr Nolan, were irreversibly dignified by his making us aware of God at work in South Africa. This late octogenarian, Catholic priest, theologian, writer and member of the Dominican Order proclaimed this in the 1980s and documented it in his book *God in South Africa: The Challenge of the Gospel*. The book was published in 1988 at the height of the Apartheid regime's oppressive rule. This period was during the ugliest days of Apartheid, characterised by the disappearance of political opponents, solitary confinements, eerie assassinations, merciless necklace murders, police brutalities, appalling poverties, biting sanctions and disinvestment, etc. These brutalities were the order of the day as part of the project of dehumanisation which was targeting the black majority. The Apartheid system and her people were unashamedly worshipping an 'omnipotent ruthless god!' Nolan instead wanted to reveal the work of the true and living God in South Africa.

I am writing this tribute at a time when our country is currently engulfed in political instability, feeling suffocated by a regime that was re-voted into power by the politically hesitant and suffrage-fatigued South African voters! In their eyes, the corrupt and wicked African National Congress (ANC) is to blame for their fatigue, for the spiritual and political lethargy we experience in South Africa. It raises the questions: Where is God in South Africa today? And what kind of a god is our present government worshipping as we speedily approach our thirtieth anniversary as a 'rainbow nation'? Those who appreciated Nolan's *God in South Africa* need to think how to reappropriate this God in this democratic era.

These questions remind me of the respected sociologists Stark and Glock in the USA, who decades ago showed that 'the more seriously Americans take their Church membership, the more racist and patriotic, and the less capable of loving their enemies they are'.[1] This god was inevitably packaged with so-called 'good news' for them. Theirs was a user-friendly god who shamelessly flirted with the powerful oppressors, not the God of the gospel of Jesus Christ.

It is in this spiritual and political context of the 1980s that Fr Nolan decided to unmask Apartheid's god and her so-called gospel. 'I decided to write (just) one book, not only because Jesus himself preached to the oppressor and the oppressed at the same time', the late bespectacled cleric asserted, 'and not only because the gospel of Jesus Christ is one and indivisible, but above all because the gospel is not, and can never be, neutral'.[2] Apartheid's god and her followers appeared to be annoyingly neutral. And as a follow-up reason for writing this book, Fr Nolan says:

> . . . in the second place, the gospel we preach will not be the gospel of Jesus Christ unless it takes sides with those who are being sinned against—the poor and the oppressed. It is from that point of view . . . that one must preach the gospel to both sides in South Africa today.[3]

These words were written thirty-five years ago, and they still reverberate to this day.

Fr Nolan's words were filled with hope for the new South Africa, which was supposed to usher in our new democratic era! 'South Africa is a land of hope and despair', Nolan continues, 'a land that paradoxically gives birth to hope while it tries to destroy all hope. So many of us have been through the experience of having our hopes and expectations crushed overnight by a blind and ruthless regime.'[4] We see a striking similarity of these two hopes in our situation today: the hope we had then when we fought against our oppression and the current crushed hopes and despair we have now in this democratic era, under the wretched ANC's turpitudes. As the hope of the major-

---

1. Kenneth (1987), 5.
2. Albert Nolan, *God in South Africa: The Challenge of the Gospel* (Gweru, Zimbabwe: Mambo Press, 1988), xii.
3. Nolan, *God in South Africa,* xii.
4. Nolan, *God in South Africa,* 139.

ity of South Africans is agonisingly crushed to smithereens, Nolan's notion of God infuses hope.

Could it be that Apartheid's god, which Fr Nolan warned us against, and the ANC's god have been strangely similar all along? We are once again sadly set for the 'Dehumanisation Project Part 2' under the democratic era, whereas the previous 'Dehumanisation Part 1' was treacherously birthed by the Apartheid regime and her capitalistic corporate bodies. 'Dehumanisation marks not only those whose humanity has been stolen', the erudite educationist Freire said, 'but also those who have stolen it'.[5] Fr Nolan fought against dehumanisation in all its forms and unmasked it. It is for this reason, I can't resist to share the lessons Freire taught about the similarities between the oppressor and the oppressed, which Fr Nolan stood against:

> How can the oppressed, as divided, unauthentic beings participate in developing the pedagogy of their liberation? ... As long as they live in the duality where to be is to be like, and to be like is to be like the oppressor, this contribution is impossible. The pedagogy of the oppressed is an instrument for their critical discovery that both they and their oppressors are manifestations of dehumanisation.[6]

Freire's words were as prophetic in 1972 as they are today. And they have not been heeded by President Ramaphosa's administration, because:

> we have now reached the stage in South Africa when anyone who is searching for signs of hope must realise that these cannot be found within the system itself. Many have known this for a long time. They were stripped of their illusions many years ago. But now everyone who is serious about change knows that we must look outside and beyond the system.[7]

Could this mean that we have to search for the true God elsewhere? Could it be that we need to be vaccinated against the current god of both the Apartheid regime and the ruling ANC administration? Fr Nolan continues,

---

5. Paulo Freire, *Pedagogy of the Oppressed* (London: Penguin, 1972), 20.
6. Freire, *Pedagogy of the Oppressed,* 25.
7. Nolan, *God in South Africa,* 140.

> What Jesus had to say was news for his time and news about his time. If the gospel for us in South Africa today is to have the shape of a prophetic message, it must proclaim news for our time, news about what God is doing and about to do in our country . . . We have seen that the gospel message today must take the shape of good news for the poor; we have seen that it must take the shape of a prophetic message for our times; and we have said that it must be shaped by what has been said about God in the Bible in order to bring us the good news of what God is doing in South Africa today. But that is not all. To be the Christian gospel for today it must be rigorously shaped by the message that Jesus preached to his contemporaries. We had put Jesus' message on a par with other prophetic messages only in order to see the general characteristics of the gospel as a prophetic message. Now we must be more specific about the characteristics that would shape our message into the gospel of Jesus Christ for our times.[8]

What Fr Nolan mentions here is not a 'nice god'; possibly we even need a wild God who is characterised by extreme mercy and sobering truth: Christ Jesus! This is the God that was served and loved by our comrade, friend, brother and teacher, Fr Albert Nolan!

We can thus say that achieving change in South Africa is not just about regime change, but about embodying the God in South Africa that Nolan advocates for and tried to emulate himself. I can illustrate this on a personal note. I only met Fr Nolan briefly in a few meetings, but a very close friend and colleague got to know Fr Nolan more personally, and shared two stories with me.

There was an incident in an all-day training event that my friend attended, with a very diverse group of keen learners. Fr Nolan was leading a social analysis and Contextual Theology process, essentially about 'doing theology' in the crisis South Africa was going through in the 1980s. A vigorous discussion broke out on the degree to which one uses, or does not use, Marxist categories of social analysis, with its underlying paradigm in Liberation Theology. What impressed was Fr Nolan's genuine inclusivity, drawing everyone into the discussion in his own effective way, giving dignity and voice to those previously marginalised in such discussions; and his ability to carefully listen to differing viewpoints, even opposing positions, responding non-

---

8. Nolan, *God in South Africa*, 15 and 17.

defensively and with insightful explanations. Fr Nolan had a very sharp mind, equal to his ability to articulate ideas clearly and concisely in words that all could understand. That, in turn, was also equal to his deep spiritual formation, seen in the way he interacted with people—a man of peace, quietness, confidence, and conviction.

This friend further shared another story when he participated in one of the first legal marches against the Apartheid regime in Johannesburg in the late 1980s. At a certain point he happened to be walking alongside Fr Nolan when a few younger protesters broke out beyond the marshals to overthrow rubbish bins on the sidewalk. Fr Nolan immediately expressed his dismay to my friend, then turned and raised his voice to rebuke the protesters, saying, 'Don't do that! It will provoke a violent response! This is a peaceful protest!' Fr Nolan had a fierce sense of justice and non-violent resistance that he applied consistently across the board. Many, including my friend, were surprised that, as gentle as Fr Nolan was, he could be decisive and assertive, for justice's sake, when he needed to be. The God for which he advocated was able to restore our stolen dignity and humanity. For this we'll be ever grateful!

Now that Fr Nolan is gone, yes, we're sad, but we're also vibrantly and radiantly comforted in that the God he followed didn't depart with him. God is abundantly and defiantly still here with us, making us humble and bold in the midst of the sewage of corruption of the current governing administration. The late Archbishop Oscar Romero reminds us:

> A Church that doesn't provoke any crises,
> A gospel that doesn't unsettle,
> A Word of God that doesn't get under anyone's skin,
> A Word of God that doesn't touch the real sin
> Of the society in which it is being proclaimed,
> What gospel is that?
> Very nice, pious considerations
> That don't bother anyone,
> That's the way many would like preaching to be.
> Those preachers who avoid every thorny matter
> So as not to be harassed,
> So as not to have conflicts and difficulties,
> Do not light up the world they live in . . .[9]

---

9. Oscar Romero, *The Violence of Love: The Words of Oscar Romero* (London: Collins Fount Paperbacks, 1989), 54.

The martyred Romero's poetic and gripping words inspire us, as the followers of Christ Jesus, to be courageous in the application of the radical gospel.

Thus, in conclusion, we can say that the god of Apartheid and the god of the current government have striking similarities in their dehumanisation projects that shamelessly still grind the poor black majority, starting with the heinous and exploitative Apartheid racial policies, and continuing in this democratic era, with ever-corroding corruption that rapes human dignity. But the God that Fr Nolan pointed to is not going anywhere, He's here to stay! We remember that during the Apartheid days, this God gave us dignity and humanised us. Now, we must watch out and listen for the rumblings of where God is subversively present and marching on in the Church of Christ Jesus today!

Rakhmah: A Palestine-Inspired Spirituality

Stiaan van der Merwe

Dear Albert,
You passed away during an ominous time. A time of fundamental uncertainty about the future globally. Our natural web-of-life, and thereby human life, is at an inflection point. The same applies to the foundations, structures and institutions designed to sustain human life. Our discernment, thoughts and 'memories of the future' hold no frames of reference to provide some certainty, clarity and meaning. This includes familiar spirituality, faith, and religion. It is as if we do not have the scientific, technological, political, economic, and spiritual tools to engage with the future. Humankind seems caught between a fear, a fascination even, with supremacist, human-centred solutions and the hope expressed by the Arundati Roys in our day, that 'Another world is not only possible, she is on her way. On a quiet day, I can hear her breathing.'

You were always radically different.

Your contemplative, scholarly spirituality taught us to first discover and then explore the essence, the root (*radix*) of things and proceed from there. An essence that often has been known but buried under layers of forgetting and denial—yet still alive.

The last time we met was a reminder of your radicalism.

You'll recall that I presented for discussion a draft text to your contemplative group exploring the pursuit of justice according to Jesus' logic of love-in-us. Your agreement with the heart of the text and your support of its vital importance for our times moved me deeply. You seriously encouraged me to pursue the wonder and mystery of Jesus' logic of love. I honour and treasure your words.

You somewhat surprised me when you shared reservations about us emphasising the ancient Aramaic word *rakhmah* as the word Jesus likely used for the word *love*. In your parting words to me, you urged me to read your book, *Jesus before Christianity*.

I did, and this book and your life and work have emboldened my quest for the *radix* of Jesus' message before Christianity: the heart of his gospel that lies hidden under layers of Church history, its patriarchal hierarchies, its doctrines with moral and thought police in tow and our socialisation. Your gift? You strengthened my understanding of love as the living and dynamic foundation, centrepiece, and capstone of our pursuit for a just peace in our country, South Africa, and in the world at large.

My journey along this unfolding path was triggered by the land of this Palestinian Jew about whom you wrote. The land where, under brutal Roman occupation, Jesus embodied his message of love—a radical alternative to and protest against superficial and even distorted practices and understanding of love. Time spent in present-day Palestine exposed me to current realties of an ongoing *nakbah* (Arabic for 'catastrophe')—a *nakbah* created, continued, and internationally supported by over seven decades of ethnic cleansing under Israel's illegal, settler-colonial, military occupation. We did not see nor experience this Apartheid in South Africa. Nor did we suffer this extent and intensity of global Christian support, enabling, and justification for Israeli Apartheid.

Blessed are the peacemakers

During my first visit to Palestine, in 2007, I walked along the 'separation wall' in Bethlehem. I noted a Biblical quote.

Blessed Are The Peacemakers,
For They Will Be Called Children Of God.

Written directly underneath was a quote from Edward Said.

Since when does a militarily occupied people
have the responsibility for a peace movement?

It wasn't until much later that I managed a response to Said's legitimate question.

In 2009, along with other South Africans, I attended the launching of the *Kairos Palestine* document (KP): *A Moment of Truth: A Word of Faith, Hope and Love from the Heart of Palestinian Suffering.* I was made aware that this document had been inspired by the South African *Kairos Document* (SAKD) that you had been so instrumental in creating.

Struck by the prophetic boldness of the Palestinian Christians, I was not prepared for its lasting impact on my life and spirituality. They offered no-nonsense, broad-ranging, truth-speaking analyses with political and faith challenges to the context at the time. Their spiritual discernment followed the message of Jesus under Roman occupation two millennia earlier. Their discernment climaxed in explicitly declaring love as central to their spiritual, theological and real-political response for liberation from Israeli occupation.

The KP document was a gauntlet thrown down to all. It seminally raised the bar for justice-pursuing activism to a quantumly different level beyond and transcending our even 'progressive', activism-as-usual.

It reads, 'We will see here "a new land" and "a new human being", capable of rising up in the spirit to love each one of his or her brothers and sisters' (KP 10). Pointing to this radically different way of being human, it seems the authors sensed that we could, and should, access our innate ability to regard every person as '. . . my brother and my sister. . . [to see] the face of God in every human being' (KP 4.2.1). and 'to see the image of God in the face of the enemy' (KP 4.2.3).

A remarkable Jesus-centred acknowledgement: In the consciousness of love there are no enemies. Everyone is family, including every Israeli soldier, settler, politician, and anyone who differs from us including from within the Christian community. Christian Zionists come to mind.

I picked up this gauntlet, signed, supported and have eagerly promoted the document as I committed myself to further explore its message. This prophetic witness of present-day Palestinian Christians remains both an inspiration and continuing challenge to pursue a just peace for both Palestine and Israel. On the one hand for Palestinians suffering rapidly deteriorating conditions under Israeli occupation and Apartheid whilst facing internal divisions; on the other hand, for Israelis who seem to be eating themselves up in internal political divisions and social strife with civil war as a real possibility with Palestinians bearing the brunt.

A pedagogy of the oppressor

In 2019, I was asked by authors of the KP document to write a piece about 'liberating the other' for a publication on the tenth anniversary of the document.

Once accepted, I knew *the writing was on the wall.* I would have to respond to Edward Said's question on the Apartheid wall.

A response came from those who suffered human-made trauma—Jews from the Nazi Holocaust and black South Africans from National Party Apartheid rule. Their cry, in words attributed to Nelson Mandela: 'Never! Never! And never again'. Theirs is a cry against an unjust past, a costly witness and protest against what many perceive to be an unbreakable law of nature: 'the vicious cycle of history'.

The KP document unwittingly dares to insist that the cycle will be broken through a way of life that has been known yet is buried under layers of forgetting and denial—the way toward 'a new land' through 'a new human being' embracing love as the real-political way going forward.

History does not repeat itself by some natural force external to humans as hapless victims thereof. History is being repeated by us through our maintaining the levels of consciousness that have created, recreated, and sustained injustice. It turns out that our struggles—our resistance—in pursuit of justice are also shaped by our having internalised the practices of 'the enemy'. When a moment of liberation arrives, as Freire already argued in his *Pedagogy of the Oppressed*, newly freed regimes and people often act out of the level of consciousness that they had internalised during struggles for liberation. He wrote '... for them, to be men is to be oppressors. This is their model of humanity ... having internalised the image of the oppressor and adopted his guidelines.'

Historic Palestine, South Africa and the whole of global history are littered with examples.

The prescient authors of the KP document had also unwittingly reframed Said's question: 'Since when does a military-occupied people have the responsibility to liberate themselves in a manner that would liberate "the other" as well?' Their perhaps unconscious response: 'Since it is our sacred, human responsibility to explicitly ensure that history would not be repeated.'

The KP document challenges Christians and humanity towards a pedagogy for practical liberation from injustice for both the oppressed and oppressors. It ultimately holds the promise of a successful outcome. Here are four of the pointers:

First, the message on the logic of love in pursuit of justice is an all-inclusive universal human message. Such is the universal mission of historic Palestine, Palestine and Israel, as declared by the authors of the KP document, 'Our land has a universal mission' (KP 2.3–2.5).

Resistance grounded in the logic of love is the only way that liberates both the oppressed and the oppressor from history's vicious cycle of injustice. The vocation of those who seek to break history's cycle of injustice toward a just and lasting peace will be defined by explicit, transparent, costly acts of love as embodied by Jesus' life, words, and witness.

Such resistance emanates from the transformed, 'new human being' (KP 10) with a radically different paradigm and level of consciousness that then pursues a radically unique path of creative, albeit fierce, resistance to *the other*. It is an approach that finds 'human ways that engage the humanity of the enemy ... [in order] to stop the injustice and oblige the perpetrator to end his aggression and thus achieve the desired goal, which is getting back the land, freedom, dignity and independence' (KP 4.2.3).

The grounding in the logic of love will thereby define what it means to be regarded as 'progressive'. Apart from our own embodying of Jesus' love, our well-intended, deeply committed progressive movements, ideologies and theologies become another repeating lesson to overcome for a next generation.

Second, this level of resistance becomes a history-defying and redefining process of change that includes solidarity with *the other*. The aim will be to overcome *the other's* destructive and ultimately self-destructive *nakba,* in this case, with Palestinians having to pay the price. Who else but the victims of injustice—and those in solidarity with them—are called and obligated to seize the initiative to 'accompany' *the other* in processes of change? We know from our own experiences that such change is existentially painful and complex as, in this case, the collapse of the collective and individual Zionist dreams—their 'memories of the future'—will be. You too know very well that change might include life-threatening and often death-imparting consequences for those who dare to change from within the oppressor's community.

Third, the oppressors carry the ultimate responsibility for their self-liberation: 'Finally, responsibility lies with the perpetrators of the injustice; they must liberate themselves from the evil that is in them and the injustice they have imposed on others' (KP 4.2.1).

Fourth, both our SAKD and the KP documents affirm: This is not an easy path. The lessons of Jesus' logic of love should not be simplistically imposed nor should they be enforced on anyone. The Christian community in Palestine and globally will have to embark together prophetically and pastorally on a journey of deconstruction as they humbly share their 'belief in God, good and just . . . to finally triumph over the evil of hate and of death that still persist . . . ' (KP 10).

Rakhmah: A deeper insight into Jesus' logic of love from his native language and culture.

I am told, the original Arabic text of the KP document uses *Almahaba (literally: The Love),* one of several Arabic words translated in English as compassion, mercy, and love. As I sought to discover what might have been the Aramaic word that Jesus used, a Palestinian Christian woman theologian, Marwa Nasser-Metzler, suggested the word *rakhmah*—one of several Aramaic words translated in English as 'love'. This, she suggested, seemed to be the word Jesus used when, for example, he summarised the essence of the law as love, including the love of one's neighbour.

Something of an epiphany arrived, when Marwa informed me that the root meaning of *rakhmah* refers to a womb. How on earth had the word love become associated with a womb?

Imagine a woman in the ancient Middle East experiencing something so profound that in the wonder, joy, and mystery of it, she associated the experience as love. In having no mind frame or word for this specific experience of love, she associated the experience with the way her and other women's womb's function. Imagine then how the word *rakhmah* might have come into more common use to refer to divine love, as womb-love. Jesus, the male, chose *rakhmah* to refer to a kind of love that can break and reshape a human heart and level of consciousness to redefine the course of human history. The word that expresses for us the logic of Jesus' life and ministry and the object of his message of love: 'the new human being capable of rising up in the spirit to love each one of his or her brothers and sisters' (KP 10).

I recall, Albert, that having shared this with the group, you gently advised me to stick to the Greek New Testament word *agape* as the word Jesus used for his love. It seemed to me that you were apprehensive that if we were to use *rakhmah* it would follow that many might think that only women could truly understand and live this love of Jesus.

To Marwa, in the pursuit of justice, the use of the word *rakhmah* is tacitly, intellectually, spiritually and theologically a sound choice when one speaks of the highest form or level of love. Other women, Christian, Muslim and Jewish, have concurred. Might this be one of the many reasons that women were drawn to and understood Jesus' message, perhaps more readily and deeper than men captured by patriarchy?

Furthermore, Paul, as a man and a Palestinian Jew, as he embraced the logic of Jesus' love, can be read to have understood the meaning of *rakhmah* as *agape* in his writings. Paul seemingly lived and experienced the life of the 'new human being', albeit warts and all by his own admission, 1 Corinthians 13:1–8 provides a credo based, not on a set of laws or doctrines, but headlines of stories from his real-life experiences. The summation of his Jesus-centred ministry is in the shortest headline: 'Love never fails.' (The definitive certainty thereof needs to sink in for all of us.)

So, dear Albert, I am persuaded that the word *rakhmah* was used by women and men as a lived experience and understanding from indigenous culture and spirituality. Just as I, a white male Afrikaner, have a lived, socialised, cultural and spiritual understanding of Apartheid. Perhaps more importantly, the word stirs a paradigm shift in our day, as the logic of Jesus' love did in the early Church. In our time, it provides for the much needed and even imperative shift away from our patriarchal, dominant Western culture and understandings of *agape*. It provides a paradigm shift away from and beyond masculine-dominated theologies, ideologies and strategies for human liberation.

Embracing the radical logic of Jesus' love

Has this core of the Christian message been lost or is it merely buried under the weight of the Church's history and practice? To use your usual guidance: We must go to the root (*radix*) of the question and proceed from there.

It is certainly not for me to attempt to describe the logic of *rakhmah* in its deepest meanings and expressions. I suggest it is the calling of those who bodily and experientially know the logic of a womb to rise and to teach, guide and accompany all of us. I acknowledge and support a calling for them to facilitate and lead this revolution in spirituality, theology, activism, resistance, and real politics. It is they, like Jesus' mother, Anna the prophetess, and Mary Magdalene who anointed him, who bear the gift and lineage of those who have known what *rakhmah*-love is before both Jesus and Christianity.

I will note a caution. There is a risk that the spirituality and theology of *rakhmah* may be lost in the Holy Land where it found its roots.

Recently, there are signs that authors and supporters of the KP document are responding to Israel's Apartheid regime by developing strategies and actions focused primarily on international law, human rights conventions and our South African history. Surely these will be essential tools and lessons that must and will shape their future. But explicit messages, strategies, and actions built on these tools or such tools alone, apart from a clear and renewed embrace of Jesus' logic of love, is amiss. I am reminded of our South African history. We have not acknowledged and explored the depth of the message and theology of love in the SAKD. We did not fully pick up the SAKD's gauntlet thrown down before us. This history dares not be repeated. I wonder how different our history in South Africa could have been had we clearly and boldly explored the SAKD's mentioning of Jesus' love also for 'the enemy'?

Our embrace of Jesus' radical, transforming, womb-like love will have to empower and create the will to change. Apart from the 'new human being', humankind is doomed to repeat our history.

Albert, you inspired us to be radical with the example you set. The times we are in demand Gospel-radical prophetic spaces, circles, networks, movements and voices. Prophetic voices and spaces are few and far between, rather muted and seemingly faltering. I trust you and others of our ancestors to walk this path with us.

Our vocation remains: a Palestine-inspired covenanting to *rakhmah*.

Who else but the authors of the KP document and all of us are to be the 'new human beings'—Alice Walker's 'the ones we have been waiting for'? The first question is not 'How?' The first question is: 'Do we want to, and indeed will we love to walk this road of liberation?' The rest will proceed from this *radix*.

We will stay in touch, dear ancestor.

In *rakhmah*.

Stiaan

Albert talking to YCS members in Gokomere, Zimbabwe (1980s).

Section Six

Challenge

Emil Blaser OP, Albert and Stephen Paradza (a student and member of the YCS at St Joseph's Theological Institute) discussing Dominican Communications, using *Challenge* as an example, at the annual assembly at La Verna, c 1996.

Telling the *Challenge* story

Renate Cochrane

Isithakazelo is a Nguni word for a poem praising important people. The praise-song is recited at the beginning of significant events, most often at the opening ceremony for a feast honouring the ancestors. Southern African culture has been an oral culture and the praise songs served as the traditional way of remembering our ancestors and their deeds. When I was asked to write an article on Albert Nolan as the founder of the *Challenge* magazine, the wisdom behind *izithakazelo* sprang to mind. Remembering *Challenge* makes me want to break forth into a praise-song for this life-affirming publication with a deep wish in my heart that this praise-song will be repeated at noteworthy occasions for future generations.

How will our children ever know about the wealth of wisdom and inspirational source in difficult times contained in *Challenge*? Albert Nolan´s books will still be with us in the years to come, while the editions of *Challenge* will probably be forgotten in a hidden archive.

Only those who lived through these 'challenging' times in which *Challenge* was published will carry this decade (1991–2000) in their memory as a precious hope-instilling gift to South Africa and the Christian world.

Challenge was the brainchild of Albert. He was at that time the 'engine driver' of the Institute for Contextual Theology (ICT) with a sensitive perception of the struggle of South Africans in their commitment to over-

come the de-humanising system of Apartheid. The context at that time was a country with hundreds of thousands of angry young people determined to fight for liberation. In 1991 the Soviet Union had collapsed and the proxy war in South Africa was no longer funded by the cold-war powers. Would this be the end of Apartheid because 'white Christians' would no longer have to fight 'black communist terrorists'? For the entrenched Apartheid-supporting white elite, a democratic South Africa was not conceivable and the politicians in charge mobilised forces of evil with the single goal of preventing a hand-over to the black majority of the country. South Africa was in turmoil. The country was in flames and civil unrest and fear engulfed our land. People needed guidance and an anchor to hold onto. The media were still controlled by the State. Where would people find a voice for their anguish? Teenage youth had disappeared, violence erupted at every corner, schools were closed, and army vehicles surrounded the townships.

How can we reach people in the townships? Albert consulted widely with activists. Can we channel such rage in a constructive way? He observed that people in the townships enjoy reading magazines. What about bringing Liberation Theology to the townships in a people-friendly magazine with eye-capturing photographs and non-academic English? Albert became an apprentice in journalism and magazine layout, taking great care in putting thought-provoking content in an appealing package.

Looking at the captivating editions today, one cannot help but be in awe of Albert's newly-developed editorial skills. Indeed, he lived the Christian call of being a *servant* of the people by venturing into a new ministry.

A fascinating product emerged. I was a Moravian pastor for several township congregations in KwaZulu-Natal during that time and I vividly remember the joy when I arrived with the latest copies of *Challenge* under my arm. Those unable to read English eagerly paged through the colourful 'mag' and asked students for translation.

The variety of topics was the strength of the magazine. For example, 'Jesus, the Great Ancestor', features next to the question of feminist theology in post-colonial Africa. Gender-based violence was a particularly painful topic as was the concept of patriarchy and polygamous households. Troubling 'untouchable' questions were discussed with deep Christian honesty in *Challenge*. Various articles on homosexuality embedded in profound Bible studies did not fail to make an impact. South Africa is still to date the only country on the African continent to have legalised same-sex marriages. Influential clergymen such as the late Anglican Bishop David Russell made this possible. *Challenge* probably prepared the ground for this remarkable achievement.

And *Challenge* gave us another precious gift, an immersion into very good English. I taught a group of lay ministers who were most grateful for studying English while reading articles related to their daily lives. Our students suffered under 'Bantu education', a system devised to exclude black people from being well-educated.

Brave headlines on the cover grabbed readers' attention: 'A Christmas Without Violence—Is It Possible?' (December 1993)—'Will Our Elections Be Free and Fair?' (March 1994).

The magazine was passionately committed to the ecumenical spirit. Most Churches were represented, also traditional African religion and other faiths were respected as partners in dialogue. The theme of the tumultuous time was *hope in despair*, yet in the Christian sense oriented to non-violent ways to 'challenge' the oppressor. Every edition contained a contextual Bible study and often a newly written 'psalm for South Africa' which Albert themed 'the people's theology'. Such interpretations helped especially young Christians in understanding the Bible as a companion when they had to 'walk in the valley of the shadow of death' (Ps 23). Biblical screams for justice in our land expressed people's suffering: 'My grief is beyond healing; my heart is sick within me' (Jer 8:18), 'O that my head were a spring of water and my eyes a fountain of tears! I would weep day and night for the slain of my people' (Jer 9:1).

In the later years of the nineties, after our 'miracle election' and the establishment of an ANC government, editor Albert had the courage to formulate in clear words the threat of another worrying cloud arising on the horizon: the new deadly disease of AIDS. Punishment from God for sinful immorality? Where are the young women in our Sunday services? The answer given by Church elders: Look for them in the graveyard.

For dubious reasons, the Minister of Health ruled out the possibility of antiretroviral treatment (ART) for people living with HIV. President Mbeki was an AIDS denialist. Imagine the agony of religious leaders who had to anticipate the death of so many young parents in their congregations knowing that 'AIDS kills both parents'. How would congregations care for the numerous orphaned children? Theologically grounded information and solid scientific debates in the editions of *Challenge* equipped pastors and faith-communities with spiritual/biblical tools to enter a new struggle for justice—the struggle for ARV treatment for all. The seed bore fruit and the first substantial financial amount for the Treatment Action Campaign was given by overseas Churches.

By that time the South African ART programme had been rolled out in 2004, our beloved *Challenge* magazine had ceased publication. The dawn of democracy, sadly, meant the dusk of the ecumenical movement. The goal of a free South Africa had been achieved and the solidarity of faith communities crumbled. Anti-Apartheid funding had decreased and keeping a magazine viable, with colour prints as a significant cost-factor, was difficult. Many contributors to the magazine were busy building the new democratic structures and had no time left for writing articles. An affordable publication was no longer possible.

As pastors and congregations, we have felt a deep loss ever since and we miss theological guidance when confronted with distressful 'challenges' in present-day South Africa.

At the same time our Christian hearts beat with the urgent need for a widely heard prophetic voice in our current world of economic crisis and political corruption embedded in the global shifts towards autocratic rulers and military power-games.

Albert was always in tune with the times, carefully researching the best channel to reach God's people on the ground. What would be the best way today? Social media, of course. But how?

A younger social-media savvy generation must take on the 'challenge' of helping Christians today to think critically and discuss our global and national problems in the context of our *TikTok* world. We cannot surrender our Christian faith to only the Spirit-guided Churches that grow enormously, yet often seem to abuse their congregations spiritually and financially. 'Prophets for profit' proclaim a prosperity cult religion in the guise of Christian faith. Such greedy business-model-Churches are dangerously misleading the flock—yet where is the voice 'challenging' these deeply disconcerting manifestations of worship?

As we remember the impact and footprint of the *Challenge* magazine, we do so as elders who lived in a time when a magazine was the most attractive means of communication for young people. This is certainly no longer the case.

All we can do as elders, is to 'tell the story' and share the value of a Christian, ecumenical, people´s theology magazine. We hope that the younger generation will hear our *izithakazelo* and conceive of a similar outreach model in our digital world. We shall soon be ancestors and can only hand over the history of this astonishing magazine as a seed for a future project.

Mentoring a Young Journalist

Khotso Kekana

I felt honoured to be shortlisted in 1992 for the position of sub-editor at *Challenge* magazine by Fr Albert Nolan, a renowned author, theologian and social justice activist. The job description in the tiny advertisement defined the vacancy as being a search for an experienced journalism technocrat to lighten Fr Nolan's workload as editor at the then newly launched publication.

Instead, the humble editor in the interview panel before me seemed mainly interested in cajoling the prospective incumbent into understanding he was not solely looking for a scribe. He had launched the magazine to provide a platform to amplify the voice of the Church beyond the pulpit to audiences grappling with daily challenges in a pre-democratic South Africa rife with Apartheid injustices.

At the end of my first week of job orientation I realised the humble and unassuming editor of *Challenge* magazine smartly omitted to declare, lest my fellow interviewers and I got cold feet, that the sub-editor was not starting a new job but rather signing up for a cause. However, even after such a realisation, Fr Nolan's demeanour remained that of a leader who was ready to engage with me on any issues that bothered me, but still leave it up to me to decide if I wanted to continue on the journey. So, rather than feel like I was having a job I felt like I had a home which I looked forward to rushing to in the mornings and with no haste to depart from in the evenings.

Fr Nolan not only helped to make my then young life more meaningful, he refocused my journalistic lens. He exposed me to a writing experience that I was neither taught in any journalism lecture nor had encountered in the newsrooms of mainstream news agencies.

Previously, I had been exposed to two forms of journalism: traditional and advocacy journalism. Traditional journalism purported to train me to engage with an ethical and legally compliant story telling genre that promotes objectively reporting on events in society. Advocacy journalism exposed me to a genre that rejects objectivism and instead promotes a reporting style that promotes a particular world view—such as what some of us did in the alternative media during Apartheid—to highlight the effect that the country's segregationist policies were having on the majority of its people.

Although he was a theologian, Fr Nolan introduced me to what did not have a name at the time, but is now referred to as 'citizen journalism'. This journalism genre extends beyond the professional journalists and manifests itself in our contemporary reality where ordinary citizens contribute to news content. An example of this is the scores of people who collect, analyse and disseminate information on events around the world using social media and various other information platforms.

The Dominican priest was ahead of his time. Fr Nolan stimulated debate in the columns of *Challenge* magazine around pressing issues of the day by critically analysing the subject and inviting readers—including subject matter experts—to contribute to debates by writing articles and opinion letters to the editor. I contend that his communication strategy contributed to the varied dialogues that evolved across black and white societies in the early 1990s. They helped to bring us closer together, despite our differences, as we strove for a peaceful transition to a 'rainbow nation' in the run-up to our first democratic elections in 1994.

Many of us got lost in the excitement of a beckoning new democracy, but Fr Nolan remained sober in his visionary focus on the challenges that awaited us. The topics we wrote about in the magazine remain relevant to this day. Fr Nolan correctly foresaw the likelihood that we were going to grapple with issues such as inequality, crime, corruption, quality education, youth unemployment and racism even after the birth of our democratic dispensation.

My editor also literally rose to the challenge when the magazine faced difficult times. Our team acknowledged that his gregarious nature and sense of humour contributed to the respect he earned and the scores of friendships he had built. In our eyes, these attributes also augured well for the sustainability of the publication in times of difficulty. An occasion that stands out for me was when we saw competitor publications publishing what was our planned lead story a day before ours. Through a combination of creative thinking and a chance meeting with a source who had not been interviewed by others on the subject gave us a new scoop. We also needed to find the appropriate pictures to illustrate the story and nobody seemed to have what we needed. The Dominican priest made a telephone call after which he merrily requested me to accompany him to allies he needed to introduce me to. They happened to be a progressive video and photography entity called Dynamic Images where we found scores of excellent footage to select from at good rates.

The affable editor of the *Challenge* magazine also kept the team spirit going with his ability to laugh at himself and gave us a good run at the game of teasing each other and giving each other nicknames. He adopted the nickname we gave him—*Ntabelanga*—after a comedic moment between us, that was linked to my journalistic assignment to Ntabelanga near Willowvale in the Eastern Cape. He reciprocated the name-calling by christening me as *Masenya* (the destroyer) and the Reverend Sipho Tselane of the Institute for Contextual Theology as *Ngema* (after the legend of a then much talked about minibus taxi driver known by that name).

Fr Nolan has not only left me with many indelible fond memories. I continue to use his principles and values to navigate my way through my adult life and our contemporary challenges. But more importantly, I try to embody them so that I can bequeath a mini toolbox of principles and values to my offspring and their contemporaries, which I hope will help them build solid foundations for their futures.

Your spirit lives on, *Ntabelanga*.

Mayfair dining room in 1984/5—Albert with YCS visitors.
Left to Right: Marilyn Sadie, Aneene Dawber, Stephen Sadie and Albert.

A Trusted Partner

Jacques Briard

It was with great sadness that I heard of the passing away of Albert, who I knew had been concerned about the burden that his declining health was imposing upon his Dominican brethren. He was always thoughtful of others.

My first memories of him date from the late 1970s when I read *Jesus before Christianity*. I read the French translation done by Jean-Marie Dumortier, who was a YCW chaplain in South Africa. I remember my joy at finding in this book the portrait of a Jesus of Nazareth who opposed the political and religious powers of his time. A portrait of Jesus who was very different from the Jesus of the Christian Church recognised by Emperor Constantine and which has been linked to political powers through the centuries.

I was also struck by the fact that in his book he did not talk about the situation under Apartheid. The same observations were shared by other readers, including members of groups who studied the book in Brussels, under the guidance of the Dominican Ignace Berten, and in Namur, with the Jesuit Gérard Fourez.

Sometime later, like other Belgian friends, I was not surprised to learn that Albert had decided to decline his election as head of the Dominican Order because he wanted to remain in South Africa among the Christian activists who opposed the Apartheid regime.

In 1987, I first met Albert as Southern African project officer for the Belgian Catholic NGO *Entraide et Fraternité*. He had been warmly recommended to me by my predecessor, Raymonde Zerghe. From 1987–2004, during a dozen missions to South Africa and during Albert's visits to Europe, I benefitted greatly from interacting with Albert the theologian and social analyst. It was through him that I discovered the work of the Institute for Contextual Theology (ICT). This organisation included members of Churches of missionary origin and of independent African Churches that opposed Apartheid. As a result, I was able to meet an archbishop who was also a taxi driver.

Having been a member of the International Cooperation for Development and Solidarity (CIDSE)'s Southern Africa Working Group during the same period, I remember my colleagues saying that they also greatly appreciated Albert's input during their missions to South Africa or on the occasion of the fiftieth anniversary of the Catholic Institute for International Relations (CIIR) in London, which he joined online. And I remember him explaining to the staff of *Entraide et Fraternité* the reasons for the creation of the Bantustans whose independence was recognised only by South Africa. He also spoke of his links with the Young Christian Students (YCS) of South Africa and assisting them in their efforts to develop partnerships in Europe.

Like my colleagues at CIDSE and at other organisations linked to the Protestant Churches, I also appreciated what Albert contributed to the development of the *Kairos Document*, even to the point of having been called its 'father' by Christelle Ortolland in her doctoral thesis in history. It was for this reason, that *Entraide et Fraternité* agreed to give financial support to the French translation of Albert's book *God in South Africa* by his Dominican brother Philippe Denis. I admit to having forgotten this book one evening on the bus taking me from Jan Smuts (now OR Tambo) Airport to the Johannesburg CBD. Fortunately, it was returned to me the next morning by the attentive bus driver.

Entraide et Fraternité solicited various CIDSE agencies and other NGOs to also fund the publication of *Towards an Agenda for Contextual Theology: Essays in Honour of Albert Nolan,* a collection of essays edited by McGlory Speckman and Larry Kaufmann and published by Cluster Publications. At the launch of the book in Johannesburg, I had the opportunity to reiterate what I had written in the donor partners' preface. I thanked Albert again and took the liberty of making the point, as a simple baptised person, that in fact, theology is always contextual.

Having also been a journalist, I found Albert's role as editor of the ecumenical magazine *Challenge* during the transition from Apartheid to democracy to be of particular importance. And while South Africans are obviously better placed than us to say so, I must say that it opened the eyes of our partners abroad and in the international context to South Africa realities. That is why, in 2006, in my first year of retirement, I gladly agreed to do an evaluation of *Challenge* with an Australian journalist who lived in South Africa. But sadly, in spite of what we proposed to the funders after meeting Albert and his successor, we were unable to secure continued funding for the magazine.

It was during this visit that I had an opportunity to talk with Albert about his book, *Jesus today*. I was pleased to hear him explain that he had expanded his previous work *Jesus before Christianity* in the light of his encounters with courageous South Africans like Mandela, with authors of spiritual books, with scientists, political scientists, women and ecologists to show the links between social, individual and spiritual liberation.

Having benefitted from the hospitality and the insights of Denis Hurley, Archbishop of Durban and president of the Southern African Catholic Bishops' Conference (SACBC), I can say that, despite Albert's involvement in the writing of the *Kairos Document*, which was critical of the Churches, this great pastor always maintained full confidence in Nolan, whom he greatly appreciated. They had in common an appreciation of the See–Judge–Act method of the Belgian priest and activist, Joseph Cardijn.

In an effort to support partners in Southern Africa, *Entraide et Fraternité* developed links with the Belgian Committee against Racism and Apartheid, the World Council of Churches, humanists, Jewish survivors of Nazi concentration camps, Protestants and other democrats. They rejoiced to see Catholics and Protestants campaigning in Belgium against four banks investing in Apartheid South Africa. But it is clear that such involvements could not have been carried out over these years, ecumenically and even more broadly, without conversations with Archbishop Hurley, Albert Nolan, Beyers Naudé, Smangaliso Mkhatshwa, Philippe Denis, Paddy Kearney, Peter Kerchhoff and others. This is why, during a lecture I gave in early 2023 on 'Nelson Mandela and other remarkable anti-Apartheid South Africans', I evoked the great Albert Nolan with gratitude and affection. Moreover, I always had an unfulfilled dream to join him and other South Africans in an immersion in Brazil among the small Christian communities doing 'theology from below' to nourish their commitments.

While I regret the withdrawal of *Entraide et Fraternité* from South Africa, I am happy that in our time working there we managed to support several of the important projects promoted by Albert.

Graduates of the 2002 Winter course, from left to right Suzanne Ramaokoka, Father Albert Nolan, Noelene van Niekerk, Zanele Mkhwanazi (who won the writing course competition in the Natal Witness and has since sadly passed away), Ruth Coggin, Euni Motsa, Elinor and baby Lowry (Patrick), Theo Coggin, Burgie Ireland, and Rosley Matlala.

Skilling Religious Journalists

Theo and Ruth Coggin

It was in the halcyon days of the liberation years immediately following 1994 that Albert Nolan approached us to discuss organising and running a religious journalism course. Theo had developed such a course and refined it when he worked for the Methodist Church of Southern Africa in the 1980s. The course had continued to be run for about six years under the umbrella of the Church's newspaper, *Dimension*, even after he left to work in corporate communications. However, it stopped being presented by the Methodists after Ruth left *Dimension*. The three of us discussed the possibilities at length. *Challenge*, the magazine edited by Albert and published monthly by Contextual Publications in Johannesburg, was a highly respected ecumenical publication whose content was on the cutting edge of theological debate. Albert had a deep love of writing and was meticulous in his work. So too were the Coggins, who by then had formed their own media company, Quo Vadis Communications.

It was a serendipitous opportunity to bring together the many skills in journalism required to run a successful religious journalism course, namely reporting, principles of communication, writing, interviewing, layout, news value, basic English—including some of the pitfalls of its idiomatic idiosyncrasies—basic photography and photographic composition, and publishing. They also brought a unique ability to train adults in an existential manner. When necessary, they included specialists in their fields, such as a professional photographer, to give the best possible input.

In the planning, it was agreed many times over that a fundamental tenet of the training was for the modules to be founded on a high standard of ethical journalism. This was backed by a progressive theological approach, led by Albert's own unique interpretation of the gospel and fully subscribed to by Theo and Ruth. As readers of this book will know, Albert's theology was contextualised in the life of the world about which people would be reporting during the course. This fundamental philosophy was a natural extension of Albert's deep-seated understanding of the life of Jesus in which he did not separate religion and politics, but regarded each as integral to the other, and a prerequisite for contemporary followers of Jesus.

It might therefore be asked how it was possible that a person like Albert, steeped in academic theological training and the theology and practices of the Catholic Church, and also an ordained priest, could work so easily and readily with two lay people who came out of the Wesleyan tradition and had both occupied executive leadership positions in the Methodist Church of Southern Africa as lay people? We pose this question only because some have asked it of us as we have spoken about writing this contribution.

The answer, of course, is simply that we had a common under-standing of the imperative to contextualise the act of following Jesus in the developing new South Africa, as much as had been the case during the Apartheid years. This would need to be reported on and written down by people in the Church, the NGO community and from other walks of life who felt called to contribute in this way. We also all had a love of teaching and sharing our skills and gifts with oth-ers. Many were the enjoyable times we experienced as we delighted in our shared sense of humour and met the challenges involved in estab-lishing such a course and keeping it running for nearly twenty years. The fact that the three of us were very down-to-earth people meant that we found a camaraderie in and with each other to celebrate the progress we saw in the course and the individual achievements of those who came on it, as well as the inevitable disappointments that happened from time to time.

Before we could get going with the course, however, it was neces-sary to secure funding. Albert, through his editorship of *Challenge*, had already been in contact with potential donors, both in South Africa and wider afield. All three of us were experienced at putting together compelling funding proposals and we put these skills to good use. Albert was masterful in networking and bringing out the best in us through his unwavering belief in our skills and Christian calling as lay people. In this respect, he never showed any doubt and an abiding memory of Albert is his complete trust in us and willingness to allow us to act independently to bring our common vision to life. In South Africa, the Christian Development Trust, under the leadership of Allan Wentzel, a former chairman of the United Congregational Church, responded to our financial need. Internationally, we received ongoing and magnificent financial support from the *Evangelischer Entwicklungsdienst* (EED) in Bonn, Germany. The funding received allowed us to subsidise the cost of training, accommodation and, frequently, travel expenses for delegates, many of whom came from far flung rural areas and others even from neighbouring countries. Many delegates came from deeply impoverished backgrounds and would not have been able to afford such a course with their own financial resources only. However, the individuals, or organisations they represented, were required to contribute a nominal amount of funding to ensure their commitment to the investment that was being made in them.

As our methodology, we took every step possible to conduct the courses in a professional manner. The courses were deliberately kept small (the largest course was fifteen delegates—never again so many, we said afterwards!) because of the intense and personal nature of the tuition. Not only were they intense for the delegates—who always worked late into the evening to finish their assigned tasks—but they were taxing on the lecturers, each of whom had other professional responsibilities, not least of which was Albert, who was running a religious order, editing a monthly magazine and was in demand as a speaker and writer, both internationally and in South Africa.

The courses were residential and divided into three sessions over a period of eight weeks. In the four weeks between each session, delegates were required to put into practice what they had learned and do the substantial homework tasks they were given. We structured the course in this way so that the process of experiential learning could be reinforced as much as possible. Tasks given included conducting an interview and writing a feature story based on this, and an additional feature on a subject of their choice, which could involve their own life journey. As each course neared its completion, delegates participated in an exercise to gather news in a highly pressurised simulated exercise with limited time available to complete the task. This taught delegates how to work under pressure, an essential element of reporting, and then to report their findings in a coherent way—the second essential element in producing good copy. A valuable aspect of the training was learning how to prioritise the value of the information they had and its relevance to the audience. The most surprising feedback often came as a result of this aspect—including more than one ordained minister telling us that this aspect in and of itself had helped them write and preach more coherent sermons!

Many of these feature stories were featured in upcoming editions of *Challenge*, a source of great pride to delegates and a way of sharing the stories of their community with a much wider audience. It was at times very moving to realise the pressures under which delegates participated in this course. One of the most memorable was that of Thomas Duane, a priest who produced a beautiful piece on his experience of living with Parkinson's Disease and its consequences for his life. Another was that of a nun from the Eastern Cape, whose name we are not using for obvious reasons, who wrote of the sexual abuse she had suffered in her ministry.

In the early days, Albert's teaching contribution was to give instruction in basic English and essential editing. Which delegates will ever forget Albert's exercise on 'The pastor's wife'—an actual article that had previously been submitted for publication—which required an editor's heavy pencil and many laughs? When Albert began to step back from his tutoring involvement (he never completely stepped back from his overall management of this project until he retired from *Challenge*), the English tuition was taken over by Elinor Lowry. She brought the same level of commitment with her, to the extent that the morning before she gave birth to her last-born child, she was still teaching English on the course! That *Challenge* baby, Patrick, attended many a graduation ceremony with Elinor as he grew from new-born to a toddler! Elinor's ability to fit so naturally into the team was a further tribute to Albert's amazing openness to the role of the laity and, in her case, of lay women in the Church in an age when this was not always the case.

The wide array of delegates who attended the courses over a period of some twelve years was astonishing. They were mostly Church people—including Mark James, who succeeded Albert as provincial of the Dominican vicariate—but the participants were always peppered with folk from other disciplines. We had trade unionists, government employees, NGOs, as well as ones that introduced us to religious organisations we had not previously heard of! Their range of education also differed widely, as were the cultural backgrounds from which they came. One unforgettable course had some highly sophisticated urban delegates attending, as well as some folk from far-flung rural areas who clearly had very different norms and values. This was the only course where we noticed a cleavage between delegates based on culture—differences that disappeared extremely fast as it became clear that the folk from the rural areas had a far better understanding of news value and the impact of the actions of bureaucracy on those not living in urban areas. As that course progressed, a new respect among the urban people for their rural counterparts dawned, and that came from the culture of inclusivity, led by Albert, that the *Challenge Quo Vadis* writers' course brought, taught and showed in practice.

The other difference worth noting was that of language skills. As tutors, we were always sensitive to the fact that the course was conducted in a language—English—which was not the first language of the majority of participants. In fact, everyone's eyes would widen during one of the presentations in which research was shared that showed that English, the *lingua franca* of South Africa, was not the most commonly spoken first language in any of the country's nine provinces. However, English was chosen as the language of tuition simply because it was the most understandable across South Africa's eleven[1] official languages. But then there were pitfalls too, not least when two delegates were sent by the United Methodist Church (UMC) in Mozambique, who were working in an important initiative there to bring basic services to isolated areas. Only one understood and spoke English, but he took on as his responsibility to translate the lectures as they were presented, as well as reading material, into Portuguese for the benefit of his colleague. What incredible commitment from two young men who are still today working for the UMC in Mozambique and have developed their project into one of the most successful in that part of the world.

In an alumni list of approximately 200 names, it is impossible to single out too many people. After much consideration, however, there is one person who speaks to the immense empowerment of this course. Zanele Mkhwanazi, who attended the course in 2002, made the news as the winner of an annual writing competition run by a

---

1. It was eleven official languages when the course was conducted. In 2023, South African Sign Language (SASL) was added as the twelfth official language.

large daily newspaper in South Africa. Her winning short story told the story of her Bushman grandmother, Makhulomhlope, highlighting the incorrect perceptions of the history and apparent disappearance of these people in the mountains of the Drakensberg range of South Africa, and the stigmas still attached to these resourceful pastoral nomads. Against stiff competition, with many from beyond the country's borders, she beat nine other finalists to win first prize—and a handsome cash prize. Zanele's elated comment on her achievement was: 'It is all thanks to the skills I learned at the *Challenge Quo Vadis* writers' course. The course was challenging and infused a lot of confidence in me.' But, probably most importantly, Zanele took those skills to empower her own community in rural KwaZulu-Natal: 'I have now started to train other people to write and prepare newsletters for the community', said Zanele, who had been sent to the course by the Women's Leadership and Training Programme (WLTP).[2]

Zanele went on to become an influential leader in her community of Ndawana, and travelled the world to raise funds to make a difference to their lives. Sadly, she died in 2008 at the tragically young age of thirty-three years.

The writing course has ensured that consistently good communication is at the hub of the information process that is a prerequisite for success. This is further underlined by the success achieved, and skills acquired, by Ntombifuthi Makhanya, who attended the *Quo Vadis* writing course in 2003. At the end of the course she, and two other course delegates, started a community newsletter, the *Centecow News*. The Zulu medium newsletter received overwhelming support from the community as it met a strong need for the community to read about itself, keeping it abreast on sports, church activities, community activities, politics and information on NGO's in the area.

---

2. The Women's Leadership Training Programme (WLTP) is an NGO founded in 1984 in KwaZulu/Natal to empower impoverished rural communities around the town of Underberg. The organisation trains women and youth in gardening, environmental awareness, tourism, HIV and Aids awareness. Its programme has made a great impact on the communities to the extent that it established branches in other towns in KwaZulu/Natal, giving rise to other community-based organisations like Centocow, which was formed in 1994 in the town of Ixopo. Centecow responded to the widespread problem of teenage pregnancies, child abuse and HIV/Aids in the community. The women devised programmes to educate youth, and also teach them on gender sensitivity, sexuality and alleviating poverty.

'Although I found the course challenging, I gained invaluable communication and layout skills. The course boosted my self-esteem, and made me more observant, looking at things with a writer's eye. I now feel that I am now making a more valued contribution to the community,' said Ntombifuthi.

Another delegate, Sibongile Mtungwa, went on to become the director of the WLTP programme.

These are but a few of the stories of how this course, which Albert initiated with such vision, took its learnings and their applications to the very heart of communities. It empowered them, inspired them to reach new heights, and sustained them for years. There are many people still in influential positions using the skills that Albert's vision and commitment brought to life.

For that was Albert: visioner extraordinaire. And that is how he will be remembered. His legacy is celebrated with fondness and great admiration.

Section Seven

Spiritual Renewal

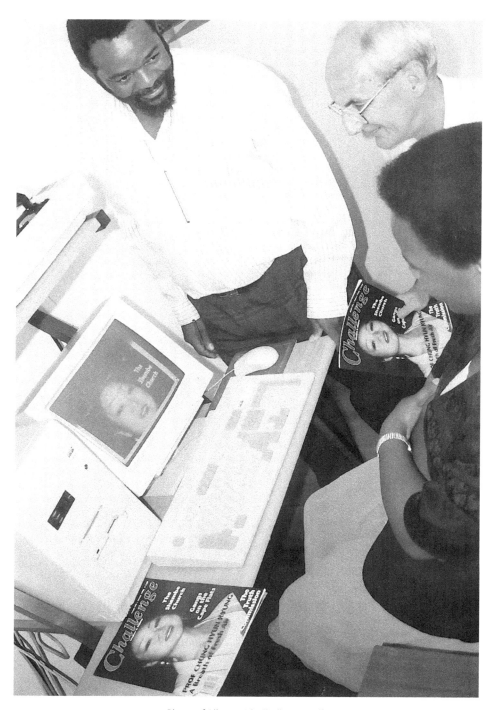

Photo of Albert with *Challenge* staff.

A Prophet for our Planet's *Kairos* Moment

Marilyn Aitken

Albert's influence on my life can be divided into two distinct but deeply connected *kairos* moments. I met him for the first time in late 1976 during the first *kairos* moment, the struggle for justice in South Africa. He had recently arrived in Johannesburg from Stellenbosch and was meeting with members of CARE (Catholic Action for Racial Education). CARE had its roots in a group of Catholic students from the 1950s Catholic Society at the University of the Witwatersrand who were deeply influenced by a legendary Franciscan Chaplain, Fr Didicus (Diego) Connery. He had three doctorates, had worked in a number of countries and together with other Church thinkers was laying the ground for Vatican Council II. He spoke fluent Hindustani and was *avant garde* in many ways. He said Mass in English (the language of the group) instead of Latin, facing those present, long before Vatican Council II in the 1960s made this practice normal in Catholic churches.

The open talks he gave drew a wide range of university students and he became so popular that the secular National Union of South African Students (NUSAS) asked the National Catholic Federation of Students (NCFS) to organise its annual conferences at different times for fear that the NCFS conferences would draw students away from the NUSAS ones. Diego opened the eyes of his students to the evils of Apartheid and gave rise to a generation of activists including Frances (Frankie) Malherbe and Tony Connell, Donovan Lowry and Etheen Ince, Peter Hunter and Lucienne O'Berle, Joan Hope and Jimmy Stewart, Paul Goller, Molly Horn, Mary Hart, Ines Ceruti and Anne Hope.

Diego was Albert's precursor. Students he influenced later married each other and gave birth to many of the student activists that Albert worked with in the 1970s and 1980s.

Diego's protegees launched CARE in the 1960s to take on the task of educating Catholics in the Diocese of Johannesburg to stand up to Apartheid. They felt that Bishop Hugh Boyle was failing in this task. Paul Goller edited an incisive magazine called *Challenge* and others created awareness in parish council meetings and other places. CARE famously organised a picket outside the Johannesburg Cathedral after Christmas midnight Mass in 1966 exhorting Catholics to stand up against Apartheid.

CARE members met monthly in the Grail Centre in Parktown and were joined by Drake Koka and Tom Manthata, teacher activists from Soweto, Jean and Eric Tyacke, trade unionists, Sydney Duval and Tony Brink, and others like me. I became a CARE member in 1969 having recently joined the Grail from rural Natal. I noticed how some of the men in the group dominated the discussions. The Women's Liberation Movement had not yet influenced this group and the women would retire to the kitchen to make the tea and find a space to have their say. During one of the meetings after a few men had dominated for about an hour, Tom exploded, 'You Non-Blacks shut up! And listen to us for a change'. Tom and Drake then had a space to talk about the realities of Apartheid in Soweto.

By the late 1960s and early 1970s the South African political scene had changed dramatically, and the Black Consciousness Movement was at its height. When CARE met Albert for the first time, the group was grappling with many challenges. They had failed to establish a Justice and Peace Commission in the diocese because the bishop had refused to allow Drake Koka to become its Chair. It was also soon after the June 16 Apartheid massacre of school students. The members were hanging onto Albert's every word: 'Please don't try to make me your guru. I am not a guru'. And he repeated Tom's message of a few years back, but in a gentler way: 'This is the time for those of us who have been privileged by Apartheid to step back from the limelight and support the leadership of the oppressed peoples in our country in whatever way we can', or words to that effect. And the CARE members' support came in many shapes and forms after that, to mention a few—personal donations and loans, support of trade unionists, peace work, safe houses for activists on the run from the security police, twinning of parishes in the affluent suburbs with those in the townships (ghettos), caring for the children of detained activists, assisting activists to go into exile, fixing and servicing cars, working for justice and peace in Church structures, supporting those suffering physically or mentally from police brutality, working with girls and women, raising funds from overseas donors for anti-Apartheid activities and organisations, initiating adult education and HIV and AIDS projects.

People who supported the oppressed in these ways attracted the attention of the Apartheid Security Police. Those of us living in the Grail Centre at 2 Loch Avenue did not escape. Early one Friday morning in December 1981, our housekeeper, Dorah Mashishi, who did a piece job somewhere else on Fridays, woke us with the news that the Security Police had blocked our driveway and refused to let her out. We found out that they were already searching Beyers Naudé's and Wolfram Kistner's homes. Dorah's husband Peter, who lived with her 'illegally' in one of the outside rooms, had meanwhile jumped over the wall and escaped along a back lane to work. We had four hours to pack into black bags anything the Apartheid agents would regard as 'subversive' and throw them over the wall into the shrubbery in our neighbour's garden. One of these items was the film, 'Generations of Resistance'. The Security Police (SP) eventually arrived at 9.30 and demanded to see 'Mr Nolans'. Pam Farrow who was very uptight by then, yelled at them, 'There's no Mr Nolans here!' So, they began with her, searching her room thoroughly and upsetting her very much by reading her private correspondence. The Dominican house in Mayfair did not get searched. The Security Police were perhaps too afraid of the pope or Archbishop Hurley to touch the Dominicans, or else they believed that by asking for Mr Nolans, Albert would understand that they had him in their sights.

Early in 1983, Albert, Smangaliso Mkhatshwa and I attended a secret meeting, called by Beyers Naudé, in the Holy Family Convent attached to the Kenridge Hospital in Parktown. As one of our ways to 'support the leadership of the oppressed peoples', we worked on a budget and plans to raise funds for the launch of the United Democratic Front (UDF), an initiative to unite and strengthen the civil society organisations that were fighting Apartheid. I worked for the Catholic Bishops' Justice and Peace Commission at that time and knew many funders, as did the other three. The budget found its way to

Europe and a few weeks later, an activist journalist, who had arrived from London that morning, came to the Grail Centre, sat down and removed from his socks a large number of the highest denomination Dutch Guilder notes. He handed them to me and I took them straight to Beyers. A few months later in August, the UDF launch took place in Mitchell's Plain, Cape Town. It was a vibrant, huge success and the UDF went from strength to strength after that.

Albert's roles extended to social activities. He was sought after by young activists to officiate at their weddings, whether or not they were Catholics. I attended a number of these at the Holy Family Convent chapel in Victory Park, which became the unofficial activist wedding venue. But the wedding I remember best was that of Kathy Bond, a Grail member, and John Stewart on 29 November 1980 at the Grail Centre in Parktown. We had a large lounge which was frequently used for meetings, and we were expert at fitting a hundred or more into that space. Albert conducted the marriage ceremony in a very relaxed and moving way. Kathy Bond-Stewart recalled:

> We chose Albert to marry us because he best represented our spirituality and commitment to social justice. He was not a marriage officer as he disagreed with the Apartheid marriage laws, so we had to get legally married the following week in Lesotho where John's parents, Joan (Hope) and Jimmy Stewart lived at their centre called Transformation. They were arrested on the way to our wedding in Johannesburg, for bringing John's books into South Africa, which included banned books, so they attended on bail. Unfortunately, their subsequent trial in South Africa prevented them from being at our legal marriage in Lesotho—a very South African wedding experience in those strange times!

I have read and absorbed the teachings from Albert's *Jesus before Christianity*. The section that stands out is the interpretation of the parable of the loaves and fishes, a story that shows how skilful Jesus was at getting people to share what they had so that no-one was in need. I believe that sharing so that 'no-one is in need' was as relevant for the Apartheid *kairos* moment as it is for the present planetary *kairos* moment.

The terms of reference for my work in the Justice and Peace Commission included 'Integrity of Creation'. I had no idea what it meant when I took on the job in 1978 and the demands of the human struggle for justice were so great that I only began to understand its meaning and importance for our times after I had left the SACBC in 1987 and had joined a group started by Dominican Sister, Angelika Laub called, 'The Earth Speaks'. In about 1991, Hannah Remke teamed up with Grail member Emilia Charbonneau to run a workshop, 'Healing the Wounded Earth' at the Lumko Institute in Germiston. One of the highlights was a ritual during which every participant traced her path from the original explosion of energy 13.8 billion years ago, through the key moments of the creation process, including the miracle of oxygen, the flowering of the planet, the emergence of human life, significant events in recent memory, and finally the participant's birth. Each stage was marked with a lit votive candle and the ritual was done with the lights off. It was very powerful! At the end of the ritual, Veronique Schoeffel noticed that two of the thirty candles had died. They were the Holocaust years 1939–1945 and the beginning of Apartheid in 1948. Very eerie!

'Healing the Wounded Earth' was an 'Ah! Ha!' moment for me as it was for many others. Marian O'Sullivan an Irish Dominican set up the *An Tairseach* Dominican Farm and Ecology Centre in Wicklow Ireland, which still exists today.

It seems that Albert was similarly very interested in finding out more about the 'Integrity of Creation' and in 1998 organised a sabbatical to the USA to study with fellow religious Thomas Berry and with Brian Swimme, who expanded on the work of the Jesuit palaeontologist, Teilhard de Chardin. Much has been written about this unfolding evolution of life, but it was Brian Swimme and Thomas Berry who put it all together as one long and exciting story in their book, *The Universe Story: The Unfolding of the Cosmos*.[1] While in the USA, Albert met also with his fellow Dominican, Miriam Therese MacGillis at Genesis Farm. Albert embraced this new way of thinking enthusiastically and on his return to South Africa, gave numerous inspiring talks on 'The Theology of Creation'.

After his 1998 sabbatical in the USA, he wrote a less well-known book published in 2006 called, *Jesus Today, A Spirituality of Radical Freedom*. In the book, he identified clearly two urgent problems for today: climate change and the loss of biodiversity. While he never used these terms in the book, he did write that:

---

1. Brian Swimme and Thomas Berry, *The Universe Story: The Unfolding of the Cosmos* (San Francisco: HarperSanFrancisco, 1992).

The most recent scientific discovery . . . is not about some future catastrophe. It is about the disaster that is already happening—global warming. I believe that it is one of the outstanding signs of our times . . . The greenhouse gases should be stopped now.[2]

The experience of oneness with other human beings would be incomplete and ineffective without an experience of oneness with the rest of the universe ... as human beings we are part of nature . . . for mystical spirituality identifying with nature and the universe as a whole is absolutely essential. There is no way that I can discover my identity, my true self without going out and making contact with nature.[3]

The urban poor are deprived of any real contact with nature.[4]

Sadly, Albert's message never entered mainstream consciousness during his lifetime. In recent years, the problem of global warming has grown exponentially, causing devastating extreme weather events as climate change has kicked in all over the globe. However, Albert identified the problem and showed us how to contextualise it in a religious way. We should be paying urgent attention to the March 2023 Intergovernmental Panel on Climate Change (IPCC) 'Survival Report' that gives human beings seven years to get their relationship to our planet right, by reducing drastically our carbon emissions.

In South Africa we have a particular obligation to reduce carbon drastically as we rank among the top greenhouse gas polluters in the world because of our politicians' stubborn reluctance to phase out coal as a matter of urgency. How shocked Albert would be to know that the parts per million of carbon in 2023 has reached 418 ppm, way higher than the safe 350 ppm.

Africa, because of its position lying mostly between the tropics, will overheat and is already suffering, more than other continents. As the Nigerian climate activist Nnimo Bassey has warned, 'We are going to fry in Africa as the temperatures rise way above the safe 1.5 degrees since pre-industrial times'. Many of Africa's political leaders

---

2. Albert Nolan, *Jesus Today, A Spirituality of Radical Freedom* (Maryknolll, NY: Orbis Books, 1998), 20.
3. Nolan, *Jesus Today,* 170.
4. Nolan, *Jesus Today,* 171.

seem to be ignorant of climate science as they hold grimly onto fossil fuels—gas, oil and especially coal, and religious people are hardly talking about this threat to God's creation and all life. The vast majority do not connect 1.5 degrees with their faith. The Southern African Faith Communities Environment Institute (SAFCEI) based in Cape Town, must be commended for working hard to raise awareness in this regard.

I thank Albert for highlighting the need for the human being to be immersed in biodiversity. The IPCC scientists, together with their counterparts in their twin Intergovernmental Platform on Biodiversity and Ecosystem Services (IPBES), are the prophets of our times. They are calling us to repent, to repudiate our present value systems and the economic activities that are causing so much hardship for the majority of the world's population and earth's creatures. The recent IPBES report warns that we have already lost sixty-nine per cent of the world's biodiversity, the planet's life support systems. Human beings too are critically endangered. We would do well to re-read and study *Jesus Today* alongside the IPCC and IPBES reports to discover how to address the twin threats of climate change and the terrifying loss of biodiversity.

The planet shares the same atmosphere, so excess carbon emissions in one part of the world affect the whole. What Africa needs is strong, informed political and civil society leadership, working together to force the Global North to honour and increase its NDCs (Nationally Determined Contributions).[5] This means fast-tracking finance for renewable energy for the 'loss and damage' we have already suffered and for the restoration and conservation of biodiversity. South Africa's NDC contains a commitment to phasing out coal rapidly from its energy mix.

A truly 'just transition' from fossil fuels to a low carbon economy will require a real 'sharing of loaves and fishes' to address the outrageous inequality that exists between rich and poor, as recently highlighted in an OXFAM UK report. A low carbon economy will go a long way to achieve an egalitarian society, providing decent work for all, clean air that ensures better health, and green spaces in cities

---

5. An NDC is the UN Party's (Nation State's) binding commitment under the UNFCCC 2015 Paris Agreement, to an action plan to cut carbon emissions and adapt to climate impacts. Each Party is required to establish an NDC and update it every five years.

where all can enjoy biodiversity. We will learn to obey the divine law of limits which human beings have grossly transgressed over the past 100 years and we will learn to recognise God manifested in natural phenomena.

To talk about Albert in the context of climate change without paying tribute to his fellow Dominican mentor, the late Finbar Synnott, would be a travesty. Finbar influenced the lives of so many of us. In the 1970s he prophetically denounced air travel and the use of cars decades before teenage girl prophet and climate guru Greta Thunberg, born at 375 ppm, did the same.[6]

This Good Friday morning, I woke up to reflect on how important an appropriate theology and spirituality is for the task ahead. I recalled the Zoom event I had participated in on the Birdlife SA 'Conservation Conversations' Platform a few days earlier. Dr Vikash Tatayah of the Mauritian Wildlife Foundation was the presenter. He began by showing us what Mauritius looked like before the advent of European settlers. It was a large completely wooded tropical island full of biodiversity—insects, tortoises, lizards, many tree species and plants, and hundreds of thousands of birds. He showed how the island became increasingly denuded of vegetation as first the Dutch, then the French and lastly the British plundered the island's resources, while at the same time slaughtering thousands of wildlife species, including the legendary Dodo, now the global symbol of extinction.

This shocking picture gave me the sensation of watching Jesus being stripped of his clothes prior to his crucifixion, until only a small loin cloth remained. In the case of Mauritius, the 'loin cloth' is a small strip of the original vegetation. We know that this 'stripping' is happening too in the Amazon, the Congo and many other parts of the world. But, in the case of Mauritius, Dr Tatayah also had a strong message of hope. Mauritian conservationists have brought back many species from the brink of extinction and are leading the world in successfully restoring the island's biodiversity.

Albert stressed the need for hope in many of his writings and talks. And that is what I will take with me into the future.

Thanks to Paul Goller and Frances (Malherbe) Connell for information about Didicus Connery and CARE.

---

6. Greta Thunberg identifies her year of birth (2003) by the amount of greenhouse gases that existed at that time. It has increased dramatically since then to about 418ppm in 2023.

Converted to the Universe Story

Miriam MacGillis OP

Albert came to Genesis Farm for two weeks during his sabbatical in 1998. When I was asked to write about his stay here and what Albert referred to as his 'conversion' (for which I felt honoured and grateful), my only memory was of the date of his sabbatical year, that it was at Easter time, and that he carried a quality of humility that is not always carried in some of the clerics who have studied here. We always caution clerics not to fulfil the needs of other more traditional participants by setting up times for alternative traditional liturgies since we stress that the universe itself is ineffable and all that emanates from it is where anything effable can be encountered. Thus, moving into that unfamiliar source of the sacred is not confined or limited by religious beliefs. I seem to remember Albert being relieved to hear that and being freed of any expectations on him. He was one searching human within a small community of humans gathered here in a common search for the ineffable.

Before he came, I knew little about him except his declining the honour of being elected Master of the Dominican Order to remain with his people in South Africa during the struggle against Apartheid. I had also heard about him from Sr Marian O'Sullivan, an Irish Dominican Sister of Cabra, who invited me to work with her and other Sisters in developing a similar programme to ours, *An Tairseach*, in Wicklow, Ireland. She had worked with him in South Africa in the 1980s.

Before continuing about Albert's experiences with us it may be necessary to outline a little about myself and what is Genesis Farm. In 1957, I entered the Congregation of the Sisters of St Dominic of Caldwell, New Jersey. During my formation years I earned a Bachelor's degree in both English and Education. In 1970, I earned a

Master's degree in Fine Arts from the University of Notre Dame in Indiana. During the racial riots in New Jersey and as a response to the Vietnam War, I left the teaching of art and joined the Archdiocesan Institute of Justice and Peace in Newark, New Jersey where I opened a new 'global issues' desk. Subsequently, I met Patricia and Gerald Mische, who had co-founded Global Education Associates in a nearby town and we worked together for many years. Through this collaboration, I first heard Thomas Berry, a Passionist priest, speak on the Universe Story at a conference in Maryknoll, New York in 1977. This talk changed my life.[1]

In 1980, on a 140-acre farm in the north-western part of New Jersey that the Sisters of St Dominic had inherited, three others and I started Genesis Farm. We were not subsidised and did not wish to be dependent on corporate or foundation support. The buildings out of which we created Genesis Farm—as a learning centre for 'reinhabiting the earth'—were in need of massive renovation and additions if they were to be able to host residential programmes. These programmes developed out of our first ten years of responding to requests from people to deepen their study of the Universe Story, through lectures, tapes, videos, basic curriculum materials and a decade of networking with different institutions, organisations and universities.

By 1990, we were able to host residential programmes and by 1992, through collaboration with the Miami-Dade College and St Thomas University in Miami, Florida we were able to provide undergraduate and post-graduate programmes in Earth Literacy.

Returning to Albert's sabbatical with us during Holy Week of 1998, I had to embark on a journey to seek out any contemporaries and to dig into our archives to uncover the courses and programmes he followed from articles, letters and reflections we received from him. From these, I will piece together some of the reflections that Albert shared with us about his own conversion to the Universe Story.

In an interview with Tom Fox, the editor of the *National Catholic Reporter* (NCR) in 2007, Albert said that after he had been exposed to the Universe Story, it had changed his perspective on his theological writings and his activism, especially among young people. Young people, he said:

---

1. Later, for a year in 1984, I was able to spend one day every month with Thomas doing a private directed reading programme, which was an enormous blessing for me.

have given up all certainties of the past: religious certainties, scientific certainties, cultural certainties, political certainties and historical certainties. This could be a tremendous opportunity . . . We have a whole new way of understanding the universe, and therefore, understanding ourselves, who we are, and how we fit in that has great potential for the future. However . . . we are going headlong into more and more selfishness and individualism. We are caught between chaos and promise . . .

In 1999, Genesis Farm sent out a questionnaire called the Earth Literacy Directory to the hundreds of people who had attended our programmes from 1992–2000. It asked them to share their efforts in living out the context of the New Story and in what area they were trying to incorporate it into their lives and work. I found Albert's response, sent in October 1999:

> We have started a sub-committee of the South African National Justice and Peace Commission on 'creation' to promote the *New Story* and ecological issues. A pastoral letter will be published soon followed by workshops and other activities. I have been trying to integrate the New Story into my retreats and lectures here and elsewhere (e.g. the Philippines). I plan to write something about it. Greetings to all at Genesis Farm, Albert.

Recently, we found a file entitled 'Letters of Endorsement'. Apparently, our Board of Trustees or Dominican Congregational Leaders were seeking these letters from a broad spectrum of people from local to global to do an evaluation of our work. It included the Summer/Fall edition of our 1998 newsletter, Volume 12/3, and on page 2, titled 'Earth Literacy Update', a number of responses given by participants who came here in 1998 were reported, including one from Albert Nolan OP, South Africa. Here is what he said:

> While I have been reading about the New Story for a number of years now, the program added many new insights like food and plants and rocks and the oneness of the universe. The challenge is to live it and to allow it to transform my theology and my writing. The program did not merely meet all my hopes and expectations, it exceeded anything that I could ever have imagined in my wildest dreams. Far and away the most formative experience of my life.

This shows that Albert's experience of conversion to the Universe Story was a cosmological transformation which would of necessity include an ecological one. If there is any vivid memory of Albert, it was his repeated expression of the depth of what had changed in him. He said it over and over.

I do not know what the rest of his life demanded of him, but I can attest to the feelings of alienation, inadequacy and isolation that often are part of the cost of such a conversion. I also say this because I know that many who have this experience find themselves returning to the world with its expectations of them. They do not receive the support or the space to go deeper into what is arising in them. They do the best they can but the work of deconstructing one's image of God and truth is enormous.

The 1998 newsletter did not tell us anything about the actual programmes he attended but it enabled us to recover roster files and to learn that he had been at Genesis Farm from 4–17 April. (Palm Sunday was 5 April, Passover and Good Friday were both on 10 April and Easter was 12 April). We also learned the names of those who attended that programme. One of them is a colleague from a local religious congregation.[2] She told me she had fond memories of Albert and sent me the total schedule for those two weeks. It included every day's activities, presentations, readings, field trips, films, rituals—all laying the context for the New Story of the evolution of the universe, Earth, life and human consciousness. These days were the necessary prelude to opening the archetypal imprints of the events of Exodus, Passover, Easter. Each is a belief created in response to the springtime renewal season by the Abrahamic religions emerging out of the Genesis story of how the world was created.

I did a review of the design of the two-week programme which Albert experienced. It attempted to provide a compressed experience of the twelve-week residential courses we had been developing since 1992. He would have been immersed in the story of the evolution of the Universe, as current astrophysicists, quantum physicists, astronomers, chemists, geologists, geographers, biologists and anthropologists have pieced it together using empirical evidence. This process of scientific learning was supported by reading, art, films, shared reflec-

---

2. Sister Melinda McDonald, a member of the Congregation of the Sisters of St Joseph of Peace.

tions, star gazing and very intentional hours alone on the lands of Genesis Farm, both wild and cultivated.

Only after a week of intensely exploring these understandings and experiences were we able to reinvent ways to enter into the archetypal wisdoms of the recent Judaic and Christian observances of the Passover, Holy Week and Easter rituals.

On Monday morning, after Easter Sunday 12 April, the programme shifted to the *implications* of discovering the reality of the Universe Story, the earth story, the human story and the terrible realisation that humans were terminating the Cenozoic era, that the last sixty-five million years of Earth's most abundant, diverse and beautiful living beings.[3] From Monday until Friday, Albert would have been plunged into the possible alternatives to our present human-centred belief systems which were unwittingly causing the devastation to the Earth, the future of life and the future of all children.

These days were devoted to understanding bioregionalism[4] and the innate capacities of Earth to becoming self-emerging, self-governing, self-healing, self-propagating, self-educating and self-fulfilling. These capacities were evolving from the very first moments of the emergence of the universe fifteen billion years ago. Each day was focused on these primary capacities of Earth within all living cells.

The programme was also designed to examine our human enterprises, such as farming, education and health care as 'derivative of the primary context of Earth and Universe'. It called for questioning and discerning whether our present industrial modes of carrying out

---

3. Years ago, Thomas Berry asked me to do one essential thing, and that was to document what was happening at Genesis Farm during the 'terminal phase of the Cenozoic era', to promote awareness of this planetary tragedy and to envision alternative possibilities for creating an ecozoic era (an era in which people live in a harmonious relationship with the earth) in the particular bio-region where we lived and worked.

4. According to Thomas Berry, a bioregion is an identifiable geographic area of interacting life systems that is relatively self-sustaining in the ever-renewing processes of nature. The full diversity of life functions is carried out, not as individuals or as species, or even as organic beings, but as a community that includes the physical as well as the organic components of the region. Such a bioregion is a self-propagating, self-nourishing, self-educating, self-governing, self-healing and self-fulfilling community. Each of the component life systems must integrate its own functioning within this community to survive in any effective manner.

these activities needed to be critiqued. Equally important, it called for discerning the newly emerging alternative to our enterprises that could become 'mutually beneficial to the natural world as well as to humans . . . not to humans at the expense of the natural world'. This describes the greatest challenge to human creativity because our Western religions separate the 'transcendent human' from the rest of crass material existing beings.

These days were complemented by experiences such as gardening, seed-saving, cooking, studying and identifying wild medicines, integrative time with art activities and a geological field trip learning to read the language of stone. The last day of Albert's stay provided a ritual where he would have entered a covenant with Earth and committed to the need to 'reinvent' himself.

All of this programme was grounded in the work of mathematical cosmologist, Brian Swimme, and cultural historian, Thomas Berry. Their insights probing the discoveries of Albert Einstein are core to the mission of Genesis Farm and the reason why we exist as an Earth Literacy Centre.

Somehow, Albert got to hear about Genesis Farm and enrolled in our Spring programme during his sabbatical. I was pleased to read that his experience here was the most transformative of his life.

Earth needs all of us to reinvent ourselves. The unravelling and aborting of Earth is pathological. This is how Thomas Berry described it:

> In the twentieth century the glory of the human has become the desolation of the earth. The desolation of the earth is becoming the destiny of the human. Therefore, all human programs, institutions, and activities must now be judged primarily by the extent to which they prohibit, ignore, or foster a mutually enhancing human/earth relationship. In the light of this:

> The Great Work of our time is
> to reinvent the human,
> at the species level,
> with critical reflection,
> in a time-development context
> within the community of life systems.
> by means of story
> and shared dream experiences.

Processes of Conversion and Hope

Malusi Mpumlwana

A giant of radical love and radical freedom, Albert Nolan was the irrepressible prophet of *Hope in an Age of Despair*.[1] This essay is a testimony to him, the gentle Elijah of our time, whose every fibre was set to defend and champion the cause of the Naboths[2] of our time—the oppressed and the dispossessed. In this he closely followed in the footsteps of Jesus Christ.

In following Jesus in his own life as a disciple, Albert's name became associated with the simplification of the relationship between faith and life, the use of social analysis and the method of See–Judge–Act that is central to the life of the Young Christian Students (YCS). I was to be inducted into his way of popular theology when I became the YCS Cape Town chaplain in 1986 at the invitation of Fr Curran, pastor of St Gabriel's Catholic Church in Gugulethu Township. This was just after Albert had left his role as National chaplain of YCS and was succeeded by Chris Langefeld.

Albert enabled ordinary young people to use the tool of social analysis to do theology in their townships, schools and universities, pursuing the truth of faith and the truth of life in ways that empowered the oppressed to take charge of their path to liberation. He also led the consolidation of reflections of ordinary Christians in the development of the *Kairos Document*. In Nolan's work, whether at community level with everyday Christians, or addressing academic audiences, or reducing his thinking into volumes of books, there is a consistency in his thinking and work that is characterised by the following three marks:

---

1. Albert Nolan, *Hope in an Age of Despair* (Maryknoll, NY: Orbis Books, 2009).
2. Read the story of Naboth in 1 Kgs 21.

First is a fundamental commitment to following the way of Jesus the Christ, in what I call the Jesus Justice.[3] Second, flowing from the praxis of Jesus, that relates faith to real life conditions, is a commitment to balancing faith and human living. Third, in order to be true to faith and living a life that follows Jesus, Albert nourished these commitments with a deep but unaffected spirituality—a process of conversion—that was not ostentatious but generally enveloped in disarming humility.

In this essay I seek to bear testimony to the essence of Albert's pastoral approach that was rooted in the historical Jesus and flowered in the Jesus of faith who is alive in the present day as a perpetual fountain of hope.

We should rightly recognise Albert Nolan as an ardent and radical disciple of the justice of Jesus—social, economic, gender and ecological justice. Albert consciously and deliberately walks in the footsteps of this Jesus Justice. This enables him to see life in our time from the perspective of the poor—those for whom Jesus cared for the most:

> the poor, the blind, the lame, the crippled, the lepers, the hungry, the miserable . . . sinners, prostitutes, tax collectors, demoniacs . . . the persecuted, the downtrodden, the captives, all who labour and are overburdened, the rabble who know nothing of the la . . . the little ones, the least, the last and the babes or the lost sheep of the house of Israel.[4]

And he concludes, 'the true history of humankind is the history of suffering . . . We must therefore try to enter into the world of the poor and the oppressed as it was in first-century Palestine.'[5] This is the foundation of Albert Nolan's radical love—the *radix* (root) of Jesus Justice.

Thus, in order to understand and to follow Jesus, Albert himself steps into his footsteps in order to apply him in the present social milieu. The choice of two of his book titles speaks directly to this commitment and the basis for Albert's theology and praxis—*Jesus*

---

3. In a dramatic conversion experience in 1977 when I was in prison, without any theological education, I came out with a grounded 'theology' of liberation. I 'discovered' the God of *Jesus Justice*.

4. Albert Nolan, *Jesus before Christianity*, 25th anniversary edition (Maryknoll, NY: Orbis Books, 2001), 27

5. Nolan, *Jesus Before Christianity*, 28.

before Christianity, and *Jesus Today*.[6] In Jesus, the person who 'turned the world, both Jewish and Gentile, upside down', he finds a model for his own life and praxis.

Albert recognised that Jesus was on to a 'social revolution that called for a deep spiritual conversion'.[7] This 'spiritual conversion' requires one to abandon the self, the ego, in favour of dedication to God's work, in order to participate in that social revolution in one's own time. And he states:

> We do this by allowing God to work in and through us. When we are radically free or on the way to radical freedom, divine energy can flow through us unhindered. We see it at work in the prophets, the mystics, and the saints, but above all in Jesus. The Holy Spirit is Jesus' spirit'.[8]

Albert firmly believed in this surrender of what he refers to as the false self, to live out the Jesus Justice to the end, as he writes, 'When I die, my ego, my false self, will be destroyed once and for all, but my true self will continue forever in God'.[9]

'Allowing God to work in and through us' is the pathway for Albert to live the Jesus Justice by taking the victims of injustice seriously. For example, he writes that Jesus,

> refused to consider women and children unimportant or inferior. This turned a carefully ordered society of status and honour upside down—even more so when he advocated moving down the social ladder instead of striving to reach the top . . . . giving women exactly the same value and dignity as men.[10]

This is following the historical Jesus in balancing teaching the faith with touching lives in their physical realities.

For Nolan, social analysis, the 'search for historical and structural causes of social behaviour',[11] is the tool for balancing faith with human living. Jesus would refer to this as 'reading the signs of the

---

6. Albert Nolan, *Jesus Today* (Maryknoll, NY, Orbis Books, 2006).
7. Nolan, *Jesus Today*, 50.
8. Nolan, *Jesus Today*, 191,
9. Nolan, *Jesus Today*, 192.
10. Nolan, *Jesus Today*, 51–52.
11. Albert Nolan, 'Social Analysis – Part 1', An undated paper on Social Analysis, 1.

times'. Nolan writes, 'Jesus preached the first truth, the truth of faith, the gospel, but he also opened our eyes to the second truth, the truth about life in this world'.[12]

This is a praxis of Jesus Justice that, for Albert, is akin to spiritual growth or conversion. In 'The Service of the Poor and Spiritual Growth',[13] he describes four stages of growth in commitment to the poor (all those sinned against by systems of social, economic and political injustice). This conversion process enables growth in appreciating one's role and limitations as an *outsider* to a situation of injustice that one is seeking to address, such as a man in the case of gender injustice, or a non-poor person in the case of economic poverty.

These stages of 'growth in commitment' begin with compassion. 'The more we are exposed to the sufferings of the poor, the deeper and more lasting our compassion becomes'.[14] Compassion leads to charitable acts and provokes a willingness to do something, removing the tendency to say, 'I can't do much about it', or it's not my business.

> Our compassion is a spiritual matter as we express God's compassion for the situation . . . enabling me to see the face of Christ in those who are suffering, and to remember that whatever we do to the least of his brothers and sisters, we do to him.[15]

An act of compassion is the *first stage* of our conversion and growth in commitment.

But then we soon realise that the cause of the injustice is structural–patriarchy for example, is rooted in cultural and religious structures and traditions. Likewise, as Nolan writes:

> Poverty in the world today is the direct result of the political and economic policies of governments, parties and big business. It has been created . . . manufactured, by particular policies and systems. This means that poverty is a political problem, a matter of injustice and oppression.[16]

---

12. Nolan, 'Social Analysis – Part 1', 7.
13. Albert Nolan, *The Service of the Poor and Spiritual Growth* (London: Catholic Institute for International Relations, 1985).
14. Nolan, *The Service of the Poor,* 3–4.
15. Nolan, *The Service of the Poor,* 5.
16. Nolan, *The Service of the Poor,* 4–5.

This realisation moves us from the charity of compassion to sharing in God's anger at this situation.

This is the *second stage*, participating in divine anger. 'Unless I can experience something of God's wrath towards oppressors, my love and service of the poor will not grow and develop.'[17] This results in different action to the charity of compassion; it leads to social action to change the unjust systems.

The *third stage* of growth in commitment follows in the discovery of the strength and agency of the poor—that the poor must and will save themselves; and that, in fact, with their own agency, they do not need to be saved by others. In South Africa, this is what Steve Biko and Black Consciousness did in the face of white South Africans that saw themselves as 'sympathetic' to black liberation. As Biko wrote against the role of 'white liberals', 'with their characteristic arrogance of assuming a "monopoly on intelligence and moral judgement", these self-appointed trustees of black interests have gone on to set the pattern and pace for the realisation of the black man's (sic) aspirations'.[18] This was to advance what Biko saw as essential for Black Consciousness without the help of white people, 'to produce at the output end of the process real black people who do not regard themselves as appendages to white society'.[19]

Nolan challenges this 'helpfulness' of the elite (for Biko, 'whites', or 'men' for feminist theologians). He writes, 'we think that we, the non-poo . . . must come to the rescue of the poor because they themselves are so pitiably helpless and powerless.'[20] The spiritual conversion demanded by this stage of growth in commitment, Nolan points out, is humility. For, 'when one is dedicated to the service of the poor, it is even more difficult to accept that it is not they who need me, but I who need them'.[21]

This growth in commitment to the cause of the poor is progressively growing to see as God sees, and letting God act through me. Albert Nolan grew in this way, recognising that God is present and acting in the struggles of the poor; a total spiritual immersion in their struggles on their terms, accepted in humility. However, he cautions

---

17. Nolan, *The Service of the Poor*, 5.
18. Steve Biko, *'I Write What I Like'* (Randburg: Ravan Press, 1996 edition), 65–66.
19. Biko, *'I Write What I Like'*, 51.
20. Nolan, *The Service of the Poor*, 5.
21. Nolan, *The Service of the Poor*, 7.

against romanticising the poor as flawless 'saints'. This results in the crisis of 'disillusionment and disappointment with the poor', who too are sinners; they have faults and make mistakes and they fail themselves even in their own set goals and objectives.

With disappointment, and growing out of romanticising the poor, we enter the *fourth stage* of solidarity with the poor and oppressed; not focusing on individual shortcomings, but rather on the systemic and structural injustices that produce and sustain their poverty and oppression. This is partaking in the solidarity of God, a spiritual conversion that surrenders one's own cause for "God to work in and through" one for the cause of the poor.

Albert thus helps us to chart a process of spiritual conversion and growth in commitment to Jesus Justice which can apply in any situation of injustice: from compassion to divine anger, to humility and finally to solidarity.

Rosemary Radford Ruether[22] presents a similar but slightly different process, that she refers to as the male journey of 'conversion from sexism'. She says the first stage is when men are first confronted with women's challenge of sexism. They respond with 'trivialisation and ridicule', a far cry from Nolan's first stage of compassion. Next, they try to co-opt the pain of sexism for women, claiming that they too are victims of sorts—again a very different reaction to that of assuming the wrath of God leading to solidarity.

Ruether's journey of male conversion, however, also reaches a spiritually 'appropriate' point in the third stage of solidarity with women. She writes,

> real conversion from sexism begins to happen only when a man is able to enter into real solidarity with women in the struggle for liberation, often by being involved in a relationship with a particular woman who is pursuing her own liberation (which is akin to Nolan's self-agency of the poor). By entering into her struggle, seeing the world of sexism from her eyes, he begins to be able to understand some dimensions of sexism.[23]

---

22. Rosemary Radford Ruether, *Sexism and God-Talk, Toward a Feminist Theology* (Boston: Beacon Press, 1983), 189–192.
23. Radford Ruether, *Sexism and God-Talk,* 190–191.

This is just the beginning, but deeper and more significant male conversion involves a readiness by the man to be vulnerable and face the risks that go with assuming the women's struggles—such as facing ridicule or loss of recognition prospects and moving upward in his career—on account of openly identifying with and living the solidarity with women.

Ruether concludes that,

> at this point, males are able to recognise, without trying to either co-opt or pander to women, that the struggle against sexism is basically a struggle to humanise the world, to humanise ourselves, to salvage the planet, to be in right relation with God.[24]

And Biko refers to this humanisation as giving the world 'a more human face'.[25]

I experienced Albert's preoccupation with processes of conversion early in 1987 when he asked to 'gate-crash' a meeting I had with Wolfram Kistner[26] in order to see me on the last day of a visit to Johannesburg. Kistner and I were to discuss my own prison conversion experience in 1977 (mentioned above), and how I was interpreting it after my seminary training since 1982. Albert joined in and then offered to buttress my spirituality of surrender with a gift of an ancient Dominican blessing, which I have treasured ever since, and which will conclude this article in honour of him.

But he had 'gate-crashed' because he wanted to continue discussing a workshop on God that I, as a YCS chaplain, had conducted with the YCS in Cape Town. YCS being so multi-denominational, the whole morning yielded no common expression of the nature of God. So, at lunch I went home, brought back thirty copies of the *Kairos Document*, and broke them into groups to name and define the nature of the God they would identify in each of the three theologies laid out in the *Kairos Document*. Albert was fascinated at how this had enabled young people from such diverse Church backgrounds to identify clearly what was communicated in the document and to

---

24. Radford Ruether, *Sexism and God-Talk,* 191–192.
25. Biko, *'I Write What I Like',* 98.
26. Director of the Division of Justice and Reconciliation of the South African Council of Churches (SACC) (1976–1988)

deepen their understanding of God. This struck a chord as he was working on what would become *God in South Africa*. I believe it was after this engaging meeting that Albert thought to invite me to write the foreword to his book.

In November 1991, Albert became editor of *Challenge* magazine that he launched and nursed as a project of the Institute for Contextual Theology (ICT), to encourage critical thinking and productive discourse that would enable conversion and inspire hope. His motivation was revealed a few months earlier when, during a break at an ICT meeting, he said to me 'Malusi, since the struggle got legalised with the unbanning of liberation movements, we seem to have stopped thinking. That would be fatal to our purpose.' I suppose he meant our purpose to be the light and salt for the transformation of society. At the launch of *Challenge* he wrote,

> Our name 'Challenge' also describes what we are trying to be. We are not interested in information merely for the sake of information. Information can be challenging, comforting, reassuring, inspiring and motivating. Theologically, we would say that God speaks to us through this kind of information— challenging, comforting or inspiring us. Would it be too much to hope that Challenge might become the channel through which we challenge and encourage one another in these difficult times?[27]

Talking of difficult times, we reflect on Albert Nolan at a time when South Africa is going through much turmoil and uncertainty, with people shackled by much anxiety, fear and feelings of despair. As though he was preparing for such a time when he would be physically absent from us, Nolan wrote in the inaugural November 1991 issue of *Challenge* about the inner struggle against feelings of despair—Hoping Against Hope! May his message of 'Hope in an age of despair' reverberate across our valleys and hills to address the despondency of our time:

Spiritually, many of us are now at a stage where we need to begin a new search for hope in a situation that provides us with very few signs of hope. How do we follow the advice of the Apostle Paul and 'hope against hope'?

---

27. *Challenge*, November 1991.

Hoping against hope does not mean pretending to be optimistic when deep down all we feel is despair. Hoping against hope does not mean trying to live a lie or turning a blind eye to the realities of life in South Africa today. The first step in a spiritual journey towards hope is honesty and truth. After that, and only after that, can we begin to discover what it means to hope against hope.

This is a charge to people of faith to take up their agency, ask searching questions and seek to have honest conversations about the current context of our time; ask 'why' until we arrive at what may be the root cause of our current situation. This is what Albert Nolan has bequeathed us: a process of conversion that can offer hope. In gratitude to God for this servant of the gospel of Jesus Christ I offer to all this Dominican blessing that he gave me:

> May God the Father bless us.
> May God the Son heal us.
> May God the Holy Spirit enlighten us,
> and give us
> eyes to see with,
> ears to hear with,
> hands to do the work of God with,
> feet to walk with,
> a mouth to preach the word of salvation with,
> and the angel of peace to watch over us and lead us at last, by
> our Lord's gift, to the Kingdom. Amen.

JESUS TODAY

A Spirituality of Radical Freedom

ALBERT NOLAN
Bestselling author of *Jesus Before Christianity*

A Prophet Micah for Today

Peter-John Pearson

With Albert it was always conversation, always a sharing, sometimes an interrogation of ideas, but always that wonderful underlining of Albert the Great's insight of 'The pleasure of seeking truth together', written so poetically in the Latin, '*in dulcedine societatis quaerere veritatem.*' Albert, true to one of the deepest Dominican charisms, will remain etched in many hearts as a seeker of Truth, a sharer of Truth and an untiring activist to implement the fruits of those searches for Truth, especially for the benefit for those on the peripheries of society.

Later as I began to read Timothy Radcliffe's writing, I realised with even greater admiration just how consciously the commitment to conversation, the vocation to listening, was indeed part of realising the vision of building a community of equals. 'Only when people learn to converse will they begin to be equal.' Looking back, it is clear that Albert relished the conversation of friends (and others), the clarification of ideas, the stretching of the imagination and the application of stored wisdom to cutting, contextual issues. It is also clear to me now that in an atrociously unequal society as is South Africa, these conversations were also a commitment on Albert's part to building communities of equals. In such a way, his conversations while intellectually rich, spiritually exciting were also profoundly subversive.

Most dictionaries agree that subversive ideas and words 'is speech that challenges and destabilises otherwise recognised authority'. As a teacher, preacher and a public intellectual Albert's words carried force and subversive intent, in that he found fellowship with others whose words released the energy for change. Another crafter of words and writer of poetry, feminist and activist Audre Lorde, writes of poetry helping, like theology I reckon, 'to name the nameless so that it can be thought'. For our feelings are the sanctuaries and spawning grounds for the most radical and daring of our ideas. Poetry makes something happen'. Albert understood that powerful process of naming, also for other forms of speech, like his teaching and preaching. It named things and thus gave them visibility. It especially named evil and oppression, the dark forces that held people in multiple chains of captivity. It was that deliberate choice of words, the precise articulation of ideas that also made of Albert a subversive, using words that made something happen and made them happen mostly through the enhanced agency of those on the peripheries.

A close reading of Albert's two major works, *Jesus before Christianity* and *God in South Africa*, underline that Albert's subversiveness lay not so much in his strident denunciation of Apartheid (although he did this fiercely) and the institutions that gave it hegemony and as such a stranglehold over the population, rather it lay in a series of paradigm shifts that gave agency to those who had long been silenced, so that those voices were included in the historical narrative. Thus the reading and writing of history shifted and powerful, robust narratives emerged from the bottom up. This threatened the privileged history of the elites and offered the marginalised a voice and tools for their liberation. Second, Albert's work underlined the critical paradigm shift from charity to the centrality of justice. I think that it was St Augustine who wrote that 'charity is no substitute for justice withheld'. The demands of justice, the sharing of resources, equal access to opportunities and the levelling of the present power imbalance all speak powerfully to the demands of justice. They were the fundamental questions which Albert raised over and over again and continued in his later years to ask even more urgently, as he, like most of us, realised that many things were not changing for the poor in our post-1994 world. Albert drew inspiration from the words of Pope Paul VI in the document *Justice in the World* that 'action on behalf of justice and participation in the transformation of the world fully appear to us as a constitutive element of preaching the Gospel'. Third, he took seriously the emerging intersections between the social sciences, Scripture and theology. An intersection that opened up the richness of the sciences and new methodologies with which to engage deep social questions and understand them more adequately, and to suggest targeted paths for action with regard to the mechanisms and abuse of power. In much of the writing of liberation and contextual theologians, as well as at the heart of social justice activists programmes, is this powerful but deceptively straight forward process born of the above shifts, called variously the pastoral circle or cycle. Albert was a strong practitioner of this participative theological and social process that unmasked hidden forces of oppression, identified institutional complicity with oppression and empowered people to act appropriately in the process of changing their realities.

In all of those insights into Albert we see the same contours of reflection and action that run through the ministries of Isaiah, Hosea, Amos and Micah, all who prophesied at roughly the same time. Theirs was a deep anger about several widely accepted practices. They sound so familiar to us today as well. These include the corrupt leadership, the abuse of power to enhance personal wealth and wellbeing, the violence against women and the dispossession of property which children should one day inherit, thus depriving them of resources on which to build a future. Together with these crimes against the marginalised and singled out by Micah, Amos, Hosea, Isaiah and others is the scandalous disregard of the plight of the poor, whose poverty was directly linked to accumulation by the rich. All of these are the focus of Micah's denunciation of the rulers and those who enable them to do so with impunity. These denunciations, we should note, include the denunciation of prophets who provided the spiritual and moral legitimacy for such treacherous actions against the poor. Those who in Albert's language practised 'State Theology.' This is the prophetic vein that Albert contributes to and expands in his writing to focus on South Africa.

Of the prophets of this persuasion or school, it is Micah whom I think resonates most deeply in Albert's ministry. Three aspects have always stood out for me in this regard. It is often remarked that Micah's ministry shows a remarkable clarity and that some aspect of the clarity is certainly rooted in disciplined study. It does not need to be emphasised just how deeply this was true of Albert and again such a charism of the Dominican identity, especially the study that emerges from engagement with context. Timothy Radcliffe puts it succinctly. He writes, 'Study is essentially the entry into a community of people who seek the truth. Central to learning to think is therefore discovering how to live with other people, how to listen to them and how to learn from them.'

This is linked to a second characteristic of Micah that I also see in Albert. Micah, even as he challenged the elites and the authorities of his time with the cry for justice, with the challenge to create hearts that could show tender love, he nonetheless is the one prophet who never in this sharpening of his focus, forgot the communities outside of the capitals of power. It is often said that Micah's origins in a small, rural village of Moresheth in south west Judah, kept him sensitive to small, almost unknown communities. Micah ministered because of this background to people who were far from power, virtually anonymous. To these groups it was not the prophets' work of denunciation but the other task of prophets, to announce hope for the future, to prepare the hearts of people and the structures in society to birth something new. It is the prophetic work of enhancing agency.

I will always admire greatly Albert's commitment to small, seemingly insignificant groups. Even as his fame grew and his international stature as a theologian increased, he never stopped working with small groups, empowering small YCS or Justice and Peace groups who were far from the international stage and national political significance, but whom Albert continued to acknowledge and honour as the unsung bearers of ground up transformation and the bulwarks of resistance to continued exploitation and oppression. This will for a very long time be one of Albert's legacies that will rightly shake us out of complacency and hold us from being seduced by the pull of power and status in our lives and ministries.

Of all the prophets, it is only Micah who mentions Bethlehem as the place from which the long-awaited Messiah will come. In identifying Bethlehem, Micah offers a sign of hope. He foresees that the long night of oppression will end, that it cannot last forever, and Bethlehem is the sign of that hope. It is also for Micah a sign that hope will emerge not from Jerusalem or the great cities and locations of institutional power, but from the margins. That surely must be one of the reasons that Albert continued to be present on the margins, to enhance capacity and do theology in such places. Small, sometimes unnoticed beginnings are often in history the well springs of change and fierce social energy. As I ponder these remarkable similarities there is thus good reason for holding Albert as a prophet, just as we acknowledge him gratefully as a student, and teacher, a spiritual guide and a priest, who not only showed us the way to heaven, but inspired us to bring bits of heaven into our fractured, unequal and environmentally destroyed world and thus hold out a bit of heaven as the rightful, already realised inheritance of the poor.

An Incarnational Spirituality

Sidwell Mokgothu

Introduction

There are many of us who were young activists in the South African liberation struggle from the period of late 1970s to the 1980s who had a problem with the notion of spirituality. The dominant view and understanding at that time was of evangelistic movements that came into the townships to set up tents to evangelise black people who were seen to be barbaric and needed to convert and 'accept Jesus Christ' as their saviour. Some of these campaigns were led by white Christian pastors who were promising the poor people a home that lay somewhere in heaven, that is, in the next life. This led to many of my generation dismissing spirituality as an escapist and otherworldly enterprise that was meant to discourage us from our commitment to the freedom of our people.

Many of my generation were involved as anti-Apartheid activists in the different sectors of the struggle. We were at the same time involved innocently in the youth structures of our different denominations. I grew up in the Wesley Guild, the youth movement of the Methodist Church of Southern Africa. We initially had to straddle the dichotomy of secular politics and Christian life that found expression in our local churches. This dichotomy is well captured by one of our comrades in the prophetic movement, McGlory Speckman:

> In practice, this meant that I saw my protests against injustice as political activism. As such, they had nothing to do with my being Christian. My Christian duty was to worship God in church during the hour appointed for that purpose. I succumbed to these distinctions because, while I could not

forever endure the pain of oppression, I also longed for the heavenly bliss that was promised to those who are faithful to their Christian duty. The result was that I became two persons at the same time—I became an activist in the community and a 'Christian' in church.[1]

These denominations were, however, part of the ecumenical movement led by the South African Council of Churches (SACC). The SACC of that time was led by luminaries of the prophetic movement who championed liberation theologies in the form of Contextual Theology, Black Theology and African Theology. The SACC had amongst its structures the youth wing, the Inter-Church Youth [ICY]—of which I was a part—that brought together the youth formations of the different denominations. The International Year of the Youth in 1985 was one event that expanded our space through the intersection and interaction of youth and student formations throughout the country. This brought together formations such as the Student Union for Christian Action (SUCA) and the Young Christian Students (YCS). All these formations, programmes and occasions cultivated in us an understanding and appreciation of the gospel of Christ that is responsive to the context in which the people of God found themselves. We were assisted to break down the duality or dichotomy that separated our faith from the concrete socio-cultural and politico-economic realities we lived in.

It was through the YCS and the Institute for Contextual Theology [ICT] that I came to know and interact with Fr Albert Nolan, who was once a chaplain and a staff member of the two respectively. It is my deep conviction that Albert Nolan's spirituality was shaped by the different Christian formations that he belonged to as a member, activist and leader. There was a reciprocal contribution between him and these structures. His spirituality was nurtured in the crucible of liberation praxis in both South Africa and the international world. Thus, the sources of Nolan's spirituality are captured in the theoretical writings and practices both of himself as an individual and of the movements to which he belonged.

---

1. McGlory Speckman, in GA Wittenberg, *Prophecy and Protest: A Contextual Introduction to Israelite Prophecy* (Pietermaritzburg: Institute for the Study of the Bible, 1993), 8.

It is this theology that was liberative in theory and practice that motivated me to register for a Masters' in Philosophy with the Catholic St Augustine College. The focus and title of my mini thesis was: 'Reopening the Wells: The Spirituality of Albert Nolan and its implications for Post-Apartheid South Africa.' This title was based on the biblical text:

> Isaac dug again the wells of water that had been dug in the days of his father Abraham; for the Philistines had stopped them up after the death of Abraham; and he gave them the names that his father had given them [Gen 26:18].

It remains my conviction that we are called to dig from the well that is Albert Nolan and will find spiritual water and that we shall find answers or pointers to the challenges the world in general and South Africa in particular are facing.

Integrated incarnational spirituality

Although neither complicated nor simplistic, Albert Nolan's spirituality is a systemic, multi-layered, integrated and holistic spirituality with many shades. His work can be summarised by the citation for the Order of Luthuli Award he received from the South African government: 'Life-long dedication to the struggle for democracy, human rights and justice and for challenging the religious dogma including the theological justification for apartheid.'[2]

Nolan's spirituality was incarnational in character. Although he was more of a sage to us, the younger activists, we interacted with him as just comrade Albert. He was not just a distant theoretical scholar and commentator. He was immersed in the political struggles of those that he served. His theological work was in dialogue with the real experiences of the political oppression and economic exploitation of the students he served as a chaplain. This incarnational spirituality located him on the margins of society where the oppressed black majority and exploited poor were located.

---

2. The Presidency. Citation of Albert Nolan. Order of Luthuli in Silver at <https://www.thepresidency.gov.za/national-orders/recipient/father-albert-nolan-1934>. Accessed 5 April 2023.

> Liberation theology can be briefly described as a form of contextual theology, in which the experience and circumstances of interpreter are given prime importance as the first step in seeking to be a disciple of Jesus.[3]

It is this understanding of liberation in context that led to Nolan articulating the South African brand of Liberation Theology called Contextual Theology. The ICT that Nolan served as a staff member emphasised the importance of the context and experiences of the oppressed and exploited. This context, located on the margins of society, is what constituted the praxis and theatre of Liberation Theology.

Grounded in the Dominican tradition

Albert Nolan was a committed member and leader of the Dominican Order. It is this Order of Preachers, founded by St Dominic, that grounded him in contemplative spirituality. He was a living example of the Order's emphasis on the importance of study inspired by the scriptures: 'Eat the book' (Ezek 3:1). Tracing from the lived experience of Dominic, Hinnebusch characterised Dominican life to be; contemplative, apostolic, liturgical, doctrinal, fraternal and sacrificial.[4] This spirituality is expressed and sustained through three practices that Albert Nolan carried out—preaching, teaching and writing.

Albert Nolan was a great teacher and a prolific writer. It is in his many books and articles and through the *Challenge* magazine that he edited that he was able to share his theological thoughts, faith convictions and spiritual practices. He wrote in a balanced way that was appreciated by academics but was accessible to ordinary people.

Rooted in the Scriptures

Whereas many of our comrades were steeped in Marxist-Leninist tradition with its dialectical materialist tools of analysis, Nolan embraced these but was more grounded in the Christian faith. This conviction he captured in the preface of a small booklet he put together as a course he taught, titled: *Biblical Spirituality*;

---

3. Christopher Rowland, *Radical Christianity* (Cambridge: Polity Press, 1988), 126.
4. WA Hinnebusch, *Dominican Spirituality: Principles and Practice* (Eugene, Oregon: Wipf and Stock, 19650.

> The Faith and Life course is an attempt to create a new spirituality for the religious who live and work in South Africa. It is an attempt to bring together and integrate faith and the experience of life in South Africa, spirituality and social justice, prayer and politics.[5]

Nolan was known in our Christian activist circles to have academically studied the Scriptures and used exegetical tools to harvest his religious beliefs and spiritual practices from them. Articulating biblical spirituality, Nolan wrote in the same booklet:

> Biblical Spirituality is an attempt to discover how the Spirit of God manifests itself or himself in the lives of Biblical figures who were moved by the Spirit, who had an exemplary spiritual life. We search for the Spirit rather than the letter in the Bible in order to give the Spirit more freedom to work in our lives and in our country today.[6]

This foundational definition captures the genuine belief in the role and power of the Holy Spirit in directing those who were engaged in the struggle for freedom. It spoke to the conviction that the Spirit of God could be manifest in the lives of South African Christian believers just as it did with the biblical characters. It is out of the scriptures that he derives such themes as the life of the Spirit, the life and ministry of the prophets, the God of justice and love, the Kingdom Spirituality and the values of the gospel.

Prophetic spirituality

Yes, Nolan's spirituality relied on the whole of the Bible, but it was the biblical prophets that shaped the prophetic movement that was his home throughout his life and ministry. The character of the prophets is what the prophetic movement went on to emulate in South Africa. Nolan lived out and practiced his theoretical understanding of biblical prophecy. He went on to articulate this radical understanding of prophecy:

---

5. Albert Nolan, *Biblical Spirituality* (Springs: Order of Preachers, Southern Africa, 1982), 5.
6. Albert Nolan, *Biblical Spirituality*, 11.

The Greek word *prophetes* has three interrelated meanings: those who speak *out*, those who speak *before*, and those who speak *for*. Prophets speak *out* because they are boldly critical of their world; they speak *before* because they foresee the future; they speak *for* because they speak for God as God's messengers.[7]

It was even in the post-Apartheid South Africa, when I interviewed him for my studies, that he wrote to me in a four-page document that he still advocated for the culture of analysis in general and social analysis, in particular:

Many of us believe that it is crucially important for us to return to the culture of analysis we had in the past—social analysis. We have lost it- for the most part. We have replaced it with a culture of blame. We no longer analyse what is happening in South Africa today—we just look around for someone to blame . . . This is called scapegoating. However, this does not mean that some people are not to blame. But the scapegoating tendency is superficial and indeed dangerous.[8]

Nolan went on to advocate for a 'more comprehensive analysis' of social forces but also of emotional, psychological and cultural forces that influence the way individual people behave. He argued that whilst the political context is important, people have moved from theological questions to more spiritual questions that deal with personal challenges.

Praxis is the theatre stage on which all the prophetic activists express their action. Prophetic spirituality expresses itself in resistance and protest. Albert Nolan and his comrades, just like the biblical prophets, never communicated God's message as neutral and disinterested commentators. They were never armchair critics or ivory tower commentators. They anchored their messages in protest that included condemnation. For Wittenberg, they protested against idolatry, oppression, false prophecy, suffering and despair.

So, prophecy in the Old Testament is always committed. There is not neutrality. There is no staying out of the conflict. Prophets take sides...They see evils in society which cannot be

---

7. Albert Nolan, *Hope in an Age of Despair* (Maryknoll, NY: Orbis Books, 2009), 89.
8. Unpublished Paper Titled: 'The Way Forward—Reflections by Fr Albert Nolan'.

swept under the carpet but which must be exposed through protest and the judgement of God's word .[9]

Solidarity with the poor

Albert Nolan and his contextual theology of liberation companions anchored their Christian faith and practice in the Gospel of the Christ, who was anointed by the Holy Spirit and identified himself with the marginalised and preached good news to the oppressed, the poor, the outcasts and the captives (Lk 4:18). He affirmed, in words and practice, the position taken by the Latin American bishops at Medellin and reaffirmed at Puebla, to take a 'preferential option for the poor'. This statement is a conviction that, in the context of oppression, God does not choose to be neutral, but take a stance against evil—a stance that places God on the side of those who are victims of powers and systems that create the poverty and squalor we see today in the world.

Nolan has written extensively about the liberation theology teaching on 'Preferential Option for the Poor'. In a speech he gave to the Catholic Institute for International Relations (CIIR) in London in 1984, he articulated to Christians how this 'option for the poor' is a form of spiritual growth. He identified four stages through which Christians can grow spiritually as they serve the poor. The first is marked by compassion, which begins with exposure to the lived reality of the poor. 'The more we are exposed to the suffering of the poor, the deeper and lasting our compassion becomes.' The second stage is one that recognises that poverty is not just a misfortune on the part of the poor, but that it is a structural problem that needs God-like anger that calls for social change. The third stage is where the middle-class exercises humility that recognises that the poor have agency and have informed solutions to their problems. The fourth stage is that of practical solidarity with the poor and oppressed. Nolan went on to elucidate his point. This experience, and it is an experience of solidarity with God's own cause of justice, can become spiritually an experience of solidarity with God in Jesus Christ. It is a way of coming to terms with ourselves in relationship to other people, with our illusions, our feelings of superiority, with our guilt, our romanticism, which then opens us up to God, to others, to God's cause of justice and freedom.[10]

---

9. Wittenberg, *Prophecy and Protest,* 20.
10. Albert Nolan, *Spiritual Growth and the Option for the Poor.* Unpublished Paper presented to the Catholic Institute of International Relations, in London 1984.

God in the new South Africa

Throughout his life, Nolan has sought to place the trinitarian God in the midst of all the theology and spiritual practice that he was engaged in. It was even in the post-Apartheid South Africa, when I interviewed him for my studies, that he wrote to me in the four-page document mentioned above that he still preached and lived a life of faith in the God who was revealed in the Lord Jesus Christ.

Even after retirement he advocated for us to 'bring God into the picture' in whatever theological reflection we are involved in. Even later, he asked his old question—What is God doing in South Africa today? Where is God? And where is God taking us with all of this? Where are the signs of God's activity—the signs of hope? He went on to answer himself: 'The trouble is that we can't even begin to do this with the old images of God. The old images of God are too childish, narrow minded and unbelievable to people today.'

> God is not dead and is not out of date. It is the images of God which are outdated. God is alive and well and very active in South Africa. The way forward will include serious thinking about the amazing mystery of God. It is only in this way that we will begin to make sense of what is happening to us in South Africa today and in Africa. The challenges of the future include money/poverty, racism, ecological concerns (earth summit 2001).[11]

Conclusion

We today evoke the name of Albert Nolan and seek to draw from his spirituality, not in a romantic and glamorous nostalgia, but out of desperate necessity to address the present context of spiritual decay in South Africa. We do this as a response to the socio-political and economic mess marked by high levels of crime, corruption and state capture that are a result of the collapse of governance through the hollowing of our democratic institutions.

We remember Nolan in the scriptural tradition of the word of the Lord that spoke to Jeremiah the prophet: 'Stand at the crossroads and look; ask for the ancient paths, ask where the good way is, and walk in it, and you will find rest for your souls . . .' (Jer 6:16). Indeed, the

---

11. Unpublished Paper Titled: 'The Way Forward—Reflections by Fr Albert Nolan'

present situation demands of us to discern the ancient paths as we are a country at a crossroads.

We seek to re-conscientise ourselves with the *kairos* spirituality that he championed in his life. Just like South Africa was in a *kairos* moment in the 1980s, it is in a similar situation today. Alan Boesak has called on us to develop and advocate for *kairos* consciousness and spirituality. We are to rediscover, just as Nolan had advocated then, the God moment of truth that discerns the context in which we are. *kairos* consciousness is:

> Discernment of what is wrong in a situation and the crisis it creates for the most vulnerable, discontent with that situation of injustice, and a refusal to leave things as they are; and dissent from the dominant judgement that the status quo is acceptable, unchangeable, or irreversible.

Albert and Chris Langefeld at Albert's 83rd birthday celebration with the Johannesburg Contemplative Book Club.

A Man who Respected Women as Thinkers

Susan Rakoczy IHM

I first learned about Albert in 1983. I was living in Ghana in West Africa as a staff member of the Centre for Spiritual Renewal in Kumasi. One day I read an article in *The National Catholic Reporter* about a South African Dominican priest named Albert Nolan, who had been elected as Master of the Order of Preachers. To everyone's shock and surprise, he did not accept the office. Instead, he said that the work of justice and opposition to Apartheid was much more crucial.

I was stunned. What kind of a person was he to turn down the most important way to serve the male Dominican Order? I would learn the answer a few years later when in 1989 I began ministry in South Africa as a staff member of St Joseph's Theological Institute in Cedara, near Pietermaritzburg.

I read his *God in South Africa* soon after it was published in 1988. The book was a revelation to me about the conditions of life in South Africa and what the gospel means there. Albert described his book as evangelisation rather than a work of theology.

One day in 1990, Albert came to visit St Joseph's. He had heard that there was a new staff member who was teaching spirituality courses and so he wanted to meet me. And I wanted to meet him! I knew that he had helped write the *Kairos Document* and of his leadership in the Institute for Contextual Theology (ICT). We met in my office and discussed Liberation Spirituality and the situation in South Africa. Mandela had walked free and hopes for the first democratic elections were strong. It was an exciting time to live in South Africa and Albert taught me a great deal that day and later through the meetings I attended of the ICT, our occasional encounters and his writings, including *Jesus before Christianity* and for *Challenge*, a journal which he edited.

From friends I learned of Albert's courage during the 1970s and later as the South African government became even more oppressive. He was on the run from the police and friends sheltered him—at their own risk. More arrests, more deaths, more violence. And more opposition from brave South Africans such as Steve Biko. The South African government tried in every possible way to crush opposition to the demonic policies of Apartheid, but for every person murdered by the State Security police, other people rose up—especially young people. This was Albert's context.

Over the years our paths crossed regularly. We led retreats together and facilitated a meeting of the Leadership Council of Consecrated Life, the organisation of female and male religious in South Africa. Working with Albert was one of the few experiences of my professional life when a man did not try to subtly (or not) undermine my ideas and suggestions. I felt relaxed and able to plan and implement our ideas without any of the anxiety I often felt, working with men who did not respect women as thinkers in our own right including myself.

Albert was interested in feminist theology and often asked me what I was writing. He was especially happy when my book on feminist theology *In Her Name: Women Doing Theology* was published in 2004. I speedily sent him a copy.

When he moved to Pietermaritzburg in the early 2000s to write what became *Jesus Today: A Spirituality of Radical Freedom*, we were able to meet more often for lunch and other visits. He and another friend had organised a book club to discuss writings on spirituality and related areas. I was invited to join this group, which was a real blessing. For all his fame and learning, Albert never touted his own accomplishments, but listened carefully to everyone's sharing. I remember that he often shared books about Scripture. Several members were psychologists and their insights intrigued him.

Eventually his manuscript was finished and the book was published in 2006. Albert returned to Johannesburg, where for a number of years he continued to give retreats and workshops. Each time I went to Johannesburg I made sure to visit him and catch up. He was always interested in my work and writing and we had wonderful conversations.

Slowly his physical health declined and he 'retired' to the Dominican facility in Boksburg.

Our last visit was in January 2022, a few days before I left South Africa and returned to the United States. He was frail, but in good spirits. We both knew that this was the last time we would see each other—so the parting was painful.

And now he is with God. All my memories celebrate a wonderful friend who embodied the Dominican charism of seeking Truth—the Truth of God, of humanity, of how to live together in that Truth and transform Church and society into places of living Truth. Rest in the fullness of God's peace and love, dear friend.

Albert with the 1987 noviciate group at the annual assembly in La Verna in 1989.
Left to Right Sylvester Lekhooa Rankhotha, Andrew Johnson,
Chris Mokolatsie, Alber, Cleophas Mudzingadutu.

A Teacher, a Colleague and a Friend

Sylvester David OMI

I first encountered Albert Nolan through his renowned book *Jesus before Christianity*. I read the book during my novitiate year. The first time I read it, I was amazed simply by the notion of Jesus, before Christianity. I read the book two more times. These subsequent readings were done with the Gospel of Mark ready to consult as the reading progressed. What emerged from that experience was a man I could not help but love and want to follow.

Many years later at the Gregorian University in Rome, John Fuellenbach SVD prescribed *Jesus before Christianity* as essential reading material for his course on the Kingdom of God. When one of the Sisters in the class asked how it was possible for there to be such a concept as Jesus *before* Christianity, Fuellenbach said that there was a South African in the class and that he ought to respond. Well, I did. I explained that what Albert had done was to look at Jesus prior to any titles being applied to him and in that way allowed Jesus to reveal himself. Later on, I told Albert what had transpired and he said that although he had not thought of it like that, it was exactly what he set out to do.

During my scholasticate years at Cedara I had the joy of having Albert as a teacher. He had the unusual ability to make complex theological concepts accessible to undergraduate students. For example, the very definition of theology as faith seeking understanding was explained by him as: 'Okay, I believe. Now what light does this belief shed on my lived experience?' In that way, he empowered many people to do theological reflection. He was always open to differing opinions and readily engaged in conversation about difficulties people had with his concepts. His *God in South Africa* was a masterpiece in

Contextual Theology and was a source of irritation to those who supported Apartheid. His talks during the struggle were keenly followed by the security forces, as he was seen as a threat. Once, when curious scholastics asked how he was able to cross the border into Lesotho, he explained that his passport contained his given name, which was Dennis. The security forces were on the lookout for Albert Nolan and simply let Dennis through without difficulty.

Albert subsequently became a friend and a dialogue partner as he re-engaged with St Joseph's Theological Institute during my term there as its President. Apart from teaching, he was a member of the formators' forum and he inspired reflections and even seminars on topics which were relevant to the time. His confidante was my confrere John Paterson OMI. Albert would come to our community at Cleland in Pietermaritzburg once every six weeks or so and after his session with John Paterson, we used to have what was called 'theological reflection'. The local superior and regular visitors like Eric Boulle OMI and Bishop Barry Wood OMI also joined in from time to time. The closest the conversation got to theology however, was the grace before meals. Albert's sense of humour was lively and he would laugh heartily during the conversations.

We kept in contact through the telephone during his stay at the convent in Boksburg and one could pick up a decline in his health. Especially after surgery, one could sense a fair amount of discomfort—but he was always gracious. Albert has left a meaningful footprint not only on South African soil, but also on the hearts and lives of the many people who had the good fortune of encountering him.

The Pietermaritzburg Spirituality Book Club

Graham Lindegger and Sharon Grussendorff

We have shared our experience of Albert Nolan's presence in our Pietermaritzburg spirituality book club in the form of a dialogue.

Graham: I had first got to know of Albert Nolan after the publication of his book, *Jesus before Christianity*, and through his work with the Institute for Contextual Theology (ICT), and already felt great admiration for him. But it was only when he was appointed to the Emaphethelweni Dominican community in Pietermaritzburg that I got to know Albert reasonably well. At that time my wife, Joan, and I would regularly join the Sunday Mass at the community. Albert frequently presided at the Mass. It was always such a blessing to have either Albert or Joe Falkiner preach, as we would leave the Sunday Mass feeling challenged and inspired by their wise words. I have seldom, if ever, experienced much inspiration from the preaching of Catholic priests, so this was such a welcome exception.

Sharon: Yes, although I had heard of Albert Nolan as a living legend in the transforming social justice landscape of South Africa, it was also when he joined the Emaphethelweni community that I met him in person for the first time. It was at the launch of his wonderful book, *Jesus Today*.

G: During Albert's time in Pietermaritzburg, Sharon and I had the great inspiration to start a spirituality book-club. We were both deeply interested in spirituality, especially contemplative spirituality, and we were both equally disillusioned with much of the Church and conventional Christian faith. We had the idea to start a book club of like-minded people, who would join an open-minded search for a deepened spirituality by sharing inspiring books we were reading.

S: Yes, I remember when the idea for the book club crystallised for us—during a supper at the Lindegger home, while Graham and Joan Lindegger, Albert Nolan and I were excitedly talking about our favourite books. We were delighted to discover a deep shared enthusiasm for contemplative literature. Rather than a serious endeavour, the beginning of the book club felt more like excited children climbing into a sandpit, sharing our favourite toys. Our meeting style was fairly informal, starting with friendly conversation over tea and snacks, followed by a time of sharing about our books. We did not all read the same book, as happens in some book clubs, but shared about the various assortment of book(s) we had each been reading the previous month. We then pooled our books and took turns in borrowing these from the communal 'book-box'. Although most of us considered ourselves to be Christian, our reading matter was not constrained by this. As a result, we had access to a wide treasury, including Sufi mystical poetry, Christian theology, Buddhist and Hindu-inspired spiritual books and reflections that explored the interface between psychology and spirituality.

G: What a wonderful and welcome contribution Albert brought to the group. On one occasion, while talking about contemplative spirituality, Albert shared an interesting observation. He reported that he had often been asked by Dutch Reformed Churches to lead retreats or give talks on contemplative spirituality, such a surprising turn of events, and yet, in the Catholic Church (arguably the origin and repository of contemplative spirituality), he had encountered much less interest in or knowledge of contemplative spirituality.

S: From our book club discussions, I soon discovered that Albert was not only a broad reader, but enjoyed exploring at the leading edges of contemplative, scientific, psychological and theological thought. Just a few of the authors that I came to know and love through Albert's introduction were Martin Laird, AH Almaas, Sandra Maitri and Gil Bailee.

G: Yes, Albert was such a valuable member of the book club, bringing with him intellectual insight, deep faith and remarkable open mindedness. I remember early in the book club being struck by Albert's remarkable capacity to hold together severe criticism of the failings of the Church, together with uncompromising faithfulness to the Church, a rare combination.

S: The depth of Albert's own spiritual journey was very clear from the way in which he shared about the books he read. I found our monthly meetings not only stimulating but also challenging, often provoking new insights that enriched my own spiritual development. Many of the avenues that Albert opened for me have widened into rich and profound areas of inner exploration.

G: It was a sad day for us when Albert announced that he was being transferred to Johannesburg, so could no longer be part of our book club—sadly Zoom was not yet available to make Albert a continued part of the book club. I will always look back with gratitude and a sense of privilege for those wonderful times spent with Albert.

S: Yes, I will forever be grateful for the few years that Albert was part of our Pietermaritzburg spirituality book club.

Albert with Roger Houngbedji OP and Quirico Pedregosa OP in Mondeor community during a canonical visitation c.2002.

A Spirituality of Simplicity and Service

Isaac Mutelo OP

The life of Albert Nolan OP can be regarded as inspiring from different perspectives. His dynamic and simple spirituality helped him to relate better with himself, others, and God. In fact, he partly understood spirituality to mean an in-depth understanding and search for God, the self, others and nature. Such a search for meaning and purpose of human life helped Albert to address one of the fundamental questions of human existence—'Who am I?' The depth of his prayer life, like that of St Dominic, portrayed his hunger and thirst for God and the salvation of souls. Conscious of his own insufficiency, he sought God and strove to centre his life on God, and through the power of the Spirit, to gratefully say 'Yes' to God again and again.

Albert cherished, nourished, and deepened his spirituality continuously. His ongoing search for the sacred partly led him to self-discovery and to conserve a profound relationship with the sacred. He was fond of saints such as St Teresa of Avila with whom he was convinced that the 'first step in a life of holiness and union with God is self-knowledge'.[1] Drawing from the spirituality and life of St Dominic, Albert's spiritual life embraced a sacramental vision that sees God in everything—other people, nature and the entire cosmos. He had a profound sense of gratitude and saw everything, including his life and existence, as a pure gift from God.

When he was my novice master in 2011, at one point I encountered a challenge which left me extremely distressed. When I shared

---

1. Bridget. Costello, *Know Thyself: St. Teresa of Avila's Essential Wisdom for a Holy Life and True Union with God.* Available from https://www.churchpop.com/2021/10/15/know-thyself-st-teresa-of-avilas-essential-wisdom-for-a-holy-life-true-union-with-god/. Last accessed April 2023.

this with Fr Albert, he advised me to consider gratitude: he encouraged me to write down a list of everything I was grateful for in my life every morning for one week. Before the end of the week, after only three days, I realised that my list was endless and went back to him. I told him that I had fully recovered from my extreme distress due to the inner sense of gratitude I developed through the simply exercise of writing down the things I was grateful to God for in my life.

Albert sense of gratitude partly helped him to live a life of joy by embracing the words of St Paul: 'Rejoice in the Lord always. Again I will say, rejoice!' (Phil 4:4 NKJV). Because he was full of gratitude, he could still smile and be happy in the midst of challenges and sickness. One of the major aspects of Albert's spirituality was contemplation. He would sometimes read scripture slowly and prayerfully through *lectio divina*, spend time in silence, and be attentive to God's presence and voice. For Albert, contemplation involved interior transformation or what he would often call 'heart-to-heart' relationship with God leading to prayerful union—'a heart's simple repose in God.' He appreciated the importance of wordless prayer, when the heart simply focuses on God's goodness in loving adoration with the eyes of faith and hope. He often talked about the centrality of resting or setting aside one's thoughts, words and intentions so that one can effortlessly respond to God while resting in God's infinite love and goodness.

Due to his love for contemplation and meditation, Albert drew from the spiritualities of other religions, especially Buddhism. He cherished the Buddhist practice of mindfulness. This meditation technique he integrated with the Dominican contemplative tradition. He understood mindfulness to mean the ongoing awareness of the present and what happens in the 'now'. As Jon Kabat-Zinn puts it, 'mindfulness practice means that we commit fully in each moment to be present; inviting ourselves to interface with this moment in full awareness, with the intention to embody as best we can an orientation of calmness, mindfulness, and equanimity right here and right now'.[2] The practice of mindfulness partly explains why Albert often appeared to be jovial, peaceful and calm with less distress and worry. Mindfulness also helped him to accomplish goals and overcome

---

2. Passfield, Ron. 2018. *Mindfulness: Commitment to Awareness*. Available from https://growmindfulness.com/mindfulness-commitment-to-awareness/. Last accessed April 2023.

major challenges due to his attentiveness to self-knowledge, self-awareness and self-reflection.

When he was my novice master, he would sometimes advise me to slow down, to frequently retreat from the noisy world and to rely heavily on experiencing the present moment. He believed that if one does not pay attention to one's surroundings, appreciate the present moment and the marvels of life, then one might find it difficult to experience joy and happiness. He extensively read both Christian and Buddhist books on contemplation and encouraged others to do the same. For example, he valued the writings of the Vietnamese Buddhist monk, Thich Nhat Hanh, who is known as the 'father of mindfulness'. When I was his novice, one day Albert made reference to a quote by Thich Nhat Hanh: 'The present moment is filled with joy and happiness. If you are attentive, you will see it.' Albert also drew inspiration from several Christian and Dominican contemplatives and mystics such as John of the Cross, St Catherine of Siena, St Teresa of Ávila (also called Saint Teresa of Jesus) and Meister Eckhart.

Albert's spirituality also heavily relied on sacred Scripture, Holy Mass, the sacraments and the liturgy, all of which he fully cherished. He incorporated traditional simplicity, and drank from the purest sources of Dominican mysticism and asceticism. His spirituality was well-grounded because it was clearly rooted in the Dominican pillars of prayer, study, community, and service for the sake of living and spreading the Truth of God's mercy and love. He did not struggle to balance these pillars since he made them part of his life and spirituality. In the words of St Thomas Aquinas, such a balanced spirituality helped him 'to contemplate and to hand down to others the fruits of contemplation.' This was evident in his own life through the love of his Dominican brothers, the leadership positions he occupied both within and outside the Dominican Order, and his love for communal prayer, service and preaching.

Albert's spirituality and life can be summarised by two words: simplicity and service. In his writings, especially *Jesus before Christianity*, he perceived Jesus as a cheerful and loving person to whom we can relate as a 'friend.' For him, the 'Kingdom of Heaven/God' can be understood to mean not only afterlife existence but also a way of living here on earth, and cherishing the present moment. While some people struggle to see themselves as sons and daughters of God who are loved and cherished, Albert often cited cases where Jesus referred to God as 'Abba' (Mk 14:36). He was convinced that like Jesus who called God 'Abba', all Christians are encouraged to refer to God as 'Daddy' so that they may enter into a loving and deeper filial relationship with Him. By regarding God as 'Daddy', Albert believed that one is able to have a deeper union with God who relentlessly pursues us and wants to know us personally, love us unconditionally and have an intimate relationship with us. Albert's spirituality helped him to understand himself and his vocation, deepen his relationship with God, and share the fruits with others through his love and service for all based on his life, sacrifices, writings, theological reflections and leadership positions he held.

Thus, as my novice master, Albert provided me with a solid foundation which has enabled me to flourish. He accompanied his novices by communicating the best of the various traditions alongside our particular Dominican charism, but he was never over-directive. As our Dominican constitutions urge, he encouraged each of us to take responsibility for our own formation and allowed us to discover our own way, path and actions.

Like Meister Eckhart, an Exemplary Dominican

Therese Sacco

My life is woven into the fabric of Dominican life: and Albert Nolan is one of the finest threads. I cannot speak of Albert Nolan without referencing my Dominican family, both horizontally and vertically. My Dominican heritage feels boundless in time and space, reaching back to Jesus, who has been bequeathed to me through connections with the Dominican Family, Albert Nolan's writings and presence, and Meister Eckhart's sermons.[1] For me, Dominican life is primarily the search for Truth, as illuminated by Jesus' life, as well as study, contemplation, and action. These four inherited dimensions of the Dominican charism are central to my life. Albert's being epitomised Dominican life.

My foundation in a Dominican charism began in high school at St Catherine's Convent, Empangeni, KwaZulu-Natal. When I was fourteen years old, Sister Justina Priess OP suggested I accompany Father Elmar Kimmel OSB in weekly visits to an Indian community facing forced removal. The visits were an outreach to show solidarity and support. This continued until I left school for university. This planted a seed which was yet to grow.

Albert Nolan's influence on the course of my journey started when I was in my early 20's and working with girls and young women in Sydenham, an impoverished 'coloured' suburb of Durban, between 1978 and 1981. Despite my encountering people facing forced removals, my political consciousness was unformed. Rick Turner

---

1. Meister Eckhart, *The Complete Mystical Works of Meister Eckhart*, Maurice Walshe, Translator, & Editor. Revised with Foreword by B McGinn (New York: Crossroad Publishing, 2009).

had been assassinated in Durban in 1978[2] and Griffiths Mxenge was assassinated in Umlazi township, Durban South in 1981. I witnessed racism daily through the girls and young women and families' experiences in Sydenham. At the same time, the 1976 South African student uprisings continued through the 1980s, and school-going students in Sydenham joined in. The cruelty and dehumanisation were overwhelming. The inhumanity and injustice enraged me, I was cut adrift. I grew up in a Catholic tradition that is patriarchal and mostly conservative: obedience to the Church conflated with obedience to the State. While I affirmed the girls' and young women's activism, I needed to understand social justice rooted in Jesus' lived values, unbound from disconnected doctrine. Albert Nolan's Liberation Theology spoke of compassion as the encounter of solidarity with the whole of creation, including the Divine. He wrote 'The secret of Jesus' infallible insight and unshakable convictions was his unfailing experience of solidarity with God, which revealed itself as an experience of solidarity with humanity and nature.'[3]

Herein lay the way, the hope: to be in solidarity with people oppressed, stripped of dignity, respect, and life. People dying to survive. Albert Nolan's Liberation Theology gave me a rootedness and an understanding that if you claim to live a life following Jesus, you live a life of compassion that includes social justice. You cannot talk about Jesus in a decontextualised way. For a young woman this was a blessing, and it emboldened me.

In 1984 I was detained under Section 29 of the Internal Security Act of 1982 and held in solitary confinement, incommunicado for sixty days before being released without explanation or preparation. Emerging from the trauma of fear that I would be forgotten and never see my loved ones again, I found several security police associated with my case present in the lobby of John Vorster Square. I said goodbye to them and shook their hands. When I got into the car, the person fetching me said: 'How dare you? How can you greet them?' I was stunned. Albert Nolan's writings taught me that Apartheid was a structural sin and must be challenged. We were opposing

---

2. He was assassinated the year his book was published. Richard Turner, *The Eye of the Needle: Towards Participatory Democracy in South Africa* (Johannesburg: Raven Press, 1978).

3. Albert Nolan, *Jesus before Christianity: The Gospel of Liberation* (Cape Town: David Philip Publisher, 1976), 125.

an unjust system, not those prisoners of lies perpetuating a brutal ideological state apparatus. I had embraced Albert Nolan's stance: making a distinction between people and unjust, violent structures, while maintaining a humanity and relational self. Albert writes, 'Jesus loved absolutely everyone he encountered and treated them all with the same respect and dignity: women and men, the poor and the rich, children and adults, those who were powerful and those who were helpless, hopeless and insignificant, the oppressor and the oppressed.'[4]

Being welcomed as a Dominican Associate into the whole Dominican family crystalised a space of searching for the real, the true, the right, as I felt disillusioned with a patriarchal Church. As a Dominican Associate I pursue study and contemplation, which shapes my work in the world. The Dominican family continues to contribute to my growing in self-knowledge: valuing inner work so that outer work is continuously refined through meditating, silence, and critical self-reflection.

Albert Nolan's impact became personal when I was invited to join his reading group. It was in this place that I experienced the aliveness of my whole being, as a woman, and as an intellectual who loves creating life's celebrations. My internal Mary and Martha were at home in his space. What he stood for, his way of being, his Dominican presence, assisted me in validating my personhood. I felt at peace in his sphere; I was fully heard, fully myself. The often-uttered statement 'you are too much' never entered our lexicon of companionship. My emotional expression, range, and vulnerability felt ordinary and accepted in his presence. I sensed the embrace of who I am: my style of creativity, my anxiety, and my identification with those in pain, as well as my social self. He contributed to my feeling a more complete version of myself. Moreover, there was an inclusion of my womanist and feminist epistemology. This values knowledge coming from all senses: including reasonable and clear articulation and experiencing personal, shared and global suffering that is not truncated by exclusive rationality, hierarchical thinking and relating.

I learned from his leadership of our contemplative book club, which was expansive yet holding. He set an easy-going convivial, as

---

4. Albert Nolan, 1 December 2018, review of the book presented to Contemplative Book Club members by José A Pagola, *Jesus: An Historical Approximation* (Miami, FL: Convivium Press. 2009).

well as a respectful tone. He generated an inquiring, open atmosphere where divergent ideas were welcomed, considered, questioned and challenged in life-giving ways. He embodied studying, contemplating, listening and deliberating over insights significant to reading the signs of the times and living meaningfully, with humour, joy and an everydayness that belied his theological and intellectual rigour. Albert led me to perceive the interconnectedness of all things as typified by the books we read and shared, as he too continuously sought to integrate insights into his life and way of being.

Albert Nolan reminds me of Meister Eckhart now that he has joined our communion of saints. They both lived exemplary Dominican lives as they remained steadfast in their commitment to pursuing and preaching the truth as revealed to them through their reading, studying and contemplation, and emanating from the ground of their beings. Both had towering intellects: The fruit of which was service through listening, engaging, guiding, and preaching. They both paid the price for acting on their truth. They both speak, write, and live by, concepts of detachment, self-knowledge and contextualising theology. They both were open to being influenced by women.[5] Albert did not just include women; he was open to deepening his humanity by our presence and noticing our absence. Their Dominican charism sparkles and is a resonant inheritance.

Choosing to live by tenets of a Dominican life and relating closely to Dominican sisters and friars has gifted me with opportunities to live a meaningful and purposeful life. My Dominican family has given me a place of belonging, a love inviting growth through expressing and witnessing vulnerability and through pursuing understanding dynamics of a constantly changing world and acting to change it so that people may flourish. It has given me strength to be true to the ground of my being, to search for the truth as I perceive it, to continue studying and learning, and to practice contemplation with the hope that as it ripens, I may take right action.

---

5. Amy Hollywood, *The Soul as Virgin Wife: Mechthild of Magdeburg, Marguerite Porete, and Meister Eckhart* (Notre Dame, Ind: Notre Dame Press, 1995).

Compassion, Humility and Justice

Lionel Green-Thompson

Every time I reflect on legends, I am reminded of the extent to which the status of a legend is determined by each of our personal encounters with such people or stories. Such has been my reflection on the legend that is Albert Nolan. Often the status of legend is emboldened by the extent to which a person or their thinking has changed the trajectory of our lives and, sometimes, the extent to which their story has changed the course of history. While I think the personal encounter with a legend is important, I do believe that we have a responsibility to translate the encounter with a legend into an enterprise for the social good, the common good that Albert Nolan often referred to as a prophetic concept within the relationship with God.

Albert Nolan was already engaged at a national level when I joined the Wits Young Christian Students (YCS) in the 1980s. My encounters with him beyond reading *Jesus before Christianity* were limited to the events he would attend from time to time or stories from those who knew him. And so I formed a view of him as the oracle that had informed so much of our reflections as middle class students engaging in a struggle for justice against Apartheid. My personal encounter with Albert was really deepened in the invitation to join the contemplative book club, which he led, first from the Dominican house in Mondeor and then from his retirement home, Marian House in Boksburg, where he later died. I mention this transition because group members shared the responsibility of fetching him and dropping him off for our monthly sessions. These trips were often spaces for conversations on health and how the issues of the day were unfolding and what we might think of them. These afternoons shared with Albert and others became my true experience of Church, a place of deep reflection and renewal of faith through shared stories. A key theme was the discussion of our own role in the South Africa of today.

It must have been an afternoon in July, soon after I had assumed duty in a senior position at a local university. There seemed to have been a misunderstanding within the group of whether we were meeting on that afternoon. So Albert and I chatted awhile and eventually established the group was not scheduled to meet that day. Albert asked how I was and how the new job was going, and I asked him if I could share something that was troubling me. I shared how I had been interviewed together with a friend. I was appointed and the friend was not. The friend was white and occupied a more senior position than myself at the time of the interview. He was really angry that he had not been appointed and felt the need to express to me how angry he was because of the process. After a long discussion, so characteristic of Albert's capacity to use a personal story as a template to create a social analysis space, he held out two reflections.

The first was that it was inevitable and expected that there would be anger and unhappiness from someone who felt a decision by a selection panel may have excluded him. These issues needed engagement and reflection. This was not the primary issue for my discussion with him.

The second was that an increased level of responsibility accrued to the person appointed in such a process. There is a duty of accountability to deliver on the promise revealed to the selection panel. This was the issue over which I had some level of authority and, he argued, should be the focus of my thinking.

It was an important idea that I could not take responsibility for the decision taken by the panel, but that I had the responsibility to respond to that statement of intent which the panel had made in the selection. The key lesson from this discussion was that I needed to be accountable for the opportunity I was being offered. I used this story quite spontaneously at the memorial for Albert Nolan held in Cape Town some months after his death. On that occasion, this story was really part of my reflection that if we remember Albert Nolan only as a heroic battle-scarred liberation theologian who contributed to liberation from the dark heart of the Apartheid beast of history, then we would fall short of appreciating his continuous contribution to understanding modern South Africa and the need for a contemporary framing of 'hope in a time of despair'. He expressed hope even as his own physical frailty was manifest.

Albert taught me to hope in the face of apparent adversity, but in that hoping three key themes emerged from both his teaching and his lived expression. The three themes were compassion as action, humility as practice and justice as expression.

Compassion as action

In *Jesus before Christianity*,[1] Albert reflects on the compassionate nature of Jesus' response to the people on the margins—the poor and the oppressed. Both Nolan in *Jesus before Christianity* and later Pagola[2] speak of Jesus' ministry as being characterised by compassion and his continuous response to the suffering of others by drawing them back into a normal society. Nolan was able to capture the need in South Africa both in the past as well as in the current reality as a call to be compassionate and so respond meaningfully to the suffering of those around us. His teaching was that responding was not sufficient, but rather that in responding we needed to become more aware of the systemic structures which caused the suffering of others. Real compassion then becomes a response against systemic suffering. Pagola reminds us that Jesus, while using images of kings and masters, taught a spirit of compassion as being opposed to cruelty and wickedness. Perhaps Pagola has captured it best as follows:

> But if all men and women live by God's mercy, will there have to be a new way of doing things, in which compassion is no longer an exceptional and admirable gesture but a normal expectation (154).

In Nolan's own words:

> Only compassion can teach a person what solidarity with human beings means (85).

---

1. Albert Nolan, *Jesus before Christianity: The Gospel of Liberation* (Cape Town: David Philip Publisher, 1976).
2. *Following in the Footsteps of Jesus. Meditations on the Gospels for Year B* (Miami, FL: Convivium Press, 2011).

Humility as practice

I last saw Albert in 2018 as part of our contemplative group discussions on how to translate our faith into action in our current South African context. He was deeply engaged in the tensions which beset the country and the extent to which there was a need for effective collective action towards a social and economic transformation. He was constantly listening. He was constantly making meaning of what each group member brought to the conversation. So much so, he chaired a discussion which the group held at the Jozi Book Fair in Johannesburg. Using the Pagola book as the template for what Jesus means for South Africa today, he led a vibrant interaction between the readers and the gathered participants. Albert's openness to being taught by others has been an essential learning for me that whatever station one holds in society, all of us have a responsibility to be open to learning and through this learning to act for the building of the Reign of God.

Albert was living through the frailty that time brings upon us all. Despite this, he showed a remarkable capacity for the group engagement. Albert offered us a clear example that humility in practice means that you do not need to be the centre of attention. Even on the occasion when one of the members read one of his books and brought this for reflection, his modesty allowed him to deflect his authorship to the need for us to be able to read the signs of the times. It has become clearer to me in the months since his passing that Albert had a reach that stretched way beyond the confines of a one dimensional framing of a legend. I have been struck by how few stories Albert told us about himself. Perhaps the message that I have heard is that humility is less about self but rather living out a simple life with accountability and integrity. He certainly role modelled that in the group and called each of us to account in the group.

Justice as expression

Justice is the most powerful enactment of love. Love enables us to see the poor and the oppressed as equally worthy of a dignified life. The definition of the poor and oppressed includes those on the very margins of society—the battered woman, the abused child, the migrant, the unemployed, the transgender communities and many others whose voices are muted in the onslaught of a system which centralises power. Nolan in *God in South Africa* speaks of the Reign of God as requiring total commitment to reordering society. He goes further to prioritise this Reign of God with an inherent commitment to justice. Nolan frequently refers to the struggle for justice in an Apartheid context where in many ways the clarity of struggle allowed for a more easily developed, albeit still costly, response to injustice. In *God in South Africa*, Albert makes a series of connections between love and the action for justice:

> Love means action (203).
> An active love cannot become an effective or efficacious love without reflection (204).
> We should never cease to reflect upon the latest strategies of the system, the new forms of cooption, the present dangers of compromise (205).

The need for an active love is ever present in our modern South African context and we can hear in these connected statements from Albert Nolan that the things which make for hope are held within ourselves, in the communities around us and the desperate need to respond to our sense of prevailing injustice. And perhaps his call is to create spaces to deepen the reflections which help us see more deeply the changing strategies of co-option, new strategies for the accumulation of wealth in place of service and the possibilities of compromise in an ethos of self-interest. Reflections which deepen our discernment of the best ways to respond. Finally, to act in strategic ways in advancing the cause of justice.

In my younger days, I had only heard people talk of a legend. In time, I read books of the wisdom from the legend. Over the years, I came to sit at a shared table and there I recognised that the legend was, indeed, humility in practice. And in his passing, I have recognised Albert Nolan as a legendary spirit now gone to join the *madlozi*—our ancestors who watch over us continually calling us to take responsibility for the common good—to the sense of restoring the 'other' to equal dignity.

My greatest tribute to Albert, and perhaps it belongs to all of us, is that we respond to his prophetic witness in our current national discourse and enterprise.

I hear the call of Albert that we continually reflect on our personal role in the restoration of the sense of 'struggle' for justice in our country.

I hear him gently remind us to think of the sin of structural injustice which leads to suffering.

I hear him suggesting that we gather in reflective spaces to reconstruct the images of justice we may have had and lost. To build ever more inclusive defining frames to help us understand and enable new communities on the margins have their rights respected, the sustainability of the earth be honoured and the asymmetrical power relationships in society overcome.

Albert Nolan, perhaps more powerfully in his passing, has become a spirit for all ages and coming generations. He calls us in the modern era to listen with compassion, walk with humility and to act with justice. I have heard his challenge that we become more socially accountable in the spaces we occupy and then join others with a similar purpose.

How we respond will enrich our hope for a just and peaceful future and fan the flames of that hope into a cleansing flame that will bring new growth and transformation to South Africa.

Over a Glass of Wine

Michael Murphy SPS

I had just arrived back from a stint in Zambia in 1982 when a certain Sr Mary Guy handed me a book saying, 'This will do something for you!' It certainly did. The book was Albert's *Jesus before Christianity*. I found the title rather strange, but I soon realised that by 'Christianity' Albert meant the huge super structure built on the humble Jesus, not least in the way he was adorned with many wonderful titles. As chaplain to a university, his students were turned off by this kind of 'Christianity' that bore little resemblance to the man who walked the roads of Galilee. Not getting anywhere, Albert changed his tactics. He invited them to get to know Jesus through one single task, namely, discover him through the decisions he made. It turned out to be a masterstroke.

Thus, the fact that Jesus chose to follow the outsider John the Baptist—a voice crying in wilderness— rather than one of the established groups like the Pharisees or Sadducees proved to be a revelation. They came in touch with a Jesus they could associate with. It opened up his vision of life, his teachings and the rationale behind his being with the down and outs of his time. And therein lies the genius of Albert; he gave us all a Jesus that was real, earthy, inspiring and compassionate. In Pope Francis' terminology, Jesus had 'the smell of sheep' about him. Like the good disciple of Jesus that Albert was, he too knew all about this 'smell.'

My first personal encounter with Albert came in 2007. I was involved in the running of a sabbatical course in Cape Town, and I invited him as a guest lecturer for a week. I was immediately struck by his warm, generous and welcoming presence. There was something modest and grounded about him. He was thrilled with the idea of having a sabbatical in South Africa because of its accessibility to the many who could not afford to go overseas. Adapting it to the local culture with local experts was an added bonus. Of course, being a Capetonian did not hurt either, as Albert could visit his family and friends there.

There was a simplicity about his lectures. He had the knack of getting straight to the point of what Jesus was really saying and demanding. He had no time for the great theological debates which had occupied great minds for centuries. As far as Albert was concerned, disputes around the two natures of Christ, *homoousias* and Christology, did not provide 'chicken soup' for the soul. That could only be found in getting in touch with Jesus as he is presented in the Gospels: his passion, his magnetism, his priorities, and the inner spirit that compelled him. In his own modest way, Albert led us to discover Jesus afresh, a very relevant Jesus for today.

In subsequent years, Pope Francis would summarise what getting in touch with Jesus meant:

> The joy of the gospel fills the hearts and lives of all who encounter Jesus. Those who accept his offer of salvation are set free from sin, sorrow, inner emptiness and loneliness. With Christ joy is constantly born anew' (*Evangelii Gaudium*, 1).

Speaking of our present Pope, Albert was absolutely thrilled with his election. Not infrequently, he used to say that Pope Francis had exceeded all his expectations!

We were overjoyed to have Albert again for the sabbatical in 2009. My meetings with him after that were very few until around June or July 2016. I got a surprise phone call telling me that we were now neighbours and would I like to come over for a glass of wine and a chat. He had just retired to Marian House. My response was immediate and positive. Soon the wine and chat became a monthly feature on the calendar and if I let it go more than a month, he was quick to pick up the phone. He always had a little table set for me with a glass on the ready and a few edibles. Just another little touch about the man.

He was always in a relaxed mood ready to enjoy retirement now that his life's work was coming to an end. He liked to reminisce, but never about himself. He said little or nothing about his own achievements, but delighted in speaking about some of the wide variety of characters he encountered and what they were up to; the good, the iffy, and the incredulous. And he would laugh heartily. He had that sense of enjoying everyone, just as they were. Gerard Manley Hopkins puts it well: 'for Christ plays in ten thousand places, Lovely in limbs, and lovely in eyes not his.' There were two incidents that he often referred to. As a young boy, he took the train to school. One Monday in 1948 the whole platform was full of police sorting out the school kids. The white kids were to move up to the two front carriages, then the coloureds and then the blacks. He could not believe that just the Friday before he used to chat freely with friends of all colours; now that freedom was taken from him. He added that even then as a young boy, he felt there was something inherently out of joint with this kind of nonsense. Perhaps he had some inkling that this Apartheid system would be one of the great challenges in his life.

The other incident was a trip to Lesotho. Thanks to his writings critiquing government policy, Albert had come to the notice of the National Party, and they were eager to pick him up. Crossing the border was therefore a risky undertaking. Four priests took the journey and Albert was the first to show his passport. Fortunately for him, the name on his passport was Dennis (Albert was his religious, not his family name) and they immediately let him through. The other three, however, endured a long and thorough examination with many questions to answer before they were allowed to pass on. He had a good smile about that one.

Retirement for Albert did not mean he switched off. His mind was as active as ever and he kept abreast of daily events. His big interest in the first few months was Sandra Schneiders' three volumes on religious life,[1] which he read from cover to cover. He was full of admiration for her clarity and depth of understanding of what religious life was all about. Contemplation, but specifically centring prayer, was his other great interest. Before coming to Marian House, he was part of a contemplative book club with lay people dedicated to centring prayer and that continued for him as they willingly provided him with transport back and forth. For a while he was confessor for the Carmelite Sisters in Benoni and had a deep interest in their welfare.

---

1. See Sandra M Schneiders, *Finding the Treasure: Locating Catholic Religious Life in a New Ecclesial Context* (New York/Mahwah, NJ: Paulist Press, 2000); *Selling All: Commitment, Consecrated Celibacy and Community in Catholic Religious Life* (New York/Mahwah, NJ: Paulist Press, 2001); and *Buying the Field: Catholic Religious Life in Mission to the World* (New York/Ma NJ: Paulist Press, 2013).

I remember him being amazed and overjoyed in 2009 at the swearing in of Barack Obama. How did someone in Hawaii whose father was Kenyan manage to get the top job? That was his big question. He was still amazed, but for very different reasons, when Donald Trump became president eight years later, but not in the least overjoyed. The same goes for Boris Johnson and Bolsonaro. The lack of integrity among global figures proved to be a very disturbing trend for him. 'What's the world coming to?' A similar scenario became evident in his beloved South Africa that left him very despondent. He had hoped the gap between the rich and poor would have narrowed, but sadly, the opposite proved to be the case.

Our little party of two began to increase in 2018. Denis Barrett, an ex-Dominican, came to retire in Marian House after spending many years in Rome. He was a linguist and had translated many Church documents into English. In his own quiet way, he had lots to say about Vatican politics. A year later Fr Emil Blaser, who spent a lifetime overcoming herculean challenges to set up Radio Veritas, also came to retire due to chronic illness. With four of us huddled together there was much to discuss: Church and local politics, the world at large, the topical and the banal, what's it all about anyway?—quite a few bases were covered and there was never enough time. The mood music was upbeat: humour, banter, jokes aplenty and the glass of wine to help with the flow. It didn't last forever. Denis died suddenly on 11 March 2019 and Emil, after much suffering, passed away a year and a half later on 16 November 2020. The empty chairs were heavy with loss.

On a personal note, I am deeply grateful to Albert as someone I could confide in. As a man of compassion and deep spiritual resources, he never failed to put my mind at ease or offer me a new perspective. I felt cared for and cherished. He gave a new depth to the meaning of friendship.

Albert knew how to die gracefully. He suffered considerably during his last few years, shattering his femur in three places at one stage, coping with a cold at another or again some other nasty ailment that lingered on forever. From walking to walking slowly, to a Zimmer frame and then to the wheelchair; it was a slow downhill movement. But he would pass it off with a wave of his hand saying that old age is not for sissies.

During the last year or so I had the privilege of having breakfast with him on a twice-weekly basis after Mass. He remained an engaging conversationalist. My last time with him was the Thursday before he died. He did not have much to say, ate little and left quickly and quietly. It was like the next chapter of his life was breaking in and that was now his focus. He did it all with ultimate grace.

Rest in peace, Albert, and thank you for your friendship. You gave me a gift beyond my wildest dreams.

Albert as a young priest and lecturer at Stellenbosch, attending a meeting in the 1960s.

A Tremendous Companion

Hyacinth Ennis OFM

Albert and I had got to know each other through Bonaventure Hinwood. Albert was sent to Rome to do post-graduate studies. There were two other South African students there at that time who got together from the different universities: Albert from the Angelicum, Bonaventure Hinwood OFM, from the Antonianum and Alan Schwarer, a diocesan priest from the Gregorian. Alan's father sponsored a car for the three of them so they could get out of town. All three of them remained friends for the rest of their lives. Albert got the name 'Bert' and Bonaventure (Bon) was 'Ted'. Albert was a great story-teller and would regale stories of the three young men in Rome. Bert and Teddy would occasionally argue about theological issues, Albert being into social justice and Bonaventure being more dogmatic.

Our paths never crossed until we were both semi-retired. I remember that it was 'an effort to retire Albert'. He was novice master in Mondeor at the time when he was already talking about possibly retiring. He found it difficult to let go of the work he was doing. However, he was beginning to have problems with his health and his ill-health tended to get him down. It did not take a lot to get him out of it but it convinced him that the time had come to go to Marian House.

When Albert retired to Marian House in 2016, we met up. I was parish priest in St Dominic's parish, Boksburg with two other Franciscans, Paddy Noonan and Dominic Hession. Albert had associations with them before and these men all had the highest respect for one another. Albert had read Paddy's books and saw Paddy and Dominic as priests who were pastorally grounded in the realities of South Africa by ministering in parishes in troubled areas during the Apartheid years. Both Paddy and Dominic would give Albert inside stories of what was taking place in the Vaal Triangle during these years. All of them were in the 'war' against Apartheid. It was a central theme of Albert's life to deal with the effects of Apartheid and with the restoration of human rights. He was against violence but was not a pacifist.

Reading was Albert's number one passion . . . and thinking. I teased Albert about his passion for reading, but I appreciated that, while there was a contentment about him, he remained a searcher.

This all came about because after Albert's move to Boksburg, I visited him there one day and said to him, 'I'm looking at this all-women environment. How would you like to come to the Franciscan friars for Sunday lunch?' Albert readily agreed. The arrangement was that I would go to Marian House after he had said Mass at the Alan Woodrow Home for the Aged in Boksburg and pick him up. Albert thoroughly enjoyed these times and the occasions were marked with story-telling, the latest in Church and Franciscan gossip, changes in the hierarchy (bishops and superiors) and never omitting the glasses of Cape red wine that Albert was particularly partial to. He was 'a tremendous companion.'

Taken from an interview conducted by Sr Stephany Thiel OP with Hyacinth Ennis OFM at the Holy Cross Home for the Aged in Lady Selbourne, Pretoria.

At Peace

Stephany Thiel OP

The content of this account of Albert Nolan's years in Marian House is mostly in the form of interviews with those who lived and associated with him. They are memories of Albert, taken mostly verbatim.

Albert Nolan was assigned as chaplain to Marian House, Boksburg, run by the Newcastle Dominican Sisters, in May 2016. He took the place of our previous chaplain, Martin Roden OP, who died on 4 January 2016.

The Sisters felt very privileged to have a priest of Albert's theological calibre assigned to them as chaplain. Besides his special personal presence, he was able to perform all the necessary priestly ministries that a facility such as Marian House needed: daily Eucharistic celebrations, benediction of the Blessed Sacrament, the sacrament of the sick, confession, ministry to the dying, officiating at burials and participating in community and Dominican congregational celebrations. All these actions he did conscientiously until his failing health prevented him from doing so.

A move to a retirement home very often means a curtailment of independence. This would have been experienced by Albert, meaning, among other things, that he did not have his own transport and could no longer move independently to wherever he might have wanted freely to go. Fortunately, there were those who were aware of this situation, and ensured that he would have transport to those events in which he used to participate or in future would participate. These events included being a member of a book club; being invited to meals with the brethren in Mondeor or Springs or to meals with a variety of friends. He participated in Dominican family events and enjoyed to be part of them.

He adapted to the community living of the Sisters, attending all community prayers, meals, teas and celebrations. He was always on time. One Sister described him as being:

> a marvellous example of common life. He enjoyed the company of the community. He was not a burden. He was faithful to religious life. He wanted to serve people. He had been a wonderful example of service to the poor. He knew the suffering of people.

Albert has been described by the Sisters at Marian House as a friend and a brother, a person 'who always had something to say to you that made you feel happy, that helped you to recognise better who you are, what you are and what you are here for. It was a pleasure to have him in our house', so said a ninety-five year-old.

'Whenever I asked Albert to hear my confession, he gave me great encouragement. I felt his compassion and I knew he had listened to me with understanding. I would make sure I got some chocolate for him—he liked chocolate—and I would give this to him after my confession. He would tease me. Albert had a great sense of humour; he enjoyed a joke. We had many a laugh together.'

'One time when I was sick and in pain, Albert came into my room and said to me, "You look awful" to which I replied, "You're a Job's comforter". He enjoyed that and laughed heartily.'

'Albert kept confidentiality. You could tell him anything.'

'Albert was a holy man. He was gentle, affable, very kind and approachable. He was thoughtful. I had great respect for him.'

'He had concern for the oldest Sisters and would go looking for one of them if she was missing from something. He was always available.'

'Albert was a man of integrity. His actions matched his words. He was a man of compassion. He showed this in his discussions. He passed on positivity. When you left him, you felt lifted up. He was full of wisdom and knowledge. He had a great knowledge of Scripture that he passed on to us particularly in his homilies. When Father preached compassion, he lifted one's spirit. His words reminded us that God walks with us and will never turn his back on you.'

What was noteworthy about Albert's homilies was that he always prepared them. One Sister described them as 'first class'. Another one stated, 'His homilies were simple, short and yet profound, accessible and given in a way that everybody could understand'. He did not skip out giving these daily well-prepared, ten-minute, food-for-the-soul inputs. There was no hint of delivering a homily, even to retired Sisters in an old age home, that had not been carefully and most thoughtfully created, based on the relevant Scriptures of the day, and surely contemplated upon in prayer.

This writer believes that Albert's spirituality in the years of his physical decline will be found in the homilies he conscientiously and faithfully wrote down and kept in a series of small notebooks written in his own hand, that are now in the possession of his brethren. Each of the homilies was prefaced by the date and the day of the particular liturgical season. I believe Albert appreciated the spiritual and mental energy that he could still muster and that was needed to continue his preaching ministry to which he had contributed so much in the books that he wrote and throughout his priestly life. When asked in 2016 if he would write another book, he said it required energy he no longer had.

'Albert kept his mind active. He kept abreast of theological developments through reading books and Catholic publications. Sometimes he would recommend that they be bought for the Newcastle Dominican Sisters' region library. He was an avid reader, but also kept up-to-date with Church and national and international news through reading newspapers and watching television. Authors sent him books to review. Past students came to visit him. He was very respected. I think Albert will go down in time as a well-respected theologian whose writings are very accessible.'

'When I prepared notes to present to the pre-novices, I asked Albert to check them for basic correct theology. He was always so helpful. Through me, he continued to teach.' The young Sisters doing studies sometimes took their assignments to him to look over.

'Albert was a very good listener. We would chat about this and that. On one occasion he and I had had challenges with our SASSA (pension) cards, and commiserated with each other. I did occasional darning and mending of clothes for him.'

Another quality that was universally found in Albert was his humility. 'He was a theologian with a brilliant mind. Yet, he never boasted about what he was, he was neither demanding of attention nor praise. He was genuine and simple.' One of the Sisters happened to mention in passing that she had bought a book entitled *Jesus. An Historical Approximation* by José A Pagola. She was really surprised when he said something to the effect that 'His book is better than mine', referring to *Jesus before Christianity*. However, she discovered that Albert's *Jesus before Christianity* was written thirty-six years before Pagola's book, and big developments in biblical research and theology had taken place, not to mention the revolution in inclusive language. Pagola had the advantage of those developments. She was gratified to find that Albert had been referred to in Pagola's book. She deeply regretted not having had discussions with Albert about questions that popped up in her scriptural and theological reflections.

Albert very seldom spoke about himself. One story, however, that he did tell about himself that the Sisters enjoyed, was the time he slipped over the country's border when the security police were looking for him. It happened in this way: he was with other brethren travelling out of South Africa. At the border, he handed in his passport. But, the sentries were looking for 'Albert Nolan', whereas his passport had his birth name 'Dennis James Harry Nolan'. After his death, one of the Marian House nurses was astounded to discover the kind of man that Albert had been. His demeanour never hinted at the greatness that she learnt posthumously about him.

At one stage, before COVID, there were two other male residents in Marian House—Emil Blaser OP and Denis Barrett. The three of them and a visitor, Mike Murphy SPS, enjoyed sociable evenings and a glass or two of something to cheer their hearts.

Albert was a man who gave the impression of being someone at peace with himself. He was appreciative of things done for him. He never complained, even when his health gave him trouble. He didn't make demands for service. He did not retaliate under some circumstances that could have been interpreted as provocative or even aggressive. When he became frail, he found it difficult to have to be helped. Yet he accepted assistance gratefully. In regard to the way in which Albert faced waning physical health one Sister expressed her deep admiration: 'I perceived him as a person who was growing frail with dignity. Illness and ill-health were met with courage. He dealt with them pro-actively, by which I mean he identified what his symptoms were, he consulted with his medical doctor, and got relevant medical remedies. He did not hide the vulnerability that debilitated him, nor feel sorry for himself. He took whatever treatment was necessary to recover. He placed himself under the care of the nurses and caregivers in Marian House who were tasked with dispensing his medication. This, despite the fact that he could have undertaken that responsibility himself.'

Albert feared losing his mind, getting Alzheimer's or dementia. God gifted him with the grace of departing this life with his full mental faculties. He slipped away unobtrusively in the stillness of the early hours of 17 October 2022.

Albert, dear brother and friend, may you experience the beatitude of fullness of life with Christ, and with the hosts of those who have preceded you: family, brethren, friends, ex-students, and readers of your works.

Albert and Theo Coggin enjoy a relaxed moment.

Section Eight

Albert welcoming a brother who had just made profession.

Conclusion

Philippe Denis OP

There is something ironic about this book. As many contributors pointed out, Albert Nolan never attracted attention to himself. To say that he was humble is an understatement. Like Nelson Mandela, he always claimed to be part of a movement bigger than himself. When pressed to answer questions about his life, he answered that there was no point in writing his biography. He would then change the subject. Yet today, over seventy friends, colleagues and fellow Dominicans tell stories about him. What we have here is a biography of sorts. Each paper highlights a particular aspect of his life. Albert, please forgive us! We could not do otherwise. We wanted to preserve your memory.

The first observation about this book is the variety of those who contributed to it. We have people from South Africa of course but also from the United States, the United Kingdom, Belgium, Australia and Sri Lanka. Men and women. Black and white people. Quite a few Catholics, including members of the Dominican Order to which Albert belonged, but also members of other Christian Churches and contributors who profess no religion and maybe even describe themselves as atheists.

Another characteristic of this book is that it describes all periods of Albert's life from birth to death. We see him as a child, a youngster and an employee in a bank in Cape Town, as a Dominican novice in Stellenbosch, as a theological student in Rome, as a newly-ordained priest and student chaplain also in Stellenbosch, as a national chaplain to both NCFS and YCS, as a provincial of the Southern African Dominican vicariate and founder of the Mayfair community in Johannesburg, as a staff member of the Institute for Contextual Theology (ICT) and editor of the *Challenge* magazine, as a provincial

415

again, as a student master and writer in Pietermaritzburg, as a novice master in Mondeor and eventually as a chaplain and then a simple resident in the retirement home of the Newcastle Dominican Sisters in Boksburg. On each period somebody has something to say.

There are two moments in Albert's life journey about which he remained particularly discreet, if not secretive. The first is his life before he joined the Dominican Order in 1954, at the age of nineteen. At that time he was called Dennis, not Albert. We are immensely grateful to Virginia Zweigenthal for having interviewed Iris Prinsloo, Albert's sister, on this part of his life and having written a fascinating account of it. We discover that Albert's sensitivity to social injustice dates from that period. He grew up in a lower middle class white environment where money was scarce. Another well-kept secret, revealed in the papers of Frank Chikane and Horst Kleinschmidt, is that Albert was not only an anti-Apartheid activist, compelled to go into hiding after the declaration of the second State of Emergency in June 1986, but an underground ANC agent, helping comrades to cross borders and gathering critical information for the organisation. He was known as operative 42.

The other papers focus on particular moments of Albert's life. Most of us knew him from a particular angle: as a student chaplain, as a theologian, as an activist, as a journalist, as a preacher or a fellow Dominican. The book enables us to discover aspects of Albert's multi-faceted biography that we did not know. For the first time we may have a fuller picture.

This collection of essays shows that, as much as Albert inspires us, he was inspired by other people, starting with his parents. That he arrived in Rome before the opening of Vatican Council II in 1962 is highly significant. His search for the 'signs of the times' dates from that period. If anybody has contributed in a significant manner to the reception of the Council in South Africa—alongside Archbishop Denis Hurley—it was Albert Nolan. Another key influence during his formative period was that of the circle of Stellenbosch academics, including some Dutch Reformed Church ministers who criticised the Apartheid ideology on theological grounds. Albert joined the Stellenbosch Christian Institute group as early as 1964. He frequently met Beyers Naudé and Johan Degenaar. From the start he was ecumenical.

From 1970–1984 Albert served as student chaplain first to NCFS, then to YCS. This period of his life was really foundational.

By listening to Catholic students, he grasped the full measure of the Apartheid heresy (if I may use a phrase coined in a different context). It was to answer students' questions that he gave the talks on 'That man Jesus' in 1972 that ultimately gave rise to the bestseller *Jesus before Christianity* in 1976. As several contributors point out, this title was a bit provocative. How can one separate Jesus from the Church? The point was that Jesus' life, as a man in a given society, full of contradictions and injustices, had to be considered for what it was: the manifestation of God's love for humankind. One could not dissociate the quest for justice from the message on the Kingdom of God. Reading the various chapters of this book, one sees how influential Albert's book has been. Many read it first, then met Albert. We hear that it was set as a prescribed reading for students by Harvey Cox in the United States and John Fuellenbach in Rome, annotated on in reading groups in Belgium, meditated upon in a spiritual centre in Ghana and discussed in Australia.

As a student chaplain, with the help of the student leaders he had trained, Albert accompanied the conversion of many young white people to a sober view of the dark reality of Apartheid. In a way he prepared the way. Also, as noted by Frank Chikane, Albert helped black activists to realise that not all white people were blind to injustice and oppression. Hence his emphasis on the common humanity of blacks and whites, which arguably contributed towards South Africa's peaceful transition to democracy with a more balanced political agenda for the nation.

In 1976, the year of the Soweto uprising, Albert was elected provincial of the Southern African Dominican Vicariate for a four-year term, renewed for a further four years in 1980. The highlight of these two terms was the establishment of a Dominican community in a dilapidated building in Mayfair, Johannesburg, close to the train station used by Soweto commuters. Three Dominican friars, later joined by Albert himself and a few others, lived a simple lifestyle there. Several contributors to the book recount how inspiring their visit to the Mayfair community was in those years.

Albert can be credited with having been one of those who gave flesh to the notion of Contextual Theology—the South African version of Liberation Theology. His encounter with Gustavo Gutiérrez and other representatives of this movement at an IMCS conference in Lima in 1975 played a major role in this respect. Albert's distinctive

418   *Reluctant Prophet*

contribution to the shaping of Contextual Theology in South Africa was his ability to combine social analysis, theology and spirituality. He was a theologian in the true sense of the word, not only a political activist. This became apparent in his second major book, *God in South Africa*, published in 1988.

The founders of ICT in 1981 were well inspired to ask Albert, who by then was starting his second term as provincial of the Dominican General Vicariate, to join the project. Always acting in the background, writing key documents, facilitating workshops, clarifying complex issues, he rapidly became an important role-player at ICT. An example is his contribution to the writing of the *Kairos Document* in 1985. Albert rightly stressed that this famous, if controversial, document was the outcome of a wide consultation process among people suffering from state repression in Soweto and elsewhere. It remains true that without his extraordinary ability to put into words what people think and feel, the *Kairos Document* probably would never have got off the ground.

For many Christian priests and pastors who saw the Church as a 'site of struggle' during Apartheid, the opening of constitutional negotiations in 1990 and the election of a democratic government in 1994 represented a challenge. Quite a few accepted positions in government and left the active ministry. All had to reinvent themselves. The way Albert navigated this transition was, in some way, unique. He declined the offer to become a Member of Parliament, critical, without saying so publicly, of those who jumped on to the gravy train. He remained a staff member of ICT, but in a new capacity. To accompany the change he learned the skills of a journalist and launched the *Challenge* magazine. This was his main activity in the 1990s. His proverbial ability to explain complicated issues clearly was utilised to the full. More than ever before, he worked ecumenically.

The Mayfair experience came to an end in 1992 and Albert moved with the new provincial to a more conventional religious house in Troyeville, east of Johannesburg. In 2000, he was elected provincial for a third time and established the provincial house in Mondeor, closer to Soweto. Later on, he was transferred to Pietermaritzburg, where he served as student master while writing his third major book, *Jesus Today*.

What strikes the reader is the manner in which Albert, far from remaining stuck in a mode of thinking that had become obsolete, took seriously the notion of 'signs of the times' he had developed in the years of Apartheid and adapted it to the new context. In the new millennium the issue no longer was political liberation—even though poverty and unemployment remained prevalent—but the emergence of new concerns, such as gender and the environment. In the same way that he had developed a spirituality for the struggle, he was now exploring news forms of spirituality relevant in a changing world. Several contributors portray him as a preacher, a retreat master and a book club member who helped them find spiritual meaning and hope in an increasingly confusing world.

Albert aged and died as he had lived. Stephany Thiel, the regional superior of the Newcastle Dominicans who are responsible for running Marian House, the retirement home where Albert spent the last eight years of his life, collected testimonies of Sisters and lay people living in the house. Until the end Albert remained a listener, a comforter, a man combining deep insights, humour and kindness in all circumstances. All remember his laughter. He suffered the indignity of seeing his body letting him down, seldom complaining.

Albert embodied the best part of religious life. On the day of his profession he promised obedience to his superiors. Throughout his life he remained loyal to his Church, but as a free man. With the other friars of Stellenbosch, he did not hesitate to distance himself from Pope Paul VI's encyclical *Humanae Vitae*, which did not sufficiently take into account the life circumstances of the women he was ministering to at the time. As already mentioned, Albert was also instrumental in the drafting of the *Kairos Document* which challenged the ambiguity of 'Church Theology' under Apartheid. Yet, at no point did the leadership of the Catholic Church lose trust in him. At one point Rome refused that he be awarded an honorary doctorate, but otherwise the Church authorities never questioned his doctrine. This is remarkable considering the audacity of speaking of a Jesus 'before Christianity' and clearly stating that the Church of his time had failed the test of prophetism.

This being said, not everybody agreed with Albert, even among the contributors of this book. He knew it and was prepared to engage with his critics. Paul Burke quotes a colleague who found that Albert's contrasting of Jesus' original message with the organised Church was misguided. Neil Mitchell questions the *Kairos Document*'s tendency to condone the use of violence. Paul Decock remarks that Albert, concerned about the urgency of the time, was unwilling to engage with scholars who had a different understanding of Jesus' relationship to apocalyptic. McGlory Speckman expresses the opinion that his choice of the phrase 'preferential option for the poor' waters down the meaning of 'option for the poor', which he thinks is more radical.

This raises the issue of poverty. Albert never idealised poverty. He had no qualms about raising funds for ICT or *Challenge*, as we read in some of the contributions. But he was not attached to fame and wealth. On three occasions he refused an honour. The first time, as pointed out in several papers, was when he chose to leave Rome before the publication of his doctoral thesis, a condition for the awarding of the degree. He felt that it was a waste of money. He could have been a leading academic. That was not for him. The second time, also highlighted many times in the book, was when he declined his election as Master of the Dominican Order in 1983 so that he could continue fighting for social justice in South Africa. The third one, as already mentioned, was when he refused a position in Parliament in 1994. Three times Albert chose to remain what he was: a Dominican friar, living a simple lifestyle, with no particular status. In post-Apartheid South Africa, this is no doubt a prophetic statement.

Time Lines

Albert Nolan OP

1934	Dennis James Harry Nolan born in Cape Town on 2 September
1950	Left St Joseph's Marist Brothers after Standard 8 to work at Standard Bank
1952	Matriculated by correspondence course
1954	Entered the Dominican Novitiate at St Nicholas Priory in Stellenbosch and takes the religious name Albert
1955	Made first profession with Gregory Brooke on 1 March
1958	Made final profession in Stellenbosch with Gregory Brooke
1961	Lectorate in Theology (STL) granted by Dominican Studium General, Oxford, but taken in Stellenbosch, South Africa
	Ordained priest with Gregory Brooke at St Mary's Cathedral, Cape Town on 18 March
	Left later that year to study at the Angelicum in Rome
1962	Licentiate in Theology (ST Lic), Angelicum, Rome
1963	Courses and thesis completed and accepted for doctorate in divinity (DD) *summa cum laude* at Angelicum, Rome, but not awarded because the thesis was never published.
1963	Lecturer in Theology at the Dominican Studium in Stellenbosch (including short periods as novice master and student master)
1964	Joined the Christian Institute
1967–1968	Worked as a parish priest at St Nicholas parish in Stellenbosch and St Mark's parish in Ida's Valley
1970	Elected Prior of Stellenbosch Priory
1970–1976	Catholic Chaplain at University of Stellenbosch
1972–1974	Catholic Chaplain at University of Western Cape
1974	Led the NCFS Conference on the theme 'That Man Jesus'

1973–1980	National Chaplain of the National Catholic Federation of Student (NCFS)
1975	Attended the IMCS Interfederal Assembly in Lima, Peru
1976–1984	Elected Provincial of the Dominican Friars in South Africa and moved to Houghton in Johannesburg
1976	Published *Jesus before Christianity* with David Phillip Publishers in Cape Town
1977	Published Jesus before Christianity with Darton Longman and Todd, and Orbis Books A founder of YCS (Young Christian Students) in South Africa
1977–1984	National Chaplain to YCS
1979	Established the Mayfair community at 124 Central Avenue
1981–1991	Research Officer at Institute of Contextual Theology (ICT)
1982	Published *Biblical Spirituality*, Order of Preachers, Springs
1983	Declined election as Master of the Order at the General Chapter in Rome
1984	Published *Taking Sides*, CIIR and CTS, London
1985	Publication of the *Kairos Document* Published *The Service of the Poor and Spiritual Growth*, CIIR, London Published 'The Option for the Poor in South Africa', in *Resistance and Hope: Essays in Honour of Beyers Nadué*, edited by Charles Villa-Vinencio, David Philip, Cape Town
1986	Went into hiding during the second State of Emergency in South Africa
1987	Published *To Nourish Our Faith: Theology of Liberation for Southern Africa*, Order of Preachers, Hilton (1989 published by CAFOD as *To Nourish Our Faith: Theological Reflections on the Theology of Liberation*) Published 'The Eschatology of the Kairos Document', in *Missionalia*, Pretoria, 15/2
1988–1996	Regent of Studies of Dominicans in Southern Africa
1988	Published *God in South Africa: The Challenge of the Gospel*, Wm B Eerdmans, Mambo Press and CIIR
1989	Published 'Theology in a Prophetic Voice', in *The Future of Liberation Theology: Essays in Honor of Gustavo Gutiérrez*, edited by Marc H Ellis, *et al*, Orbis, New York. First published in: *Hammering Swords into Ploughshares: Essays in Honour of Archbishop Desmond Tutu*, edited by B Tlhagale *et al*, Skotaville, Johannesburg 1986

1990	Granted an honorary doctorate by Regis College, Toronto, Canada after the Holy See would not allow the University of Fribourg in Switzerland to grant him one
	Published *Contextual Theology: One Faith, Many Theologies*, Regis College, Toronto
1991	Editor *Challenge* magazine, owned by Contextual Publications, Johannesburg
	Published 'Conflict and Community', in *Becoming a Creative Local Church*, edited by PJ Hartin *et al*, Cluster Publications, Pietermaritzburg
	Published 'Poor in Spirit', in Grail: A Ecumenical Journal, Waterloo, Canada, 6/4
1992	Published 'Evangelism, Mission and Evangelisation', in *The Scandal of the Cross: Evangelism and Mission Today*, edited by WS Robins *et al*, USPG, London
1992–1994	Co-ordinator of Communications Department at Institute for Contextual Theology
1994	Started the Challenge Quo Vadis religious journalism course, Johannesburg
1998	Went on sabbatical to the United States
2000–2004	Elected for a third term as Provincial of the Dominican Friars in South Africa
2003	Awarded the 'Order of Luthuli in Silver' by then President Thabo Mbeki for his 'life-long dedication to the struggle in South Africa'
2005–2010	Student Master at Emaphethelweni Dominican Priory, Pietermaritzburg
	Member of the Pietermaritzburg Spirituality Book Club
2006	Published *Jesus Today: A Spirituality of Radical Freedom*, Orbis Books
2008	Recognised as a Master of Theology and granted a STM by the Master of the Order, Carlos Azpiroz Costa OP
2009	*Hope in an Age of Despair*, edited by Stanslaus Muyebe OP, is published, Orbis Books
2011	Novice Master in Aquinas Priory, Johannesburg
2013	Started the Contemplative Book Club in Johannesburg
2014–2015	Novice Master in Aquinas Priory, Johannesburg
2016	Chaplain to the Newcastle Dominican Sisters in Marian House retirement home,
2022	Died on 17 October

Albert and Mike Deeb 25 August 2021 at Marian House.

Biographical Details of Contributors

Kevin Ahern is a public theologian and Professor of Religious Studies at Manhattan College in New York, USA where he directs the Dorothy Day Center for the Study and Promotion of Social Catholicism. He is the author of *Structures of Grace: Catholic Organizations Serving the Global Common Good* and editor of several books. From 2003–2007, he served as president of the International Movement of Catholic Students (IMCS).

Marilyn Aitken joined the International Grail Movement (IGM) in 1969. She practises eco-spirituality, is an eco-feminist and a climate activist. She promotes biodiversity through birding activities with young people. She works as a volunteer in the Women's Leadership and Training Programme (WLTP), website www.wltp.co.za, an NGO she co–founded nearly forty years ago. She has documented WLTP's work in three manuals.

Edwin Arrison is a South African Anglican priest for more than thirty years after being ordained to the priesthood by Archbishop Tutu in 1992. He currently serves as the Director of the Volmoed Youth Leadership training programe after having served as Development Manager at the Desmond and Leah Tutu legacy foundation from 2020. He is also the General-Secretary of Kairos SA and a member of the leadership team of the South African Christian Leaders' Initiative (SACLI).

Jacques Briard was the Southern Africa project officer of the Belgian NGO *Entraide et Fraternité* from 1986–2005. He was a member of CIDSE Southern Africa's working group during the same period. He published an article on 'Albert Nolan *un grand dominicain anti-apartheid*' in the Belgian magazine *L'appel* in December 2022.

Paul Burke started his professional career as an Aboriginal legal aid and land council lawyer before converting to anthropology. His first book *Law's Anthropology* (2011) examined the role of anthropologists in native title claims and his second book *An Australian Indigenous Diaspora* (2018) is an ethnographic study of *Warlpiri* matriarchs who migrated to towns and cities. He currently is a consulting anthropologist working on native title claims and is an honorary lecturer at the School of Archaeology and Anthropology at the Australian National University (ANU).

Frank Chikane at the University of the North (Turfloop) he played a leadership role within the Student Christian Movement (SCM) thereby became part of the national leadership of the movement. He has been a national youth leader of his church, a pastor at local congregations and national and international president of his Church. At an ecumenical level, he became a Director of the Institute for Contextual Theology (ICT), a General Secretary of the South African Council of Churches (SACC), participated in various programmes of the World Council of Churches (WCC) and has been a member of the Ecumenical Association of Third World Theologians (EATWOT). The ICT facilitated the processes which resulted in the publication of the celebrated *Kairos Document*. Frank was one of the founders of the *United Democratic Front* (UDF) where he was elected Vice President of Transvaal Region as well as chaired meetings of the National Executive Committee of the UDF. During the transition period he was appointed as a Commissioner of the *Independent Electoral Commission* (IEC), which was responsible for the first democratic elections in South Africa. He was elected to the National Executive Committee (NEC) of the African National Congress (ANC) in 1997 and served for two five-year terms. Frank was Special Advisor to Deputy President Mbeki and later, Director General in his Office; Deputy Secretary of Cabinet during Mandela's Presidency and Director-General and Secretary of Cabinet during Mbeki's Presidency), and the current role as the Moderator of the Churches Commission on International Affairs (CCIA) of the WCC.

James R (Jim) Cochrane is Emeritus Professor (religious studies) and Senior Scholar (School of Public Health), University of Cape Town, as well as Adjunct Professor, Wake Forest School of Medicine, NC, USA. Convenor of the Leading Causes of Life Initiative, a loose transdisciplinary international collaboration of sixty-five plus fellows, he has authored or edited over 180 books, essays, articles and reports. He currently lives in Cape Town but also spends time in Germany.

Biographical Details of Contributors

Renate Cochrane grew up in Germany and studied theology with Jurgen Moltmann in Tübingen. She came to South Africa in 1977 researching Christianity and racism. During that time, she met her future husband James who was working with the anti-Apartheid organisation: The Christian Institute of Southern Africa. She settled in South Africa and became a pastor in the Moravian Church. During the time of the liberation struggle she ministered in various townships in Kwa Zulu. After the first free elections in 1994, a new enemy emerged: AIDS. Reverend Cochrane became an AIDS activist campaigning for the churches´ involvement in the struggle for health-justice. She is retired but remains actively involved with AIDS orphans projects in rural areas.

Theo and Ruth Coggin have worked together in media-related work since the early 1980s. They have full-time heads of their own communication consultancy since 1996, serving a variety of clients, including religious organisations, heads of Churches, NGOs, corporate businesses and government. They remain highly active in their field. Ruth is a qualified musician and recently formed the Johannesburg Queer Chorus, one of the fastest growing choirs in the city. Theo still writes extensively and is at present completing a book about the work of the head of one of the then largest relief agencies in the world's most troubled hotspots. In his spare time, he tends his large collection of beloved roses in his beautiful garden in Johannesburg, South Africa.

Brian Currin BA LLB graduate from the University of Stellenbosch, is a South African Human Rights lawyer and international mediator who, since the end of apartheid in 1994, specialised in international political conflict resolution. He has shared lessons learnt in South Africa in mediation, reconciliation, transitional justice, trust building, amnesty and release of political prisoners in many countries including Northern Ireland, the Basque Country, Columbia, the Middle East, Turkey/Kurdistan, Liberia, Ethiopia and Madagascar.

Sylvester David OMI was born in Durban, South Africa where he joined the Oblates of Mary Immaculate. He now lives in Cape Town as the Auxiliary Bishop of the Archdiocese of Cape Town, and is the Vicar General of the Archdiocese. His previous positions have been Parish Priest; Mission and Retreat Preacher; President of St Joseph's Theological Institute (SJTI), Cedara; Vicar General of the Archdiocese of Durban; and President elect of Oblate School of Theology in San Antonio, Texas, USA.

Paul B Decock OMI was born in Belgium and after studies at the Catholic University in Leuven and studies at the Gregorian University in Rome came to South Africa to lecture at St Joseph's Theological Institute (SJTI) at Cedara in 1969. He continued his studies in South Africa at the University of Natal and after three years returned to Rome to complete doctoral studies in biblical theology. At present he is an honorary professor at the University of KwaZulu-Natal (UKZN) and still lectures at SJTI. He has published regularly in the area of biblical studies (Apocalypse; Luke-Acts) and the reception of the Scriptures during the time of the Church Fathers (particularly Origen) and occasionally during the Middle Ages (Bernard of Clairvaux) or the Renaissance (Erasmus). At present he is the Vice-President of the Pan-African Association of Catholic Exegetes and the Chairperson of the Board of Management of the *Journal of Theology of Southern Africa*, and also a member of the advisory board of the series *Patristic Studies in Global Perspective* published by Brill Schoeningh.

Mike Deeb OP is a Dominican, born in Welkom in South Africa, and has lived in all corners of the country, ministering in parishes in Kroonstad diocese, as a university chaplain in Pietermaritzburg, and as the Coordinator of the Justice and Peace Department of the Southern African Catholic Bishops' Conference (SACBC) in Pretoria. After working for many years with National Catholic Federation of Students (NCFS), Young Christian Students (YCS) and Association of Catholic Tertiary Students (ACTS) as a student leader and chaplain, he was appointed as the International Chaplain to the International Young Catholic Students (IYCS) and International Movement of Catholic Students (IMCS–Pax Romana) based in Paris for eight years. He has most recently worked as the General Promoter of Justice and Peace & Permanent Delegate to the United Nations for the Dominican Order, based in Rome and Geneva for seven years. He currently lives in Cape Town.

Philippe Denis OP is a member of the Dominican Order in Southern Africa. He is Emeritus Professor of History of Christianity at the University of Kwazulu-Natal, Pietermaritzburg, South Africa. He currently works as Research and Development Manager in the KwaZulu-Natal Christian Council. He has authored or co-authored several books on the history of the Reformation, on mission, colonialism and Apartheid in South Africa, on psycho-social support to children affected and infected by HIV/AIDS and on the Churches' response to the genocide against the Tutsi in Rwanda.

Biographical Details of Contributors

Leslie Dikeni was a senior researcher at Mistra in the faculty of Humanities. He has an MSc in Rural sociology (University of Wageningen, Netherlands) and was a doctoral candidate at *Ecole Practique des Hautes Etudes en Sciences Sociale* (school for advanced studies in the Social Sciences). Dikeni is a visiting research fellow at the school of public and development management at the University of Witwatersrand (Wits) and a research associate at the University of Pretoria (UP). His research interest is the social construction of knowledge and its dynamics. Dikeni has co-edited with William Gumede *The Poverty of Ideas: The Retreat of Intellectuals in New Democracies* and is the author of *South African Development Perspective in Question* and also *Habitat and Struggle: The Case of the Kruger National Park in South Africa.* His fourth upcoming book working title is called *Music Agency and Power.* He is currently a Senior Analyst for Palladian Advisory Services.

Kevin Dowling CSsR, is Emeritus Bishop of Diocese of Rustenburg, North West Province, South Africa. He was ordained a priest in the Catholic Church in 1967 by Archbishop Denis Hurley OMI. He was elected as Vice-Provincial of the Redemptorists in South Africa and Zimbabwe and served in that capacity from April 1975 to December 1985. He was then elected to the General Council of the Redemptorists and moved to Rome, and worked all over the world from January 1986 to December 1990 when he was appointed Bishop of the Diocese of Rustenburg and ordained Bishop in 1991, serving in that role until 2021.

Anthony Egan SJ is a South African Jesuit priest currently teaching theology at Hekima University College in Nairobi, Kenya. By training a historian and moral theologian, he worked for fourteen years at the Jesuit Institute South Africa in Johannesburg. He has written or co-written a few books, a number of articles (academic and popular) and chapters in books. He is the author of *Signs of the Times: The Church and War in the 21st Century* (2012) and *The Politics of a South African Catholic Student Movement, 1960–1987* (1991). He received his Master's degree in history from the University of Cape Town (UCT) and his PhD in Political Studies from the University of Witwatersrand.

Robert Ellsberg is the long-time editor in chief and publisher of Orbis Books (the publishing arm of the Maryknoll Fathers and Brothers), where he worked with Albert Nolan on several of his books. He is the author and editor of over twenty-five books of his own, including *All Saints: Daily Reflections on Saints, Prophets, and Witnesses for Our Time*; *The Saints' Guide to Happiness*; *A Living Gospel: Reading God's Story in Holy Lives* and *Dearest Sister Wendy . . . A Surprising Story of Faith and Friendship* (based on his correspondence with Sister Wendy Becket). He has edited five volumes of writings by Dorothy Day, including her diaries, letters, and selected writings.

Hyacinth Ennis OFM is an Irish Franciscan friar who has worked in South Africa since 1968. He has been involved in the formation of Franciscan students and has taught Moral Theology at St John Vianney National Seminary in Pretoria for many years. He also spent many years as the Catholic Chaplain to Pretoria University. After his retirement, he worked in parish ministry in Pretoria and Boksburg.

Joseph (Joe) Falkiner OP is a member of the Dominican Order in Southern Africa and has been a Dominican for sixty years, after having previously graduated as a geologist and worked in that capacity for four years for a big mining house. As a priest he has dedicated himself to helping exploited, underpaid and ill-treated young workers by working full-time for many years as chaplain to the Young Christian Workers (YCW) Movement at both regional and national levels in South Africa. He was a founding member of the Mayfair Dominican Community described in this book and was at various times Postulant Master and Novice Master for the Dominicans in Southern Africa. He has published two books: *The First Dominican Friars in Boksburg, Brakpan and Springs, South Africa (1917–1927)* and *A Priest for Workers: Memoirs of Joseph Falkiner OP*.

Lionel Green-Thompson joined Young Christian Students (YCS) at Wits university in 1986. He had been the chair of the Black Student Committee at Wits at the time. This was the equivalent structure for Black student representation at the Health Science campus. He was the representative of YCS to both the Johannesburg Diocese Justice and Peace Commission as well as to the United Democratic Front Johannesburg North Area Committee. Lionel was part of the Dominican Contemplative Book Club led by Albert Nolan between about 2013 till 2019. He currently serves as Dean: Faculty of Health Sciences at the University of Cape Town since March 2020. Previously as Dean: School of Medicine at Sefako Makgatho Health Sciences University (2018–2020) and Assistant Dean: Teaching, Learning and Undergraduate Affairs (2014–2018) at Wits University. He is a specialist anaesthesiologist and completed a PhD in 2014 entitled: The nature of social accountability in South African medical education and practice. Lionel is currently (2022–2023) the Chairperson of the SA Committee of Medical Deans (SACOMD). A long-time councillor, he was SAAHE national co-chairperson for the 2010 to 2013 triennium and co-chaired the national conference held at Wits in 2010 titled Making Education Matter'.

Sharon Grussendorff has a PhD in quantum computational physics. In 2003 she left her position as a university lecturer to engage in rural science teacher development and to found Solitude Retreat Centre, a beautiful space in nature for contemplative practice. Sharon leads Dove Fellowship, a contemplative community based in Pietermaritzburg, South Africa, which focuses on contemplative spiritual development. She has been practicing centering prayer and other contemplative practices for more than twenty years and is an experienced retreat facilitator. She has recently completed a two-year training with the Living School for Action and Contemplation. In addition to her scientific publications, she is the author of the book *Deeper: Finding the Depth Dimension Beneath the Surface of Life*, published by Anamchara Books in 2022.

Mark James OP is a member of the Dominican Order in Southern Africa and lives in Manzini, Eswatini, Southern Africa. He was a member of the National Catholic Federation of Students (NCFS) and Young Christian Students (YCS) while a student in Johannesburg (1981–1985) and at St Joseph's Theological Institute, Cedara, KwaZulu-Natal (1987–1991). Mark was National Chaplain of YCS in South Africa (1999–2004). He has been the Novice Master (1995–2004, 2012–2013) and Provincial (2004–2012) of the Dominicans in Southern Africa. Mark has worked as a chaplain to the Deaf community in the Archdiocese of Johannesburg (2011–2014) and since 2018 is ministering as chaplain to the Deaf community in the Diocese of Manzini, Eswatini, South Africa.

Roxane Jordaan lives in Gqeberha, formerly Port Elizabeth, in the Eastern Cape, South Africa and is an ordained clergy person in the United Congregational Church of South Africa. She has worked as a minister in local churches, taught Social Analysis at the College of the Transfiguration when she worked as the Women's Ministries Coordinator with the Institute for Pastoral Education in Grahamstown.

Roxane has worked as a programme leader at the East Cape Council of Churches, participated in the South African Council of Churches' Women's ministries and as the Programme Officer for the Church Community Leadership Trust. She did her first degree at the Federal Theological Seminary and holds a Masters degree in Theological Studies from Vanderbilt University in Nashville, USA. Her study focus was The Church and the Poor. She is a Womanist Theologian and one of her articles was published in the *Journal of Black Theologies* in the 1980s.

Larry Kaufmann CSsR is a Catholic priest and member of the Redemptorist order. He has a licentiate in systematic theology and a doctorate in moral theology and has lectured at St Joseph's Theological Institute, Cedara, University of KwaZulu-Natal, and Rhodes University. He joined the Institute for Contextual Theology (ICT) in 1990 where he worked with Albert Nolan for three years. His most recent publication is a book, *Become Love*, on the Gospel of John interpreted through the lens of 'the law of gradualness', a concept espoused by Pope Francis. Other publications include *Keep it Light: Praying Through Suffering into Joy*, and *A Life and a Prayer*. Larry is currently leader of the Redemptorists in South Africa as well as director of Redemptorist Pastoral Publications. He lives in Mossel Bay, in Western Cape Province, where he also serves a parish.

Khotso Kekana worked as a journalist for more than twelve years in print, media and radio. He describes himself as a backbencher activist who had the privilege to meet Anti-Apartheid stalwarts such as Fr Albert Nolan. He has had the privilege to get a foretaste to the end to Apartheid rule in South Africa through his assignment as one of the international observers who reported on Namibia's transition from Apartheid rule to democracy under United Nations Resolution 435. He transitioned from journalism into the role of spokesperson for diverse organisations where he steadily grew into occupying executive management positions. Dr Kekana now does advisory/consulting work and spends some of his time supervising post-graduate university students and helping high school students prepare for matric examinations and for university life. He also coaches young sprint athletes during school holidays. He has a PhD in Business Management, an MBA in Strategic General Management and a Diploma in Advertising Management.

Biographical Details of Contributors

Horst Kleinschmidt worked at the Christian Institute from 1972. In 1975 he became Assistant to the Director, Ds Beyers Naudé, but was detained under the Terrorism Act a month later. He was never charged or tried. In 1976 he escaped from South Africa. Holland offered him political asylum from where he represented the Christian Institute abroad. After the 1977 bannings he worked closely with Beyers Naudé to help him and his associates when they helped build both legal and underground resistance.

Lois Law was part of the Young Christian Students (YCS) at the University of Witwatersrand, Johannesburg in the late 1970s and early 1980s. On graduating she was part of the Christian Action Movement (CAM). She has a BA (Social Work) and a BA Hons in Sociology from Wits University, Johannesburg and a Masters in Social Science from the University of Cape Town. She has practiced as a Social Worker and worked for various NGOs. She currently works for the Southern African Catholic Bishops' Conference (SACBC) Catholic Parliamentary Office as a Project Coordinator.

Michael Lewis SJ was born in Cape Town. He joined the Society of Jesus. In 1983 he became Superior of the Jesuits in South Africa and worked closely with Emil Blaser the Dominican Superior in South Africa. He has worked in parishes, prisons, seminaries and formation houses. He is presently the Jesuit Tertian Director in Zinkwazi South Africa.

Graham Lindegger is a Clinical Psychologist, Professor Emeritus Psychology at the University of KwaZulu-Natal, and a long-time friend, colleague, admirer of Albert Nolan.

Ian Linden is a former General-Secretary of the Catholic Institute for International Relations (CIIR) based in London. From 1978–1986 he worked on its Southern Africa desk. He has been an adviser on Europe and Southern Africa for the Department of International Affairs of the Catholic Bishops' Conference of England and Wales (CBCEW). His book *Global Catholicism* (2012) discusses the role of the Church in the Anti-Apartheid struggle. He was awarded a Companion of St Michael and St George (CMG) for work on human right in the UK New Year's Honours List 2000. He is currently a visiting Professor at St Mary's University, Twickenham, London, UK.

Miriam MacGillis OP is the co-founder of Genesis Farm in Blairstown, NJ, USA, where she lives and works. It was left as a bequest to the Dominican Sisters of Caldwell, NJ. She is the Interim Coordinator of the Earth Literacy Center, founded in 1980 for the mission of 'studying and communicating the evolutionary story of the Universe, Earth, Life and Consciousness as a single, seamless process', as articulated in the writings of cultural historian Thomas Berry and mathematical cosmologist Brian Swimme. They were both steeped in the work of Albert Einstein. As a bioregional centre it has offered residential, undergraduate and graduate programs in exploring a new cosmology and fostering alternative human activities, institutions and programmes to reflect those understandings.

Mike Mailula lives in Pretoria, South Africa. He worked for YCS as a regional organiser from 1981–1984, nationally from 1984–1986, SA Catholic Bishops Conference 1987–1991, and worked for Theology Exchange Programme from 1991–1994. From 1995–1999 he worked for Wits Technikon and is currently at Tshwane University of Technology.

Norman Malatjie lives in Spruitview, Germiston, in Gauteng province, South Africa. He is married with three adult children, two sons and a daughter. Previously, he lived in Mokopane, Tembisa (East Rand), Ga Rankuwa, Mamelodi, and Soshanguve (all in Pretoria).
He has a Bachelor Degree in Training and Development (HRD) obtained from Northwest University and a higher certificate (NQF Level 7) in Management Strategy, obtained from the same institution. Norman currently works as an independent contractor and previously worked for YCS, Saint Charles Catholic Church, Soshanguve Residents Organisation, South African Breweries, Junior Achievement South Africa, the Nations Trust and Jesuit Refugee Services.

Shepi Mati lives in Cape Town but works at the School of Journalism & Media Studies, Rhodes University, Makhanda. He has a special passion for community journalism and specifically audio as a medium to promote citizen agency and reflect a diversity of voices in community development. Shepi was a militant in the YCW and a student activist in the Congress of South African Students (COSAS) and a community media producer and cultural activist in the 1980s.

Biographical Details of Contributors

Neil Mitchell OP is a member of the Dominican Order in Southern Africa and has worked in education as an English and Religious Education teacher, principal of a Catholic school in Soweto, and fieldworker for an NGO doing development work in rural South African schools. He has trained candidates for the permanent diaconate in the Diocese of Kroonstad and for a time was assistant parish priest in Welkom and Bronville (Welkom is the second-largest city in the Free State province of South Africa). He is currently Master of Students at the Order's Southern African formation house in Pietermaritzburg, and lectures in Church History and Moral Theology at St Joseph's Theological Institute in Cedara, KwaZulu-Natal.

Smangaliso Mkhatshwa lives in Pretoria and is a Catholic theologian educated by the Dominicans at St Peter's seminary in Pevensey and then Hammanskraal. After ordination he co-founded the Black Priests Solidarity Group to pressurize the Catholic Church to de-racialise its institutions by adopting a vibrant anti-Apartheid stance. He was appointed to the South African Catholic Bishops' Conference (SACBC) and was finally made its Secretary General before assuming the leadership of the Institute for Contextual Theology (ICT). He co-sponsored the *Kairos Document* of which Albert. Nolan played a key role. He studied at the University of Leuven, Belgium. He returned to South Africa and actively participated in anti-Apartheid struggles and after 1994 was Deputy Minister of Education and then the Mayor of the capital, Tshwane. After retiring from public life he immersed himself in the struggle aganst corruption using the Charter of Positive Values as a vehicle.

Sidwell Mokgothu is the Bishop of the Limpopo District of the Methodist Church of Southern Africa in Pretoria. Sidwell is a passionate trainer, speaker, coach, retreat leader who has presented at international platforms. He is a former liberation struggle activist in the different formations of the Liberation Movement, United Democratic Front, Student, Youth, Civic; Institute of Contextual Theology, and an Ecumenical leader grounded in social justice. He is an ardent proponent of a spirituality that balances the contemplative and the prophetic action. He strongly believes in inter-faith spirituality with emphasis on African Spirituality. The title of his research paper for Masters in Philosophy in Christian Spirituality was: 'Reopening the Wells: The Spirituality of Albert Nolan and its Implications for Post-

Apartheid South Africa.' His PhD studies focused on racial integration in the Methodist Church and its contribution to Social Cohesion in South Africa.

Malusi Mpumlwana is a retired diocesan bishop of the Ethiopian Episcopal Church. Along with Steve Biko, he and his wife Thoko Mpumlwana were activists in the Anti-Apartheid Black Consciousness Movement in South Africa. He is currently the General-Secretary of the South African Council of Churches (SACC). Trained at the Federal Theological Seminary, the University of Cape Town and the University of Notre Dame, Mpumlwana follows the contextual theology approach that reflects on momentous challenges and distills those elements that cry out for intervention, failing which history would judge adversely a Kairos Theology. He was an active member of the ICT led by Reverend Frank Chikane and Fr Albert Nolan; and he served as Chaplain of the very ecumenical Cape Town chapter of the YCS, which played a key role in thwarting necklace attacks on people at the confluence of the Nyanga–Gugulethu townships.

Aaron Mokabane is a social justice activist based in Roodepoort, Johannesburg and a member of the West Rand Lutheran Church. He has been active in the Student Union for Christian Action (SUCA) starting at Wits in the late eighties and into the early nineties at Turfloop. He is currently serving on the Board of the Evangelical Alliance of South Africa (TEASA). He is married to Ria and blessed with three children.

Isaac Mutelo OP is a member of the Dominican Order in Southern Africa. He is Regent of Studies for the Dominican Vice Province of Southern Africa. He is a Senior Lecturer and Director of Quality Assurance at Arrupe Jesuit University in Harare, Zimbabwe. A graduate in Theology, Philosophy and Education, he acquired his MA and PhD degrees in Philosophy with a specialisation in religion and politics from the University of KwaZulu-Natal in South Africa. At present, he is pursuing studies in human rights. He is author of *Muslim Organisations in South Africa: Political Role Post–1948* published in January 2023 by Domuni Press.

Michael Murphy SPS is a member of St Patrick's Missionary Society (Kiltegan), who was ordained in 1973 and spent the first five years after this in Zambia as a teacher and then in parish work. In 1978 he was appointed as spiritual director for students in his Society and was based in Ireland for seventeen years except for 1986–1988 when he gained an STL in spirituality from studies in Rome. In 1996 he moved to South Africa and was in 2008 appointed leader of his Society in Southern Africa and held that position until the end of 2022. He presently is in parish work in Johannesburg.

Moss Ntlha is the General-Secretary of The Evangelical Alliance of South Africa (TEASA) and has passion for justice, reconciliation and transformation in the South African society. His faith journey and vocation was shaped by his insertion in the struggle against Apartheid. In Post-Apartheid South Africa, he participates in several initiatives aimed at strengthening Civic agency for Democratic renewal. His passion is to see the gospel impact lives at personal and public levels. To that end, he is a church planter and disciple maker. A keen student of the evangelical movement, he holds degrees in theology (Mth) and natural Science (BSC).

Trevor Peter (Amafu) Ntlhola is originally from Soweto, South Africa. Born and lived in the days of Apartheid, when he had to learn how to apply his faith in Christ Jesus' Anti-Apartheid struggle for truth, justice, solidarity, and love. This led him to a multiracial reconciliation community called Johweto Vineyard Church, where he was ordained as a pastor in 1996 within the Association of Vineyard Churches of South Africa (AVSA). He pastored a few Vineyard Churches and most of his ministry has been dedicated to serving the poor, youth and marginalised through Emthonjeni-Fountain of Life HIV/AIDS, a community farm south of Gauteng province. His long journey of studies in theology culminated in a MPhil in Christian Spirituality through St Augustine Catholic College and an PhD from the UP.

John O'Leary lives in Cape Town, South Africa with his wife Elsabe. He is an Attorney specialising in mediation and dispute settlement. He was born in Lesotho in 1960 and graduated with a Master's degree in Religious Studies from the University of Cape Town before starting law studies through the University of South Africa. He was a conscientious objector to military conscription in South Africa in the mid-1980s. He contributed to a book published by SACBC called *The Things That Make For Peace* (1985, Pretoria) and later published a book on *Mediation in Family and Divorce Matters* (2014, SiberInk, Cape Town).

Benita Pavlicevic was a student in the 1970s when Albert Nolan was NCFS chaplain. She was influenced by his theological writing and teachings, and in the late 1970s and early 1980s lived in a commune called Joceto (Johannesburg Central Township) that tried to follow gospel values through radical sharing, collective decision making and collaborative activism against Apartheid. Tried—because this is more difficult than we expected. Benita was involved in the United Democratic Front (UDF) primarily in an education capacity, and worked on campaigns to influence whites to turn away from Apartheid. She has worked in support of non-profit and community-based organisations, initially by working for the Human Awareness Programme (HAP) which trained many community, youth and faith-based organisations and activists involved in the struggle against Apartheid. Since leaving the HAP, Benita has worked as a consultant supporting the management of social justice NGOs. She is winding down in her work life, but looking to get involved in climate change activism, albeit in a supportive capacity. Benita is married to Mike (who also lived in the commune) and they have four children—three biological and one who joined our family after his mother, who had also been part of Joceto, died.

Peter-John Pearson is a priest in the Archdiocese of Cape Town, the city of his birth. He holds a degree in law from the University of Cape Town, a post graduate degree in Canon Law and is the Director of the Southern African Catholic Bishops' Conference Parliamentary Liaison Office, which is the office that engages the South African Parliament on policy legislative issues.

Andrew Prior was a Dominican student at St Nicholas' Priory Stellenbosch with Albert Nolan. He subsequently studied in Switzerland and the United Kingdom and became a Professor in Political Studies at the University of Cape Town. He wrote *South African Politics* with Leonard Thompson (Yale University Press), *Revolution and Philosophy* (David Philip publishers) and edited *Catholics in Apartheid Society* (David Philip publishers). He lives and works in Cape Town.

Nicholas Punch OP is an itinerant preacher at the Thomas Moore Center for Preaching and Prayer in Webster, Wisconsin, USA, where he has been since 1991. From 1981–1989 he was Dominican provincial in Australia. Prior to that he worked in a parish in Melbourne, Victoria, was Dean of Mannix College, Melbourne, a teacher at Blackfriars Priory School in Adelaide, South Australia and the prior of various Dominican communities in Australia.

Biographical Details of Contributors

Timothy Radcliffe OP is a friar of the English Province of the Order of Preachers, living in Blackfriars, Oxford. After teaching scripture at Blackfriars for twelve years, he was elected Provincial in 1988, and Master of the Order in 1992. He is an itinerant preacher and lecturer. His books include *What is the Point of Being a Christian*, which won the Michael Ramsey Award for theological writing in 2007. His latest books are *Alive in God: A Christian Imagination* (2019) and *Questioning God* (2023), co-authored with Lukasz Popko OP. His books have been translated into twenty-four languages. He has an honorary doctorate from Oxford University and twelve other universities. He is a Board Member of the Las Casas Institute for Social Justice.

Susan Rakoczy IHM recently completed thirty-nine years of ministry in Ghana and South Africa. In South Africa she was a faculty member of Saint Joseph's Theological Institute and continues to be an Honorary Professor in the School of Religion, Philosophy and Classics of the University of Kwazulu-Natal. She has published widely in the areas of feminist theology, spirituality and ecofeminism. She now resides in Detroit, Michigan in the United States.

Brian Robertson was a student at St Nicholas' Dominican Priory, Stellenbosch, from 1962 to 1965. He is now Emeritus Professor of Psychiatry and Mental Health at the University of Cape Town and lives in Cape Town with his wife, Francoise, and their extended family.

Therese (Terry) Sacco is President of St Augustine College, a Catholic Higher Education Institute in South Africa. She is a Dominican Associate and treasures the Dominican heritage of study, contemplation, and action. She is an activist academic, who fosters education that encourages students to delight in their thinking, connect with their truth, manifest social agency, think critically and forge lives that contribute to the common good. She is married to Martin Connell and is mother to Gabriela Connell Sacco and Tebogo Moroe Maphosa.

Peter Sadie is a Director and Founder of Imsimbi Training. He has a rich experience of leading in the field of spiritual/moral leadership. He developed a values-based multi-faith curriculum for SA schools (*Rainbow religions*), worked in healing juveniles as principal of a juvenile detention centre and integrated self-awareness into leadership and management training programs as director of Imsimbi. He lives and works in Johannesburg with a team of YCS graduates. He is author of *Faith in our Struggle: A Memoir of Hope*, Polity, 2023.

Celia Smit OP was born in Duiwelskloof, Limpopo, but her family travelled about during growing up years—Johannesburg, Bloemfontein, Kimberley and Durban. She was educated by a combination of Dominican and Holy Family Sisters as the family moved about, and entered the Oakford Dominicans and made her first profession as a Religious in 1968. After studying Theology in Rome, she worked in the north of England for a Catholic Youth Service. In South Africa she has assisted in a parish and held administrative roles at the SACBC, ICT and the Catholic Institute of Education (CIE). Celia has also been engaged in the ministry of leadership within her own Congregation. From 1991 she was a member of Community Consulting Services which offered facilitation in Systemic Organisational Development and Group Formation to several Religious Congregations across South Africa, Namibia, Zimbabwe and Zambia. Since the end of 2019 and until recently, she has been at Villa Assumpta Residential Care Home in Pietermaritzburg, first as Director of the Home and local prioress in the Dominican community, and has recently been appointed as Pastoral Co-ordinator for her congregation with Sisters who are in retirement/resident at Villa Assumpta.

Cecil Sols was a YCS organiser in the 1980s. Currently he is self-employed, focusing on Farming and Youth and Children Art Education. From 2006–2021 he was working as the Chief Director at Department of Home Affairs and working in International Relations, Cluster Management and Parliament and Cabinet Support. From 1996–2006 he served at the South African High Commission in Botswana and Tanzania.

McGlory Speckman is Professor Emeritus of New Testament Studies at UP, South Africa. He has been involved with contextual theology through lecturing at different universities, the ICT and the Institute for the Study of the Bible (ISB), now Ujamaa Centre for Research and Community Development. He has published two books as sole author and three as contributing co-editor in addition to a number of peer reviewed journal articles and book chapters. McGlory is currently employed as a Research Professor at Walter Sisulu University, Mthatha, South Africa.

Peter Stewart: A child of Church activists—Jimmy and Joan Stewart—Peter grew up outside South Africa in neo-colonial Africa and Britain and the USA. He returned to South Africa in 1982 at the age of twenty-six and soon joined CAM and the Christian commune Joceto, and was an activist in Catholic Justice and Peace, the Johannesburg Democratic Action Committee (JODAC), the National Educational Union of South Africa (NEUSA) and the Five Freedoms Forum. In 1987 he started a doctorate studying white South Africans. In 1988 he started an academic career at Unisa which continued to 2022. At Unisa he was also an activist in Udusa, the Union of Democratic University Staff Associations. He is currently writing on regressive political phantasy in South Africa. Peter is married to Paula Risi, and has two grown-up sons, Dylan and Laurence. His publications include: *Segregation and Singularity: Politics and its context among white middle class English-speakers in late apartheid Johannesburg,* University of South Africa Press, 2004; 'Why Science Does Not Get You. The Nonergodic Social World and the Limit to Measurement', in *World Futures* 2023 Volume 79/1 (2023); 'South Africa in the Installation Phase of a New Techno-Economic Paradigm', in *Perspectives on Global Development and Technology*, 20/3 (2021) and 'Discordant dreams: the spirit of the times in contemporary South Africa', in *Safundi The Journal of South African and American Studies,* 2019.

Raymond Suttner is an Emeritus Professor at the University of South Africa and a Research Associate in the English Department at the University of Witwatersrand (Wits). He holds BA, LLB, LLM degrees from the University of Cape Town (UCT) and an inter-disciplinary PhD from UW, in sociology, history and political studies. He served lengthy periods in prison and house arrest for underground and public Anti-Apartheid activities of the African National Congress, South African Communist Party and the United Democratic Front. His books include *Inside Apartheid's Prison* (2 edition 2017), *Recovering Democracy in South Africa* (2015*)* and *The ANC Underground* (2008).

Brigid Rose Tiernan SNDdeN (BA, BEd, MEd) was born in Bulawayo and grew up in Ndola (Northern Rhodesia). She met the Sisters of Notre Dame de Namur while attending their High School in Kroonstad, South Africa. After obtaining her first degree at Rhodes University she joined that SNDdeN Congregation. Brigid Rose has taught in several secondary schools around South Africa and has worked in Justice and Peace ministry in the Archdiocese of Cape Town and with the SACBC. She was the second Director of the Catholic Institute of Education from 1988–1999 and has served in leadership in her Congregation for several terms. She has written a number of books about the lives and ministries of SNDdeNs in Southern Africa and is currently the archivist for the SNDdeN Congregation in this part of the world.

Stephany Thiel OP joined the Newcastle (South Africa) Dominican Sisters in 1963 and did most of her formation in the UK. She completed a diploma in Education and taught in various primary schools owned by the Newcastle Dominicans. Her BA honours degree was completed majoring in Anthropology and Psychology. She became a member of a collaborative Dominican Sisters' novitiate in which four congregations undertook to train their novices, and also lived in a Dominican women's collaborative community. For a number of years, she undertook prison ministry, co-ordinating a team of priests and religious who supplied liturgical services to Catholic inmates. At present she is Region Prioress of the Newcastle Dominican Sisters of South Africa.

Molefe Tsele is an ordained Lutheran Minister. He worked in Soweto Parishes during the years of the State of Emergency (1984–1989). He worked as Research Officer at ICT alongside Father Albert Nolan at the time of the writing of the *Kairos Document*. He served more than two years of detention during the State of Emergency. He served as the General-Secretary of the SACC. He served as South African Ambassador to the Democratic Republic of Congo (Kinshasa) and the Hashemite Kingdom of Jordan (Amman).

Stiaan van der Merwe, was involved in resistance to South African Apartheid from within the white Afrikaans community, and in particular from within the white Dutch Reformed Church and Reformed ecumenical structures. He joined the staff of the Institute for Contextual Theology in 1992, upon his return to South Africa from Zambia and lectured theology in Lusaka at the Justo Mwale Theological College (1981–1992). He was a signatory of the South African *Kairos Document* and remains committed to and is part of initiatives to pursue and sustain a prophetic tradition, discernment and action in post-1994 South Africa. Stiaan became involved in Palestine solidarity initiatives in South Africa and beyond, following an international inter-faith solidarity visit to Palestine. He co-signed the Palestine *kairos* document in support of this prophetic testimony in the context of military, settler-colonial occupation as Israeli Apartheid.

Biographical Details of Contributors 443

Charles Villa-Vicencio is Professor Emeritus in Religion and Society at the University of Cape Town (UCT) and former Visiting Professor in the Conflict Resolution program at Georgetown University, Washington DC, and former national research director of the South African Truth and Reconciliation Commission. Recent publications include *Living Between Science and Belief: The Modern Dilemma* (2021).

Ravi Tissera Warnakulasooriya is currently the International President of IMCS Pax Romana. He is a young Sri Lankan lawyer who graduated from the University of Colombo, Sri Lanka. He joined the Sri Lanka University Catholic Students Movement (SLUCSM), the national affiliate member of IMCS Pax Romana during his university days. Ravi also served as the IMCS Pax Romana Asia Pacific Coordinator from 2016–2019.

Gerald O West is Professor Emeritus in the School of Religion, Philosophy, and Classics at UKZN, South Africa. He has worked with the UKZN-based Ujamaa Centre for Community Development and Research for more than thirty years, a project in which socially engaged biblical scholars and ordinary African readers of the Bible from poor, working-class, and marginalised communities collaborate for social transformation. His most recent book is *The Stolen Bible: From Tool of Imperialism to African Icon* (2016).

Ann Wigley OP is a King Dominican Sister. She has been a teacher, a consultant, a retreat giver and the organiser of a spirituality centre. For ten years she was involved in the formation of young religious in her own and other Congregations. For nineteen years she was in General Leadership of the King Dominican Sisters. In that position she was also involved in the Association of Women Religious, the Leadership Conference of Consecrated Life and in the initial creation of Joint Witness. She has been active in the creation and ongoing life of the Federation of Dominicans in Southern Africa and also of Dominican Sisters International. Throughout her various involvements she has been active in justice work especially in the 1970's to 1994. She was involved in the End Conscription Campaign and also in Free the Detainees. With others, she visited political prisoners and helped families to know where their family members were detained as little information was given them. At present she is retired and lives with her community in Westdene, Johannesburg.

She is a dreamer, an activist and a visionary and never fails to hope for and to work for a more peaceful, more harmonious and more just world.

Michael Worsnip was born in Johannesburg, South Africa and fled the country for Lesotho in 1979 as a War Resister. There he was ordained in the Anglican Church and also secretly joined the banned African National Congress (ANC) to work in its underground structures. After the Pretoria-aided coup in Lesotho, Michael was deported from Lesotho for speaking out against South African Army death squads, who were abducting refugees and taking them back to South Africa to torture and kill them. The ANC then asked Michael to return to South Africa to the then war-torn area of KwaZulu-Natal. He taught theology in the ecumenical Federal Theological Seminary, once again avoiding the draft by taking steps to have his racial classification changed to ensure that he would avoid conscription. Michael has degrees from Rhodes, Cambridge and Manchester Universities. He has worked extensively in the areas of HIV/Aids prevention; Land Reform Advocacy; Restitution; as Programme Manager for the Cradle of Humankind World Heritage site; Director of Social Cohesion programmes for the 2010 FIFA World Cup; CEO of the Cape Town Carnival, Land Claims Commissioner for the Western Cape and most recently CEO of Maropeng, the visitor centre for the Cradle of Humankind World Heritage Site.

Vusumuzi Francis Zitha lives in Cleland Pietermaritzburg KwaZulu Natal. He worked as an organiser for Young Christian Students where he visited youth clubs and students in parishes in the suburbs of Soweto and Robertsham in Johannesburg. Later he moved to his home-town in Pietermaritzburg where he worked with the Federal Theological Seminary students in Imbali township forming YCS groups and facilitating learning of the See–Judge–Act method to integrate their life and faith. He facilitated a group of young girls at Oakford Priory in Verulam, Durban with the assistance of the Dominican Sisters. There was also a YCS group that was formed at the University of Zululand (Ongoye) with which he worked. At present he is employed by North-West University, Potchefstroom campus, as Centre Manager for the Learner Support Centre, Unit of Distance Learning, facilitating learning programmes for teachers.

Virginia Zweigenthal is a Public Health Medicine specialist living in Cape Town, South Africa. For the past thirty years she has worked in public sector health departments firstly as a clinician, then as a manager as well as an academic at the University of Cape Town (UCT). She first met Albert Nolan as a student in the 1970s in Johannesburg and became intensely involved in social justice in the ecumenical movement, mostly in Cape Town, where she first worked as an organiser for YCS. This led to her detention in Pollsmoor prison and was banned while a medical student. She chose to become a doctor to serve communities affected by social determinants of health and continues to work with students. She has one son, Daniel, and a life partner, Jean.

Albert at the 30th anniversary of the *Kairos Document*.

Section Nine

Albert with Neil Mitchel OP, January 2014

Index of Names

A

Achebe, Chinua, 144.
Ahern, Kevin, 35, 37, 425.
Alonso, Anicetus Fernandez, 98.
Althaus-Reid, Marcella, 292, 293, 294.
Anselm of Canterbury, 139.
Aquinas, Thomas, 105, 239, 387.
Aristotle, 281.
Arrison, Edwin, xxii.
Armstrong, Karen, 281.
Avila, Teresa, 385, 387.

B

Balasuriya, Tissa, 33, 37, 46, 47.
Barth, Karl, 282.
Bassey, Nnimo, 342.
Benedict XVI, Pope, xxii, xxiii.
Berry, Thomas, 341, 346, 349, 350, 432.
Berten, Ignace, 323.
Betto, Frei, 92.
Biko, Steve, 26, 160, 179, 230, 231, 233, 234, 355, 357, 376, 433.
Blaser, Emil, 87, 100, 101, 102, 114, 123, 131, 402, 410.
Boesak, Allan, 154, 191, 232, 273.

Bonhoeffer, Dietrich, 165, 192, 225, 226, 233, 234.
Borg, Marcus, 282.
Bond, Kathy, 340.
Botha, PW, 172, 185.
Brink, Tony, 338.
Brooke, Gregory, 7, 98, 118, 421.
Bultmann, Rudolph, 265, 267.
Burke, Paul, xxii.
Byrne, Damian, xxi, xxiii, 102, 107, 108.

C

Caledon, Harold, 101.
Camara, Helder, 68, 91, 230, 328.
Cardijn, Joseph, xxxv, 28, 39, 34, 60, 91, 219, 325.
Ceruti, Ines, 337.
Charbonneau, Emilia, 341.
Che Guevara, 93.
Chikane, Frank, xxvii, xxix. 77, 78, 104, 132, 154, 161, 163, 165, 167, 169, 171, 172, 173k 187, 191, 230, 231, 233, 273, 416, 417, 433.
Chikane, Moses, 77.
Cochrane, James (Jim), 32, 153, 155, 156, 157, 159, 191, 269, 271, 274, 426

Cochrane, Renate, 313–317, 426.
Collins, John, 230.
Comblin, J, 261, 263.
Cone, James, 54, 146.
Connell, Luke, 203.
Connell, Tony, 237.
Connery, Didicus (Diego),
    337, 344.
Connor, Bernard F, 282.
Costello, Bridget, 385.
Creamer, Terence, xxv, 241, 256.

D

de Gruchy, John, ii.
de las Casas, Bartolomé, 88, 436.
de la Torre, Ed, 106.
Dear, John, 252.
Decock, Paul B, 419.
Deeb, Mike, iv, xxx, 35, 37, 428.
Denis, Philippe, xxv, 19, 273, 428.

E

Eckhart, Meister, 387, 389, 392.
Egan, Anthony, 36, 428.
Ellsberg, Robert, xx, xxiii, 429.
Esquivel, Adolfo Pérez, 70.

F

Feeny, Peter Paul, 101.
Fischer, Bram, 230.
Fourez, Gérard, 323.
Fox, Tom, 346.
Francis, Pope, xix, 38, 40, 70, 124,
    137, 138, 139, 199, 251, 252, 399,
    431.
Franzidis, Jean-Paul, 29.
Freire, Paulo, 297, 305.
French-Beytagh, Gonville, 293.
Frostin, Per, 270.

G

Gaybba, Brian, 262.
Giddy, Patrick, 101.
Gigacz, Stefan Robert, 29, 34.
Gill, Walter, 191.
Glenny, Misha, 158.
Goba, Bonganjalo, 154, 172, 215, 216.
Goller, Paul, 337, 338, 344.
Gottwald, Norman K, 223.
Gqubule-Mbeki, Thandeka, 92.
Gutiérrez, Gustavo, xxxv, 33, 36,
    37, 44, 46, 47, 54, 57, 104, 125,
    135, 250, 251, 252, 253, 254, 257,
    417, 423.

H

Hanekom, Kallie, 25, 26.
Hanson, JS, 223.
Hardiman, Áine, 90.
Hart, Mary, 237
Hartin, PJ, 423.
Heschel, Abraham Joshua, 237.
Hinnebusch, WA, 368.
Hollywood, Amy, 392.
Hope, Anne, 35, 213.
Hope, Joan, 340.
Hopkins, Gerard Manley, xxii,
    119, 122.
Horn, Molly, 337.
Horsley, RA, 223.
Hortop, Peter, 101.
Huddleston, Trevor, 230, 293.
Hunter, Peter, 337.
Hurley, Denis, 10, 134, 325, 339,
    416, 428.

J

James, Mark, xx, xxiii, xxv, 72,
    101, 430.
Jeannotat, Claire-Marie, 90.

Index of Names

John XXIII, Pope, 9, 17, 181.
John of the Cross, 387.
Johnson, Lulu, 93.
Jones, Dave, 93.
Jordan, Roxanne, 430.

K

Kafity, Samir, 198.
Kasrils, Ronnie, 123.
Kaufmann, Larry, xix, 324, 430.
Kearney, Paddy, 325.
Kerchhoff, Peter, 64, 325.
Kierkegaard, Søren, 159.
King, Martin Luther Jr, 237.
Kistner, Wolfram, 172, 230, 232, 339, 357.
Kleinschmidt, Horst, xxvii, xxix, 163, 416, 431.
Koch, Klaus, 265.
Koka, Drake, 338.
Kotze, Theo, 229.

L

Laird, Martin, 194, 382.
Langefeld, Chris, 75, 203, 213, 238, 242, 244, 351.
Lapsley, Michael, 290.
Linden, Ian, xxix, 102, 162, 432.
Lorde, Audre, 361.
Lowry, Elinor, 330.
Lowry, Stephen, 101.
Luthuli, Albert, i, 4, 103, 208, 230, 240, 367, 424.

M

Mabaso, Charles, 203.
Magdalene, Mary, 308.
Mailula, Mike, 203, 432.
Makhanya, Ntombifuthi, 332.
Makhathini, Nhlanhla, 203.

Malano, Christopher Derige, 37.
Malatjie, Norman, 203, 432.
Manchidi, Peter, 77, 101.
Mandela, Nelson, 11, 13, 184, 190, 191, 193, 230, 325, 375, 415.
Manthata, Tom, 338.
Marquard, Leo, 222.
Marx, Karl, 92, 147.
Mavimbela, Vusi, 92.
Mayer, Rupert, 225.
Mayson, Cedric, 94, 191, 229.
Mbeki, Thabo, i, 78, 103, 104, 163, 231, 315, 424.
Mboweni, Tito, 290.
McCann, Owen, 20.
Mencken, HL, 285.
Mendel, Charles, 101.
Metz, Johann, 282.
Mische, Patricia and Gerald, 346.
Mkhatshwa, Smangaliso, xxix, 51, 83, 104, 123, 229, 231, 339, 435.
Mokgoebo, Zak, 201.
Mokuku, Phillip, 290.
Moltmann, Jürgen, 253, 426.
Mosala, Itumeleng J, 275, 276.
Mpetha, Oscar, 92.
Mtungwa, Sibongile, 333.
Mulder, Benedict (Ben), 87, 98, 103.
Mayathula, Mashwabada, 233.
Muyebe, Stan, 56, 424.
Mxenge, Griffiths, 390.

N

Nasser-Metzler, Christian Marwa, 306.
Naudé, Beyers, 18, 78, 104, 154, 155, 166, 172, 229, 231, 232, 234, 269, 325, 339, 416, 431.
Newman, John Henry, 139.
Niemoller, Martin, 225.
Nolan (Prinsloo), Iris, 2, 3, 4, 6, 7, 416.

Nolan, Dennis James Harry, xxxi, 3, 410, 421.
Nolan, Dorothy, 3, 5, 6, 7, 8.
Nolan, James, xxxi, 3.
Nolan, Ronnie, 2, 3, 4, 5, 6, 7, 8.
Nondumo, Zim, 93.
Nunes, Roddy, 94.
Nxumalo, Jabulani Nobleman, 92.

O

O'Berle, Lucienne, 337.
O'Riordan, Richad (Dick), 94.
O'Sullivan, Marian, 341, 345.
Ormerod, Neil, 61.
Origen of Alexandria, 281, 427.
Osei-Tutu, Mahlape and Tony, 75.
Osmers, John, 230, 290.

P

Pagola, José A, 391, 396, 409, 410.
Paul VI, Pope, 20, 119, 362, 419.
Paz, Nestar, 90.
Pelegri, Buenaventura, 36, 45, 46.
Pityana, Barry (Barney), 94, 179, 229.
Putin, Vladmir, 283, 284.

R

Radcliffe, Timothy, 361, 363, 436.
Radebe, Mandla, 92.
Rahner, Karl, 282.
Ratzinger, Joseph, xxii, 138.
Reeves, Ambrose, 293.
Remke, Hannah, 341.
Robertson, Rob, 113.
Romero, Oscar, 134, 135, 299, 300.
Rowland, C, 368.
Ruether, Rosemary Radford, 356, 357.
Russell, David, 315.

S

Sadie, Peter, 221, 437.
Saddington, Tony, 191.
Sanders, Stuart, 154.
Scheid, Anna Floerke, 225.
Scott, Michael, 293.
Schweitzer, Albert, 265.
Sebidi, Lebamang, 172.
Seekings, Jeremy, 221.
Segundo, Juan Louis, 273.
Shiel, Paul, 101.
Sider, Ron, 146.
Simelane, Themba, 27, 36.
Sobrino, Jon, 135, 251, 253, 254, 256.
Sobukwe, Robert, 230, 234.
Speckman, McGlory, 156, 324, 365, 366, 420, 438.
Spruyt, Carel, 102.
Stanley, Cuan, 93.
Stewart, Jimmy, 337.
Stewart, John, 340.
Stompjes, Wilhelmina, 198, 199.
Struthers, Trish, 29, 36.
Suttner, Raymond, 221, 242, 256, 438.
Swimme, Brian, 341, 350, 432.
Synnott, Finbar, 98, 105, 112. 344.

T

Tatayah, Vikash, 344.
Taylor, Charles, 62.
Tema, Elia, 172, 191.
Thunberg, Greta, 344.
Timmel, Sally, 213.
Torres, Camillo, 90.
Tshenkeng, Drake, 233.
Turner, Rick, 389, 390.
Tutu, Demond, 78, 168, 229, 293, 423, 425.
Tyacke, Jean and Eric, 338.

V

Van Kessel, Ineke, 221.
Von Rad, G, 264.
Vorster, BJ, 155.
Vorster, Koot, 155.

W

Wallerstein, Immanuel, 222.
Wallis, Jim, 146.

Weiss, Johannes, 265.
Williams, Brian, 101.
Williams, Vincent, 92.
Winter, Colin, 293.
Wittenberg, GH, 366, 370, 371.

Z

Zerghe, Raymonde, 323.
Zweigenthal, Virginia, xxvi, 416, 445.

Index of Subjects

A

A Theology of Liberation, xxxv, 36, 54, 252, 254.
Ackerville, 179.
ACTS (Association of Catholic Tertiary Students), xiii, 35, 45.
AFM (Apostolic Faith Mission of South Africa), xiii, 161, 162, 164.
African Independent Churches, 284.
African Initiated Churches, 197.
Aggiornamento, 13.
Alphonsian Academy, Rome, the, 138.
An Tairseach, 341, 345.
ANC (African National Congress), xiii, 18, 75, 104, 123, 212, 214, 222, 223, 229, 231, 250, 297, 441.
ANC Youth League, 233.
Angelicum, the, xxxii, 9, 421.
Apartheid, i, ii, Xx, xxi, xxvi, xxvii, xxvii, xxxiii, xxxiv, xxxvi, xxxvii, 5, 11, 12, 16, 17, 19, 25, 26, 27, 28, 30, 45, 50, 51, 54, 62, 63, 68, 69, 73, 74, 75, 78, 82, 84, 90, 91, 93, 99, 103, 105, 106, 108, 109, 111, 112, 114, 115, 117, 127, 131, 132, 133, 141, 142, 143, 144, 147, 148, 149, 153, 154, 155, 157, 158, 162, 164, 165, 166, 169, 172, 173, 174, 175, 176, 177, 179, 180, 182, 184, 185, 186, 187, 191, 208, 211, 214, 215, 217, 220, 221, 223, 224, 225, 229, 231, 232, 233, 234, 240, 241, 242, 244, 250, 259, 261, 262, 264, 266, 276, 279, 280, 283, 288, 289, 293, 295, 296, 297, 299, 300, 302, 304, 308, 314, 316, 319, 320, 323, 324, 325, 328, 340, 341, 362, 365, 367, 370, 372, 375, 376, 380, 393, 394, 397, 401, 406, 416, 417, 418, 419, 425, 428, 431, 432, 433, 435, 436, 438, 440.
Apocalyptic Christianity, 261, 263, 264, 265.
Apophatic tradition, the, 216.
Atteridgeville, 84.

B

Bible Study, 175.
Black Consciousness Movement, xiii, 26, 44, 229, 235, 338.
Black Priests' Manifesto, 180.
Black Priests Solidarity Group, 180.
Black resistance, 113.
Black Sash, 235.
Black theologians, 155, 156, 180, 232.
Black Theology, 54, 146, 163, 277, 366.

Bophuthatswana homeland, 134.
Boer resistance, the, 156.
Boksburg, 81, 117, 376, 380, 405, 406, 416, 429.
Braamfontein, 145, 153, 171, 189, 240, 273.

C

Call-box, 163, 231.
Christian Action Movement (CAM), xiii, 75, 132, 185, 212, 213, 214.
Cape Town, i, ii, xxxi, 3, 4, 5, 6, 9, 10, 64, 92, 94, 99, 105, 115, 133, 179, 183, 191, 204, 227, 294, 340, 343, 351, 357, 394, 399, 415, 427, 433, 441, 442.
Cape Town, University of, 30, 36, 154, 426, 429, 436, 438, 440.
Catholic Student Association (CASA), xiii, 29, 35, 44, 100
Catholic Action, specialised, 28, 33, 34. 30, 26.
Catholic charismatic renewal, 111.
Catholic Institute for International Relations (CIIR), xiii, 102, 103, 162, 219, 234, 371, 422, 423, 432.
Catholic Student Society (Cathsoc), xiii, 26, 27, 28, 30, 101, 111, 112, 116, 118, 147.
CenteCow, 332.
Challenge: Church and People, 105, 124, 145, 147, 183, 193, 197, 198, 207, 313–317, 319–321, 324, 325, 327, 338, 358, 368, 375, 415, 423.
Church Theology, 276.
Christus Vivit, 40.
International Cooperaton for Development and Solidarity (CIDSE), xii, 324, 425.
Circles of Dignity, 157, 274.

Climate change, xiv, 38, 137, 341, 342, 343, 344, 436.
Christian Life Group (CLG), xiii.
Cloetesville, 17.
Colonialism of a Special Type, 222.
Compassion, I, xi, xxii, xxxv, 5, 40, 57, 65, 69, 73, 113, 114, 137, 139, 253, 306, 354, 355, 356, 371, 390, 393–398, 399, 402, 408.
Conference of Major Religious Superiors in South Africa, 133.
Confessing Community, 232.
Congregation for the Doctrine of the Faith (CDF), xiii, 138.
Congress of South African Students (COSAS), xiii, 79, 104, 433.
Conscription, 75, 113, 211, 212, 227, 435, 441.
Constantinian Orthodox Church, 283.
Contemplative Book Club, 117, 194, 391, 401, 424.
Contextual Bible Study (CBS), 269, 270.
Contextual Publications, 327.
Contextual Theology, 85, 132, 140, 141–149, 153, 156, 171, 182, 189, 190, 192, 213, 250, 298, 366, 380, 417, 433.
Contextualisation, 116.
Conversion, 57, 356.
Congress of South African Student (COSAS), xiii, 104, 432.

D

Decree on the Apostolate of Lay People, 35.
Democratic Alliance, 284.
Dicastery for Promoting Integral Human Development, 139.
Dispensation, 148, 149, 184, 216, 320.

Index of Subjects

Dominican pillars, 387.
Dominican Sisters of Cabra, 345.
Dominican Sisters of Caldwell, 345, 434.
Dominican Sisters of Newcastle (South Africa), xxiv, 407, 409, 416, 423, 439.
Dutch Reformed Church, xiv, 10, 11, 12, 13, 18, 19, 104, 155, 283, 382, 416, 439.
Dutch Province of the Dominicans, 98.

E

Earth Literacy, 346, 347, 350, 432.
East Rand, 98, 99.
Ecumenical Association of Third World Theologians, xiv, 153, 164.
Ecumenical Youth Leadership Training programme, 197.
Ecumenism, 13, 197–201.
Emaphethelwemi community, 381, 423.
Edanyana, 90.
English Province of the Dominicans, 14, 436.
Entraide et Fraternité, 323, 324, 325, 425.
Evangelicals for Social Action, 146.
Evangelischer Entwicklungsdienst, xiv, 329.
Exegesis, 267.

F

Fedsem, xiv, 215.
Freedom Charter, 112, 239.
Freedom Front Plus, xiv, 284.
Freedom Square, 101.

G

Gaudete et Exsultate, 38.
Gauteng, 164, 432, 434.
General Chapter, 31, 107, 108, 121, 176, 220, 422, 428.
General Law Amendment Act, 90.
Genesis Farm, the, 341, 345, 346, 347, 348, 349, 350, 432.
German Confessing Christians, 165.
Germiston, 341, 432.
God in South Africa, 114, 121, 123, 145, 147, 153, 186, 192, 200, 219–227, 240, 244, 250, 259, 260, 262, 263, 264, 295, 296, 297, 298, 324, 358, 362, 375, 379, 396, 397, 418, 422.
Grace and Truth, 260, 262.
Grail, the, 338, 339, 340, 341, 423, 425.
Gratitude, 194, 270, 325, 383, 385, 386.

H

Hammanskraal, 98, 179.
Heavenly Valley, 112.
Hermeneutics, 271, 274, 277, 281
Hope in and Age of Despair, 56, 143, 151, 226, 351, 370, 423.
Houghton, 65, 73, 102, 103, 121, 212, 256, 422.
Humanae Vitae, 20, 120, 419.

I

Institute of Contextual Theology, xiv, xxvi, xxxvi, 31, 68, 83, 120, 123, 142, 145, 153, 161, 167, 171, 174, 182, 189, 204, 220, 271, 321, 324, 366, 375, 381, 415, 422, 430.

Inter Federal Assembly, xiv, 29, 31, 33, 36, 44, 422.

IMCS-Pax Romana, xxvi, 27, 33, 34, 35, 36, 43, 44, 45, 47, 427.

In Her Name: Women Doing Theology, 376.

Internal colonialism, 222, 223.

Internal Security Act, the, 172, 222, 390.

International Young Catholic Students, 33, 43, 44.

Inter-Church Youth [ICY], xiv, 366.

Ipelegeng Community Centre, 172.

Institute for the Study of the Bible (ISB), xiv, 272, 273, 438.

Isithakazelo, 373.

International Yung Catholic Students (IYCS), xiv, 38, 40, 45, 46, 84, 427.

J

Jabavu, 172.

Jesuits (Society of Jesus), the, xxvi, 3, 4, 131, 132, 162.

Jesus Today: A Spirituality of Radical Freedom, xv, 38, 40, 55, 143, 193, 217, 226, 238, 240, 259, 341, 342, 353, 376, 424.

Jeunesse Ouvrière Chrétienne (JOC), xiv, 34.

John Vorster Square, 101, 166, 390.

Journal of Theology for Southern Africa, xiv, 269, 273, 275.

Just War Theory, 139, 224.

Justice and Peace Commission (South Africa), 99, 100, 134, 185, 251, 338, 339, 347.

K

Kagiso, 161, 162.

Kairos Document, the, xv, xxix, xxxiv, 19, 32, 69, 74, 78, 84, 105, 114, 115, 120, 134, 145, 146, 153, 154, 155, 156, 167, 168, 171, 173, 174, 175, 177, 178, 182, 183, 192, 240, 241, 244, 259, 273, 276, 279, 284, 324, 325, 337, 351, 357, 375, 416, 419, 422, 423.

Kairos moment, xxxiv, 83, 140, 201, 260, 263, 264, 265, 274, 337–344, 439.

Kairos Palestine Document (KP), xiv, 198, 303.

Kairos spirituality, 373

Kairos theology, 199, 200, 433.

Kingdom of God, the, xxviii, xxxi, 25, 26, 36, 65, 67, 68, 70, 73, 74, 113, 116, 129, 166, 167, 215, 237, 250, 251, 254, 259, 266, 280, 359, 369, 379, 387, 417.

Kroonstad, Diocese of, 98, 101, 433.

Krugersdorp (now Mogale City), 161.

Kwazulu Natal, 27, 193, 314, 389.

Kwazulu-Natal, University of, xvi, 427.

Kweekskool, xiv, 10.

L

Laudato Si', 124.

Leadership Council of Consecrated Life, 376.

Lectio divina, 75, 281, 386.

Lesotho. 101, 123, 289, 290, 291. 340, 380, 401.

Liberation spirituality, 56, 104, 308, 365, 366, 375. 419.

Liberation theologians, 29, 87, 135, 213, 239.

Liberation Theology, xxiii, xxxv, 32, 45, 54, 61, 63, 68, 89, 104, 135, 213, 249, 250, 261, 270, 271, 298, 417.

Lumko Institute, 341.

M

Magaliesberg, 64, 65, 82, 83, 86.
Mamashianoka, 82.
Mamelodi, 77, 82, 84, 231, 232, 432.
Marian House, 117, 393, 400, 401, 402, 405, 406, 407, 408, 410, 419.
Marxism, xxv.
Marxist-Leninism, 85, 239.
Master General, xv, 107.
Master of the Dominican Order, xiv, xxi, xxii, xxxvi, 31, 32, 98, 102, 107, 108, 110, 121, 132, 133, 208, 241, 256, 345, 375, 420, 422, 424.
Mauritian Wildlife Foundation, the, 344.
Mayfair, xii, xxvi, xxvii, 65, 73, 78, 87, 95, 96, 97, 98, 99, 101, 102, 103, 103, 104, 105, 112, 121, 123, 129, 256, 415, 417, 418, 422, 429.
Mayibuye, 93.
Medellin, 249, 251, 253, 254, 255, 256, 371.
Message to the People of South Africa, 155.
Methodist Church of Southern Africa, 327, 328, 365.
MIEC-JECI, xv, 35.
Millenarianists, 263.
Minister United for Christian Responsibility (MUCCOR), xiv, 165.
Mokopane (Potgieterust), 81, 82, 432.
Modder B prison, 233.
Mondeor, 102, 194, 279, 393, 405, 416, 418.

N

Nyanga East, community of, 90, 92.
Nakbah, 302.
National Catholic Reporter, the, 252, 346, 375.

National coordinator, 84, 203, 427, 431, 440.
National organiser, 30, 203, 432.
National Party, the, 304, 401.
National Catholic Federation of Students (NCFS), xv, xxvi, xxxiii, xxxiv, 25, 26, 27, 28, 29, 30, 31, 32, 33, 35, 36, 44, 45, 49, 50, 53, 73, 100, 127, 185, 211, 337, 415, 416, 422, 427, 430, 435.
New Brighton Police Station, 90.
New Kairos: Challenge to the Churches, 192.
New Testament Society, the, xxxii.
Nederduitse Gereformeerde Kerk, Dutch Reformed Church, (NGK) the, 155.
Non-governmental organisation (NGO), xv, 206, 323, 324, 328, 330, 332, 425, 426, 431, 435.
No Life of My Own, 273.
Novice master, xxvi, 16, 115, 118, 385, 387, 388, 405, 421, 424, 429, 430.
Naboom Spruit (Mookgopong), 81.
National Union of South African Students (NUSAS), xv, 337.

O

Orthodox Church of Ukraine (OCU), xv, 284.
Operation Plecksy, 171.
Option for the poor, the, 17, 59, 61, 64, 79, 91, 125, 135, 159, 216, 217, 249–257, 250, 251, 252, 253, 254, 255, 256, 257, 269, 270, 272, 371, 420, 422.
Order of Preachers/Dominican Order, the, i, xii, xiv, xv, xx, xxi, xxii, xxxiii, xxiv, xxv xxvi, xxviii, 3, 5, 8, 9, 10, 12, 13, 14, 15, 17, 18, 19, 21, 30, 31, 32, 56, 57, 59, 73, 75, 78, 89, 91, 92, 94, 97, 100, 101, 102, 103, 104, 105, 112, 114, 115,

119, 120, 121, 124, 127, 129, 133,
142, 179, 193, 194, 198, 208, 212,
216, 220, 227, 241, 250, 279, 281,
298, 320, 321, 323, 330, 334, 339,
341, 344, 347, 357, 361, 363, 368,
369, 375, 377, 381, 386, 388, 389,
391, 392, 393, 407, 409, 415, 416,
417, 420, 421, 422, 424, 428, 429,
430, 432, 433, 434, 436, 439, 441.

P

Palestinian Jew, 302, 307.
Pan Africanist Congress (PAC), xv,
229, 230, 250.
Parktown, 338, 339, 340.
Parousia, the, 263.
Patriarch of Constantinople, 283,
284.
Pax Christi International (PCI), xv,
134.
Payneville, 16, 19, 98.
Pedagogy, 36, 37, 46, 297, 304, 305.
Pentecostal, 143, 168, 273.
Pietermaritzburg, 193, 215, 381, 416
Pietermaritzburg Agency for
Christian Social Awareness
(PACSA), xv, 64.
Preaching, xxiii, xxxiv, 10, 53, 63,
64, 68, 105, 109, 129, 136, 198,
220, 225, 251, 281, 287, 299, 362,
368, 381, 387, 392, 409, 436.
Pretoria, 27, 30, 51, 77, 78, 82, 98,
164, 185, 292, 406, 423, 427, 428,
432, 435, 441.
Pretoria Central Prison, 113.
Pretoria Cultural Forum, 84.
Pro Veritate, 229.
Prophet, xxvii, xxviii, xix, 76, 116,
144, 192, 238, 264, 282, 286, 308,
337–344, 351, 353, 363, 354, 369,
370, 372.
Prophetic action. 120.

Prophetic boldness, 303.
Prophetic Church, 135, 216, 220.
Prophetic concept, 393
Prophetic ecumenism, 197–201.
Prophetic insight, 174.
Prophetic movement, 365.
Prophetic process, 269–277.
Prophetic proclamation, 223.
Prophetic relevance, 142.
Prophetic role, 240.
Prophetic spaces, 309.
Prophetic stance, 133, 182.
Prophetic statement, 273, 284, 420.
Prophetic tradion, 265, 440.
Prophetic theology, 115, 154, 156,
157, 159, 176, 177, 273, 274, 276,
285.
Prophetic vision, 183.
Prophetic voice, 316. 423.
Prophetic witness, 304, 397.
Prophetic words, 297.
Prophetism, 419.
Provincial, xxi, xxii, xxvi, 16, 18, 19,
20, 30, 97, 98, 101, 102, 103, 108,
113, 121, 131, 174, 236, 279, 330,
415, 418, 422, 424, 428, 430, 436.
Puebla, 249, 250, 251, 256, 371.

Q

Quakers, the 113.
Queer Chorus, the, 426.
Quo Vadis, writing course, 331, 332,
423.

R

Rakhmah, 301–309.
Rainbow Nation, xxxviii, 295, 320.
Redemptorists, the, xxvi, 133, 428,
431.
Russian Orthodox Church, 283, 284.
Rustenburg, 133, 190, 428.

S

South African Communist Party (SACP), 93, 211, 222, 223, 229, 242, 439.

South African Catholic Bishops' Conference (SACBC), xv, xxvi. 99, 123, 179, 180, 181, 182, 185, 212, 220, 325, 341, 427, 432, 435, 437, 439.

South African Defence Force (SADF), xv, 113, 171.

Second Vatican Council (Vatican II), the, xxxii, 9, 29, 35, 91, 137, 179, 181, 416.

Security Branch (South Africa), 77, 78, 93, 103, 186, 187, 235.

See–Judge–Act, method, xxxv, 28, 29, 33, 34, 35, 37, 44, 60, 63, 65, 67, 77, 82, 182, 191, 192, 209, 211, 212, 216, 219, 261, 325, 351, 441.

Sensus fidelium, 67–71.

Seventh Day Adventist Church, the, 92.

Signs of the times, the, xxvii, xxviii, 8, 16, 17, 18, 73, 105, 116, 128, 142, 143, 177, 191, 192, 193, 207, 238, 282, 342, 392, 396, 416, 419, 429.

Sin, Suffering, Salvation, 219–227.

SNDdeN, Congregation of, xv. 185–187, 439.

Soshanguve, 77, 81-84, 86, 432.

South African Council of Churches, 205, 357, 366, 430, 433.

South African Liberal Party, 222.

Soweto, 30, 64, 97, 98, 99, 100, 101, 102, 112, 161, 172, 187, 191, 231, 232, 238, 338, 417, 418, 433, 434, 439, 441.

St Peter's Old Boys Association (SPOBA), xv, 179, 180.

St Joseph's Theological Institute, 193, 375, 380, 427, 430, 433, 436.

St Nicholas Priory, 7, 10, 12, 24, 421, 422, 436.

State capture, 51, 158, 372.

State of Emergency, 83, 103, 142, 155, 172, 175, 176, 185, 212, 240, 416, 439.

State theology, 19, 74, 114, 115, 176, 276, 363.

Stellenbosch, xxvi, xxxii, xxxiii, 7, 10, 11, 13, 15, 16, 17, 18, 19, 20, 21, 24, 29, 30, 48, 49, 118, 126, 337, 415., 416, 419, 421, 422.

Studium, xxxii, 421.

Students Union for Christian Action (SUCA), xv, 146, 147, 366, 433.

T

Tamatievlei, 112.

Tertiary Catholic Federation of Australia (TCFA, the, 59–62.

Terrorism Act (South Africa), the, 64, 229, 431.

Theology Exchange Programme, 32, 79, 84, 204, 432.

Training for Transformation, 213.

Transitional Justice, 134.

Troyeville, 102, 418.

Truth Commission Report, the, 171.

U

Ujamaa Centre, 269, 270, 272, 273, 276l 277, 438, 440.

Ujamaa Institute, 157.

United Democratic Front (UDF), xvi, 79, 152, 170, 176, 181, 211, 221, 234, 439.

V

Vaal Civic Association, xvi, 176.
Vaal Triangle, 175, 176, 406.
Verulam Catholic School, 64.
Victory Park, 132, 340.
Voortrekkerhoogte, 113.

W

Wesley Guild, the, 365.
Western Cape, 15, 17, 197, 422, 431.
Women's Leadership and Training
  Programme (WLTP), the, xvi,
  332, 425.
World Council of Churches, the, 325.

Y

YCS, the, ii, viii, xvii, xxvi, xxxv, 25,
  29, 30, 31, 32, 35, 36, 38, 40, 44,
  63, 64, 65, 67, 74, 77, 79, 81, 82,
  83, 84, 86, 87, 88, 91, 92, 100,
  101, 130, 147, 161, 203, 204, 211,
  212, 219, 238, 234, 351, 357, 366,
  393, 415, 416, 422, 427, 430, 431,
  432, 433, 437, 441, 442.
YCW, the, 28, 30, 35, 36, 87, 88, 89,
  91, 92, 93, 99, 100, 231, 261, 323,
  429, 430, 434.

Printed in the USA
CPSIA information can be obtained
at www.ICGtesting.com
JSHW070504261023
50712JS00002B/25